Trustees and Officers
of Indiana University

Volume III
1982–2018

TRUSTEES AND OFFICERS OF INDIANA UNIVERSITY

VOLUME III
1982–2018

Keith Buckley · Derek F. DiMatteo
Linda Fariss · Kelly Kish · Colleen Pauwels
editors

1820–2020
INDIANA UNIVERSITY
BICENTENNIAL

Editors: Keith Buckley, Derek F. DiMatteo, Linda Fariss, Kelly Kish, Colleen Pauwels

Trustees and Officers of Indiana University, Volume III: 1982–2018
ISBN 978-0-578-48788-5

Printed in the United States of America.

Published by Indiana University.

Indiana University and the IU trident logo and seal are registered trademarks
of Indiana University.

While every precaution has been taken in the preparation of this book, the publisher, the editors and the contributors assume no responsibility for errors or omissions, or for damages resulting from the use of the information contained herein.

Indiana University
107 S. Indiana Avenue
Bloomington, IN 47405-7000
812-855-4848

www.iu.edu

Contents

PREFACE

This manuscript follows the format of the two previous informative volumes edited by Burton Myers in 1951 and Eleanor Roehr in 1983 chronicling the trustees and officers of Indiana University from 1820 to 1950 and 1950 to 1982, respectively. In this volume, we maintained the useful format of brief biographical sketches and photographs of each trustee or officer. Officers include the secretaries of the Board of Trustees and all those holding positions at the level of president, vice president, and chancellor on IU-administered campuses.

This volume contains several changes from the previous volumes. The most significant changes are the alphabetical presentation of the biographies and the inclusion of a Period of Service chart that shows each person's period of service as an officer or trustee along a common timeline. This fold-out chart is fascinating, as it shows a significant number of trustees and officers whose university work has spanned over twenty-five years. Collectively they represent institutional memory, continuity, and stability—factors that undoubtedly contributed to the success of IU as an institution during this thirty-six-year period. We have also included Tables of Roles to make clear the genealogy of who served in any given position over time. An index is provided to facilitate finding information.

The biographies have been written to be both less and more than simply a transcription of someone's CV. Rather than an exhaustive listing of every association or organization, every accolade or honorary degree, we have attempted to be judicious. To give greater dimension to people beyond their accolades and community service, we have included some family history and anecdotes along with specific accomplishments and challenges overcome. Note that either due to the timing of their employment at IU or due to the length of their service to IU, some people listed in this volume are also included in Volume II (edited by Eleanor Roehr). Thus, in their entries in this volume, we have tried to focus on their lives during the target period of 1982–2018; therefore, in most of those cases, Roehr's volume will have earlier biographical details not included here.

The remarkable individuals who are featured in this volume have inspired us through their leadership and their tireless efforts on behalf of Indiana University. We hope their stories will inspire you, too.

ACKNOWLEDGMENTS

Unlike Dean Burton Myers' struggles with identifying individuals who served in leadership positions from 1820 to 1950 for the first *Trustees and Officers* volume, our work was eased by the impeccable record-keeping of the Office of the Board of Trustees, especially Robin Gress, Terri Crouch, and Teresa Barnett, and the University Libraries' Office of University Archives and Records Management, especially Phil Bantin, Dina Kellams, Carrie Schwier, Bradley Cook, and all of their predecessors and colleagues. Thanks to Anthony C. Warner for database assistance; Dr. Jason M. Gold for creating the Period of Service Gantt chart; Rebecca Torstrick for ensuring access to Qualtrics; James Brosher, Angela Lindauer, Thomas Weinzerl, and others at IU Communications for their help acquiring photographs; Peggy Solic and Laura Christina Hohman at IU Press for assistance in the early stages of production; our colleagues in the IU Office of the Bicentennial for their patience and support; the staff at IU Communications, especially Mary Spohn and Dennis Hill, who did the final design and production of the book.

Our thanks to the many individuals who contributed biographies for friends, family, colleagues, and mentors: Jeff Alberts, Yvette M. Alex-Assensoh, Elisabeth Andrews, Gerald Bepko, Clarence Boone Jr., Trevor Brown, Keith Buckley, Greg Buse, James Capshew, Anita Cast, Terry Clapacs, Gayle Cook, L. Cindy Dabney, Derek F. DiMatteo, Sarah Engel, Linda K. Fariss, Patrick Furlong, G. Frederick Glass, Gerardo Gonzalez, Cameron J. Harris, Brian Hawkins, Gordon Lynn Hufford, Wendell Johnting, Susan Joiner, Christopher Kauffman, Kelly Kish, Sherry Knighton-Schwandt, Julia Lamber, Eric Love, Michael Maben, Karen L. Mackenzie, Lisa McKinney, Scott Miles, Kathy Morrison, Emily Myrick, Dave O'Guinn, Pamela Perry, William M. Plater, Simon Rhodes, Al Ruesink, William Schneider, Carol Seaman, Linda Showalter Balthaser, Curt Simic, Jacqueline A. Simmons, Ken Turchi, Richard Vaughan, Nonie Watt, Steve Watt, and Rob Zinkan.

Thanks also to the many people at Indiana University who commented on and reviewed bios or who contributed other items, such as CVs and photographs, to help with the research process including: Nathan Daniel Albert, Kylie Ayers, Terri Belden, Kirsten Ruth Bowden,

Stephanie Brater, Ryan Carlberg, Hali Noel Cartee, Kip Drew, Lisa Frank, Ben Fulton, Jeremy Gray, Jan C. Halperin, Carol Hobbs, Nancy Larkin, Anne Marie McGee, Vicki D. McLaren, Sharon Rogers, Michael Sheets, Alison Stankrauff, IU's University Student Services and Systems Kimberly M. Wagner, Kathy Wilson, Catherine Winkler, Becky Wood and Denise Wyatt. Thanks also to those beyond IU, including: the Registrar's Office at Butler University; Jonathan Potts at Robert Morris University; Melinda Doehrman and Brenda Lawson at Pacers Sports & Entertainment; Kim Rohlfing at Cook Medical; Janet S. Wood at Eli Lilly and Company and Jayne Ann Dennis at Lilly USA, LLC; Carin Olah at the James W. and Betty Dye Foundation; Zoullin Ballman at Tsuchiya Group North America; and Anne Hartung Spenner at the University of Missouri-Kansas City.

Much of the early work of this volume was completed by Indiana University students Meggan Houlihan, Scott Miles, and Sarah Taylor. We are thankful for their assistance on this project and their appreciation for the distinguished history of leadership at Indiana University. Our colleague Colleen Pauwels, Maurer School of Law librarian, was originally commissioned to prepare this volume by President Michael McRobbie and Vice President John Applegate. Her conception of this manuscript and diligent efforts laid the groundwork for our subsequent success. Regrettably, she passed away in April 2013 after a brave battle with cancer that consumed her energy—but not her spirit—for the last several years. She was proud to serve the university in this important editorial capacity.

The development and printing of this volume was financially supported by the Indiana University Foundation, the Office of the Bicentennial, and the Office of the President; we are grateful for their assistance.

Keith Buckley, Derek F. DiMatteo, Linda Fariss, Kelly Kish

Tables of Roles

Administrators

PRESIDENTS

Name	Years held	Page
John W. Ryan	1971–1987	357
Thomas Ehrlich	1987–1994	108
Myles Neil Brand	1994–2002	47
Gerald L. Bepko	2002–2003 (*Interim*)	27
Adam W. Herbert	2003–2007	191
Michael A. McRobbie	2007–	253

UNIVERSITY CHANCELLORS

Name	Years held	Page
Herman B Wells	1962–2000	441
Kenneth R. R. Gros Louis	2006–2011	169

TREASURERS

Name	Years held	Page
John D. Mulholland	1974–1991	279
Steven A. Miller	1991–2004	262
MaryFrances Moriarty McCourt	2005–2015	246
Donald S. Lukes	2015–	236

Tables of Roles

EXECUTIVE VICE PRESIDENTS

Name	Title	Years held	Page
W. George Pinnell	EVP of the University	1974–1988	324
Charles R. Bantz	EVP and Chancellor, IUPUI	2006–2015	20
Karen Hanson	EVP and Provost, IUB	2007–2012	182
Lauren K. Robel	EVP and Provost, IUB	2012–	354
John S. Applegate	EVP for University Academic Affairs	2013–	5
Nasser H. Paydar	EVP and Chancellor, IUPUI	2015–	308
Jay L. Hess	EVP for University Clinical Affairs	2018–	197

VICE PRESIDENTS FOR PLANNING, FACILITIES, FINANCE, HUMAN RESOURCES, AND LEGAL AFFAIRS

Name	Title	Years held	Page
W. George Pinnell	VP and Treasurer	1971–1974	324
Edgar G. Williams	VP for Administration VP for Finance and CFO	1974–1986 1986–1988	454
Judith G. Palmer	VP for Planning VP for Planning and Finance Management VP and CFO	1986–1991 1991–1994 1994–2007	299
John T. Hackett	VP for Finance and Administration	1988–1991	176
Neil D. Theobald	VP and CFO	2007–2012	413
MaryFrances Moriarty McCourt	VP and CFO	2013–2016	246
John A. Sejdinaj	VP and CFO	2016–	371
J. Terry Clapacs	VP for Facilities VP and Chief Administrative Officer	1986–1991 1991–2009	80
Gerald L. Bepko	VP for Long-Range Planning	1994–2002	27
Charles R. Bantz	VP for Long-Range Planning	2003–2006	20
John S. Applegate	VP for Planning and Policy VP for University Regional Affairs, Planning, and Policy EVP for University Regional Affairs, Planning, and Policy	2008–2010 2010–2011 2011–2013	5
Thomas A. Morrison	VP for Capital Planning and Facilities	2009–	274
Dorothy J. Frapwell	VP and General Counsel	2006–2012	132
Jacqueline A. Simmons	VP and General Counsel	2012–	380
John J. Whelan III	VP for Human Resources	2018–	448

Tables of Roles

VICE PRESIDENTS FOR INTERNATIONAL AFFAIRS, STUDENT AFFAIRS, INFORMATION TECHNOLOGY, AND ATHLETICS

Name	Title	Years held	Page
Charlie Nelms	VP for Student Development and Diversity	1999–2003	282
	VP for Institutional Development and Student Affairs	2003–2007	
Edwin C. Marshall	VP for Diversity, Equity, and Multicultural Affairs	2007–2013	242
James C. Wimbush	VP for Diversity, Equity, and Multicultural Affairs	2013–	460
Michael A. McRobbie	VP for Information Technology and CIO	1997–2007	253
Bradley C. Wheeler	VP for Information Technology and CIO	2007–	444
Patrick O. O'Meara	VP for International Affairs	2007–2011	290
David Zaret	VP for International Affairs	2011–2018	467
Hannah Buxbaum	VP for International Affairs	2018–	70
G. Frederick Glass	VP and Director of Intercollegiate Athletics	2009–	149

VICE PRESIDENTS FOR EXTERNAL RELATIONS

Name	Title	Years held	Page
Danilo Orescanin	VP for University Relations	1983–1988	293
Douglas M. Wilson	VP for University Relations and External Affairs	1988–1996	457
Christopher Simpson	VP for Public Affairs and Government Relations	1996–2001	383
William B. Stephan	VP for Public Affairs and Government Relations	2001–2004	392
	VP for University Relations and Corporate Partnerships	2004–2005	
	VP for Engagement	2007–	
Thomas C. Healy	VP for Government Relations	2004–2007	188
Michael M. Sample	VP for University Relations	2005–2007	362
	VP for Public Affairs and Government Relations	2007–2018	
	VP for Government Relations	2018–	
Bradley C. Wheeler	VP for Communications and Marketing	2018–	444

VICE PRESIDENTS FOR RESEARCH AND CLINICAL AFFAIRS

Name	Title	Years held	Page
George E. Walker	VP for Research and Dean of the Graduate School	1991–2003	432
Michael A. McRobbie	VP for Research	2003–2007	253
Ora H. Pescovitz	Interim VP for Research Administration	2007–2009	319
Robert Schnabel	Interim VP for Research	2009–2010	364
Jorge V. José	VP for Research	2010–2015	208
Fred H. Cate	VP for Research	2015–	77
D. Craig Brater	VP for Life Sciences VP for University Clinical Affairs	2006–2010 2010–2013	51
Jay L. Hess	VP for University Clinical Affairs EVP for University Clinical Affairs	2013–2018 2018–	197

CHANCELLORS AND PROVOSTS

BLOOMINGTON

Name	Title	Years held	Page
Kenneth R. R. Gros Louis	VP and Chancellor, IUB	1980–1988	169
	VP for Academic Affairs and Chancellor, IUB	1988–2001	
	Senior VP and Interim Chancellor, IUB	2004–2006	
Sharon Stephens Brehm	VP for Academic Affairs and Chancellor, IUB	2001–2003	60
Michael A. McRobbie	Interim VP and Provost, IUB	2006–2007	253
Karen Hanson	EVP and Provost, IUB	2007–2012	182
Lauren K. Robel	EVP and Provost, IUB	2012–	354

The position of Provost and Vice President for Academic Affairs for the IUB campus was created in January 2006 by President Herbert and the Board of Trustees, eliminating the position of Chancellor for the Bloomington campus and making the President the CEO of the Bloomington campus.

INDIANAPOLIS

Name	Title	Years held	Page
Glenn W. Irwin Jr.	VP and Chancellor of IUPUI	1973–1986	205
Gerald L. Bepko	VP Indianapolis and Chancellor of IUPUI	1986–2002	27
William M. Plater	Acting Chancellor, IUPUI	2002–2003	*
Charles R. Bantz	Chancellor, IUPUI	2003–2006	20
	EVP and Chancellor, IUPUI	2006–2015	
Nasser H. Paydar	EVP and Chancellor, IUPUI	2015–	308

Biographies are not included for individuals who held positions for fewer than twelve months.

Tables of Roles

EAST

Name	Years held	Page
Glenn A. Goerke	1981–1986	15*
David J. Fulton	1986–1987 (*Acting*)	13*
Charlie Nelms	1987–1994	28*
David J. Fulton	1994–1995 (*Acting*) 1995–2007	13*
Nasser H. Paydar	2007–2012	30*
Laurence D. Richards	2012–2013 (*Interim*)	34*
Kathryn Cruz-Uribe	2013–	10*

KOKOMO

Name	Years held	Page
Hugh Lee Thompson	1980–1990	41*
Arthur C. Gentile	1990–1991 (*Acting*)	
Emita Brady Hill	1991–1999	20*
Ruth J. Person	1999–2008	31*
Stuart M. Green	2008–2010 (*Interim*)	16*
Michael Harris	2010–2012	18*
Susan Sciame-Giesecke	2012–	36*

NORTHWEST

Name	Years held	Page
Danilo Orescanin	1975–1983	29*
Peggy Gordon Elliott Miller	1983–1984 (*Acting*) 1984–1992	25*
Lloyd A. Rowe	1992–1993 (*Acting*)	
Hilda Richards	1993–1999	34*
Bruce W. Bergland	1999–2010	3*
William J. Lowe	2010–	23*

*Biographies are not included for individuals who held positions for fewer than twelve months.

SOUTH BEND

Name	Years held	Page
Lester M. Wolfson	1969–1987	463
H. Daniel Cohen	1987–1995	83
Lester C. Lamon	1995–1997 (*Interim*)	224
Kenneth L. Perrin	1997–2002	312
Una Mae Reck	2002–2013	333
Terry L. Allison	2013–2018	2
Jann L. Joseph	2018– (*Interim*)	212

SOUTHEAST

Name	Years held	Page
Edwin W. Crooks	1968–1985	99
Leon Rand	1986–1996	330
F. C. Richardson	1996–2002	349
Sandra R. Patterson-Randles	2002–2013	305
Barbara A. Bichelmeyer	2013–2014 (*Interim*)	34
Ray Wallace	2014–	438

BOARD OF TRUSTEES

SECRETARIES OF THE BOARD OF TRUSTEES

Name	Years held	Page
Robert E. Burton	1981–1988	67
Janet C. Shirley	1988–1990	374
Susan Parrish	1990–1998	303
Robin Roy Gress	1998–2014	164
Deborah A. Lemon	2014–	227

TRUSTEES

Name	Years held	Page
Robert E. Gates	1969–1990	142
William G. Bannon	1971–1983	17
Joseph M. Black	1972–1993	41
Richard B. Stoner	1972–1992	398
Carolyn P. Gutman	1974–1986	173
Clarence W. Long	1975–1984	230
Harry L. Gonso	1976–1994 2017–	155
Elizabeth Blumberg Polley	1980–1986	327
James W. Gray	1981–1983	158
Emerson Kampen	1983–1989	216
John R. Talley	1983–1985	410
James W. Dye	1984–1990	105
Thomas R. Haley III	1985–1987	179
Edgar F. Kettler	1986–1989	219
Ann Whitlock Swedeen	1986–1992 1994–1997	404
Joseph R. Motherwell	1987–1989	277
Susanne P. Bair	1989–1991	14
Milton J. Fineberg	1989–1994	126
Robert H. McKinney	1989–1998	249
Frederick F. Eichhorn Jr.	1990–2005	112
John D. Walda	1990–2001	429
Eric A. Todd	1991–1993	423
P. A. Mack Jr.	1992–1998	239
R. Ray Richardson	1992–2001	352
J Thomas Forbes	1993–1995	129
Cynthia P. Stone	1993–1996	395
William A. Cook	1995–1998	92
Frank D. Otte	1995–1997	296
James Thomas Morris	1996–2002 2013–	271
Cora Smith Breckenridge	1997–2006	54
Rose E. Gallagher	1997–1999	136
Stephen A. Backer	1998–2004	13

TRUSTEES, *continued*

Name	Years held	Page
Stephen L. Ferguson	1998–2010	122
Peter L. Obremskey	1998–2004	287
Dean A. Hertzler II	1999–2001	194
Sue H. Talbot	2001–2010	407
Sacha I. Willsey Urban	2001–2003	426
Jamie B. Belanger	2002–2005	24
Patrick A. Shoulders	2002–	376
Erin Haag Breese	2003–2005	57
Clarence W. Boone Sr.	2004–2007	44
Jeffrey S. Cohen	2004–2007	86
William R. Cast	2005–2014	74
Casey B. Cox	2005–2007	96
Thomas E. Reilly Jr.	2005–2014	336
Philip N. Eskew Jr.	2006–2018	115
Jack M. Gill	2007–2010	145
Arthur D. King	2007–2009	222
Derica W. Rice	2007–2016	340
Abbey Rae Stemler	2009–2011	389
MaryEllen Kiley Bishop	2010–	38
Bruce Cole	2010–2013	89
William H. Strong	2010–2013	401
Cora J. Griffin	2011–2013	166
Janice L. Farlow	2013–2015	119
Randall L. Tobias	2013–2016	420
Michael J. Mirro	2014–	265
Andrew F. Mohr	2014–2017	269
Anna M. Williams	2015–2017	451
William Quinn Buckner	2016–	64
Melanie S. Walker	2016–	435
Zachary D. Arnold	2017–	8
Donna Spears	2018–	386

ABBREVIATIONS

IU	Indiana University
IUB	IU Bloomington, Indiana University Bloomington
IUPUI	the Indianapolis campus, Indiana University–Purdue University Indianapolis
IPFW	the Fort Wayne campus, Indiana University–Purdue University Fort Wayne
IUE	IU East, Indiana University East
IUK	IU Kokomo, Indiana University Kokomo
IUN	IU Northwest, Indiana University Northwest
IUPUC	IUPU–Columbus, Indiana University–Purdue University Columbus
IUS	IU Southeast, Indiana University Southeast
IUSB	IU South Bend, Indiana University South Bend
AA	Associate of Arts
BA	Bachelor of Arts
BS	Bachelor of Science
MA	Master of Arts
MBA	Master of Business Administration
MEd	Master of Education
MFA	Master of Fine Arts
MLS	Master of Library Science
MPA	Master of Public Administration
MS	Master of Science
DDS	Doctor of Dental Surgery
DMD	Doctor of Medical Dentistry
EdD	Doctor of Education
JD	Doctor of Jurisprudence
MD	Doctor of Medicine
PED	Doctor of Physical Education
PhD	Doctor of Philosophy

Biographies of Trustees
and Officers

TERRY L. ALLISON
1955–

Chancellor, IU South Bend,
2013–2018

As a librarian, professor, and university administrator, Terry Allison has seemingly spent his life organizing and planning both inside the academy and beyond its ivied walls.

Terry L. Allison was born October 2, 1955, in Fort Worth, Texas, to Betty Burnett, an administrative assistant, and Franklin D. Allison, a chief petty officer in the U.S. Navy and a golf assistant pro. Allison grew up in the U.S. Navy, living in Texas, California, Hawaii, and Japan. He attended public schools, including Barber's Point Elementary School in Hawaii during 3rd–6th grades, an experience that he credits as influencing his whole life; he also attended Lemoore Union High School in California, the high school of Tommie Smith, who won a 1968 Olympic Gold Medal in the 200m sprint and famously protested the state of human rights by raising his fist during the national anthem. Allison has also been inspired by a long line of ancestors that he traces back to 1589 and which includes the sixth governor of the Massachusetts Bay Colony, the female Quaker preacher Charity Grubb, and several who fought in the Revolutionary War. After high school, Allison attended the University of California Berkeley, earning a BA in economics and political science with honors (1977), followed by a Master of Library and Information Sciences (1983). He then went to UC San Diego, where he earned a Master of Arts in comparative literature (1992) and a PhD in literature (2000).

Allison worked as a library assistant at UC Berkeley (1977–1983) and then as a librarian at the New York Public Library (1983–1986) and at UC San Diego (1986–1991). As one of its first thirty-five faculty members, he joined fledgling California State University San Marcos (1991–2006), where he was a faculty member in the library, chair and co-chair of women's studies, university planning officer, and interim vice president for administration and finance. From 2006 to 2010, Allison held the positions of dean of arts and letters and professor of English at California State University Los Angeles, where he implemented a new MFA in television, film, and theatre. He then became provost and professor of English at Governors State University in Illinois (2010–2013), where he helped the university gain reaccreditation as well as approval to begin lower division studies.

In 2013, Terry Allison joined Indiana University South Bend as its fifth chancellor. He developed an academic master plan and campus strategic plan. Under his leadership, the campus implemented a number of new majors and graduate programs, and it also completed major renovations of the Administration Building and Riverside Hall. The campus also received its largest gift to name the Vera Z. Dwyer College of Health Sciences (2014) and subsequently received a second endowed Dwyer Chair (2016). Allison stewarded the campus through its Jubilee Year (2016–2017), which celebrated 100 years of offering classes, fifty years of awarding degrees, and twenty-five years since the founding of the Raclin School of the Arts. After successfully guiding IUSB through its reaccreditation process in fall 2017, Allison resigned as chancellor at the end of the school year in 2018, returning to a faculty position.

Beyond the university, Allison has been active in community and civic organizations. Over the years, these have included Federation of Gay Games, for which he served on the board of directors (1990–1996) and as co-chair of the Archives Committee (1991–1995); City of San Marcos Creekside Specific Planning Committee (2005–2006); South Metropolitan Higher Education Consortium (2010–2013); Complete the Degree College Leadership Council of Chicago (2011–2013); Cook County/Foundations Economic Development Working Group (2011); Village of Flossmoor, Illinois, Public Arts Commission (2011–2013); Riley Children's Hospital Foundation, South Bend Region Committee (2014–2017); LGBTQ Presidents in Higher Education (2013–), including various committees; AASCU New Presidents' Academy Advisory Committee (2014–2015); South Bend Symphony Orchestra, board member (2014–); Regional Cities Northern Indiana steering committee (2015–2016); North Central Indiana Regional Development Authority, Workforce Development Committee, co-chair (2017–). ◌▨

JOHN S. APPLEGATE
1957–

Executive Vice President for University Regional Affairs,
Planning, and Policy, 2011–2013

Vice President for University Regional Affairs, Planning,
and Policy, 2010–2011

Vice President for Planning and Policy, 2008–2010

LAWYER, EDUCATOR, AND ACADEMIC ADMINISTRATOR John S. Applegate has served Indiana University in multiple capacities since 1998, from professor of law to executive vice president.

John Applegate comes from five generations of Hoosier stock on his father's side. His paternal grandparents were born in Clay County, and his father (James Earl Applegate) was born in Mount Ayr, Indiana. John was born in Elmira, New York, the eldest of four children, but grew up largely in Chambersburg, Pennsylvania, where his father was a professor of English and a dean at Wilson College, and his mother, Joan, was a professor of music at Shippensburg University. The family spent sabbatical years in England (1962–1963, 1971–1972). John graduated from Chambersburg Area Senior High School, where he was active in orchestra and singing groups, and in several political campaigns. He received a BA in English from Haverford College in 1978, where he was a member of Phi Beta Kappa and recipient of the S.P. Lippincott Prize in History. He earned a JD, magna cum laude, from Harvard Law School in 1981.

After graduation from Harvard, Applegate served as a clerk for Judge Edward S. Smith of the U.S. Court of Appeals for the Federal Circuit (1981–1983) before joining the firm Covington & Burling in Washington, D.C., to practice environmental law (1983–1987). He entered academia as an assistant professor of law in 1987 at the University of Cincinnati College of Law. He advanced to the rank of professor in 1992 and was appointed the James B. Helmer Jr. Professor of Law (1994–1998), twice receiving the Goldman Prize for Excellence in Teaching (1991 and 1995).

Applegate joined the IU faculty in 1998 as the Walter W. Foskett Professor of Law and, from 2002 to 2009, served as executive associate dean for academic affairs for the Indiana University School of Law–Bloomington (in 2008 it became the Maurer School of Law). In 2003 he was a CIC academic leadership development fellow, and in 2006 he was an inaugural member of the IU Leadership Development Program. Over the years, he has taught regularly at the Institut de Droit Comparé, Université Panthéon-Assas in Paris, France; Cardiff University in Wales; and Friedrich-Alexander-Universität Erlangen-Nürnberg in Erlangen, Germany. In addition to his responsibilities in the law school, in 2006 Applegate was appointed by IU President Adam Herbert as presidential fellow, a position he held until IU President Michael McRobbie appointed him vice president for planning and policy in 2008. This title was changed in May 2010 to vice president for university regional affairs, planning, and policy (and then to executive vice president in 2011), before evolving into the position of executive vice president for university academic affairs. In this role, Applegate has overseen the coordination of strategic plans, external academic relations, and policies that enable the university to serve the citizens of the state and nation. Applegate's office works to develop a shared identity for all of IU's regional campuses that incorporates and retains each campus's individual identity. It is also responsible for promoting university-wide collaboration in academic affairs and government relations on academic matters. Additionally, the office is charged with executing IU's public safety mission through the IU Police Department, the Office of Emergency Management, and Office of Environmental Health and Safety.

Active in numerous professional and public organizations, Applegate has served as chairperson of the Fernald Citizens Advisory Board and as a member of the Department of Energy's National Environmental Management Advisory Board. He has been vice chair of the board of directors of the Hamilton County Ohio Environmental Priorities Project. He also worked in various capacities with the Society for Risk Assessment, the Monroe County PCB Task Force, and the League of Women Voters, among others. Since 2010, he has worked extensively with the National Academy of Sciences, serving on multiple boards and committees including the Nuclear and Radiation Studies Board (2010–2014) and the National Research Council (2014–2016).

Applegate is the author of numerous books and articles on environmental law, including the textbook and teacher manual for *The Regulation of Toxic Substances and Hazardous Wastes*, Third Edition (2018). He has also written on the role the public plays in the participation of environmental decisions, including the chapter "Embracing a Precautionary Approach to Climate Change" in *Economic Thought and U.S. Climate Change Policy* (2010).

Applegate lives in Bloomington with his wife, Amy G. Applegate, who is clinical professor of law at the IU Maurer School of Law and director of the Viola J. Taliaferro Family and Children Mediation Clinic. Married since 1980, they have three children: Jesse, Jamey, and Gillian. ꙮ

ZACHARY D. ARNOLD
1993–

Trustee, 2017–

ASPIRING PHYSICIAN AND IU ALUMNUS Zachary Arnold is the third generation of his family to attend the IU School of Medicine and the first of them to serve as a student trustee.

Born June 30, 1993, in Dayton, Ohio, Zachary David Arnold was raised in Indiana by his mother, Julie, the CFO of Indiana Geriatric Associates, and father, William Arnold, a geriatric psychiatrist. He attended public schools in Carmel before completing high school at Brebeuf Jesuit Preparatory School in Indianapolis. His desire to become a doctor came while still in elementary school, when at age nine he helped his Alzheimer's-stricken grandfather navigate using the restroom in a restaurant and then walked him back to the table. This experience, recalls Arnold, helped him to realize that "medicine requires compassion and caring," and motivated him to "aspire to be a physician who takes the time to comfort, listen, and help those who need it." He began studying at Indiana University Bloomington in the Hutton Honors College and graduated in 2016 with a BS in biology and in neuroscience, with minors in psychology and chemistry. Arnold then matriculated to the IU School of Medicine (IUSM), from which he plans to graduate with an MD in 2020, and in so doing follow in the footsteps of his father (MD, 1986) and paternal great-grandfather, a family medicine doctor in rural Indiana who earned his MD in the 1920s.

While at IU, Arnold has held many leadership roles in community and campus organizations. As a graduate student at the IUSM, Arnold was appointed to the IU Board of Trustees in June 2017 by Governor Eric Holcomb for a two-year term. Arnold also serves on the Medical Student Council as an elected class representative for the IUSM—Muncie campus (2016–). In this role, he works as a liaison between students, faculty, and staff as well as organizing events for the Medical Undergraduate Mentoring Partnership with Ball State University students. As an undergraduate at IU Bloomington, Arnold was elected to serve for four years on the IU Student Foundation (2012–2016) and served as vice president of the steering committee. While a member of the foundation, he helped to coordinate events and fundraising initiatives, including the 66th Little 500 Bicycle Race and the promotion of the IU Bicentennial Campaign. He was vice president of communications and social chairman of the Indiana Beta Chapter of the Sigma Phi Epsilon Fraternity (2014–2016). Arnold also volunteered as a mentor at

Templeton Elementary School in Bloomington (2013–2016) and was a certified autism mentor in the Hutton Honors College Autism Mentoring Program (2012–2014).

Arnold's early work experience includes positions as clinical research assistant in the IU Department of Psychiatry (2015), laboratory technician analyzing data in a study of brain networks in cannabis users (2014–2015), medical scribe at Indiana Geriatric Associates (2014), and teaching assistant in for L112 Foundations of Biology at IU Bloomington (2014–2016).

Honors and awards that Arnold has received include the National Merit Scholarship, Curtis R. Simic Leadership Scholarship, Christine Eder and Virgie Neizer Scholarship, Indiana University Excellence Scholarship, and Child of a Disabled Veteran (CVO) Scholarship.

Zachary Arnold and Victoria West were married in Indianapolis in December 2018. ⌘

Stephen A. Backer
1946–2009

Trustee, 1998–2004

A TTORNEY AND LIFELONG HOOSIER Stephen Backer was committed to his family, his profession, and his roots, supporting education in Indiana both as an IU trustee and on the Carmel Clay School Board.

Born in 1946 in Indianapolis, Indiana, Stephen A. Backer lived his whole life in the state where he was born until his passing on March 15, 2009. A graduate of North Central High School, Backer continued his education at Indiana University Bloomington where he earned undergraduate and law degrees in 1968 and 1971, respectively. While at IU Bloomington, he was a member of the Sigma Alpha Mu fraternity and the Student Athletic Board. With a great love for the outdoors, he worked his way through school as a travel and tour guide. Throughout his life, he seldom missed an IU home football or basketball game and was a frequent visitor to the press box during Carmel Greyhound football games.

An accomplished attorney, Stephen Backer practiced law at Backer and Backer PC, which he established in 1974 with his father, Herbert Backer. They specialized in real estate, construction, corporate, commercial, and commercial transaction law. The two worked together until Herbert's death in 1995. Prior to forming the law firm, Stephen Backer was deputy prosecutor in Marion County and was a member of the Indianapolis Bar Association, the Indiana State Bar Association, and the American Bar Association.

Stephen Backer served Indiana University in several capacities. He was first appointed to the Indiana University Board of Trustees in 1998 by Governor Frank O'Bannon and served two terms, stepping down in 2004. In addition to his position as a trustee, Backer was a member of the Indiana University Alumni Association, Varsity Club, and the Well House Society. He also served on the National Board of Visitors at the Indiana University School of Education.

Known as a dedicated public servant, Backer was admired for his staunch commitment to the community in which he lived. Prior to serving as an IU trustee, Backer had been elected to two terms on the Carmel Clay School Board, and after his term as an IU trustee ended he was re-elected to the board and served as president (2006–2009). He also served on the Carmel Clay Parks and Recreation Board and was a member of the Corporate Board of Directors of Salin Bank and Trust Co. He was also a volunteer and board member of Big Brothers Big Sisters of Central Indiana. His community and civic involvement included positions on the Hasten Hebrew Academy board of directors, Indianapolis Hebrew Congregation board of directors, Broadmoor Country Club board of directors, Indiana State Criminal Justice Institute—Juvenile Task Force, Indiana Lottery Commission, and the Central Indiana Community Foundation Legacy Fund. He was twice named a Sagamore of the Wabash by Governors Evan Bayh and Frank O'Bannon.

With his wife, Susan, Stephen Backer had three children—Benjamin, Andrew, and Elizabeth—and from a previous marriage he had two children, Ryan and Jaime. ✍

SUSANNE P. BAIR
1958–

Trustee, 1989–1991

A n accomplished higher education administrator, Susanne Bair began her career at IU and ended it twenty-eight years later at Buffalo State (The State University of New York).

Susanne P. Bair was born November 21, 1958, to Richard Paul and M. Jeanette (Schlunz) Bair in Rochester, Indiana, where she grew up. A first-generation college student, she attended Indiana State University, earning a BA in physical education and business in 1981. She later earned an MA in 1985, also from Indiana State University, before finally earning a Doctor of Physical Education (PED) with a minor in higher education awarded by the School of Health, Physical Education, and Recreation (now School of Public Health-Bloomington) at IU Bloomington in 1991. While working toward her doctorate, she served as the administrative assistant to the associate athletic director for women's sports at IU Athletics.

During Bair's doctoral studies at IU, she served as student trustee from 1989 to 1991. When Indiana Governor Evan Bayh appointed Bair as the eighth student to serve on the IU Board of Trustees, he had no way of anticipating the long career in higher education administration that Bair would achieve. While on the board, she served on the hospitals, real estate and legal, and student affairs committees, and she was the trustee representative to Indiana University–Purdue University Fort Wayne. In recognition of her outstanding service to Indiana University, President Thomas Ehrlich awarded her the Thomas Hart Benton Mural Medallion in 1991, citing her wise counsel, faithful attendance at university functions, significant contributions as an advisor and decision maker, and her unique stature not only as the first trustee to earn a doctorate during her term on the board but also as the first female student trustee.

After receiving her bachelor's degree, Bair took a job teaching at Attica High School in Attica, Indiana, where she coached basketball and volleyball and was eventually appointed the school's athletic director—the fourth female in the state to hold this position. After receiving her doctorate, Bair became associate athletic director at Northeast Missouri State University (now Truman State University) from 1991 to 1993. In 1993, she returned to Indiana University, working as associate director of development and external affairs for the School of Health, Physical Education, and Recreation (HPER). In 1995 Bair was promoted to director, and in 2000 she held the additional position of assistant dean; she held both positions until 2002. She also held a part-time faculty title of assistant professor of kinesiology and adjunct faculty member at the IU Center on Philanthropy (now the IU Lilly Family School of Philanthropy). While at HPER, she created the strategy for a major academic endowment campaign, secured gifts for faculty chairs and professorships, and was responsible for the solicitation of the largest monetary gift the school had ever received. She left HPER to become vice president of development at the Indiana University Foundation in 2002. While in Bloomington, she was a member of the Bloomington Development Council, served on the board of directors for the Lutheran Campus Ministry, and was a member of the Rotary Club.

In 2005 and 2006, Bair served as vice president of development at Fletcher Allen Health Care in Vermont. In 2007, she was appointed vice president of institutional advancement at Buffalo State and served ten years before retiring. At Buffalo State, Bair oversaw the offices of development, alumni affairs, college relations, government relations, and serves as the executive director of the Buffalo State College Foundation Inc. In the fall of 2012, she led Buffalo State into the public phase of Transforming Lives, the college's first-ever comprehensive campaign which exceeded by over $7 million its goal of raising $20 million when it concluded in 2015. Bair also served on the board of directors of the Richardson Olmsted Complex (2014–2017).

Susanne Bair enjoys reading, woodworking, and gardening and currently resides in Buffalo, New York. ༄

William G. Bannon
1921–2007

Trustee, 1971–1983

A S STUDENT, PROFESSOR, TRUSTEE, and abiding supporter of IU athletics, William Gregory Bannon had a long and passionate relationship with Indiana University.

Son of Freeman R. and Nell (Gregory) Bannon, William was born in Kokomo, Indiana, on December 18, 1921. His father received a medical degree from Indiana University in 1911 and his mother was a nurse. William graduated from Kokomo High School in 1939 and entered Indiana University, where he obtained a BA in 1943 and an MD in 1945. He later earned an MS in medicine at the University of Minnesota (1952) after serving in the United States Army from 1943 to 1948. He completed a three-year fellowship at the Mayo Clinic in 1952 and became a Diplomate of the American Board of Internal Medicine in 1955.

Bannon began his internal medicine practice in Terre Haute in 1952 and was a member of the Union Hospital staff for thirty-eight years, serving as its president in 1972. Deeply committed to the quality of patient care, Bannon received the Physician of the Year award from the Indiana Mental Health Association in 1968; he donated the monetary award that accompanied the honor to the IU Scholarship Fund. His medically related activities included directorships on the State Cancer Board, State Mental Health Association, State Maternal Mortality Commission, and State Regional Health Planning Commission for Nursing Education; membership on the Mayor's Commission on Human Relations, American Board of Internal Medicine, and the American College of Physicians; and a term as president of the Medical Alumni Association.

William Bannon's relationship to Indiana University deepened when Governor Edgar Whitcomb appointed him to the IU Board of Trustees in 1971. He was reappointed three times by Governor Otis Bowen in 1974, 1977, and 1980. After his last term as trustee, Bannon continued to serve the university in the IU School of Medicine as clinical professor of medicine at the Terre Haute Center for Medical Education from October 1 1987, to June 30, 1990. Throughout his life, Bannon maintained an intense interest in IU sports, and often voiced his opinion on athletic matters to the university administration even before becoming a trustee. He served as president of the Vigo County Varsity Club and was a member of the Varsity Club's Hoosier 100.

William Bannon also devoted himself to his community. He was a member of Phi Kappa Psi, Rotary, Elks, Central Presbyterian Church, a board member of the IU Foundation, and a life member of the Indiana University Alumni Association, where he served as a member of the Executive Council. He also found time to serve the community as president of the United Fund for Terre Haute, the Terre Haute Chamber of Commerce, and the Terre Haute Council of Churches, and as Chairman of the Vigo County Commission on the Aged and Aging. He was a director of the Fort Harrison Savings and Loan Association of Terre Haute and of the Valley Federal Savings and Loan. For his service and contributions to Terre Haute, Bannon received the Chapman S. Root Award and an honorary Doctor of Science from Rose-Hulman Institute of Technology in 1999.

On July 4, 1942, William Bannon married Jane Gertrude Alexander, who obtained a BA from Indiana University in 1943 but preceded her husband in death in 2000. They had three children, all of whom graduated from Indiana University: Sue Bannon Latham (AB psychology 1966), Pamela Bannon Denning (BS education 1971), and Lynn Ellen Bannon Crawford (AB Spanish 1975, MSW social work 1989).

William Bannon passed away on March 24, 2007 in Terre Haute. The William G. Bannon Scholarship at Indiana University was established to honor his memory by providing access to higher education for graduates of Terre Haute high schools. ❧

CHARLES R. BANTZ
1949–

Executive Vice President and Chancellor, IUPUI,
2006–2015

Vice President for Long-Range Planning and Chancellor,
IUPUI, 2003–2006

T WELVE YEARS OF LEADERSHIP for Indiana University culminate Charles Bantz's lifetime career in higher education as a distinguished professor and administrator. Under his leadership, IUPUI more clearly distinguished itself as Indiana's urban higher education campus.

Born October 5, 1949, to parents Harriett Bernice Dowdell and Douglas William Bantz, Charles grew up in Aberdeen, South Dakota. Harriett was an investor and homemaker while William was a practicing attorney at Bantz, Gosch & Cremer, a firm that he helped launch in 1963. Growing up, Charles Bantz was inspired by his grandmother Ethel Dowdell Abild (1888–1989), who regaled her grandson with stories of her life as a teacher, public servant, historian, and author, including serving during the Great Depression as state director of the professional and service division of the Federal Work Projects Administration, publishing articles on South Dakota history (including on Calamity Jane, whom she met), and her experience of having to jump out of a burning hotel in her 90s. Charles Bantz was also deeply influenced by his lifelong friendship with John Edward Hasse, a PhD in folklore from IU Bloomington and co-founder of the Smithsonian Masterworks Jazz Orchestra with the late David Baker, the IU jazz legend. Bantz received a BA in English education from the University of Minnesota in 1971, as well as an MA in speech-communication in 1973. He received a PhD in communication from The Ohio State University in 1975.

Charles Bantz has had a long and distinguished career in higher education, beginning as an assistant professor at the University of Colorado, Boulder (1975–1977). He joined the University of Minnesota, Twin Cities, first as an assistant professor and was promoted to associate professor in the Department of Speech-Communication (1977–1988). He taught at Arizona State University (ASU) from 1986 to 2000 as associate professor and then professor in the Department of Communication (renamed the Hugh Downs School of Communication in 1999). He gained administrative experience at ASU as director of graduate studies for the Department of Communication (1988), department chair (1989–1995), director for university continuous improvement (1996–2000), and vice provost (1995–2000). From 2000 to 2003, Bantz served as provost and senior vice president for academic affairs at Wayne State University in Detroit.

Indiana University hired Bantz in June 2003 on the recommendation of then-Interim President Gerald L. Bepko to lead IUPUI as chancellor (succeeding Acting Chancellor William M. Plater) and to serve the entire university as vice president for long-range planning, in which capacity he functioned as the chief academic officer for the campuses of IU Northwest, IU South Bend, IU East, IU Kokomo, IU Southeast, and IUPUI until 2006, when the campuses gained their own chief academic officers. In January of 2006, President Herbert and the Board of Trustees decided that the title of the vice president for long-range planning would be modified to executive vice president and the duties expanded; these duties included, for example, addressing the full range of university-level policy and administrative issues, providing coordination and consultative services to campus chancellors and academic vice chancellors, and monitoring the conduct of all undergraduate academic programs. Bantz also received additional academic appointments as professor of management, of communication studies, and of organizational leadership and supervision.

During Bantz's time as chancellor of IUPUI, the campus was able to generate over $400 million in external funds as well as raise over $2 billion in two capital campaigns. He implemented numerous undergraduate and graduate degree programs, increased the number of graduates holding each type of those degrees, and was active in fostering on-campus diversity. Under his leadership, the campus initiated seven new facilities projects, received a Presidential Award for community service, and was listed several times in the *U.S. News & World Report* annual college rankings. As executive vice president, Bantz expertly addressed a full range of university-level policy and administrative issues, in addition to serving as a liaison between Indiana University and the Indiana Commission for Higher Education, as well as a presidential liaison to the Board of Trustees' Academic Affairs Committee. He served as the chair of the Academic Leadership Council. In December 2009, Bantz represented the university in signing a strategic alliance with Sun Yat-Sen University in Guangzhou, China.

Bantz has been involved in a wide range of professional and community service organizations. He served as editor for the quarterly journal *Communication Monographs* and on several committees for the National Communication Association, including as chair of the Organizational Communication Division and the Mass Communication Division. He also served as chair for the Publications Committee of the International Communication Association. From 2005 to 2011 he served the NCAA as a member of the Executive Committee, Division I Board of Directors, and the Presidential Advisory Group. He also helped lead the Coalition of Urban Serving Universities as president (2013–2015), president-elect (2010–2013), and director (2004–2015). Deeply involved with community matters, Bantz has served as a board member for numerous local committees, including the United Way of Central Indiana, Indianapolis Downtown Inc., the Greater Indianapolis Chamber of Commerce, the Greater Indianapolis Progress Committee, the Indiana Sports Corporation, the Skyline Club, and the Indiana Campus Compact. He was also a publicly elected trustee for the town of Crow's Nest, Indiana (2003–2015).

Charles Bantz has been recognized multiple times for his contributions as a scholar, as an administrator, and to the State of Indiana. Some of these recognitions include being the recipient of the National Communication Association's Outstanding Book Award, a Recognition Award from the Academic Senate at Arizona State University, the Gerald L. Bepko Outstanding Administrator Award from the IUPUI Faculty Council (2015), the IU President's Medal (2015), and the Sagamore of the Wabash (2015). Upon retiring, Bantz was named executive vice president and chancellor emeritus.

Since returning to the faculty in 2015, Bantz has worked as executive director of the Center for Translating Research into Practice (TRIP), and in 2016 became an affiliate faculty member at the IU Lilly Family School of Philanthropy. He has also continued serving on the board of directors for Downtown Indy, Inc.

In 1984 Charles Bantz married Dr. Sandra Petronio, who holds faculty appointments at IUPUI and at the Indiana University School of Medicine, and together they raised Kristen E. Petronio. ❧

JAMIE B. BELANGER
1978–

Trustee, 2002–2005

O NLY TWO YEARS AFTER RECEIVING his undergraduate degree, Jamie B. Belanger served as an alumni-elected member of the Board of Trustees of Indiana University.

Born in Canada, Belanger and his parents moved to Michigan when he was in elementary school. He attended Indiana University Bloomington, earning a BS in business in 2000. He took classes in the Honors College; was treasurer and president of the Pi Kappa Phi fraternity, president of the Order of Omega Honorary Society, a member of the Blue Key Honor Society; and rode twice in the Little 500 bicycle race.

Belanger's service on the IU Board of Trustees is remembered for his professionalism mixed with youthfulness. In 2002, he became the youngest person ever to be elected to the Board of Trustees, at the age of 24. That year, he ran a very successful election campaign and was elected by alumni of Indiana University by a huge margin—he received more than 7,000 votes, beating his closest competitor by over 3,000 votes. At the time of Belanger's election, approximately 81 percent of all IU alumni were under the age of 55. In addition to being the youngest member-elect on the board, he was the first non-Indiana resident to serve on the board since state legislators enacted a law in 1999 allowing alumni from outside the state to serve on the IU Board of Trustees. That being the case, Belanger traveled every month from Ohio to Indiana to fulfill his role on the Board of Trustees. During his time as trustee, Belanger worked closely with President Myles Brand, and was able to bring to the board fresh perspectives generated by his ability to relate first and foremost to the viewpoint of current students, keeping in mind the impact the Board of Trustees' decisions would have on them.

Belanger has also served on the IU East Board of Advisors, and has been a member of the Hoosiers for Higher Education. In addition, he has been active with the nonprofit Push America, has volunteered with the Aullwood READS Program, and was the fundraising director for the Pi Kappa Phi Alumni Corporation. He has also been a member of the Iams Company Charitable Contributions Committee.

After leaving IU, Belanger was a financial analyst and profit forecaster for North American Pet Health and Nutrition Sales and Marketing at Procter & Gamble, as well as a senior cost analyst for Folgers coffee and a senior financial analyst for Global Fabric Care, also with Procter & Gamble. In July 2007, Belanger went to work for LexisNexis, a corporation that provides computer-assisted legal research services. With LexisNexis, he has served as lead financial analyst, finance manager, director of financial planning and analysis for research and litigation solutions, and director of finance. He is currently a senior director and the head of global reporting, planning, and analysis (2016–).

Jamie Belanger lives in Ohio with his wife, Amy. ✺

GERALD L. BEPKO

1940–

President (Interim), Indiana University, 2002–2003

Vice President for Long-Range Planning,
1994–2002

Vice President Indianapolis and Chancellor,
IUPUI, 1986–2002

Gerald L. Bepko

A FORMER FBI SPECIAL AGENT, Gerald Lewis "Jerry" Bepko joined Indiana University in 1972 as a professor in the IU School of Law–Indianapolis (renamed in 2011 as the Robert H. McKinney School of Law) and served the university in multiple positions before retiring in 2004; since then he has continued to serve the university in various capacities as Indiana University Trustee Professor Emeritus.

A native of Chicago, where he was born on April 21 in 1940 to Louis V. Bepko and Geraldine Fanstill, Gerald Bepko earned a BS from Northern Illinois University (1962), a JD with high honors from Illinois Institute of Technology (IIT) Chicago-Kent College of Law (1965), and an LLM from Yale University (1972). Bepko practiced law in Chicago in 1965 with Ehrlich, Bundeson, Friedman, and Ross before becoming a special agent for the Federal Bureau of Investigation from 1965 to 1969. After suffering a near-fatal accident while undercover in New York City, Bepko made the decision to leave the FBI in order to work for equity, justice, and fairness through law and education. In 1969, he became an assistant professor of law and director of the Institute for Criminal Justice at the Chicago-Kent College of Law. In 1970 he was appointed a Ford Urban Law Fellow at the Yale Law School.

At Indiana University, Bepko was first appointed in 1972 to the School of Law–Indianapolis. During his tenure, Bepko served as associate professor (1972–1975), professor (1975–), associate dean for academic affairs (1979–1981), and dean (1981–1986). From September 1, 1986, to January 1, 2003, Bepko served as vice president Indianapolis and chancellor of Indiana University–Purdue University Indianapolis. In August 1994, he was given the additional title of vice president for long-range planning, which he held until the end of 2002. As chancellor, Bepko oversaw significant changes on the urban campus including increases in enrollment and external research support, the physical consolidation of the campus to West Michigan Street, the construction of more than twenty new buildings, enhanced campuswide attention to undergraduate education and student performance, increased connections between the campus and the community, and a successful Campaign for IUPUI that generated more than one billion dollars—the first university campus to reach this milestone in Indiana. When IU President Myles Brand resigned in late 2002, Gerald Bepko stepped down as chancellor and vice president in order to serve as interim

28

president from December 2002 through June 2003, guiding the university's transition between the presidencies of Brand and Adam Herbert. Vice Chancellor William M. Plater became acting chancellor of IUPUI from December 2002 to May 2003. In 2004, Gerald Bepko retired with the titles chancellor emeritus, IU Trustee Professor Emeritus, and professor emeritus.

In retirement, Bepko has remained active at Indiana University, working on special assignments both inside the university and in allied organizations under the designated title of Indiana University Trustee Professor Emeritus (2004–). He has continued teaching at the IU McKinney School of Law in Indianapolis and at the IU Kelley School of Business at IUPUI. From 2004 to 2006, he served as inaugural director of the IU Randall L. Tobias Center for Leadership Excellence, which he continues to support in an advisory role. From 2006 to 2016 he served on the Indiana Commission for Higher Education, where he chaired the commission's Academic Affairs and Quality Committee.

Gerald Bepko has served on numerous civic boards; professional committees and councils; higher education task forces, boards, and consultancies; governmental commissions; and corporate boards. Examples include chairing the executive committee of the Riley Children's Foundation Board and serving on the board of the Lumina Foundation for Education, as well as the boards of the Indianapolis Children's Museum, Indianapolis 500 Festival Committee, United Way of Central Indiana, Black Expo, the Indianapolis Chamber of Commerce, American United Life, and Citizens Gas & Coke Utility. Over the years, Bepko has also been active in law reform, government service, and legal education through a variety of organizations. His work in these areas include the Law School Admission Council and American Bar Association/Association of American Law Schools accreditation activity, the National Conference of Commissioners on Uniform State Laws (NCCUSL), the American Law Institute, and the Permanent Editorial Board of the Uniform Commercial Code.

Bepko's service to the nation, his community, and the university has been celebrated with many awards. He has received three Sagamore of the Wabash awards from Indiana Governors Frank O'Bannon, Evan Bayh, and Mike Pence in recognition of his service. Other awards have ranged from teaching awards to honorary degrees and include the Black

Cane Award for outstanding teaching (1976), the Daughters of the American Revolution Medal of Honor (1991), Columbia Club's Benjamin Harrison Award for Public Service (1996), Indiana Black Expo President's Award (2002), Greater Indianapolis Progress Committee Charles L. Whistler Award (2004), and the Anti-Defamation Man of Achievement Award (2005). Bepko has received an honorary Doctor of Laws degree from the Illinois Institute of Technology Chicago-Kent College of Law in 2003; an honorary Doctor of Laws degree from Indiana University in 2007; and an honorary Doctor of Humane Letters from Purdue University at the IUPUI commencement ceremony in 2009. In 2015, IU President Michael McRobbie awarded Gerald Bepko with the University Medal, the highest recognition Indiana University's president and Board of Trustees can bestow on an individual.

Bepko's contributions to Indiana University are memorialized through three named chairs and programs. In 2013 Indiana University created a chair in intellectual property, made possible by the gifts that caused the school to be named the Robert H. McKinney School of Law. The new position was designated the Gerald L. Bepko Chair in Intellectual Property. In 2008 the position of Gerald L. Bepko Professor of Law was created and designated for the dean of the Robert H. McKinney School of Law. In academic year 2004–2005 Indiana University created at IUPUI the Bepko Scholars and Fellows Program, which provides undergraduate Bepko Scholars a tuition scholarship and automatic admission to the Honors College. Bepko Scholars who continue into graduate studies become Bepko Fellows with scholarship support. As of 2017, more than 100 students have been Bepko Scholars.

Throughout Gerald Bepko's service to the university and to the community, he was supported—and sometimes led—by his wife, Jean B Cougnenc, whom he married February 24, 1968. Together they had two children, Gerald L. Bepko Jr. and Arminda. Over the years, Jean Bepko was just as active and engaged as Jerry in both the community and the university. While supporting inter-faith dialogue and understanding, Jerry and Jean Bepko were active in their own spiritual community based at St. Luke's Methodist Church, where Jean taught Sunday school for twenty-six uninterrupted years and was recognized by the naming of the church's children's library in her honor. ⟨≈⟩

BRUCE W. BERGLAND
1944–

Chancellor, IU Northwest,
1999–2010

APPOINTED CHANCELLOR of Indiana University Northwest in 1999 by IU President Myles Brand, Bruce W. Bergland served eleven years en route to the longest chancellorship at the campus until his retirement in 2010.

Born October 6, 1944, at Fitzsimmons Army Hospital in Denver, Colorado, Bruce Bergland moved frequently in his youth—living in Western Minnesota, South Dakota (where he attended elementary school), and Iowa (where he attended high school). Bergland's mother, Lois Margaret Bethke, was a telephone operator when he was growing up, and his father, William Ashley Bergland, had a career as a developer of training systems for B-29 Army-Air Force flight engineers. It was his father that led Bruce to Iowa State University to pursue a BA in psychology with a minor in math. At Iowa State, where he played freshman football, Bergland discovered the joy of working with people and graduated in 1966 as a member of Psi Chi, the psychology honor society. This led him to Stanford University and a PhD in counseling in 1970.

Bergland's first professorship was at Northwestern University (1969–1972), followed by academic and administrative appointments at the University of Colorado at Denver (1972–1995), the University of Hawai'i–West O'ahu (1995–1997), and Trinity College of Vermont (1997–1999). In these appointments, Bergland was responsible for strategic planning, academic affairs, and day-to-day administration; he also served as a special advisor for presidents and chancellors.

In July 1999, Bergland was named chancellor of Indiana University Northwest. At IUN, he is credited with enhancing the quality of arts and culture, creating partnerships between the community and the campus grounded in a shared planning process that involved over 800 individuals, obtaining funding for IUN's first endowed faculty chair, establishing critical assessment and accountability offices on campus, and prioritizing issues of diversity and equity throughout the campus and the community. An important representation of Bergland's commitment to the arts is the IU Northwest sculpture garden, a project designed by his wife, Cynthia, a landscape architect, and containing sculptures by IUN Professor Neil Goodman. In 2005, the Dunes Medical/Professional Building was completed and houses the IU School of Medicine—Northwest. In 2007, the College of Health and Human Services was established, filling a need for highly skilled health professionals in the community and serving as a testimony to Bergland's dedication to IUN students and the region.

In 2010, at the time of his retirement, Bergland was granted the titles chancellor emeritus and professor emeritus of psychology and presented with a permanent sculpture in the Savannah Center (a building dedicated during his chancellorship) marking the dynamism and energy he brought to the campus; the Bruce W. Bergland Arts Scholarship was created in his honor for students in the fine and performing arts; the Board of Trustees named the Savannah Center Auditorium as the Bruce W. Bergland Auditorium; Governor Mitch Daniels named him a Distinguished Hoosier and a Sagamore of the Wabash; and IU President Michael McRobbie awarded the President's Medal for Excellence to Bruce and Cynthia Bergland for their distinguished service to IUN.

Bergland's professional affiliations include the American Association of State Colleges and Universities, American Council on Education, Association of American Colleges and Universities, Beta Gamma Sigma, and the Coalition of Urban and Metropolitan Universities. In Northwest Indiana, he has been deeply involved in community affairs and has served as a member of the board of directors of South Shore Arts and the Urban League of Northwest Indiana in addition to his participation in the NAACP, Northwest Indiana Empowerment Zone, Northwest Indiana Forum, Northwest Indiana Quality of Life Council, Lake Area United Way, Boys and Girls Clubs of Northwest Indiana, Tradewinds, Gary Educational Development Foundation, Mayor's Hall of Fame Advisory Committee, and the University Club. ❧

BARBARA A. BICHELMEYER
1960–

Chancellor (Interim), IU Southeast,
2013–2014

P ROFESSOR OF EDUCATION and university administrator Barbara Bichelmeyer served IU for nearly twenty years, earning many accolades along the way.

The youngest of ten children, Barbara Anne Bichelmeyer was born November 3, 1960, in Kansas City, Missouri, to Mary Helen Matson, a homemaker, and John Floyd Bichelmeyer, owner of Bichelmeyer Meat Company. Her parents have served as a lifelong inspiration due to the hardships they overcame. Her father, also one of ten children, grew up during the Great Depression and was sent to work at a butcher shop and later a stockyard packing plant in Kansas City to send money home to the family. It was in the city that her father met her mother, an only child who worked at a factory in the garment industry. They married in 1938 and started their own business in 1946, which not only survived the 1951 Kansas River flood but grew to include livestock, real estate, and, eventually, real estate development. Barbara's sister Mary wrote a book about customer service based on her conversations with their father, *Lunch Meat and Life Lessons: A Butcher's Wisdom.*

Bichelmeyer's parents valued education greatly, although her father completed only the 8th grade and her mother finished the 12th. Like her siblings, Bichelmeyer attended the St. Joseph Roman Catholic elementary and secondary schools in Shawnee, Kansas. When she went to university, she earned all of her degrees from the University of Kansas—Lawrence: BS in journalism (1982), BA in English (1986), MS in educational policy and administration (1988), and PhD in educational communications and technology (1991). As an undergraduate, she was active at the St. Lawrence Catholic Center as a peer mentor, served as a resident assistant in Naismith Hall, was a student writer for the *Jayhawk Journalist*, and participated in co-ed intramural basketball and softball. She was inducted into the Phi Kappa Phi Honor Society in 1991. While completing her second BA degree, Bichelmeyer worked as a teacher and girls basketball coach at Aquinas High School (1983–1986). While a graduate student, she worked in the Department of Curriculum and Instruction as a research and teaching assistant (1986–1989) and in the Instructional Technology Center as the UNITE project coordinator for training and evaluation (1989–1990). During her final year of graduate school, she worked at U.S. Sprint Telecommunications Corporation as a technical training group training development specialist (1990–1991).

After completing her PhD, Bichelmeyer worked at Sprint United Management Company's University of Excellence as an educational consultant (1991–1993) before founding her own company—Synthesis/ Human Performance Improvement Consulting LLC—for which she was president and principal consultant (1993–1996). During this period, she began her first academic position at the University of Kansas School of Education Department of Curriculum and Instruction as a visiting assistant professor (1994–1996) as well as director of technology (1995– 1996). In 1996, she left Kansas for Indiana.

In 1996, Barbara Bichelmeyer joined IU Bloomington's School of Education in the Department of Instructional Systems, where she rose steadily in rank from assistant professor (1996–2002) and associate professor (2002–2009) to professor (2009–2015). During her nearly 20-year tenure at IU, Bichelmeyer held several administrative positions, including IU Bloomington's associate dean of the faculties (2007– 2009), in which capacity she worked with Professor Russ Hanson to co-chair a 50-person committee to design, develop, and implement the first campuswide general education curriculum. She then served as associate vice president for university academic planning and policy (2009–2013) and founding director of the Office of Online Education (2011–2013). In the latter position, she was responsible for establishing a new office to lead, manage, and coordinate online education on and across IU's seven campuses. She also took on the roles of interim chancellor of Indiana University Southeast (2013–2014) and executive associate vice president for university academic and regional campus affairs (2014–2015).

Since leaving IU, Bichelmeyer has been provost and executive vice chancellor (2015–) at the University of Missouri-Kansas City, where she also holds the rank of professor in the Henry W. Bloch School of Management's Department of Management.

Bichelmeyer has been involved in a variety of community and civic organizations. She has been an ACT National Workforce Solutions Advisory Board member (2013–). In the past, she has served on the Kinsey Institute Board of Trustees (2013–2016) and Executive Committee (2013–2015); Academic Impact Committee (co-chair, 2013–2016); Indiana Supreme Court Commission on Continuing Legal Education's Program Development Committee (2005–2010) and Specialization Committee (2005–2010). She also served on the Habitat for Humanity of Monroe County Board of Directors (2010–2011) and Women's Build Committee (2006–2008, chair 2008–2010), receiving the Leaving a Legacy Award in 2011.

For her service and teaching, Bichelmeyer has been nominated and received many awards. Some of those for service include the IU Distinguished Service Medal (2015); Friend of Ivy Tech Community College (2014); honorary member, National Society of Leadership and Success, awarded at IU Southeast Induction Ceremony (2014); Coin of Recognition, IU Southeast Student Veterans Organization (2014); IU Committee on Multicultural Understanding Award of Excellence (1988–1999). Some of those for teaching include IU Trustees Teaching Award (2000–2001 and 2004–2005); IU School of Education nominee for Excellence in Mentoring (2000–2001 and 2001–2002); IU Teaching Excellence Recognition Award (1998–1999 and 1999–1900). While in graduate school, Bichelmeyer also received the University of Kansas School of Education Dissertation of the Year (1990-1991) and was University of Kansas Dissertation of the Year finalist (1990–1991); she also won the Association of Educational Communications and Technology, Special Research Award (1991) and the Region 7 Leadership Award (1989).

After being in domestic partnership since 1995, Barbara Bichelmeyer and Emily Raeburn Ward were married December 30, 2013.

MaryEllen Kiley Bishop
1957–

Trustee, 2010–

Beginning her long relationship with IU as a student, MaryEllen
Bishop made many contributions to the university over the years as
a trustee and as a member of the IU Alumni Association.

MaryEllen Kiley Bishop was born in 1957 in Marion, Indiana. She
earned a BS in marketing from the IU School of Business in 1979
(renamed the Kelley School in 1997) and a JD from the School of Law–
Indianapolis in 1982 (now the IU Robert H. McKinney School of Law).
She is a member of Alpha Chi Omega Sorority.

Bishop's service to Indiana University has been broad. She was elected
by alumni as an Indiana University trustee in 2010 to a three-year term,
endorsed by Sue Talbot as Talbot's replacement on the board. With
Bishop's election, the board continued to include at least one woman, as
Bishop served at least part of her term alongside student trustee Cora J.
Griffin of Cass County, Indiana. Bishop was reelected in 2013 and served
as vice chair of the board as well as interim chair (June–August 2014),
the first woman to serve as chair of the Board of Trustees at IU. Bishop
has also been the international chair and a member of the board of managers and executive council of the IU Alumni Association, including
serving as chair (2007–2008). She has served as a member of the board
of visitors of the IU Robert H. McKinney School of Law, as a member of
the board of visitors to the Lilly Family School of Philanthropy, and as
the alumni representative to the Indiana University Athletics Committee
and Athletic Director Search Committee in 2008. Additionally, she was
co-chair of the Planned Giving Committee of the IU School of Medicine.
She is a member of the Indiana University Women's Colloquium Planning
Committee and a member of IU Women's Philanthropy Council.

Prior to serving as a trustee, Bishop began her legal career as a tax
associate at Coopers & Lybrand (1983–1987) before becoming a partner
with her husband at Bishop & Bishop (1987–2007), and then a partner
at Bose McKinney & Evans LLP (2007–2009). She is currently a partner at Cohen Garelick & Glazier, serving as a board-certified trust and
estate lawyer, as well as representing clients in individual and fiduciary
taxation. She is admitted to practice law before the Indiana Supreme
Court, both United States District Courts of Indiana, the United States
Tax Court, and the United States Supreme Court.

Bishop has served two terms on the Indiana Probate Code Study
Commission and is a fellow of the American College of Trust and Estate

Counsel, a fellow of the Indiana State Bar Foundation, and a distinguished fellow of the Indianapolis Bar Foundation. Bishop has been named an Indiana Super Lawyer in the practice area of estate planning and trusts since 2004, and is listed in *Best Lawyers in America* in the practice area of estates and trusts and estate litigation since 2006. She has had numerous titles published by the Indiana Continuing Legal Education Forum (ICLEF) and the Indianapolis Bar Association (IBA), and has presented many seminars for ICLEF and IBA. Bishop has also served in several leadership positions within the Indiana State Bar Association and the Indianapolis Bar Association. Bishop's pro bono contributions include serving as secretary of the Kiwanis Club of Meridian Hills (Indianapolis) and as a member of the board of directors of the Visiting Nurse Association.

MaryEllen Bishop resides in Carmel with her husband, Michael Bishop (JD 1980, IU McKinney School of Law). They are parents to Elizabeth (BS 2007) and John (BS 2010, JD 2013). ᑫᔆᑌ

JOSEPH M. BLACK
1918–1999

Trustee, 1972–1993

D ISTINGUISHED FAMILY PRACTICE PHYSICIAN Joseph Black was a key figure in Indiana's health care system, an Indiana University graduate, a president of the IU Alumni Association, and a member of the IU Board of Trustees for over twenty years.

Joseph Morton Black was born to Morton Colfax and Mae (Baker) Black in Seymour, Indiana, on September 17, 1918. In 1937, he graduated from Seymour High School, which inducted him into their hall of fame in 1996. He matriculated to Indiana University, where he earned a BA in 1941 and an MD from the IU School of Medicine in 1944. He served his internship and residency at Indianapolis General Hospital (1944–1946) and, upon completion, entered the United States Army Medical Corps where he served from 1946 to 1948.

After an honorable discharge from the Army, Joseph Black returned to Indiana and began a lifelong career as a physician. In 1962, he became active in the development of statewide medical education. He was one of the founders of the Indiana State Medical Education Plan, president of the Indiana State Medical Association (and received its outstanding service award), a member and vice chairman of the Board of Governors of the Riley Memorial Association, founder and treasurer of the Indiana Medical Political Action Committee, and chairman of the Indiana Blue Shield Board.

Joseph Black was first elected to the IU Board of Trustees in 1972 and was re-elected six additional times, for a total of twenty-one consecutive years of service that stretched to 1993. He also served as president of the IU Alumni Association, a member of the IU Foundation Board of Directors, and a member of the Indiana University Southeast Board of Advisors. He was a member of the Columbia Club in Indianapolis, the Varsity Club's Hoosier Hundred, the IU Foundation's Pacesetter Club and its Well House Society and Woodburn Guild. Joseph Black's involvement with IU as an adult was an extension of his already deep involvement with the university as a youth. As a student, he participated in freshman football and basketball, was senior baseball manager, and was a member of several organizations including Sigma Alpha Epsilon (which bestowed upon him the Order of the Phoenix), Blue Key, the Sphinx Club, Nu Sigma Nu medical fraternity, and the I-Men's Association. At IU, he also worked as a chauffeur for President Herman B Wells and Kelley School of Business Dean Clare Barker.

Joseph Black's contributions to Indiana University, to the State of Indiana, and to the field of medicine have been recognized many times over. He was cited as a Sagamore of the Wabash by several governors and was a fellow of the Royal Academy of Health in Great Britain. In 1978, the I-Men's Association presented him with the Zora G. Clevenger Award. In 1980, he received the Distinguished Alumni Award from the IU School of Medicine; in 1994, he received the Distinguished Alumni Service Award from Indiana University; in 1995, he accepted the Chancellor's Medallion from Indiana University Southeast; and in 1999, he received the J. O. Ritchey Medal for outstanding service to the medical profession by the Ritchey Society of the IU School of Medicine.

Beyond serving the university and the state, Joseph Black was active in his local community. He was a member of the United Methodist Church, Rotary Club, Masons, Elks, Eagles, and American Legion. He also held several community leadership positions, including serving as a director and vice president of the Seymour Community School Holding Corporation. In addition, he was a board member of the Seymour Boys Club (and served a term as president of the board), an officer and a director of the Seymour Chamber of Commerce, and a director of the Jackson County Bank.

On December 27, 1942, Joseph Black married Mary A. Elsner, whose father, Edward Peter Elsner, received an LLB in 1904 from Indiana University. Mary's grandfather and mother, Mae MacDonald, also attended Indiana University. Joseph and Mary had three children, all of whom attended Indiana University: Deborah Ann Divan (BS 1969), Susan Annette Black Edwards (BS 1970), and Joseph M. Black Jr. (BS 1977; JD 1981). Mary Elsner died in June 1969, and Joseph Black married Jane L. Thompson on February 7, 1971.

On December 20, 1999, Joseph M. Black passed away, leaving behind a legacy of exemplary service to Indiana University and to health care in the State of Indiana. ❧

CLARENCE W. BOONE SR.
1931–

Trustee, 2004–2007

T HROUGH A LIFETIME OF CIVIC ENGAGEMENT, Clarence Boone gave of himself not only to his medical patients but also to IU and to his community.

Born in Bryan, Texas, in 1931, Clarence W. Boone came to Indiana to study anatomy and physiology, receiving a BA from Indiana University in 1953 followed by an MD from the IU School of Medicine in 1956. While a student, Boone worked closely with his mentor, IU President Herman B Wells, and was a member of the Student Senate as well as a brother in Kappa Alpha Psi fraternity.

After completing his education, Boone was determined to give back to the university that had helped him fulfill his dreams. From 1984 to 1996, he was on the Executive Council of the Indiana University Alumni Association (president, 1997–1998). From 1984 to 1985 he was president of the Neal-Marshall Alumni Club, a club that he also co-founded. In addition, Boone has been on the Chancellor's Advisory Council at Indiana University Northwest and the Vision Task Force for Indiana University Northwest, as well as on the Advisory Council to the Dean of Indiana University School of Medicine and the Indiana University Medical Center Hospital Committee. From 1990 to 2004, he was a director of the Indiana University Foundation. He served on the IU Board of Trustees from 2004 to 2007, appointed by Governor Joe Kernan.

A physician by vocation, Boone opened his private practice in Gary, Indiana, in 1964, finally retiring from a long career in 1999. Prior to opening his practice, Boone worked at the U.S. Air Force Regional Hospital, Elmendorf Air Force Base in Anchorage Alaska (1961–1964). While practicing medicine, Boone also devoted much of his career to local and national civic engagement, serving as medical director of Planned Parenthood of Northwest Indiana, as well as serving on the National Medical Committee of the Planned Parenthood Federation of America. In addition, he was president of the Lake County Medical Society, president of the medical staff for the Methodist Hospitals of Gary, chairman of the Department of Obstetrics and Gynecology for the Methodist Hospitals of Gary, and president of the National Medical Association—NWI. Boone has also been a Fellow of the American College of Obstetricians and Gynecologists and was Diplomat of the American Board of Obstetrics and Gynecology. Boone's social work has extended beyond the realm of medicine. He has been a member of the Reorganization of the State

Department of Public Instruction, the Gary Housing Authority, the director of the Gary Citywide Development Corporation, and a member of the Gary Community School Corporation's Drop-Out Prevention/At Risk Collaborative Committee.

Boone has been the recipient of many awards, including the Alan Guttmacher Distinguished Service Award from the Planned Parenthood Federation of America (1979), the Dudley Turner Physician of the Year Award (1990), the Sagamore of the Wabash (2000), a Distinguished Hoosier Award (2000), and a Spirit of Scouting Award from the Calumet Council of the Boy Scouts of America (2004). Since 1977, he has been a life member of the NAACP. Boone's service to Indiana University has been recognized with the 1998 Chancellor's Medallion from IU Northwest, the 2003 Distinguished Alumni Service Award, the 2006 School of Medicine Distinguished Alumni Award, and the IUAA President's Award in 2009. In May of 2018, he was honored with a placard introducing the newly named Dr. Clarence Boone Lecture Room on the second floor of the Dunes Medical and Professional Building on the Gary campus, home to IU School of Medicine—Northwest.

He resides in Gary, Indiana, where he enjoys spending time with his wife, Blanche (BS 1952), and their children and grandchildren. ᕦ

MYLES NEIL BRAND
1942–2009

President, Indiana University, 1994–2002

C OMMITTED EDUCATOR AND PERCEPTIVE ADMINISTRATOR, Myles Brand served as the sixteenth president of Indiana University. Under his leadership, the university experienced remarkable growth and increased national recognition.

Born in Brooklyn, New York, in 1942, Myles Neil Brand attended Rensselaer Polytechnic Institute, where he played lacrosse and basketball, earning a BS in philosophy in 1964. Brand went on to earn a PhD in philosophy from the University of Rochester in 1967.

Brand's career in higher education began in 1967, when he was a professor in the department of philosophy at the University of Pittsburgh, a position he held until 1972. He next taught philosophy at the University of Illinois at Chicago, and served as the chair of the Philosophy Department, until 1980. Brand then took his experience and expertise to the University of Arizona, where he stayed until 1986, working as both an educator and administrator, taking on positions including dean of social and behavioral sciences, coordinating dean of the College of Arts and Sciences, director of the Cognitive Science Program, and head of the Department of Philosophy. From 1986 to 1989, he was provost and vice president for academic affairs at the Ohio State University, and from 1989 to 1994, he was the president of the University of Oregon. Brand published widely during his career, and he was the author of over forty-nine book chapters, articles, and reviews.

Myles Brand's tenure as president at Indiana University began in August 1994 and lasted eight years. Under his leadership, total student enrollment rose from 92,769 to new heights of 98,710 in fall of 2002 research grants and contracts rose from $175.1 million in 1994 to $329 million in 2002–2003; and the Lilly Endowment awarded a $105 million private gift to the school to fund the Indiana Genomics Initiative (INGEN), the largest private gift in the university's history at that time Brand oversaw the consolidation of the IU Medical Center Hospitals and Methodist Hospital to form Clarian Health Partners in 1997. The IU Bloomington campus was given the College of the Year distinction by Time magazine in 2001, when IU was the leading public university in private-sector support. Brand is remembered for his yearly contest among students in which the winner switched roles with Brand for the day. The student acted as IU president for the day, and Brand attended classes according to the winner's schedule, immersing himself in daily student life on campus. Brand is also remembered for his role in dismissing long-time IU basketball head coach Bob Knight, and in doing so making clear the university's priorities about academics and athletics. Among faculty and administrative colleagues, Brand was also known for his formidable argumentative skills, through which he engaged in discussion and exploration of important issues essential to both the university and American education. Myles Brand resigned as president in December 2002 with the title president emeritus. At this time Gerald Bepko, chancellor of IUPUI and vice president of long range planning for IU, relinquished those titles and responsibilities in order to step into the role of interim president of Indiana University (January 1– June 30, 2003).

Upon President Brand's retirement, the University Faculty Council honored him for his commitment to improving the university, and they thanked him for being a staunch protector of tenure, a defender of academic freedom and of the academic integrity of IU. One of Myles Brand's great legacies at Indiana University is to have made the university a national leader in information technology, including having established the nation's first school of informatics and having recruited IU's first vice president for information technology Michael McRobbie, who went on to become president in 2007. Another of Brand's legacies is to have created the university's first vice-presidential position of diversity and to have increased outreach, retention, and graduation of students from underrepresented populations. Reflecting on Brand's diversity efforts, former Vice President for Student Development and Diversity Charlie Nelms noted that Brand "understood that excellence and diversity are part of the same fabric, and that you cannot have one without the other. He walked the talk." For his many contributions to Indiana University, Brand received an honorary Doctor of Humane Letters degree in 2009.

When Brand left IU at the end of 2002, he did so seeking to influence higher education at the national level by taking an appointment as the fourth president of the National Collegiate Athletic Association (NCAA), a position he held from 2003 to 2009. During his tenure, Brand transferred the values he instilled at IU to the national stage. Dubbed the NCAA's "education president," Brand placed new emphasis on the education of student-athletes while advocating for greater integration of intercollegiate athletics into the mission of higher education.

Myles Brand was a leader in many community and professional organizations. Always conscious of his community's needs, Brand worked with numerous organizations and councils in support of his neighbors, including the Metro Leaders Task Force on Human Rights and Affirmative Action, the League of Women Voters of Lane County (Oregon), the United Way, the Red Cross, and the Arizona Humanities Council, among many others. Professionally, Brand held memberships on boards and committees for many organizations, including the American Philosophical Association, the Philosophy of Science Association, the Committee on Institutional Cooperation, the American Council of Education, the National Association of State University and Land Grant Colleges, and the Association of American Universities.

On January 17, 2009, it was announced that Myles Brand had been diagnosed with pancreatic cancer; he passed away from the disease on September 16, 2009, at age 67. In his free time, Brand was an avid outdoorsman and equestrian. He loved opera, progressive jazz, folk music, and Japanese food. Together with Peggy Zeglin Brand, Myles Brand had one son, Joshua.

Former first lady of IU Peggy Zeglin is an artist and a professor who taught at The Ohio State University, the University of Oregon, IU Bloomington, and IUPUI in the areas of philosophy, gender studies, and women's studies. She is the first presidential spouse to hold a PhD (philosophy, University of Illinois at Chicago, 1985). She advocated nationally through the Association of American Universities (AAU) for the role of presidential spouse to be recognized as a formal position with a job description, salary, and benefits. At IU, she established several women's initiatives for alumnae including the Colloquium for Women of Indiana University (IUB), Insights Colloquium (IUPUI), *The Caryatid* newsletter, The Academy educational outreach program for women in Indiana, and the Sarah Parke Morrison Society and Fund, which provides scholarships for women at IUB. In 2013 she became emerita associate professor and adjunct associate professor of philosophy and women's studies at IUPUI. Since the fall of 2017 she has been visiting professor of philosophy at the University of Arizona, along with her husband, Dr. Edward Weiser, who is also adjunct associate professor of obstetrics and gynecology at the Indiana University School of Medicine. ℘

D. CRAIG BRATER
1945–

Vice President for University Clinical Affairs,
2010–2013
Vice President for Life Sciences,
2006–2010

PHARMACOLOGY RESEARCHER AND PROFESSOR Craig Brater served IU for over twenty years, leading the IU School of Medicine and life sciences initiatives.

D. Craig Brater grew up in Oak Ridge, Tennessee, in the late 1940s and 1950s, the son of Donald Carl Brater, a chemical engineer and wholesale florist, and Lois Caldwell Brater, a homemaker. Brater attended Duke University, where he earned a BA in chemistry (1967) and an MD (1971) as well as an internship in internal medicine (1971). He completed his residency in internal medicine in 1973 at the University of California, San Francisco (UCSF) and a research fellowship in clinical pharmacology at UCSF in 1976.

After a brief stint as a junior faculty member at UCSF, Craig Brater spent nine years on the faculty at the University of Texas Southwestern Medical School before receiving a call from August Watanabe, MD, who was then chairman of the Department of Medicine at Indiana University School of Medicine. At Dr. Watanabe's urging, Brater joined the IU faculty in 1986 as professor of medicine and director of the Section of Clinical Pharmacology. Upon his arrival in Indiana, he became the seventh generation of his family to live in the Hoosier State.

Brater's research at Indiana University focused on renal pharmacology in general, with an emphasis on the mechanisms of diuretic response and the effects of non-steroidal anti-inflammatory drugs on renal function. In January 1991, he was appointed chairman of the Department of Medicine. In 2000, he was selected as the ninth dean of the IU School of Medicine. During his tenure as dean, he oversaw a 40 percent growth in faculty and the addition of more than 600,000 square feet of research space. He oversaw nine medical campuses comprising nearly 2,000 students, more than 1,100 residents and fellows, and more than 1,800 full-time faculty.

In addition to serving as dean of the School of Medicine, Brater held the title of Walter J. Daly Professor and in 2006 became IU vice president for life sciences, which was renamed IU vice president for university clinical affairs in 2010. In this capacity, Brater was a formal spokesperson and university leader for its life science efforts, convened the deans of the university's clinical affairs units, and coordinated their partnerships with Indiana University Health, Eskenazi Health, the Richard L. Roudebush VA Medical Center, and Larue D. Carter Memorial Hospital.

Brater retired from IU in October 2013 with the titles of vice president emeritus of university clinical affairs and dean and Walter J. Daly Professor Emeritus, Indiana University School of Medicine.

Since his retirement from IU in 2013, Brater has served as president of the Regenstrief Foundation, vice president for programs of the Walther Cancer Foundation, and as president of the Alliance for Academic Internal Medicine.

While Craig Brater is passionate about many of the IU School of Medicine's programs and endeavors, he has a particular affinity for its partnership with the Moi University School of Medicine in Eldoret, Kenya, which has evolved into one of the world's most successful responses to the crises of global health and poverty. Primed by the example of his maternal grandfather, an Indiana farmer who believed strongly in helping communities and individuals who were down on their luck, Craig Brater and his wife, Stephanie, along with their daughter, Aimee, began making regular visits to Eldoret. It was there in the mid-1990s that they met a 12-year-old Kenyan named Michael and his family. The Braters arranged for him to come to Indianapolis to become a member of their family and complete his undergraduate and graduate degrees.

Craig Brater has been the recipient of many honors during his career, including an honorary doctorate from the Purdue University College of Pharmacy, a Research Career Development Award from the NIH, the Rawls-Palmer Progress Award in Medicine from the American Society for Clinical Pharmacology and Therapeutics, and the Burroughs Wellcome Clinical Pharmacology Award. He has served or currently serves on the boards of the United States Pharmacopeia, BioCrossroads, the Fairbanks Institute, and the Regenstrief Institute, and was a member of the Ethics Committee of the U.S. Olympic Committee. ❧

CORA SMITH BRECKENRIDGE
1937–

Trustee, 1997–2006

D ETERMINATION, PERSEVERANCE, AND LOVE for Indiana University are three traits that aptly describe Cora Lee Smith Breckenridge, the first African American ever elected to the IU Board of Trustees. Rather than being intimidated by this fact, she was determined to use her skills as an educator to make her alma mater an institution committed to inclusive excellence.

In many respects, Breckenridge's determination to succeed against all odds was instilled in her by her parents as well as the broader network of aunts, uncles, cousins, and friends, who cared for one another. Her parents, Major Smith and Estella (Andrews) Smith, "came out of the cotton fields of Alabama" to make their home in East Chicago, Indiana, where they reared nine children. Cora Lee Smith was born on June 24, 1937, at the tail-end of the Great Depression. For a living, her father sorted metal at U.S. Reduction Company in East Chicago, Indiana, while her mother, a housewife, reared the children. The Smiths raised their children to love God and value education by working hard on their studies.

Upon graduation from Roosevelt High School in East Chicago, Cora Lee Smith studied at Indiana University through its extension program at the Calumet Center in East Chicago, taking as many courses as possible before transferring to Indiana University Bloomington as a sophomore to complete the requirements for her degree. She earned a BS in speech and language pathology (1959) and an MA in education (1963). To support herself, she worked as a part-time student secretary for Lee Norvelle of the Department of Speech and Theatre and also for Dr. Frye of the Department of Zoology. While a student, Cora Lee Smith developed leadership skills as vice president of the Pleiades Honorary Society, the secretary of her senior class, a board member of the YWCA, a member and secretary of the Alpha Kappa Alpha (AKA) Sorority, a member of the IU Student Foundation, a member of the Speech and Hearing Club, and as an elected member of the prestigious Mortar Board. Her participation and leadership in the multitude of organizations instilled in her a deep appreciation for the way IU enhanced the quality of student lives. Apart from keeping up with her studies and her involvement in extra-curricular events, she was also involved generally in the Bloomington community. She was a member of Second Baptist Church, where she attended church services and also sang in the church choir.

After completing her MA in education in 1963, Breckenridge worked for over three decades as a speech language pathologist in East Chicago, Kokomo, Indianapolis, and Elkhart Community Schools of Indiana as well as in Royal Oaks, Michigan. She retired in 1998; retirement meant not the end of work, but rather the continuation of her work, on a broader scale, for she had just won election to the IU Board of Trustees.

With enduring drive, Breckenridge campaigned for a seat on the board twice before she was elected in 1997 to serve as trustee, becoming the first African American to serve. Her election was not only a personal testimony of perseverance, determination, and vision but also a historical occasion for the State of Indiana because her presence integrated the last all-white bastion of a public university governing board in the state. During her three-term tenure on the board, Breckenridge focused on three major issues: keeping higher education accessible and affordable, retaining and recruiting students, and recruiting and retaining top-notch faculty and administrators. Breckenridge's leadership is reflected in IU's commitment to inclusive excellence, vitality, and international strength. In 2012, Indiana University awarded her the Distinguished Alumni Service Award.

Breckenridge has also served communities beyond IU. She has been president and secretary of the Elkhart Branch of the NAACP, and in 2000 she was elected to the National Board of Directors of the NAACP for four consecutive terms, until 2012. She has been an active member of St. James African Methodist Episcopal Church of Elkhart since her husband retired in 2014 from the pastorate of Olivet AME Church in South Bend (which celebrated its 140th anniversary in 2010).

On June 13, 1964, Cora Lee Smith married Franklin Eugene Breckenridge (BS 1963, JD 1968). He was a practicing attorney and an ordained AME pastor. They are parents of three children: Lejene Elise Breckenridge-Peete (BA 1988), Franklin Eugene Breckenridge Jr. (JD 1994, MBA 2004), and Emma Estel Breckenridge (BS 2001). ᑐᔑᐧ

ERIN HAAG BREESE
1978–

Trustee, 2003–2005

THE FIFTEENTH STUDENT to be appointed to the IU Board of Trustees, Erin Haag Breese served a two-year term while completing an MD/PhD before beginning a career as an oncologist.

Erin Marie Haag Breese was born to Marilyn (Sheehan) and Mark Haag on March 17, 1978, in Indianapolis, Indiana. She attended Our Lady of Mount Carmel Catholic School and Carmel High School, where she graduated as valedictorian. Her academic achievements continued at the University of Notre Dame, where she earned a BA in French and pre-professional studies in 2000 magna cum laude. She also she holds a Diplôme Supérieur d'Etudes Françaises from the Alliance Française. Breese received both a PhD (2006) and an MD (2008) in biochemistry and molecular biology from the IU School of Medicine, studying under the tutelage of Maureen Harrington, a professor in the Department of Biochemistry. Breese was elected as a member of the Gold Humanism Honor Society and received the Lyman T. Meiks Research Award.

Appointed by Governor Frank O'Bannon to a two-year term as student trustee in 2003, Breese served on the Trustees' Academic Affairs and University Policies Committee, Campus Community Committee, Facilities Committee, and Long-Term Planning and External Relations Committee. Breese completed her term on the board while working on her MD/PhD. Breese became well versed in many aspects of IU, including regular board functions, state regulations, and the intricate nature of how all eight campuses operate.

During her time at IU, she was active in recruiting students for medical school, the MD/PhD program, and the graduate school as an admissions ambassador, and she also served on the Executive Council of the Pediatric Student Interest Group. While completing her graduate studies, she received a Graduate Assistance in Areas of National Need (GAANN) Fellowship in 2002–2003 and a Cancer Biology Pre-Doctoral Fellowship in 2003–2004.

After medical school, Breese completed her residency in pediatrics at Riley Hospital for Children in the IU School of Medicine Department of Pediatrics (2008–2011). During this time, she served on the Teacher Learner Advocacy Committee and was selected as a Morris Green Scholar by the Department of Pediatrics. From 2011 to 2014 she held a pediatric hematology/oncology fellowship through Stanford University at the Lucile Packard Children's Hospital. From 2012 to 2014, she held a postdoctoral fellowship in the Division of Hematology/Oncology within the Department of Pediatrics at Stanford University, where her research focused on understanding the pathogenesis of childhood leukemia. Following these fellowships, Breese taught as an instructor in the Division of Hematology/Oncology within the Department of Pediatrics at the Stanford University School of Medicine (2014–2015) before taking a position as assistant professor of clinical pediatrics in the Division of Oncology at the Cancer and Blood Diseases Institute in the Cincinnati Children's Hospital Medical Center (2015–).

Breese has been active in several organizations. She has served as a grant reviewer for the St. Baldrick's Foundation (2015–) and an ad hoc reviewer for *Blood*, the journal of the American Society of Hematology (2015–). She has also published in multiple journals, including *Molecular and Cellular Biology*, *DNA and Cell Biology*, and *Pediatric Neurology*.

In 2003 Erin Haag married Marcus R. Breese (PhD 2011), a bioinformatician/staff scientist at Stanford University whose work focuses on personalized genomics. Together they have a son, Jack Robert Breese, and a daughter, Lauren Michelle Breese. ᑫᔑᒪ

SHARON STEPHENS BREHM
1945–2018

Vice President for Academic Affairs and Chancellor,
IU Bloomington, 2001–2003

D ESCRIBED BY SOME AS A "friendly workaholic with an infinite amount of energy and commitment to excellence," Sharon Stephens Brehm was the first woman to be appointed chancellor of the Indiana University Bloomington campus.

Brehm was born and raised in Roanoke, Virginia. Attending Duke University from 1963 to 1967, she graduated Phi Beta Kappa with a BS degree in psychology. After receiving an MA in social relations (clinical psychology) from Harvard University in 1968, she returned to Duke from 1970 to 1973, earning her PhD in clinical psychology, and then completed a clinical psychology internship at the University of Washington Medical Center.

Before coming to Indiana University, Brehm had an outstanding career that included fifteen years on the psychology faculty at the University of Kansas, where she was also director of the college honors program (1987–1990). She held subsequent posts as dean of the Harpur College of Arts and Sciences at the State University of New York, Binghamton (1990–1996) and as provost at Ohio University (1996–2001). Brehm was also a Fulbright Senior Research Scholar at the École des Hautes Études en Sciences Sociales and a visiting professor in Germany and Italy. She chaired the governing board of Ohio's statewide higher education library consortium, was the founding chair of the governing board of the Ohio Learning Network, and served as a member of the American Council on Education's Commission on International Education.

Brehm arrived at Indiana University in March 2001, when she was named chancellor of the Bloomington campus and vice president for academic affairs by President Myles Brand. In addition to her administrative roles, Brehm also held a tenured position in the College of Arts and Sciences as professor of psychological and brain sciences and a position as adjunct professor in the School of Public and Environmental Affairs. As chancellor, Sharon Brehm worked on many difficult issues such as the aftermath of the September 11 terrorist attacks in 2001, the Thomas Hart Benton mural controversy in 2002, and the transition from the Brand presidency to the Herbert presidency in 2002–2003. She helped expand international opportunities for students, engaged in strategic planning processes, and promoted diversity. One major hallmark of her chancellorship was the initiation of the Commitment to Excellence program which saw the first major student tuition increase on the Bloomington campus in decades, earmarked around strategic uses of financial aid, faculty retention and recruitment, and a robust investment in academic and student service programs on campus. In January 2004, Brehm stepped down from her administrative positions in order to return to teaching full time. She also continued to provide advice and counsel to President Herbert as senior advisor to the president. On December 31, 2011, Brehm retired, becoming professor emeritus.

Brehm's retirement was a difficult decision, made after being diagnosed with Alzheimer's disease, from which her mother passed away at age 68. In September 2013, Brehm gave her first public talk about her life with Alzheimer's at the Walk to End Alzheimer's. In an interview with Dann Denny of the *Herald-Times*, Brehm reflected on her new reality: "This is who I am now, and I want to make a difference," she said. "I think it's important for the community to understand more about Alzheimer's and what happens to people who have it. If I can help with that by going public, then that's what I want to do." She also expressed her hope that someday researchers would find a cure.

In her own research, Brehm examined the effects of psychological reactance, empathy, and self-focus. She specialized in child clinical psychology, focused increasingly on social psychology, advocated the integration of clinical and social psychology, and encouraged a stronger dialogue between developmental and social psychology. She authored numerous books, chapters, and articles in both clinical and social psychology. Her work includes six editions of the popular textbook *Social Psychology* and editing a collection of papers by feminist scholars, *Seeing Females: Social Roles and Personal Lives*.

In 2007, Brehm served as president of the American Psychological Association (APA). During her tenure, Brehm initiated the creation of the Presidential Task Force on Integrative Health Care for an Aging Population, the Joint APA-Society of Research on Child Development Task Force on Math and Science Education, and the Presidential Task Force on Institutional Review Boards and Psychological Science. Brehm's presidential year came more than 100 years after the APA presidency of William Lowe Bryan in 1903, who served as Indiana University's tenth president, from 1902 to 1937.

In November 2013, Brehm was awarded the IU Foundation President's Medallion during a special luncheon tribute by IU President

Michael A. McRobbie and IU Foundation President Dan Smith. "During her notable career in higher education, Sharon has served with great dedication as an academic administrator, a pioneering scholar, and an enthusiastic teacher," McRobbie said. "She also has been a great friend and extremely generous supporter of Indiana University, and we are honored to be able to recognize her accomplishments and commitment to IU in this way." Brehm created an estate gift that funds an endowed chair in the Department of Psychological and Brain Sciences at IUB.

Sharon Stephens Brehm was married to Jack Brehm, professor emeritus at the University of Kansas. Jack died in 2009 in Lawrence, Kansas, at age 81. Sharon passed away on March 30, 2018. She was an avid fan of opera and ballet, and enjoyed reading biographies and mystery stories. ⟪🦢⟫

WILLIAM QUINN BUCKNER

1954–

Trustee, 2016–

F ROM HIS TIME AS A STUDENT AND ATHLETE to his role as a member of the Board of Trustees, Quinn Buckner has had deep connections to Indiana University.

William Quinn Buckner was born in Phoenix, Illinois, to educators Jessica and William Buckner Sr. He attended Thornridge High School in Dolton, Illinois, where he played football and basketball, winning two state basketball championships. Buckner then attended IU Bloomington, majoring in business. As an undergraduate, he played for the football team, like his father, who had been a member of the 1945 undefeated IU football team. But it was his four years on the IU basketball team under Coach Bob Knight that catapulted Buckner to national recognition and a career in the NBA after he co-captained the 1976 Hoosiers to an undefeated NCAA championship season. That year, he was the seventh overall pick in the first round of the NBA draft, but before he joined the Milwaukee Bucks that fall, he played in the 1976 Olympics as captain of the U.S. men's basketball team, winning the gold medal.

In 1976, he began a ten-year career in the NBA. He started at the Milwaukee Bucks and played with them for six years, during which time he earned a reputation for defensive prowess. He was named to the NBA All-Defensive Second Team three times while with the Bucks, ranking as high as third in the league in steals (1980–1981). Buckner was traded to the Boston Celtics in 1982, where he played regularly off the bench and helped the team to the NBA Finals in 1984 (which they won) and again in 1985. He was then traded to the Indiana Pacers for the 1985–1986 season, after which he subsequently retired. After his playing days ended, Buckner became a broadcaster and analyst for major networks that included ESPN, ESPN Radio, NBC, and CBS, where he called both NBA and college basketball games (e.g., for CBS's March Madness coverage). He made one return to the NBA as a coach of the Dallas Mavericks for the 1993–1994 season.

Buckner was an analyst with the Cleveland Cavaliers briefly before joining the Pacers' television staff, where he became a longtime analyst and color commentator for the Pacers' television broadcasts on Fox Sports Indiana. In July 2004, he was named vice president of communications for Pacers Sports & Entertainment (PS&E). Buckner also leads the Pacers Youth Basketball program, a PS&E initiative to support youth basketball in Indiana. On November 19, 2015, he was inducted into the

National Collegiate Basketball Hall of Fame in Kansas City, Missouri. Buckner's community activities have included serving on the boards of various charities, as well as the Indiana University Board of Trustees (appointed by Governor Mike Pence), Indiana University Foundation, Center for Leadership Development, Pacers Foundation, Community Health Network Foundation, Indianapolis Children's Choir Advisory Council, National Basketball Players Association, First Tee of Indianapolis, USA Basketball, Indiana Youth Institute, Special Olympics of Indiana, YMCA, Indianapolis Zoological Society, and the Big Ten Advisors Council, as well as being a member of Old National Bank Advisory Board. Buckner is also a partner in Mack Financial.

Quinn Bucker and his wife, Rhonda, have four children: Jason, Cory, Lauren, and Alexsandra. ॐ

ROBERT E. BURTON
1918–2007

Secretary of the Board, 1981–1988

E DUCATOR AND ADMINISTRATOR Bob Burton served IU and the Board of Trustees for forty-seven years.

Robert E. Burton, son of Loring Ermer Burton and Edith Roberts, was born in Kearney, Nebraska, on April 28, 1918. His parents were natives of Hamilton County, Indiana, and his father obtained an MS in education from Indiana University in 1940. In 1924, the family moved to Muncie, where his father was a teacher. Robert Burton graduated from Burris High School in Muncie (1935) and Ball State Teachers College, where he obtained his BA in education (1939).

Robert Burton was active in a number of college activities. He was editor of *"B" Book* as well as managing editor and summer editor of *Ball State News*. While working part time in the college business office, he was involved in the YMCA, Pi Omega Pi business education fraternity, Kappa Delta Pi education fraternity, Alpha Phi Gamma journalism fraternity, Blue Key, and the Wesley Foundation. After graduating from Ball State, Burton taught at Bremen High School from 1939 to 1941.

Burton's long relationship with Indiana University began in 1941, when he left teaching to become assistant cashier and ticket manager at Indiana University Bloomington. In 1942, he became assistant to the vice president and treasurer. His work at IU was interrupted during his military service in the Antiaircraft Command Section of the 15th U.S. Army Headquarters (1943–1946). Honorably discharged as a sergeant, Burton received the Army Commendation Medal, the Good Conduct Medal, and four service ribbons. Then he returned to his position at IU. In 1951, Burton also assumed the duties of the assistant secretary to the Board of Trustees until July 1974, when that position changed to assistant secretary-treasurer. He served in that capacity until 1981, when Charles E. Harrell retired as secretary of the board and Burton succeeded him as secretary of the board and platform marshal. At the same time, Burton had been serving as assistant secretary of the Indiana-Purdue Fort Wayne Foundation since 1962. Bob Burton retired from his positions at IU in 1988, and the board unanimously recognized "his insight, his knowledge of Indiana University, and his keen recognition of the purposes and mission of the institution," thanking him for his forty-seven years of service to IU.

While at Indiana University, Burton held leadership positions in the Employees Credit Union, IU Retirement Community, Indiana

Association of College and University Business Officers, Scholarship Committee, and Halls of Residence Committee, and was a member of the Indiana Memorial Union Board of Directors (1969–1972). In 1976 he received the E. Ross Bartley Award for distinguished staff service to IU, in 1986 he received the Leather Medal Award of Sigma Delta Chi, and he was named a Sagamore of the Wabash in 1988.

Burton was active in community affairs and was president of the Greater Bloomington Chamber of Commerce, the United Way (which awarded him the Mary Alice Gray Award in 1995), the Monroe County Historical Society, and the Community Service Council, and served on the boards of the MCCSC Building Corporation and the Hospital Authority of Monroe County. He was a 57-year member of the Bloomington Kiwanis Club and was named a life member of Kiwanis International. He was honored with the award for Outstanding Volunteer of the Year of the City of Bloomington in 1985 and the Citizen of the Year Award of the Bloomington Board of Realtors (with Joan Burton) in 1982.

On May 26, 1940, Robert Burton married Mary Joan Smith of Westfield, Indiana. Mary Joan served as the first executive director of Stone Belt Arc from 1965 to 1985 and made a remarkable impact on the Bloomington community through her advocacy on behalf of individuals with developmental disabilities. Together the Burtons had five children: Ann E. Grimes (BA 1966, MAT 1971), John E. Burton (BS 1968), Nancy E. Morales (BA 1968), William L. Burton, and James E. Burton.

Robert Burton passed away on December 15, 2007, in Bloomington. He and his family enjoyed camping and traveling. He and his wife visited all fifty states and more than sixty countries. He enjoyed football, basketball, and classical music. He attended the First United Methodist Church for sixty-five years and was a leader in the congregation. ᥫᩣ

HANNAH BUXBAUM
1966–

Vice President for International Affairs,
2018–

THROUGHOUT HER CAREER, from attorney to law professor to university administrator, Hannah Buxbaum developed and maintained an international orientation that she has brought to the service of Indiana University and its students.

Born in Cologne, Germany, in 1966 to mother, Wiebke, an attorney, and father, Richard Buxbaum, a law professor, Hannah L. Buxbaum was raised in Berkeley, California. She attended Emerson Elementary School, Malcolm X Elementary School, The Academy (Berkeley), and The College Preparatory School (Oakland). She graduated cum laude from Cornell University (BA in English 1987), and then graduated magna cum laude from Cornell Law School (JD 1992) and summa cum laude from University of Heidelberg (LLM 1993). She was admitted to the Bar in New York (1993) and is also a member of the American Bar Association. As an undergraduate, she performed with the Cornell Savoyards (a Gilbert and Sullivan company) and with the Sage Chapel Choir. She also played club volleyball. In law school she was a member of the moot court board, a finalist in the Cuccia Cup Moot Court Competition, a teaching assistant (constitutional law, freedom of expression, torts), and articles editor at the *Cornell Law Review*; she also performed with the Heidelberg University Chorus.

Buxbaum's graduate school and career choices were inspired by her parents. Her father was a professor at University of California, Berkeley School of Law, and served as dean of international and area studies (1993–1999). He was one of the defense counsel for the 773 members of the Free Speech Movement in Berkeley from 1964 to 1967, represented various campus organizations and individuals in cases arising out of Vietnam War protests, and was defense counsel in a large number of criminal proceedings that accompanied the Third World Strike of 1969–1970. Her mother, Wiebke, was also inspirational, having started over again to earn a law degree at UC Berkeley as one of only a handful of female law students in the class of 1966, after having already earned a law degree at the University of Cologne in Germany. She joined the San Francisco law firm of Brobeck, Phleger & Harrison, where she became the first female partner, and she later served as lead outside counsel for Wells Fargo Bank.

Prior to her IU tenure, Buxbaum practiced law in the area of international securities transactions in the New York and Frankfurt, Germany, offices of Davis Polk & Wardwell as an associate in the Corporate Department, 1993–1997. She was active in areas of banking, mergers and acquisitions, and securities law, with an emphasis on global capital-market transactions.

Indiana University hired Buxbaum in 1997 to join the faculty at the School of Law (now the Maurer School of Law). She held the positions of associate professor of law (1997–2003), professor of law (2003–), associate dean for research (2007–2009), and executive associate dean for academic affairs (2009–2012). In 2011 she was named the John E. Schiller Chair in Legal Ethics. Her research focused on the areas of private international law and international litigation and jurisdiction. She taught conflict of laws, contracts, international business transactions, and international litigation. Buxbaum also served as the school's interim dean from January 2012 to December 2013. During her tenure at the law school, Buxbaum also held visiting scholar posts and lectureships overseas, some of which included conducting research in Germany as a fellow of the Alexander von Humboldt Foundation (2005–2006); teaching as a visiting professor at Humboldt University (2016) and the universities of Cologne (2002), Nürnberg-Erlangen (2001), and Kiel (2000); and delivering a course on international regulatory law at the Hague Academy of International Law (2013). From 2015 to 2018, Buxbaum served as the inaugural academic director of the IU Europe Gateway office in Berlin. In 2018 she was appointed to the post of vice president of international affairs. In this position, she promotes global engagement at IU across all aspects of the university's mission and oversees the offices that manage international admissions and student services, study abroad, international partnerships, and international development, as well as the university's Global Gateway Network.

Beyond Indiana University, Buxbaum has held leadership roles in a number of national and local organizations. Professionally, these include the American Society of International Law, the American Society of Comparative Law, and the Association of American Law Schools. She has been elected to membership in the American Law Institute, where she is currently an advisor for the Restatement (Fourth) of Foreign Relations Law: Jurisdiction and Judgments, and is a titular member of the International Academy of Comparative Law. She has also served as a member of the advisory Board, University of Cologne U.S. office;

member of the advisory board, Max–Planck–Institut für ausländisches und internationals Privatrecht, Hamburg, Germany; member of the advisory board, SSRN Transnational Litigation/Arbitration eJournal. Aside from professional activities, Buxbaum has been involved in several local civic organizations. She has been a member of the boards of directors of the Indiana University Credit Union, Indiana University Children's Choir, and the Monroe County YMCA.

Among the honors and awards that Buxbaum has received, teaching awards are prominent. She has won the Teaching Excellence Recognition Award (1999–2000), Leon H. Wallace Teaching Award (2000–2001), and the Trustees Teaching Award (2007–2008). She is a five-time recipient of the law school's Gavel Award for outstanding contribution to the graduating class (2003, 2005, 2012, 2013, 2014).

Hannah Buxbaum married Edward W. Herrmann in April 1989. Together they have two daughters, Susanna and Julia.

WILLIAM R. CAST
1937–

Trustee, 2005–2014

A PPOINTED TO THE IU BOARD OF TRUSTEES in August 2004 by Governor Mitch Daniels, William Cast served as chair of the board from 2009 to 2013 and retired from the board in 2014. In addition, he served on the board of Indiana University Health until 2015 and on the Indiana-Purdue Fort Wayne Foundation.

Born to parents Alvin Carter Cast (BA 1923) and Marjorie Rose (Miller) Cast in Logansport, Indiana, on September 15, 1937, William R. Cast grew up in Kentland, Indiana, and attended Kentland High School. He earned a BA from Indiana University Bloomington and then graduated from Indiana University School of Medicine in 1962 with a specialization in otolaryngology. While an undergraduate at IU, his activities included memberships in the Board of Aeons, IU Student Foundation, Blue Key, Skull and Crescent, Student Senate, and the Sigma Nu fraternity. After receiving his MD, he interned at Methodist Hospital in Indianapolis and then completed a four-year residency in otolaryngology at the IU medical school. He spent the next two years serving in the Army, stationed at Fort Jackson in South Carolina. He was chief of eye, ear, nose, and throat (ENT) during the two years in the Army.

In 1969, Cast and his family moved to Fort Wayne, Indiana, where he practiced ENT as a physician for forty years. During this time, Cast was involved in many companies and projects both locally and out of state. Some of his major accomplishments include serving as the founding chairman of the board of DuPont Hospital, president of the Fort Wayne Medical Society, and founding president of Tri-State Medical Independent Practice Association. From 1980 to 1991, he edited and published the *Medical Business Review*, a medical management newsletter focused on medical economics and practice management. He has also served as chair of the board of directors of Fort Wayne Medical Surety, a medical liability company in Fort Wayne; a director of Octamer Biotechnology Company, Tiburon, California; a director of Indiana Health Information Exchange, a digital repository for health records in central Indiana; and a venture partner of the Regenstrief Institute. Since 2005, Cast has worked at NoMoreClipboard, a digital personal health records company that is a division of Medical Informatics Engineering, Inc. in Fort Wayne, where he became chief medical officer in 2006. During this time, the company has grown to a top-ranked company that received a key federal grant from the U.S. Department of Health and Human Services, Office of the Coordinator for Health Information Technology (HHS, ONC) to demonstrate patient engagement, identification, and authentication. As of 2017, he is also president of Reduxx Pharmaceutical, LLC.

William Cast has been active in medical volunteer work. He served the Indiana State Medical Association as speaker of the House of Delegates. He was also chair of the lobbying committee that oversaw passage of Indiana's Patient Compensation Act, the first legislation in the country that established a cap for medical liability reimbursement. He served on the board of the American Academy of Otolaryngology, Washington, D.C., and also as an examiner for ENT board certification. One of his proudest accomplishments is being a founder and president for the first seven years of Canterbury School, a private K–12 school in Fort Wayne (1977–1984). The school started in a church basement with eighty-nine students. As of 2017, Canterbury has expanded to two campuses with an enrollment of over 1,000 students. Cast continues to serve on Canterbury Foundation's board of directors.

On April 1, 1961, William Cast married Anita Hursh, and they have three children (Jennifer, Carter, and Meghan) and five grandchildren. A graduate of DePauw University, Anita has adopted IU and served over twenty years with the IU Jacobs School of Music Friends of Music (two separate terms as president) and on the school of music dean's advisory board. She is also a founding member of the Indiana University Foundation's Women's Philanthropy Council. ᗢ

FRED H. CATE
1963–

Vice President for Research, 2015–

P ROFESSOR AND HIGHER EDUCATION ADMINISTRATOR Fred Cate has served IU for over twenty-five years.

Fred H. Cate was born in 1963 in McRae, Georgia, to Dorothy (an antiques dealer) and Robert Cate (a pastor, professor, and academic dean). His family moved a few times in his youth, and Cate attended public schools growing up, including Aiken Elementary School (Aiken, South Carolina), and Mill Valley Middle School and Tamalpais High School (Mill Valley, California). He attended Oxford University for a year, working towards a BA in modern history before completing a BA in history at Stanford University in 1984 with departmental honors and distinction. He was elected to membership in Phi Beta Kappa. Cate earned a JD at Stanford Law School in 1987. His scholarship focuses on information security and privacy law and policy issues.

Cate first came to Indiana University as an associate professor at the IU School of Law in 1990 (later renamed the Maurer School of Law), rising through the ranks to become distinguished professor and C. Ben Dutton Chair in the IU Maurer School of Law, adjunct professor of informatics and of computer science in the School of Informatics and Computing (now the School of Informatics, Computing, and Engineering), and senior fellow in the Center for Applied Cybersecurity Research (founding director, 2003–2014). During his tenure as director, IU was recognized by the federal government as a National Center of Academic Excellence in both information security research and information security education. He also served as founding managing director of the IU Center for Law, Ethics, and Applied Research in Health Information from 2011 to 2015. In 2015, Cate was appointed vice president for research, succeeding Jorge José. During his tenure, Cate has overseen the launch of the university's Grand Challenges initiative and has conducted a review of the vice president for research's role and responsibilities within Indiana University. Cate also worked to expand and diversify support for research and creativity at IU, facilitate public-private partnerships and technology transfer, and increase collaborative research opportunities.

Cate is a member of the National Academies' Forum on Cyber Resilience, the Department of Homeland Security's Data Privacy and Integrity Committee Cybersecurity Subcommittee, the National Security Agency's Privacy and Civil Liberties Panel, the Organisation for

Economic Co-operation and Development's (OECD) Panel of Experts on Health Information Infrastructure, and Intel's Privacy and Security External Advisory Board. He serves on the board of directors of The Privacy Projects, the International Foundation for Online Responsibility, and the Kinsey Institute. Cate is an elected member of the American Law Institute, a fellow of the American Bar Foundation, and appeared on *Computerworld*'s Best Privacy Advisers list. Cate is also one of the founding editors of the Oxford University Press journal *International Data Privacy Law*. He is a senator, fellow, and past president of the Phi Beta Kappa Society.

Cate served on the Department of Defense Advanced Research Projects Agency's Privacy Oversight Board, the National Academies' Committee on Technical and Privacy Dimensions of Information for Terrorism Prevention, the Federal Trade Commission's Advisory Committee on Online Access and Security, and Microsoft's Trustworthy Computing Academic Advisory Board, and as counsel to the Department of Defense's Technology and Privacy Advisory Committee and reporter for the third report of the Markle Task Force on National Security in the Information Age. He chaired the International Telecommunication Union's High-Level Experts on Electronic Signatures and Certification Authorities, served as a member of the United Nations Working Group on Emergency Telecommunications, and was principal drafter of the Tampere Convention on the Provision of Telecommunications Resources for Disaster Mitigation and Relief Operations.

Cate received the IU Trustees Teaching Award in 2004 and 2010, the IU Maurer School of Law Public Interest Faculty Award in 2010, and the IU Teaching Excellence Recognition Award in 1999. The Phi Beta Kappa Society presented Cate with its President's Award and Judith F. Krug Medal in 2015.

Fred Cate married his wife, Beth, a member of the faculty in IU's School of Public and Environmental Affairs and previously associate general counsel to the university, on September 18, 1993. ❧

J. TERRY CLAPACS
1943–

Vice President and Chief Administrative Officer,
1991–2009
Vice President for Facilities, 1986–1991

AFTER A CAREER SPANNING forty-three years at IU, John Terry Clapacs retired in 2009 as vice president emeritus, having served as vice president and chief administrative officer for twenty-five years.

A native of Cleveland, Ohio, Clapacs spent his formative years in Goshen, Indiana. He enrolled at Indiana University in 1961 and never left. His undergraduate days were filled with classes, extracurricular activities, rider training for the Little 500, and fraternity life. In 1965 he earned a BS from the IU School of Business (later renamed the Kelley School of Business), followed by an MBA in 1968.

In 1966, Clapacs joined the IU staff and became one of the guardians of the Herman B Wells legacy. His portfolio included most of the non-academic units at IU. He began as a space assignment coordinator and space analyst (1966–1969), moved to manager of construction contracts and administration (1970–1976), and later was named vice president for facilities (1986–1991). These were not new positions, but rather title re-designations to better match the shifting portfolio for which he was responsible. In 1991, Clapacs was promoted to vice president for administration, a title that was changed in 2001 to vice president and chief administrative officer, a post he held until his retirement in 2009, when he was granted the title vice president emeritus.

Despite these changes in title, Clapacs' main responsibilities remained facilities planning and management. In this capacity, he supervised the development of over two-thirds of the physical assets of the university, including two new campuses in Richmond and New Albany. He planned and implemented 661 major building projects (more than half of all buildings) on the eight IU campuses. He worked diligently to preserve the natural beauty of the campuses, instilling the Facilities Committee with an identity as "the aesthetic watchdogs" of the entire university.

Aside from facilities, Clapacs also had other responsibilities, which included human resources, the university police department, travel management, internal auditing, purchasing, property and casualty insurance, and environmental health and safety, as well as being the liaison between IU's president and the Department of Intercollegiate Athletics. He also served as the athletic director (2002–2004), a position he held along with his duties as vice president and chief administrative officer. One of the most critical of his assignments was his responsibility for the guiding, development, and presentation of the university's capital appropriation requests to the Indiana State Legislature.

Throughout his career, Clapacs' expertise was tapped by twenty-seven IU committees, including the University Names Committee (he succeeded Herman Wells as chair) and the IU Foundation's Board of Directors Real Estate Committee. He also contributed to twenty-three boards and programs in Bloomington and throughout Indiana. Successful leadership in all of these assignments required earning and maintaining the trust of every person, department, and bureau. Terry had a reputation for integrity regardless of pressures from special interests inside or outside of the university, and he was known for keeping his equilibrium in the face of sometimes hostile and inflammatory rhetoric.

Although retired and holding the title vice president emeritus, Clapacs has not lost his passion for the university, the community, or for building and architecture. He served as a consultant for the Bloomington Convention Center expansion, the First United Methodist Church expansion, and the Monroe County YMCA renovation and expansion. He serves on the Wawasee Area Conservancy Foundation Board, has become board chair of the Bloomington Volunteers in Medicine Clinic, and has been appointed to the Indiana High School Athletic Association Foundation Board of Directors. Governor Daniels appointed Clapacs as a consultant to the Lucas Oil Stadium construction commission. Clapacs has recently completed work on a book about the architectural history of the IU Bloomington campus titled *Indiana University Bloomington: America's Legacy Campus* (IU Press, 2017).

Clapacs has received much recognition for his services both within the university and outside, including being named Sagamore of the Wabash by two Indiana governors, election to the Goshen Hall of Fame, honorary membership in the American Institute of Architects, and receiving the Thomas Hart Benton Mural Medallion, the IU Foundation President's Medallion, the Bill Armstrong Ambassador Award, and the University Medal conferred by the Board of Trustees. In 2015 Indiana University recognized Terry with the Distinguished Alumni Service Award.

In 1966 Clapacs married his college sweetheart, Phyllis Wiseman (BA 1965, MS 1976). They have two sons: John Terry Clapacs II, MD, who is married to Ayesha Chaudhary, MD; and Grantland Mathew Clapacs, who is married to Dr. Marla Smith. They have five grandchildren. ᦰ

H. DANIEL COHEN
1937–

Chancellor, IU South Bend, 1987–1995

A LIFELONG EDUCATOR, Daniel Cohen served IU for fourteen years as a professor of physics and campus leader.

H. Daniel Cohen served as the chancellor of Indiana University South Bend from 1987 to 1995. Cohen was born in New York in 1937, and received his BS from Antioch College in 1959. He went on to receive a PhD in physics from Stanford University in 1966, where he was a teaching assistant from 1959 to 1961 and held both pre- and postdoctoral fellowships from the National Science Foundation.

Before coming to Indiana University, Cohen built a career teaching physics that saw him slowly transition into administration. From 1967 to 1972, Cohen was an assistant professor of physics at Brandeis University. During the summer of 1970, Cohen served as the staff director for Joseph Rhodes Jr., commissioner on the President's Commission on Campus Unrest. From 1972 to 1977, Cohen was an associate professor of physics at the University of Vermont, where he got his first taste of administrative work as an associate dean for the College of Arts and Sciences from 1975 to 1977. In 1977 he joined the State University of New York at Binghamton, where he was the associate dean for academic affairs, the dean of Harpur College, and an associate professor of physics until 1982. From 1982 to 1987, he was the executive vice president and vice president for academic affairs at the University of Redlands as well as professor of physics. He was also a visiting professor of physics at Harvey Mudd College in the spring of 1987. Cohen came to Indiana University in August of 1987.

At Indiana University South Bend (IUSB), Cohen improved both the facilities and the grounds. During his tenure, the Schurz Library was built in 1989, and a former Army Reserve center was renovated into the Purdue Technology Building. The first parking garage for the campus was built, and the Playland Golf Course was acquired and turned into recreational fields. In addition, student enrollment grew by 30 percent; the number of academic programs at the campus grew to over one hundred; associate and bachelor degrees were established in nursing, liberal arts, and fine arts; and a master's degree in social work was added. After resigning as chancellor, Cohen continued to serve as professor of physics at IUSB until 2001.

Cohen has been a member of numerous professional associations, including the American Association for Higher Education, the American

Association of Physics Teachers, the American Conference of Academic Deans, the American Physical Society, and the Association of American Colleges. Cohen has also served on the boards of numerous community organizations, including the Memorial Hospital of South Bend, the Michiana Arts and Sciences Council, the Michiana Public Broadcasting Corporation, the Midwest Commerce Bank, Project Future, Rotary International, and the South Bend Symphony Orchestra.

Aᴛᴛᴏʀɴᴇʏ ᴀɴᴅ ᴀᴛʜʟᴇᴛᴇ Jeffrey Cohen has long supported IU and the Indianapolis community through professional and civic service. Cohen was born December 30, 1963, in Wilmington, Delaware, to Lorraine and Gerald, a homemaker and entrepreneur, respectively. A natural athlete, Cohen traveled the world competing in tennis competitions between the ages of 11 and 18. After his graduation from Wilmington Friends School in Delaware, Cohen came to Indiana University Bloomington on a four-year varsity athletic scholarship, where he was a letter-winner for the men's varsity tennis team four years in a row. In 1986, Cohen received his BS in business, and went on to receive a JD from IU's School of Law (later renamed the Maurer School of Law) in 1989. He was a member of the Sigma Phi Epsilon fraternity.

The dedication and resulting success that Cohen experienced as a tennis player translated into his professional career. After completing law school, Cohen joined the Dann, Pecar, Newman & Kleiman firm in Indianapolis from 1989 to 1991. He then spent five years at Johnson, Smith, Densborn, Wright & Heath, where he was partner. In 1997, he joined David Knall (BS 1966) in what was formerly known as McDonald & Company Securities. The duo later formed the Knall/Cohen Group and joined with the financial services firm Stifel Nicolaus. Cohen has been partner in the Knall/Cohen Group and managing director of Stifel Nicolaus' Indianapolis Office since 2005. He works closely with families, foundations, and endowments to manage more than $6 billion in assets.

Jeffrey Cohen has been an ardent supporter of Indiana University. Cohen was appointed to the Board of Trustees by Governor Joe Kernan for three years (2004–2007), during which time he was chairman of the Finance and Audit Committee. In addition to his service on the IU Board of Trustees, he has served as a steering committee member of the Athletics Capital Campaign, as a member of the board of directors of the Varsity Club, and on the IUPUI Board of Advisors. In 2013, he served as national co-chair of the Athletics Capital Campaign. Cohen himself is a significant financial supporter of the university and its athletics program, volunteering and fundraising whenever called upon. In addition, within the IU Kelley School of Business, Cohen established the Knall Cohen Fund, which affords students real-world practice in portfolio management. He is also a regular guest speaker at the Kelley School.

Cohen is also engaged in professional and civic service. He has served as a board member for several Indianapolis community organizations, including Park Tudor School, the Indianapolis Marion-County Public Library Foundation (and previously served on its investment committee), the Jewish Federation of Greater Indianapolis, and Visionary Enterprises, Inc. (a subsidiary of Community Hospital). He is also a former member of the American, Indiana, and Indianapolis Bar Associations and was an appointee of the Marion County Judicial Nominating Committee.

In 1999, Cohen was recognized in the *Indianapolis Business Journal*'s "Forty under 40" list for his accomplishments within the community. In 2008, he was recognized by the *Indianapolis Business Journal* as one of the Best Wealth Managers, as well as one of the Best in Client Satisfaction. Cohen was listed in Who's Who in Banking and Finance by the *Indianapolis Business Journal* in 2011.

Jeffrey Cohen and his wife, Jennie, have two children: Kendall, who enjoys dance, and John, who enjoys lacrosse.

F OR OVER THIRTY YEARS Bruce Cole served Indiana University as a professor and as a trustee, as well as serving the nation as chairman of the National Endowment for the Humanities (NEH).

Bruce Milan Cole was born in Cleveland, Ohio, on August 2, 1938. In his youth he loved motorcycles, but he became inspired to study Renaissance art after seeing Sassetta's painting *The Meeting of Saint Anthony and Saint Paul.* Cole earned a BA from Case Western Reserve University (history and art history), followed by an MA from Oberlin College and a PhD from Bryn Mawr College, both in art history.

Cole first taught art history at the University of Rochester in New York from 1969 to 1973, when he came to IU Bloomington as associate professor of fine arts with tenure. He advanced to distinguished professor of fine arts (1988) and professor of comparative literature (1991), the title he held until his retirement in 2001. His scholarship can be seen in numerous articles and fourteen books, including *Giotto and Florentine Painting, 1280–1375* (1976), *The Renaissance Artist at Work: From Pisano to Titian* (1983), and *The Informed Eye: Understanding Masterpieces of Western Art* (1999). In 1971, Cole received an NEH fellowship to conduct research on "The Origins and Development of Early Florentine Painting." He later served as an NEH peer review panelist and was appointed as a member of the National Council on the Humanities, the 26-member NEH advisory board.

From 2001 to 2009, Cole served as the chairman of the NEH, where he managed a budget of $150 million and a staff of 170 and was responsible for awards totaling over $800 million. Appointed by President George W. Bush and unanimously confirmed by the Senate in 2001 and again in 2005, Cole was the longest-serving chairman of the NEH up to that point in time. Under Cole's leadership, the NEH launched key initiatives, including We the People, a program designed to encourage the teaching, study, and understanding of American history and culture, and the Picturing America project, which uses great American art to teach the nation's history and culture in 80,000 schools and public libraries nationwide. He also created the NEH's Digital Humanities Initiative and Office, which made the NEH a national leader in this new frontier of humanities access and knowledge. Under his tenure, partnerships were developed with several foreign countries, including Mexico and China.

After leaving the NEH, Cole was appointed to the IU Board of

Trustees by Governor Mitch Daniels for one term (2010–2013). He was president and CEO of the American Revolution Center in Philadelphia (2009–2011) and also served as a senior fellow at the Hudson Institute in Washington, D.C., before becoming a senior fellow at the Ethics and Public Policy Center in Washington, D.C.

Cole held fellowships and grants from the Guggenheim Foundation, the American Council of Learned Societies, the Kress Foundation, the American Philosophical Society, and the Center for Medieval and Renaissance Studies at the University of California, Los Angeles. He was a member of the Accademia Senese degli Intronati, the oldest learned society in Europe. For two years he was the William E. Suida Fellow at the Kunsthistorisches Institut in Florence, Italy.

Cole served on the U.S. National Commission for the United Nations Educational, Scientific, and Cultural Organization (UNESCO), the Woodrow Wilson Center board, and is a member of several other boards, including American Heritage, the Norman Rockwell Museum, and the Villa Firenze Foundation. He has been appointed by the U.S. Senate to the National Advisory Committee on Institutional Quality and Integrity. In August 2013, Cole was appointed by President Barack Obama to be a member of the Dwight D. Eisenhower Memorial Commission.

For his service to the nation, state, and university, Bruce Cole has been recognized with many prestigious honors. In November 2008, President George W. Bush awarded Cole the Presidential Citizens Medal "for his work to strengthen our national memory and ensure that our country's heritage is passed on to future generations." The medal is one of the highest honors the president can confer upon a civilian. Earlier in 2008, he was decorated Knight of the Grand Cross, the highest honor of the Republic of Italy and received the President's Medal from Michael McRobbie at IU. In 2006, Governor Mitch Daniels awarded Cole the Sagamore of the Wabash. Upon early retirement from IU in 2001, Cole was named distinguished professor emeritus. He is recipient of nine honorary degrees including four Doctor of Humane Letters degrees from Aquinas College (2005), the University of North Texas (2005), the University of Missouri (2007), and Washington College (2008).

In 1962, Bruce Cole married Doreen Luff of Fairfax County, Virginia. They had two children: Ryan and Stephanie. On January 9, 2018, at age 79, Bruce Cole passed away while vacationing in Cancun, Mexico. ⌒🐌

WILLIAM A. COOK
1931–2011

Trustee, 1995–1998

A^N INTERNATIONALLY KNOWN ENTREPRENEUR, philanthropist, and historic preservationist, William A. "Bill" Cook served as an IU Trustee—just one undertaking on a list of countless projects from one of Indiana's most celebrated, passionate, and decorated personalities.

Born on January 27, 1931 in Mattoon, Illinois, to Cleo and George Cook, a homemaker and a grain elevator owner, respectively, the young Bill Cook attended high school in Canton, Illinois, where he lettered in football, basketball, and track. He had a part-time job at the local pharmacy's soda fountain, in a building he would one day restore, and he worked as a lifeguard at the town's public pool. At an early age, he had already begun to show signs of greatness. He was named MVP for the school's football team, was a member of the 1948 Illinois Sweet Sixteen basketball team, and was a competitor in the State Division I Music Competition, highlighting his gift for playing the piano.

Bill Cook attended Northwestern University, where he received a BS in biology in 1953, and where he later was the recipient of an Alumni Merit Award in 1995 and an honorary doctorate of science in 2003. While at Northwestern, Cook was a member of the Beta Beta Beta National Biological Honor Society and Beta Theta Pi social fraternity, an award-winning choral director, and a part-time Chicago taxi driver. From 1953 to 1955, he served in the U.S. Army as a medic at Brook Army Hospital while teaching physics of anesthesia to Army resident anesthesiologists at Trinity University in San Antonio.

After his Army service, Cook worked as an engineering recruiter for Martin Aircraft and then as a catalog editor and a scientific products salesman for American Hospital Supply Corporation. In 1958, Cook moved to Chicago and co-founded MPL Inc., which would become the third largest manufacturer of hypodermic needles in the United States. In 1963, he left the Chicago area and founded Cook Incorporated in Bloomington, started in a spare bedroom in an apartment, with just two employees—himself and his wife, Gayle.

Today, Cook Group's history has taken on what seems like mythical proportions, having grown to become the world's largest family owned medical device manufacturer, with over fifty U.S. and international companies. Working with some of the most renowned medical pioneers in the field of interventional radiology, the small company began by manufacturing and selling percutaneous wire guides, needles, and cardiovascular catheters that Bill made at home with a blowtorch, soldering together iron and plastic tubing. Today, Cook Group has annual revenue of nearly $2 billion and has over 11,000 employees.

Bill Cook was appointed to the IU Board of Trustees in 1995 by Governor Evan Bayh. While a trustee, Cook focused his efforts on continuing to develop a world-renowned faculty and administration, as well as serving on the Finance and Hospital Committees and acting as the trustee liaison to the IU Kokomo and IU Southeast campuses. An extensive and generous supporter of Indiana University, Cook donated countless resources to the university, specifically to the School of Medicine, the Jacobs School of Music (including the William and Gayle Cook Music Library), the Herman B Wells Scholars Program, the FASE Mentoring Program, Memorial Stadium lighting, the School of Education, Cook Hall, and various causes and endowments. He was awarded the honorary Doctor of Laws degree from Indiana University in 1993 and the Herman B Wells Visionary Award in 2000.

An active volunteer and philanthropist, Cook served on numerous boards, including Bloomington Utility Services, Lake Monroe Regional Waste District, Indiana Corporation for Science and Technology, Oregon Health Sciences University Foundation Trustees, and the Marshfield Clinic Foundation. He invested much time and effort personally and through Cook companies to help restore and improve downtown Bloomington, and he was instrumental in the building of the Monroe County YMCA.

For his commitment to using his companies and his knowledge to better society, Cook received numerous awards and accolades over his career. In 1992 he received the honorary doctor of engineering degree from Rose-Hulman Institute of Technology in Terre Haute, Indiana, and in 1993 he was awarded the Oregon Health Sciences University Distinguished Achievement Award. In addition, he received the Bill Orwig Medal from the Indiana University Athletics Program, was an Honorary Speaker of the Indiana House of Representatives, and a Sagamore of the Wabash multiple times. Bill Cook has the distinction of being the first non-physician to receive the Gold Medal from the Society of Cardiovascular and Interventional Radiology as well as from SCIR's European counterpart, CIRSE. In 1999 he was awarded the Indiana Chamber of Commerce Businessman of the Year Award.

Bill Cook married Indiana University Phi Beta Kappa, fine arts alumna, and Evansville native Gayle Karch. Together they have a son, Carl, who grew up to become an engineer, a philanthropist, and historic preservationist in his own right, while also succeeding his father as Cook Group CEO. Bill and Gayle published *A Guide to Southern Indiana* from 1972 to 1982, which led to their efforts to preserve historic landmarks across Indiana, over forty of which are listed on the National Register of Historic Places. The Cook family received the National Trust's highest honor award in 1998 and again in 2008 for their restoration of the historic West Baden Springs/French Lick Springs Resort. In addition to the built environment, the Cooks are also preserving over two thousand acres of southern Indiana forestland.

Cook was also a licensed jet pilot, a sometime driver of the John Mellencamp tour bus, the owner of a professional basketball team in Great Britain (the Manchester Giants, who were national champions in 2000), founder of the 1991 international champion Star of Indiana Drum and Bugle Corps, and producer of the Tony and Emmy award–winning musical *Blast!*

Bill Cook passed away at his home on Friday, April 15, 2011. He is remembered for working tirelessly to use his success to brighten the lives of anyone and everyone around him. ᵔᶰᵕ

CASEY B. COX
1982–

Trustee, 2005–2007

WHEN HE WAS APPOINTED as the sixteenth student trustee of Indiana University, Casey Cox said in an interview with the *Indiana Daily Student* that "I want this university to continue to play a greater role in the foundations of the state. I can't ever see a time when IU is not a part of my life."

Casey Cox was born in 1982 to Judy and Michael Cox and grew up outside of Fort Wayne, Indiana. He attended Leo Junior/Senior High School in Leo, Indiana, graduating in 2000. He then enrolled at Indiana University Bloomington, where he majored in political science and history, graduating in 2004. During his time as an undergraduate, he became involved in student government, culminating in serving as president of the IU Student Association during the 2003–2004 academic year. His term as IUSA president focused on a variety of issues, including an expanded late-night campus bus service, an online book exchange, and a library drop box for returning material. In addition, he served as a special assistant for civic engagement with the Division of Student Affairs, an undergraduate legislative assistant for Hoosiers for Higher Education, a member of the Dean of Students Advisory Board, and Delta Chi Fraternity.

In 2004, he enrolled at the Indiana University Bloomington Maurer School of Law. After his first year of law school, he applied for the student trustee position on the Board of Trustees. On July 27, 2005, Governor Mitch Daniels announced Cox's appointment to the Board of Trustees. He served on the Board of Trustees from 2005 to 2007, while in his second and third years of law school. One major agenda item that occurred during his tenure on the board was the selection of Michael McRobbie as the eighteenth president of Indiana University.

Cox graduated cum laude from law school in 2007. That same year he was admitted to the Indiana State Bar Association, and he began his career as an attorney with the Fort Wayne law firm of Beers Mallers Backs & Salin. His practice focused on business law, corporate law, municipal law, and litigation. He also serves as the city attorney for the City of Woodburn, Indiana.

In January 2008, Cox was appointed to the Fort Wayne Redevelopment Commission by the Fort Wayne Common Council. The commission is charged with promoting development projects in Fort Wayne, particularly in the downtown area. Among the successful projects during his tenure on the commission has been the construction of the new Parkview Field at Harrison Square, a new baseball park in the downtown section of Fort Wayne. Connected to this was the construction of a new parking garage and hotel as a part of the project. This development has been recognized by the International Downtown Association, the Indiana Society of Landscape Architects, and the Professional Sports Stadium accreditation group. Cox has also served as Indiana State Representative (HD85) from 2013 to 2016 as well as chairman of the Campaign Committee for Congressman Jim Barber.

Casey married his wife, Melissa, in 2006, and together they have three children: Adrianne, Andrew, and Abigail. ᢙᢩ

EDWIN W. CROOKS
1919–2011

Chancellor, IU Southeast,
1968–1985

E DUCATOR AND ADMINISTRATOR Edwin "Ed" William Crooks was the first person to hold the title of chancellor of Indiana University Southeast, a position he held with distinction, in addition to teaching as a professor of business.

Ed Crooks was born in 1919 to Rebecca Dils and Edwin Crooks Sr. in Parkersburg, West Virginia. He grew up with three siblings: Mrs. Catherine Roberts, a homemaker and teacher; Dr. H. Nelson Crooks, a physicist; and Dr. Robert D. Crooks, a pediatrician. Ed Crooks' success began early—he was active in Boy Scouts as a child, and he was a drum major for a champion marching band in high school. In 1937, he enrolled at West Virginia University, where he was a member of the Beta Theta Pi Fraternity, the cadet regimental adjutant of ROTC, and selected for the Phi Beta Kappa honorary society. In 1941 he received a BS and in 1942 an MA in economics. Crooks served in the United States Naval Reserve, where he was called to active duty (1942–1946) and attended several naval schools before serving on the staff of Commander Air Pacific at Pearl Harbor. In 1946, he enrolled in the Harvard Business School, graduating in 1947 with an MBA. From 1956 to 1959 he earned a DBA from Indiana University while holding a Ford Foundation Fellowship.

Crooks' first professional position was with the Halle Brothers Company, a department store in Cleveland, Ohio, where he worked as an assistant to the president, and as merchandise controller. In 1954, he began his career in higher education at West Virginia University as assistant professor of marketing (1954–1956) and then assistant dean in the School of Business (1958–1966). In 1966, he became dean and director of Indiana University Southeast, which was located at that time in Jeffersonville. By order of IU President Elvis Stahr, all deans of regional campuses became acting chancellors on June 7, 1968. Crooks was appointed chancellor permanently in September 1969, a position that he held until retiring in 1985.

Over the course of his nineteen years as head of the IU Southeast campus, Crooks oversaw numerous milestones. Two of the most significant are IU Southeast's move in 1973 from its original location in Jeffersonville to newly constructed facilities in New Albany, a move that coincided with its evolution from being an IU extension center to being a full-fledged campus of the university. Other milestones include the adoption of the Grenadier as the official IU Southeast mascot, increasing the number and quality of faculty and staff, almost doubling the student enrollment (from 2,408 to 4,467), and the awarding of the first associate, bachelor's, and master's degrees. During his years of service at IUS, he also held an academic appointment as professor of business administration, regularly teaching courses in marketing. When he retired in 1985, Crooks was named chancellor emeritus.

Always highly involved in community matters, Crooks volunteered his time and expertise with numerous organizations such as the Clark County Youth Shelter, the Jeffersonville Township Public Library board, the Clark County Center for Lay Ministries board, the Southern Indiana Chamber of Commerce, the Athenaeum, and the Southern Indiana Model Railroad Club. He also worked with the South Indiana Conference of the United Methodist Church and was an active Rotarian. He was named a Sagamore of the Wabash by Indiana Governor Otis R. Bowen.

Edwin Crooks and his wife, Joan Schleuniger, had three children together (Edwin, Ann, and Alice), all of whom graduated from Indiana University. Edwin Crooks passed away in his home in Oklahoma in 2011 at the age of 92.

At the first commencement ceremony held at IU Southeast, Chancellor Crooks told the graduating class, "We hope that the knowledge and skills you acquired while among us will equip you to better serve mankind, to improve this world for the benefit of all, and to give you a most satisfying career." Thanks to Edwin Crooks' dedicated service, generations of IU Southeast graduates have achieved these life milestones, reflecting the legacy of the institution he created in Southeastern Indiana. ❧

KATHRYN CRUZ-URIBE
1956–

Chancellor, IU East, 2013–

ANTHROPOLOGIST AND UNIVERSITY ADMINISTRATOR Kathryn Cruz-Uribe joined Indiana University as the sixth chancellor of IU East—the first woman to serve as chancellor of the campus.

Born in Niskayuna, New York, to Gloria Aurichio, a homemaker, and Joseph Allwarden, an electrical engineer and aerospace industry marketing executive, Kathryn Cruz-Uribe attended public Lloyd Harbor elementary school in Huntington, New York, and Cold Spring Harbor High School in Cold Spring Harbor, New York. She earned a BA in anthropology and art from Middlebury College in Middlebury, Vermont (1974–1978), before attending the University of Chicago for graduate school, where she earned an MA (1980) and PhD (1987) in anthropology. She was elected to Phi Beta Kappa as an undergraduate, won a National Science Foundation Graduate Fellowship (1978–1981), and was elected to Sigma Xi academic scientific society (1990). Her academic area of expertise is the analysis of animal bones from archaeological sites, and for more than twenty years during her career she has conducted field and laboratory research in South Africa.

Cruz-Uribe began her career at the University of Rhode Island as a lecturer in anthropology (1988–1989), before finding a home at Northern Arizona University in Flagstaff, Arizona, from 1989 to 2007, where she rose from assistant professor to professor of anthropology and served in administrative positions that included dean of the College of Social and Behavioral Sciences, interim associate provost of research and graduate studies, and graduate dean. She implemented a successful academic reorganization in which the college grew significantly by adding the previously independent School of Communication, the Department of Geography, Planning and Recreation, as well as other units. In addition, she oversaw significant growth in online programs as well as college participation in off-campus programs in Tucson, Phoenix, and Yuma, aimed at serving nontraditional, place-bound students.

She next moved to California State University Monterey Bay, where she served as provost and vice president for academic affairs (2007–2013). In that role, she was responsible for leading the academic programs of the university, including the development and implementation of the new University Strategic Plan for 2008–2018. During her tenure, Cruz-Uribe oversaw the implementation of eight new academic programs, as well as a significant revision of the university's general education program, the successful re-accreditation by the Western Association of Schools and Colleges, enrollment growth of 50 percent, and a significant improvement in student retention.

In 2013, Kathryn Cruz-Uribe joined Indiana University as the sixth chancellor of IU East. One of her first responsibilities was to lead the development of the IU East Strategic Plan (2016–2019), which focuses on increasing student success and continuing to foster meaningful community connections. In the first four years of Cruz-Uribe's leadership, the campus has made gains in numbers of graduates (from 589 to 766), minority student enrollment (from 9 percent to 11.4 percent), and new degree programs. Capital projects Cruz-Uribe has overseen include a renovation of the campus quad, installation of outdoor sculptures in the quad area, and the construction of the Student Events and Activities Center—the fifth building on the campus and the first since 1999, when the campus's fourth building, Springwood Hall, was dedicated. Athletics has grown to include men's and women's soccer as well as men's and women's track and field, bringing the total number of athletic teams competing in the KIAC and NAIA conferences to thirteen.

Committed to her communities, Cruz-Uribe has served on several civic boards in both Monterey and Flagstaff, and now in Indiana. She currently serves on the board of the Wayne County Area Chamber of Commerce (chair 2016), the Richmond Art Museum, Reid Health, and First Bank Richmond.

Over the years, Cruz-Uribe has been recognized with several honors and awards including the Northern Arizona University Teaching Scholar Award (1994), College of Social and Behavioral Sciences Outstanding Teaching Award (1996), and Charles and Ellie Meister Award for outstanding service to the Honors Program (2001). California State University at Monterey Bay awarded her the President's Medal for Outstanding Administrator in 2011.

Kathryn and Eugene Cruz-Uribe (d. 2018), an Egyptologist, married in 1981 and have two daughters, Alicia and Mariana. ꝯ❧

JAMES W. DYE
1931–

Trustee, 1984–1990

A LIFELONG HOOSIER AND IU ALUMNUS, James W. Dye served two terms as an Indiana University Trustee, influenced the university's architectural planning, and sponsored several scholarships. James Dye Jr. was raised in Hammond, Indiana, following his birth on October 13, 1931, to Edna Eudora Dye and James William Dye. He attended Hammond public schools and eventually IU Bloomington, graduating in 1953 with a BS in business as a real estate major. As a student, Dye was a member of the Sigma Chi Fraternity, I–Men's Club, basketball manager, chairman of Student Spirit, and in Army ROTC. In 1954, he joined the United States Army Corps of Engineers and served as an active-duty first lieutenant until 1956.

Dye credits his experience working various odd labor jobs as a boy during World War II as shaping him into a successful entrepreneur and business owner. He has served as president of ten businesses and organizations, including Griffith Materials Corporation; Mansards, Inc.; Standard Lumber Company (founded by his late brother, Richard James Dye); and Dye Family Farms. Dye also served as chairman or managing partner for several other Indiana-based real estate, construction, and property management companies. As of 2017, he serves as president of JWD Management, Inc. and as president of the James W. and Betty Dye Foundation, both of Munster, Indiana.

In 1984, Governor Robert Orr appointed James Dye to the Indiana University Board of Trustees. During his tenure as a trustee, Dye assisted in the hiring process of the master architect position with the university and served on the Visiting Committee on University Architecture, the Faculty Relations Committee, the Investment Committee, and the Fiscal Committee. He also acted as a representative on the IU Northwest Campus Advisory Board. Eager to share his success with his alma mater, Dye has given generously to Indiana University. He has sponsored a number of scholarships, including the Reverend Robert Lowery Scholarship Program (IUN), the IUN Non-Traditional Student Scholarship Program, the James W. Dye Entrepreneurial Scholarship, and the Herman B Wells Scholars Program. He also established his own Dye Entrepreneurial Seminar Series, which gives students the opportunity to hear and interact with successful entrepreneurs. Through his own James W. and Betty Dye Foundation, he established the Jim and Betty Dye Scholarship Program and the NWI Non-Traditional Student

Scholarship, which has provided scholarships to more than 350 students at Indiana University, Purdue University, IU Northwest, Purdue Calumet, IUPUI, and Ball State University. He has also been a member of Indiana University's Varsity Club, the 1820 Society, Hoosiers for Higher Education, the President's Circle, and the Well House Society.

Recognized for his leadership and philanthropy, James Dye has received many awards, ranging from the 1972 Griffith Boss of the Year to the 2010 Individual Philanthropist Award from the Association of Fundraising Professionals (Indiana Northwest Chapter). Notable awards include being named a Sagamore of the Wabash by Governor Robert Orr in 1981 and the St. Margaret's Hospital Man of the Year in 1997 (Hammond, Indiana); receiving the Z. G. Clevenger Award from IU in 2003, the Calumet Region Sportsmanship Committee Humanitarian Award in 2007, and being inducted into *The Times'* Northwest Indiana Business and Industry Hall of Fame in 2010. In 2009, Dye received an honorary Doctor of Humane Letters, presented at IU Northwest by IU President Michael McRobbie.

James Dye has been active in community, state, and national organizations in various capacities including: commissioner, Aeronautics Commission of Indiana; member, Advisory Committee to the Executive Council for State Planning; delegate to the Republican National Convention in 1976, 1980, and 1988; member, Executive Board of Directors and chairman, Finance Committee, St. Margaret's Hospital; founding chairman and president, Northern Indiana Apartment Council; president, Northern Indiana Homebuilders Association; vice president, Home Builders Association of Indiana; president, Indiana Easter Seal Society; Hammond Optimist Club; Orak Shrine; McKinley Lodge Masons; and the Tradewinds Rehabilitation Center, over fifty years on the board of directors.

James Dye married Betty Olson on December 14, 1957. Over the next fifty years, the couple raised five children: James, Eudora (BS 1980 IUB), Debra (BS 1990 IUB), Jennifer, and Jay (BGS 1996 IUN). Betty passed away in 2007. In his free time, Dye enjoys the outdoors through activities such as golf, fishing, hunting, and various kinds of aviation, including bush piloting and floatplanes. Dye has been an avid pilot for over fifty years. ⌁

THOMAS EHRLICH
1934–

President, Indiana University, 1987–1994

D RESSED IN HIS ICONIC RED BOW TIE, Thomas Ehrlich led Indiana University for seven years, striving for increased quality and higher expectations despite a fiscally challenging period.

Born in Cambridge, Massachusetts, on March 4, 1934, Thomas Ehrlich attended Philips Exeter Academy for high school. Thanks to his second-grade teacher, Mrs. Scattergood, Ehrlich thought about teaching from an early age, but it wasn't until his grandmother loaned a biography of Louis Brandeis to him when he was 15 that he was inspired to study and teach law. He graduated magna cum laude from Harvard College (BA 1956) and Harvard Law School (LLB 1959). He was a member of Phi Beta Kappa, article editor for the *Harvard Law Review*, and the recipient of the Erich Firth Prize.

After law school, Ehrlich served as a clerk for Judge Learned Hand of the U.S. Court of Appeals for the Second Circuit in New York City. From 1960 to 1962, he was an associate for Foley, Sammond, and Lardner of Milwaukee, and from 1962 to 1965 he was a special assistant to the legal advisor for the Department of State. From 1964 to 1965, he was a special assistant to the undersecretary of state for the Department of State. From 1965 to 1975, he was a professor at the Stanford University Law School, serving as dean from 1971 to 1975. He left Stanford and returned to Washington, D.C., where he was appointed by U.S. President Jimmy Carter to be the first president of the Legal Services Corporation (1976–1979) and then the first director of the International Development Cooperation Agency (1979–1980). During that time, he was also a guest scholar at the Brookings Institution. He then returned to academia, serving as provost and professor of law at the University of Pennsylvania from 1982 to 1987.

In 1987, Thomas Ehrlich joined Indiana University as its fifteenth president, serving in this post for seven years. During his time at IU, the university continued to prosper, with enrollment reaching a new high of more than 96,000 students across eight campuses. He launched the Minority Achievers Program (now known as the Hudson and Holland Scholars Program), the Indiana Partnership, and a student advisory council on issues of campus-related racism. He helped to lead the implementation of Responsibility Center Management at the university. He oversaw the completion and funding of the Herman B Wells Scholars Program. Although the early 1990s were difficult financially, Ehrlich was able to secure state funding for major projects such as the renovation of three buildings in the Old Crescent and the Multi-Campus Technology Project. He oversaw an increase of more than 50 percent in outside research funding as well as an increase in private gifts that helped place Indiana University tenth among public universities in total endowment. Ehrlich hosted a PBS television show called *Pro & Con* in which Ehrlich and IU faculty members discussed topics of concern to the general public. He retired from IU in 1994 with the title president emeritus.

Ehrlich is said to have quipped that the greatest asset he brought to IU was his wife, Ellen. Their partnership is remembered as a collaborative leadership of the university. For example, in order to demonstrate the importance of funding higher education, the Ehrlichs hosted regular dinners at the Lilly House in Indianapolis for legislators. Ellen was unflagging in her efforts on behalf of IU, including as an advocate and a fundraiser. However, her activities reached far beyond IU. She chaired the United Way of Monroe County 1989 campaign, co-chaired the 1990 campaign, founded the United Way Vanguard leadership giving program, and in 1992 she was elected to the fifteen-member national board, United Way of America. The United Way presented her with the Mary Alice Gray Memorial Award in 1994. She also served for several years as a trustee of Radcliffe College, her alma mater, from which she graduated with a BA magna cum laude in 1956. Prior to coming to IU, Ellen taught grade school for 12 years before working as a development officer for the Georgetown University Law School Institute for International and Foreign Trade Law and as an assistant to the dean at Johns Hopkins University's School of Advanced International Studies, among other positions. Ellen Ehrlich received the IU East Chancellor's Medallion (1994), an honorary Doctor of Humane Letters from IU (1994), the Gertrude Rich Award from the IU Alumni Association (1994), and the University Medal (2013).

After his tenure at Indiana University, Thomas Ehrlich became a distinguished university scholar at California State University and taught community service learning courses for five years at San Francisco State University. Inspired by Ernest Boyer's *Scholarship Reconsidered* (1990), Ehrlich began focusing on the processes of effective teaching and learning. From 2000 to 2010, he was a senior scholar at the Carnegie Foundation for the Advancement of Teaching. Since 2010, he has been a visiting professor at the Stanford University Graduate School of Education, where he trains future teachers. Over the years, Ehrlich published widely, most recently as co-author of *Preparing Undergraduates for Business: Liberal Learning for Professional Education* (2011), which won the Ness Prize for the best book of the year on liberal education; and *Civic Work, Civic Lessons: Two Generations Reflect on Public Service*, with Stanford student Ernestine Fu (2013).

Thomas Ehrlich has been active in both professional and civic organizations at all levels. Professional service has included boards, societies, and associations such as the American Association of Law Schools, the American Association for Higher Education, the Association for American Universities, the Council of Ten, CAUSE, the University of Maryland Law School, and the Midwest Universities Consortium for International Activities (MUCIA). Ehrlich's commitment to community service has included work as co-chairman of the Monroe County effort for Red Ribbon Week, fundraising efforts for Planned Parenthood of Philadelphia, the Indiana Adult Literacy Coalition, and volunteering for the United Way. While in Bloomington, Tom and Ellen Ehrlich launched the campus campaign for Monroe County United Way, propelling faculty and staff into leadership positions among nonprofits in the Bloomington community. In 1991, President George H. W. Bush appointed Ehrlich as a member of the board of directors of the Commission of National and Community Service.

Ehrlich has been the recipient of numerous awards, honors, and distinctions, including an IU East Chancellor's Medallion (1994), a Thomas Hart Benton Mural Medallion (1988), and was named a Sagamore of the Wabash. He is the namesake of Indiana University's Thomas Ehrlich Service Learning Award, the recipient of which becomes IU's nominee for the national Thomas Ehrlich Civically Engaged Faculty Award the following year. In total, he holds five honorary degrees, including one from IU (1994). He received the University Medal from IU President McRobbie in 2013.

Thomas Ehrlich and his wife, Ellen, have three children—David, Elizabeth, and Paul—and nine grandchildren. He and Ellen currently reside in Palo Alto, California. ⌘

FREDERICK F. EICHHORN JR.

1930–2012

Trustee, 1990–2005

Appointed to the IU Board of Trustees in 1990, Frederick F. Eichhorn Jr. was to become one of the university's most cherished and influential trustees, serving as both vice president and president of the Board of Trustees before retiring his services after fifteen years of dedication and commitment.

Born in Gary, Indiana, on October 16, 1930, Eichhorn received his BS from Indiana University in 1952, and after earning his degree, he served in the United States Air Force during the Korean War (1952–1954). Upon returning, he began working toward a JD degree from the Indiana University School of Law in Bloomington (now the Maurer School of Law), which he completed in 1957. During his time as a student at IU, Eichhorn was selected as a Krannert Fellow and was elected president of the Law Club.

Eichhorn's career as a lawyer was long and prosperous, beginning in 1957, when he joined his father's prominent law firm, Gavit and Eichhorn (now known as Eichhorn and Eichhorn, LLC). In 1963, he became a partner and was a senior partner from 1977 until his retirement in 1996. The firm changed names over time, from Lawyer Schroer & Eichhorn to Schroer, Eichhorn, & Morrow, and then later, Eichhorn, Eichhorn, & Link. He also served as general counsel for Northern Indiana Public Service Company from 1977 to 1993, and as general counsel for *The Times* (Hammond, Indiana). In 1985, Eichhorn and several other Hoosier attorneys visited London and were granted the honor of meeting the Queen of England.

During his life, Eichhorn tirelessly served as member and officer of numerous societies and clubs, including the Skyline Club, University Club, Columbia Club, and the Indiana Society of Chicago. Eichhorn served on the Indiana Sesquicentennial Commission and was president of the board of the Northwest Indiana Symphony and the Gary Housing Authority (1972–1975). In addition, Eichhorn served on the Indiana Commission on State Tax and Financing Policy (1977) and the Gary Police Civil Service Commission (1975–1982), and was a chairman for the Lake County Community Development Committee (1984), the World Affairs Council, the Lake 2000 Committee (1989), and the Gary Regional Airport Task Force (1989). Eichhorn's extensive service with the Indiana Bar Association included his election as treasurer (1977–1979), as member of the Board of Managers (1979–1980), as vice president (1983–1984), and as president (1985–1986). Eichhorn was also a trustee with the Lincoln Legal Foundation, a fellow of the American Bar Foundation, and a commissioner on the National Conference of Commissioners on Uniform State Laws.

In 1993, for Eichhorn's exemplary contributions to the Hoosier heritage, Indiana Governor Evan Bayh bestowed upon him the distinguished Sagamore of the Wabash Award. In 1997, to recognize Eichhorn's extensive contributions to IU Northwest and the Gary community, IUN Chancellor Hilda Richards awarded him the Chancellor's Medallion. Recognizing outstanding personal achievements and his deep commitment to the highest possible professional standards, the IU School of Law inducted him into its Academy of Law Alumni Fellows in 2002. In 2006 he received the IU Distinguished Alumni Service Award, the highest recognition of alumni achievement.

On August 27, 1955, Mr. Eichhorn married Julia "Judy" Abel (BA 1953, MS 1956). Together, they raised four children: Jill (BA 1981, MA 1985, PhD 1994), Thomas (MD 1986), Timothy (BS 1985, MBA 1998), and Linda (MA 1995). After a lifetime of public service, Frederick F. Eichhorn Jr. passed away on October 3, 2012.

PHILIP N. ESKEW JR.
1941–

Trustee, 2006–2018

Doctor, professor, and administrator Philip Eskew has spent a lifetime in service to others through his professional and civic activities.

Born in Wabash, Indiana, in 1941 to Elsa Barker (BA 1932), a homemaker, and Philip N. Eskew Sr. (MS 1933), commissioner of the Indiana High School Athletic Association, Phil Jr. was raised in Sullivan, Indiana, and graduated from Sullivan High School. A three-sport athlete in his youth, Eskew played football and basketball, and ran track. At DePauw University, he played football, ran track, and was a member of Beta Theta Pi Fraternity while earning a BA in pre-medical sciences (1963). He then earned an MD at the IU School of Medicine in 1970 before launching a distinguished career in medicine and a lifetime of service to higher education in the State of Indiana.

After medical school, Eskew spent six years as a captain in the United States Army Reserves (1971–1977), earning the Army Commendation Medal "for organizing and successfully moving 102 patients from the old St. Vincent Hospital to a new hospital ten miles away in three hours and twenty minutes." He was the founder and managing senior partner from 1974 to 1994 at the Carmel, Indiana, OB/GYN, Inc. He then worked at St. Vincent Hospital in Indianapolis for over two decades, serving as the Ob/Gyn Residency Program director (1994–1999), medical director of Women and Infant Services (1996–2003), and director of Physician and Patient Relations (2004–2007). Eskew was a volunteer clinical professor of obstetrics and gynecology at the Indiana University School of Medicine, rising from clinical assistant professor (1989–1995) and clinical associate professor (1996–2004) to clinical professor (2004–2013).

In 2006, the year before his retirement from private practice, Eskew was elected by the alumni of Indiana University to serve on its board of trustees. While on the board, he served as chair of the Long Range Planning Committee (2006–2009) and chair of the Facilities Committee (2009–2018). He was re-elected three times. In addition, he has served on the IUPUI Board of Advisors, the IU South Bend Board of Advisors, and the Varsity Club National Board of Directors.

Beyond IU, Eskew has served on the boards of countless organizations and committees. Foremost among them is the American College of Obstetricians and Gynecologists, in which he served extensively on committees at both local and national levels (1971–2016). Other organizations he served include the American Medical Association (1977–2004), the Indiana State Medical Association (1970–), the March of Dimes (1982–2016), and Rotary International (1981–). Additional organizations include: Ascension Health (1999–2007), the Prenatal–Perinatal Subcommittee of the Task Force on the Prevention of Handicapping Conditions for the Indiana State Board of Health (1980–1985), the Marion County Health Department (1995–2007), and the Indiana Basketball Hall of Fame (1993–). He was the governor's appointee to the Indiana Medicaid Drug Utilization Review Board (2002–2014).

Eskew has also volunteered with many community organizations. Over the years, he has served on the Carmel Clay School Board (1982–1994), the Carmel Clay Parks and Recreation Board (1992–1994), the Carmel Clay Public Library Foundation Board of Directors (2004), the St. Elizabeth's Home Board of Directors (1995–2000), the Carmel Rotary Club, and the Board of Directors of the McDowell House of Danville, Kentucky (1997–).

Philip Eskew's service at all levels has been recognized by numerous awards. Some of these honors and awards include: the American College of Obstetricians and Gynecologists Outstanding District Service Award (1995), the American College of Obstetricians and Gynecologists Distinguished Service Award (2007), a Sagamore of the Wabash (1996), a Distinguished Physician Award from the St. Vincent Hospital (2000), a Mark of Distinction Award from the March of Dimes (2001), and a Burgess L. Gordon Memorial Award from the American Medical Association (2003). He has also been inducted into the Sullivan High School Athletic Hall of Fame (1997) and the Indiana Basketball Hall of Fame (2005). A colonel and battalion surgeon with the Indiana Guard Reserve (2001–), Eskew was recognized by the governor in 2011 with the Indiana Commendation Medal for service to the Indiana Guard Reserve and then, in 2014, with the Indiana Guard Reserve Merit Medal. In 2006, he was honored by receiving the Masonic 33rd degree from the Supreme Council of Scottish Rite Masonry. An active DePauw University alumnus who has served on the alumni board and as president of the "D" Association, Philip Eskew was elected to the DePauw University Athletic Hall of Fame and has received an Alumni Citation from his alma mater. Since 2005, DePauw annually grants the Phil Eskew Award to one outstanding male senior athlete who best exemplifies effort and excellence in academics and athletics as well as involvement in campus and community.

The Eskew family is well connected to Indiana University. Eskew's father and mother received degrees from Indiana University, as did his wife, Ann (BS 1978, MS 1982) and all three children: Kelly (JD 2001, MA 2012); Philip III (BA 1997, MLS 2003), and Kevin (MBA 2001). Phil Eskew Sr. received the Distinguished Alumni Award from the School of Education in 1983 and the Distinguished Alumni Service Award from IU in 1984. Ann Eskew, a distinguished nurse and hospital administrator, received the School of Nursing Excellence in Nursing Award in 2010.

An avid fan of athletics, Philip Eskew has volunteered as a photographer's assistant with NFL Films at thirty-four Super Bowls and for twenty-eight years at Indianapolis Colts home games. He coordinates credentials and stadium access, and he handles film and the occasional staging of shots of the sideline or stands. ॐ

JANICE L. FARLOW
1987–

Trustee, 2013–2015

THE TWENTIETH STUDENT to serve on the Board of Trustees, Janice Farlow has served IU in a variety of capacities both during and after her years as a student.

Janice Lin-Lishin Farlow was born July 20, 1987, in State College, Pennsylvania, to Jane Tsai and William Lin. Her mother is a senior vice president for international affairs at YFY Biotech Management Company in Taiwan and her father is on the faculty at the Purdue School of Engineering and Technology. They immigrated to the United States separately, with a suitcase apiece, met, and raised three children together. As a child, Farlow attended Barley Sheaf Elementary School in Flemington, New Jersey, before moving to Indianapolis and attending Craig Middle School and Lawrence North High School. She and her two siblings all attended Indiana University through the IUB Herman B Wells Scholars Program. Farlow herself attended Indiana University Bloomington from 2005 to 2009, graduating with a dual degree: BS with honors in biology and BA with honors in the Individualized Major Program (romance languages). She then attended Indiana University School of Medicine from 2009 to 2017, earning an MD (2017) and a PhD in medical and molecular genetics (2015). Since June 2017, Farlow has been working as a resident physician in the Department of Otolaryngology–Head and Neck Surgery at the University of Michigan.

Farlow's positions at IU have included: executive president of the Medical Student Council (2012), member of the Administrative Review Committee for Dean of the school (2011–2012), member of the Search and Screen Committee for Dean of the school (2012–2013), student representative on the Curriculum Council Steering Committee (2015–2017), and student lead on the Independent Student Analysis Committee of the Accreditation Self-Study Task Force (2014–2017), all at the IU School of Medicine; and steering committee member of the Colloquium for Women of Indiana University (2015–2017), student trustee on the IU Board of Trustees (2013–2015, appointed by Governor Mike Pence), and member of the IU Bicentennial Steering Committee (2016).

During her student years, Farlow was involved in a wide range of activities and organizations. As an undergraduate, her service included the IU Board of Aeons and the March of Dimes National Youth Council; membership in Circle K International, Alpha Chi Sigma, and the Asian American Association; and volunteering at Volunteers in

Medicine, Shalom Community Center, Pages to Prisoners, Bloomington Community Kitchen, and Riley Hospital for Children; and playing piano, cello, and bassoon. As a graduate student, Farlow served on the Association of American Medical Colleges board of directors and the Organization of Student Representatives National Administrative Board; Indiana University Student Outreach Clinic and the Society for Student-Run Free Clinics; American Medical Women's Association; and the Medical Student Service-Learning Group.

For her scholarship and her leadership, Farlow has been recognized with various awards and honors. As an undergraduate, she was Phi Beta Kappa and a Founder's Scholar, received a Hutton Honors College Research Grant and a Hutton Honors College/Individualized Major Program Capstone Award, won the Norton-Mavor Classical Studies Prize, and was named a Presidential Scholar. As a graduate student, she received a Clinical Translational Sciences Institute Pre-Doctoral Training Grant, a Wells Graduate Fellowship, and a Medical Scientist Training Program Fellowship, and was named to the Gold Humanism Honor Society. She also won the Excellence in Public Health Award from the United States Public Health Service, the Dr. Charles R. Bantz Award for Excellence at IUPUI, the American Medical Association Foundation Leadership Award, the Class of 1985 and Todd B. Taylor Leadership Award, and the IU School of Medicine William M. Plater Civic Engagement Medallion.

Janice Lin-Lishin married Nathan Rhys Farlow and together they have two children, Layla Yehlin Farlow and Eleanor Eilin Farlow. ᕗ

STEPHEN L. FERGUSON
1941–

Trustee, 1998–2010

A MIDWESTERN WORK ETHIC, a solid Hoosier education, and respect for his roots placed native son Steve Ferguson in a position to make a difference in Indiana and at Indiana University.

Living in Bloomington, Indiana, from his birth on January 3, 1941, and with Indiana University sitting in his front yard, Steve Ferguson developed a deep and abiding affection for his hometown and for IU. Both his parents and his siblings are IU alumni. His father, Luther, an executive at Scribner Publishing Company, instilled a love of books and learning in his young son. Weekends, holidays, and summers were spent on the family homestead farm in Springville, Indiana, learning the value of family and hard work. Steve attended Wabash College, graduating with distinction in 1963. He completed a JD at Indiana University in 1966, with distinction, Order of Coif. From 1966 to 1991, he practiced law at Ferguson Ferguson & Lloyd with his older brother, Jim.

In 1966, Ferguson was elected to the Indiana House of Representatives. During his four terms as a representative (1966–1974), Ferguson worked in leadership, ran for speaker and, among other things, chaired the Transportation Committee. He also appeared before Congressional committees testifying on transportation as well as on healthcare, medical device, and FDA issues. He sponsored the first increase in the gasoline tax since the 1930s to eliminate the "killer highways" in Indiana, which made possible the four-lane construction of Indiana's primary roads, including State Road 37 from Mitchell to Indianapolis.

Beginning in 1963, Ferguson developed an enduring professional and personal relationship with Bloomington entrepreneur and philanthropist William A. Cook. Because of that relationship, he spent a great deal of time working on Cook legal matters and diverse projects related to Cook philanthropy. This included the Monroe County YMCA, the only one of its kind with a cardiac rehab program and a focus on heart health, for which he served as president during construction and membership development (1979–1989); and the Star of Indiana Drum and Bugle Corps, a summer music program for students that developed into the touring Broadway show *Blast!* that opened in London and won a Tony Award (2001). As president of CFC, Inc. (a Cook company) from 1972 to 1993, Ferguson oversaw the restoration of several downtown properties in Bloomington (e.g., Graham Plaza, Fountain Square, and the Cochran House). He was also a key leader in the restoration of downtown Bloomington including the creation and construction of the Bloomington Monroe County Convention Center and the conversion of the former Showers furniture factory into a government center, commercial office space, and university research center. Since 1996, Ferguson has worked on the enormous Cook restoration project that came to be known as the French Lick Resort, which includes two historic hotels with spas, the creation of a Pete Dye golf course, and a casino.

In 1991, Ferguson left the family law firm to work at Cook full time as executive vice president and chief operating officer. In 2003, he became chairman of the board. While working at Cook, Ferguson has spent countless hours in Washington, D.C., lobbying for medical device legislative reform, including numerous appearances before committees and sub-committees of the U.S. Senate and House of Representatives to give testimony regarding issues confronting medical device companies in the United States. His efforts contributed to the passage of the 1990 Safe Medical Device Act and the FDA Modernization Act of 1997, in addition to various life sciences projects designed to increase opportunities for students and create jobs. Ferguson continues to be active within the industry in both state and national organizations, in 2017 joining both the board of directors for the Medical Device Innovation Consortium and the board of directors of the Applied Research Institute.

Over the years, Ferguson has been a leading figure in higher education for the State of Indiana. He was appointed to the State of Indiana Commission for Higher Education (1992–1998, vice chair 1994–1995, and chair 1996–1998) by Governor Evan Bayh and to the Indiana Education Roundtable by Governors O'Bannon and Kernan (2002–2004). He served on the State Chamber Board (1994–2011; chair, 2009–2010). In 1998 Ferguson was appointed by Governor O'Bannon to the IU Board of Trustees and re-appointed by Governor Kernan in 2004 and Governor Daniels in 2007. While on the Board of Trustees, he was elected vice president (2003) and then president (2005–2007), helping to guide the university's search for a new president, as well as improving relations with faculty and the State of Indiana, and establishing the 21st Century Scholars Program. In 2004, he served on the Governor's Task Force on College Affordability. Together with his wife, Connie, he has also promoted higher education in Indiana through Ivy Tech Community College with both time and philanthropic gifts. In 2011 he also joined a group of eleven investors to create IUB's Building Entrepreneurs in Software Technology competition for students who develop startup companies focusing on internet and software technology.

Ferguson's contributions to Indiana have been recognized with several awards. In 1976, he was awarded his first Sagamore of the Wabash by Governor Otis Bowen. As a testament to his bipartisan work, he went on to receive the same honor from Governors Frank O'Bannon (2003), Joseph Kernan (2005), Mitch Daniels (2012), and Mike Pence (2016). In 2002 he received the Lifetime Achievement Award from the Bloomington Chamber of Commerce. He was also inducted into the Indiana Academy in 2004, and is a 2005 laureate of the Central Indiana Business Hall of Fame. His dedication to IU earned him the prestigious Maurer School of Law Academy of Alumni Fellows Award in 2011. In 2013 the Indiana Chamber of Commerce named him Business Leader of the Year. In 2014 he received an honorary Doctor of Humane Letters from Wabash College, and in 2018 he received an honorary Doctor of Humane Letters from Indiana University.

In May 2012, Ferguson granted the State of Indiana a conservation easement for his 1,500-acre property near Springville to become part of the Bicentennial Nature Trust Conservancy. He served on the Indiana Bicentennial Commission (2011–2016), which was charged with planning and executing events for Indiana's Bicentennial celebration.

Ferguson married high school classmate Jean Byrd in the summer of 1962, starting a family beginning with Betsy, Matthew, and Amy. They divorced in 1986. In 1992, Ferguson married Connie Mungle, becoming stepfather to Ty and Eric. ᝍ

MILTON J. FINEBERG
1911–1998

Trustee, 1989–1994

ONE OF INDIANA'S MOST SUCCESSFUL builders and developers, Milton J. "Josh" Fineberg was a loyal and dedicated friend to Indiana University. His legacy lives on in IU's Jewish Studies Program and in the Indiana Memorial Union's John Whittenberger Society.

Fineberg's path to IU began when his parents emigrated from Russia in 1881. He was born in Trenton, New Jersey, on June 22, 1911. The Finebergs were one of the first Jewish families to settle in Trenton, and it was there that he spent his youth. After working odd jobs as a youngster, he graduated from Trenton High School in 1929, with honors and as class valedictorian, and headed to the University of Wisconsin. Two years later, he transferred to Indiana University Bloomington and earned a BA in political science in 1933. He then enrolled in the Indiana University School of Law (now the Maurer School of Law), where he received an LLB in June of 1936. Upon being admitted to the Indiana Bar, Fineberg had a brief career as an attorney. In 1942 he decided to forgo a legal career and follow his passion: building homes. That passion grew over the next fifty years and resulted in The Fineberg Group.

As a professional real estate developer, Fineberg contributed to the growth and expansion of Indianapolis. During his career, Fineberg was responsible for the development of thousands of residential homes, apartments, and subdivisions in the Indianapolis area. His firm also developed several neighborhood shopping centers in the Carmel area, including Keystone Square, Hunter's Quest, Carmel Walk, Hunter's Run, and Vista Run. In 1965 the Marion County Residential Builders named him Builder of the Year, and in 1968 he was president of the Builders Association of Greater Indianapolis. Fineberg also served for many years as a national director of the National Association of Home Builders, and in 1972 was elected a life director.

Over the years, Fineberg received numerous awards and presentations for his public service work. He was a tireless fundraiser for the Indianapolis Jewish Welfare Federation and was an active member of Beth-El Temple, the Anti-Defamation League, and Indianapolis B'nai B'rith Lodge No. 58. He was appointed to the Builder's Taskforce Sub–Committee of Greater Indianapolis, the Governor's Advisory Commission of LaRue Carter Hospital, and the Athletic Advisory Council of the Indiana White River Park Development Commission. Fineberg was twice awarded a Sagamore of the Wabash by Indiana governors (1965 and 1980). On a national and international level, he was a recipient of the National Conference of Christians and Jews Brotherhood Award, the Eleanor Roosevelt Humanitarian Award, and the B'nai B'rith Guardian of the Menorah Award.

As a student at IU Bloomington, Fineberg was a member of the varsity debating club, president of the Jewish Student Union, and president of the Indiana State Jewish Student Society. He was treasurer of his freshman class, a member of Tau Kappa Alpha, Blue Key, and Phi Epsilon Pi. As an alumnus, Fineberg served on a variety of boards and committees, including the Advisory Board of the College of Arts and Sciences, the President's Council, the Indoor-Outdoor Alumni Education Committee, the Varsity Club, and the IU Indianapolis Club. He was an original member of both the Well House Society and the Woodburn Society.

Josh Fineberg has left a lasting legacy at Indiana University. He was instrumental in the IU Foundation's Indiana Council campaign as well as in the creation of IUB's Jewish Studies Program, serving on its board of governors for many years. Perhaps his most passionate legacy can be seen in his involvement with the Indiana Memorial Union. As a student, Fineberg was a Union Board director from 1933 to 1936, serving one year as vice president and then one year as president (1934–1936). While an alumnus, he continued to be an avid supporter of the Union Board as a member of the John Whittenberger Society (JWS). In recognition of his years of service to the Union, the JWS created its first endowed scholarship, the Milton J. "Josh" Fineberg Scholarship, which it awards annually to a Union Board member who exemplifies Fineberg's high standards of leadership. It was first awarded in 1968. Fineberg was also instrumental in the Indiana Memorial Union's 75th Commemorative Project. In 1985, Fineberg was named a Distinguished Alumni of the College of Arts and Sciences. In 1989, Indiana Governor Evan Bayh appointed Fineberg as an IU Trustee, and he served until 1994.

Fineberg passed away in Indianapolis on July 21, 1998. He is survived by three children: Susie, Daniel, and Mark. ᔕᕈ

J Thomas Forbes
1966–

Trustee, 1993–1995

S ERVING ON BEHALF OF A WIDE RANGE of constituents, primarily those affiliated with Indiana University, J T. Forbes has spent his career building relationships.

J Thomas Forbes was born on July 5, 1966, and reared on a farm near the town of Blackhawk, Indiana. He was influenced greatly by his maternal grandfather, farmer Ewing Allen Brinton, who had a major impact on his upbringing. Forbes learned the value of education and the importance of family from his mother, Donna L. Brinton, an English teacher. Forbes' proclivity to enchant and entertain others is derived from his father, an itinerant salesman and tavern owner.

Forbes served as student council president and machine politician at Dixie Bee Elementary School, and as drum major and thespian at Terre Haute South High School. Despite annual defeats in student government elections from sixth grade through high school, Forbes was inspired to pursue the political stage by his high school history teacher. He graduated from Indiana University with a BA in political science (1990). While an undergraduate, he was a member and president of the IU Student Association, president of his pledge class of Acacia Fraternity, a member of the Presidents' Roundtable, a representative to the Bloomington Faculty Council and University Faculty Council, a member of the Athletics Committee, and a member of the Academic Appeals Committee. His first paid position at IU was as an hourly staff member in the Dean of Students Office at IU Bloomington. He was selected to Order of Omega Greek leadership and received the Dean of Students Outstanding Student Award and the Student Recreational Sports Award for advocacy on behalf of the Student Recreational Sports Center.

Forbes took a research associate position at the Center on Philanthropy in Indianapolis (now the Lilly Family School of Philanthropy), which led to his earning a Master of Public Affairs in nonprofit management from the School of Public and Environmental Affairs at IUPUI in 1996. In graduate school, he spent a year as a policy analyst for the Indiana General Assembly. In 1993 he became the tenth student trustee, appointed by Governor Evan Bayh to a two-year term on the IU Board of Trustees, where he was chair of the External Relations Committee and helped select IU's sixteenth president, Myles Brand. At the conclusion of his term on the board, Forbes was appointed special assistant to the president and coordinator of federal relations for IU, a position he held for two years. From 1997 to 2001, as assistant vice president for public affairs and government relations, Forbes oversaw integrated creative services, marketing, media relations, and government relations.

In 2001, Forbes left IU to take a similar position at Michigan State University as assistant vice president (2001–2004), where he gained insight into the land-grant traditions and values of higher education in the United States. He returned to Indiana University from 2004 to 2007 as assistant vice president for government relations and executive director for state relations under President Adam Herbert. Under President Michael McRobbie, Forbes was named associate vice president for public affairs (2007–2008). From 2008 to 2010, Forbes worked at Cummins, Inc. as their first director of state government relations, where he ultimately served as the lead private sector staff member of the U.S.-Brazil CEO Forum, chartered by the two governments to foster innovation and trade between these two global economic powers.

The opportunity to return to IU as executive director and CEO of the IU Alumni Association (IUAA) drew Forbes back to Bloomington, where he has served as IU's "chief enthusiast" since June 2010. In the first three years of his tenure, he refocused the organization to bring alumni together to serve IU and each other through a program that stabilized IUAA membership and finances. In 2013, he was nominated by his peers from Michigan, Stanford, and Wisconsin to the board of the Council of Alumni Association Executives.

During his various tenures working at Indiana University, Forbes has served on the I-Association Board, the Varsity Club Board, the IUAA Board of Managers, the IU Lilly Family School of Philanthropy Deans Advisory Council, the University Committee on Names, the Strategic Directions Charter Steering Committee, several senior leadership search committees, and the IU Foundation.

Forbes has also been involved in civic activity with the Bloomington Board of Public Safety, Habitat for Humanity of Monroe County, the Indiana Commission for Community Service, and as administrative council chair of First United Methodist Church of Bloomington.

J T. Forbes married Martha Shedd on May 19, 2017. She graduated from DePauw University in 1987 and frequently reminds J T. that he went to a state school, while he reminds her that she did take summer courses at IU. They have three children: Meghan, Rachel, and Ben. ৎঌ৴

DOROTHY J. FRAPWELL
1947–

Vice President and General Counsel,
2006–2012

Attorney and trusted advisor Dorothy Frapwell served IU and the community for over thirty-eight years.

Dorothy Jane "Dottie" Frapwell was born October 17, 1947, in New York. She graduated from Penn State in 1969 with a BA in biology and chemistry. She worked for one year for General Motors in New York before attending the IU School of Law–Bloomington (now Maurer School of Law) and earning a JD in 1973. After graduation, she worked for two years as chief deputy prosecutor for Monroe County.

In 1975, she joined the Indiana University legal staff, where she served for three years as associate university counsel. Beginning in 1978, she served as associate university counsel and medical center attorney (1978–1990). In that capacity, she advised doctors and administrators on matters of patient care, ethics, hospital law, and medical education. In 1990, Frapwell was named special counsel to the president and associate university counsel. In 1994, she was selected to be university counsel, heading the Office of University Counsel, where she supervised six associate counsels in Bloomington and Indianapolis. The title vice president was added to her portfolio in 2006, but she had effectively served in that capacity since 1994, advising the university and the Board of Trustees on legal matters.

During Frapwell's tenure, the Office of University Counsel was a safe space for trustees, administrators, faculty, staff, and students to seek advice. The unique combination of Frapwell's knowledge of the law, coupled with her long institutional memory, made her an effective and trusted advisor to five university presidents: Tom Ehrlich, Myles Brand, Gerry Bepko, Adam Herbert, and Michael McRobbie. Frapwell was known for having a strong moral compass and for her ability to see multiple sides of an issue. After retiring, she continued serving of counsel to the university until June 30, 2013, working as special advisor to her successor, Jacqueline A. Simmons. Frapwell became vice president emeritus in 2013.

Throughout her career, Dorothy Frapwell has engaged in service both within and beyond the university community. Examples include sixteen years on the Maurer School of Law Board of Visitors, serving a term as president of the Maurer Alumni Board, and serving on the IU Foundation Legal Affairs Committee. Her service extended into the surrounding community. Frapwell served as a member of the board of directors of the

Indiana University Credit Union, the Old Crescent Insurance Company, the American Council on Graduate Medical Education, the Indiana Supreme Court's Character and Fitness Committee, the National Association of College and University Attorneys, the NCAA Legal Advisory Committee, and the Board of the Community Foundation of Bloomington and Monroe County.

President Ehrlich honored Frapwell with the Thomas Hart Benton Mural Medallion in 1994. She was inducted into the Maurer School Academy of Law Alumni Fellows in 2012, and received the President's Medal for Excellence from Michael McRobbie in that year.

DAVID J. FULTON
1942–2016

Chancellor, IU East, 1995–2007
Acting Chancellor, IU East, 1994–1995
Acting Chancellor, IU East, 1986–1987

WITH HIS CHARACTERISTIC ENERGY AND WIT, David Fulton began a long and successful relationship with Indiana University that lasted over forty years, first as a graduate student in the Department of History at IU Bloomington and culminating as the fourth chancellor of Indiana University East.

A native of Willoughby, Ohio, David Fulton graduated from Willoughby South High School in 1960 and received a BA with honors in history from Allegheny College in Pennsylvania. He studied European political institutions at the University of Manchester for two years, and was awarded a fellowship for graduate study at Indiana University Bloomington, from which he received an MA (1968) and a PhD (1975), both in history. As a specialist in Balkan history, Fulton spent considerable time in Yugoslavia in the 1960s, including as a Fulbright Fellow in Zagreb, Yugoslavia, in 1969–1970.

Upon returning from Yugoslavia and while still a graduate student, Fulton taught history as an associate instructor from 1970 to 1971 at Indiana University Bloomington. When Indiana University East was founded, he jumped at the opportunity to move to Richmond in 1971 and become one of IU East's earliest faculty members, as an instructor in history and political science. He was soon promoted to the rank of assistant professor of history and political science. During his tenure as an assistant professor, Fulton took on administrative duties as assistant for campus planning and academic development to Chancellor Alex Schilt. He was later named director of planning and budget by then-Chancellor Glenn Goerke. Fulton served as acting chancellor of IU East in 1986–1987 and became vice chancellor for administrative affairs in 1988. In addition, from 1989 to 1990, he was an American Council on Education Fellow in the president's office at Metropolitan State College of Denver. Fulton served as acting vice chancellor for student services in 1990–1991. From 1972 to 1995, Fulton served on numerous committees for Indiana University, including the Task Force on Career Education, the University Business Officer's Group, the Academic Planning and Policy Committee, the President's Senior Planning Group, and the University Operations Cabinet. In 1994–1995, Fulton once again served as acting chancellor of IU East until IU President Myles Brand appointed him as chancellor permanently in 1995.

David Fulton served as the fourth chancellor of Indiana University

East from 1995 to 2007. While at IU East, Fulton oversaw tremendous growth, as the campus completed its transition from being a two-year college into being a full regional university with sixteen baccalaureate programs and two new master's programs. During this time, Fulton managed the construction of Springwood Hall in Richmond and oversaw the dedications of Middlefork Hall, the Connersville Center, and the celebration of the 30th anniversary of IU East. Fulton also oversaw the development and opening of IU East's second off-campus instructional site, the Henry County Danielson Learning Center in New Castle, an effort spearheaded by former trustee Daniel Danielson and funded largely by community sources. Fulton's leadership produced the first online courses by IU East campus faculty, the Tuition Reciprocity Agreement with select counties in Ohio, and a $2.5 million Campaign for Community fundraising effort that established the Center for Entrepreneurship, the Art Gallery, and Meijer Artway.

While chancellor, Fulton formed and fostered partnerships between IU East and its surrounding areas, including the Community Education Coalition in Connersville and the Post-Secondary Education Council in Henry County. He was active in developing relationships with Ivy Tech Community College, which is on the Richmond campus. IU East was the first campus to transfer Ivy Tech credit toward an IU degree and continued to lead in developing the course transfer arrangements demanded by the Commission for Higher Education. Under Fulton's leadership, the Master Plan for the Richmond campus was renegotiated, facilities-sharing agreements were put in place in Connersville and New Castle, and a two-plus-two degree program was established in Lawrenceburg, enhancing the educational opportunities for citizens in southeast Indiana. Fulton retired in 2007 with the title chancellor emeritus.

Even before his work as chancellor, Fulton was known for his efforts in weaving the university into the communities it serves by building community partnerships. He served on the Greater Richmond Progress Committee, United Way (president, campaign chair, vice president), Social Services Planning Board, Community Services Council, and as chair of the task force dealing with the city's master plan, performing arts center, and neighborhood development. He co-authored the original grant that established the outreach program Area 9 Agency on Aging, and served on its council. Fulton served the community as a member of the board of the Richmond Wayne County Chamber of Commerce and as a member of its CEO Roundtable. He also served on the board of Historic Landmarks of Indiana and on the board of Reid Hospital and Health Care Services.

After retiring as chancellor, Fulton remained active in the Richmond community as a member of the board of directors of Wayne Bank and Trust, chair of the Steering Committee of the Countywide Partnership for Youth, member of the Mayor's Council on Economic Vitality, chair of the Certified Technology Park Committee, and as president and treasurer of the Starr-Gennett Foundation Board. In 2012, he was appointed co-chair of the Joint Commission on City-County Government.

Fulton received numerous awards for community work. In 1995, Indiana Governor Evan Bayh recognized Fulton as a Sagamore of the Wabash. In 2006, the Chamber of Commerce presented him with the Art Vivian Distinguished Community Leader award, in recognition of which the Indiana Senate passed a resolution in 2007 describing his dignity and distinction. Upon Fulton's retirement in 2007, IU President Adam W. Herbert awarded him the Thomas Hart Benton Mural Medallion, recognizing that his entire professional life has been in service to IU.

David married Marilyn Kay (Ritz) Fulton, a registered nurse and IUPUI graduate (1982), with whom he raised five children: Alex, Ben (AS 1987, IU East; BA 1989, IUB), Kate, Alison, and Brian. David Fulton passed away September 11, 2016, after a lifetime of service to Indiana University. Marilyn passed away on July 21, 2018, at her home in Centerville, Indiana. ᑶ

ROSE E. GALLAGHER
1974–

Trustee, 1997–1999

W ITH TIES TO INDIANA UNIVERSITY that have run strong and deep over the years, including her time as an undergraduate at IU Bloomington, Rose Gallagher served as IU's twelfth student trustee.

Rose Gallagher was born in April of 1974 in Chicago to Robert and Beverly Gallagher, both educators, who encouraged Rose to pursue college and graduate school. She enrolled at Indiana University in 1992, majored in political science, and earned a BA cum laude in 1996. During her time as an undergraduate, she was involved in numerous extracurricular activities, including serving on the Indiana University Student Foundation steering committee and as secretary for the organization. She was a member of the sorority Kappa Kappa Gamma and she served on the Fraternity and Sorority Judicial Board. She also received several awards during her time as an undergraduate, including the Honors Division Senior Achievement Award and membership in the Mortar Board Senior Honor Society and Phi Beta Kappa. In the fall of 1996, Gallagher enrolled at the Indiana University Maurer School of Law in Bloomington. When the student trustee position opened in 1997, she applied and was appointed by Governor O'Bannon, effective July 1, 1997. She served on the Board of Trustees during her second and third years in law school. Gallagher graduated with a JD cum laude in 1999.

After graduation, Gallagher was admitted to the Indiana State Bar Association and began her legal career with the Indianapolis firm of Ice Miller, LLP. In 2003 she joined the Chicago, Illinois, law firm of Chapman and Cutler, where she concentrated her practice in municipal finance, including acting as bond counsel, disclosure counsel, issuer's counsel, and underwriter's counsel. She also chaired the firm's employment committee. She was admitted to the Illinois State Bar Association in 2004. In April 2008 she became partner at Chapman and Cutler and served as chair of the employment committee (2009–2011), but left in February 2013 in order to pursue an MA at the University of Chicago's School of Social Service Administration (2014–2016). Upon graduation, she joined Ounce of Prevention Fund (Chicago, Illinois) as a policy specialist (2016–).

Over the years, Gallagher has continued to give back to Indiana University and to the legal profession. She was on the Maurer School of Law Alumni Board from 2001 to 2007, and she was a member-at-large on the Indiana University Alumni Association's Executive Council from

2008 to 2011. She was a member of the National Association of Bond Lawyers and served as a panelist and faculty member for their annual Fundamentals of Municipal Bond Law Seminar. In 2010 she received Chapman and Cutler's Pro Bono Achievement Award for her pro bono service as a guardian ad litem with Chicago Volunteer Legal Services.

In 2012, Rose E. Gallagher wed Patrick D. Gallagher (whose last name is conveniently her maiden name). Together, they care for Patrick's children from his first marriage: Brendan, Ian, and Cara. ᔕᎲᏉ

ROBERT E. GATES
1920–1994

Trustee, 1969–1990

A TTORNEY AND CIVIC LEADER Robert Gates served Indiana University for over twenty years as a trustee.

Robert Edwards Gates, son of Ralph and Helen (Edwards) Gates, was born November 19, 1920, in Columbia City, Indiana. He graduated from Columbia City High School where he was the 1938 valedictorian. During the summers of 1935, 1936, and 1937, he attended the Culver Summer Naval School. In 1938, Gates entered Indiana University, where he received a BS in business four years later. After graduation, he spent four years in the Navy, completing his service as a lieutenant aboard the USS New Mexico in the Pacific. After World War II, he returned to Indiana and enrolled at the IU School of Law–Bloomington (now the IU Maurer School of Law). Upon receiving his law degree in 1949, Robert Gates joined the family law firm in Columbia City and worked there for the next forty-five years alongside his father and uncle.

Both as a student and as an alumnus, Robert Gates was very active at Indiana University. As a student, he served as president of his senior class and president of the Union Board. He was business manager of the University Theatre, senior swimming manager, and a member of the I-Men's Association. He was president of Sigma Alpha Epsilon, as well as a member of the Sphinx Club, Blue Key, and Skull and Crescent. As a law student, he was a member of the legal honor society Phi Delta Phi. After Gates' student days, his university ties and interests continued, as he served on the IU Executive Council (1956–1959), the Indiana-Purdue Fort Wayne Foundation (1969–1990), and the IU Foundation Board of Directors (1971–1990). Gates was awarded IU's Clevenger Award in 1987 and the Distinguished Alumni Service Award in 1991. Gates served for twenty-one years as a trustee of the university, first appointed by Governor Whitcomb in 1969 and then reappointed by Governors Bowen and Orr. He served as board vice president from 1975 to 1980.

Like his father, who was governor of Indiana from 1945 to 1949, Robert Gates was active in politics, serving as Whitley County Republican Chair (1959–1977) and twice as Fourth District Republican Chair. He was a delegate to the Republican National Convention in 1968 and 1976, an alternate delegate in 1980, and sergeant-at-arms in 1940, 1952, and 1960. He was a Republican Indiana gubernatorial candidate in the 1964 primary. He was a member of the American, Indiana, and Whitley County (president 1969) Bar Associations.

Always active in city, county, and state service, Gates served as Columbia City's city attorney (1951 to 1955), as a director of the Farmers Loan and Trust Company, as a member of the Columbia City Chamber of Commerce, the Columbia Club, and the Indiana Society of Chicago. He held the following offices in the American Legion: Post #98 commander, fourth district commander, state judge advocate, state northern vice commander, state commander (1957–1958), and national membership chairman (1958–1960). He served on the board of directors of Culver Summer Schools (1972–1975) and belonged to the Indiana Masons Mizpah Shrine, as well as Rotary (president 1954–1955), Elks, Eagles, Moose, and Post #2919 of the Veterans of Foreign Wars. Gates was twice awarded the Sagamore of the Wabash (1969 and 1975) and was made a Kentucky Colonel in 1969.

On June 9, 1948, Gates married Harriett Kunkel Brown of Bluffton, Indiana (BA in speech and hearing, 1947). The couple had three daughters, all of whom attended Indiana University: Marjorie B. Gates (Giffin), BA in English, 1974; Anne E. Gates (Redman), BS in education, 1977, and MS in education, 1985; and Mary Ellen Gates (Osborne), BS in physical education, 1982.

Robert Edwards Gates passed away March 22, 1994, in Columbia City, Indiana, and was still seeing clients at home during the final weeks of his illness. ᐭᕈ

JACK M. GILL
1936–

Trustee, 2007–2010

C HEMIST, PROFESSOR, AND ENTREPRENEUR Jack M. Gill began his affiliation with Indiana University as a graduate student in the 1950s before going on to teach at many universities and to found Vanguard Venture Partners.

Jack Morris Gill was born March 25, 1936, on a farm in Lufkin, Texas, to Samuel G. and Beulah (Dominy) Gill, who raised Jack alongside five siblings. Gill's parents worked extremely hard to provide for their family—his father worked twelve-hour days, six days a week in construction. Although no family members in their generation had ever graduated from high school, Gill's parents instilled in their children the notion that the way to a better life was through education, and four of the six children went on to earn college degrees. Gill took an early interest in chemistry, staying up late and studying, tinkering at all hours of the night with a chemistry set in the family garage. This led him to graduate as the top chemistry student in his high school and to earn a BS in chemistry and engineering from Lamar University in 1958, where he was on the dean's list and in the honor society all four years. To finance his studies, he worked full time. While at Lamar, he was affiliated with Alpha Tau Omega Fraternity. Deciding to pursue a PhD in chemistry, he received scholarships from the National Institutes of Health and the National Science Foundation as well as a teaching assistantship at Indiana University. He graduated from IU in 1963 with a PhD in organic chemistry. Gill also participated in the Special Seminars in Nuclear Magnetic Resonance at Stanford University.

From 1963 to 1965, Jack Gill worked as a research scientist for Monsanto in St. Louis, and from 1965 to 1970 he was the vice president of research and development for Wilkens Instruments in Walnut Creek, California, as well as the director of research and engineering for the Aerograph Division of Varian Associates. In 1971, he founded Autolab Inc. (acquired by Spectra Physics) in Mt. View, California, and served as the CEO until 1981. Then, in 1981, he founded Vanguard Venture Partners in Palo Alto, California, a venture capital firm that has founded or financed over one hundred startup high-tech companies.

Over the years, Jack Gill has been a professor or visiting professor at various universities including Stanford University; the University of California, Berkeley and the University of California, Davis; Harvard University; Massachusetts Institute of Technology; Rice University;

Indiana University (adjunct professor of chemistry, College of Arts and Sciences, 1998–2001); Purdue University; University of Kentucky; University College of London; the London Business School; Boston University; and Lamar University, among others. Gill is credited with pioneering and teaching an entrepreneurial curriculum and courses for MD, PhD, and MBA students at Harvard, MIT, Rice, and Stanford. Jack Gill was appointed to the Indiana University Board of Trustees by Governor Mitch Daniels in 2007 and served until 2010. Gill has also taught for the IU School of Medicine, been a member of the board for the Indiana University Foundation, and served on the dean's advisory boards for the IU Kelley School of Business, the College of Arts and Sciences, and the IU Jacobs School of Music. He and his wife, Linda, created and endowed the Gill Center for Biomolecular Sciences at Indiana University and the Gill Heart Center at the University of Kentucky.

Outside of Indiana University, Gill's service is equally extensive. He has served on the boards for numerous organizations, including the Boston Symphony Orchestra, the Houston Symphony Orchestra, the President's Circle of the National Academies, the Project Hope Board, the Texas Emerging Technology Fund, the Lamar University Foundation Board (president, 1988–1991), and the senior advisory board to the Center for Innovation, Commercialization, and Entrepreneurship (CICE) at Lamar University. He has also served as a director of the University of Texas MD Anderson Cancer Center, the Horatio Alger Association, and Project HOPE. He is a member of the President's Circle of the National Academy of Sciences, the National Academy of Engineering, and the National Academy of Medicine.

Gill's work has been widely recognized with honors and awards. He has been awarded an honorary Doctor of Science degree from Indiana University (2001), the Distinguished Alumnus Award from Lufkin High School, the Distinguished Alumnus Award from Lamar University (1999), the Distinguished Alumnus Award from the College of Arts and Sciences at IU (2001), the Distinguished Alumni Service Award from IU (2002), the Velocity Entrepreneurship Award from the IU Kelley School of Business, the Horatio Alger Award for Distinguished Americans (1999), and numerous other awards in entrepreneurship and teaching.

Together, Jack Gill and his wife, Linda Challis, are the founders of the Gill Foundation of Texas, which focuses on educational philanthropy.

They have made gifts totaling more than $30 million to high schools, colleges, and universities, and have endowed over twenty-five chairs or professorships, as well as more than two hundred four-year scholarships for students. Their legacy includes the creation of numerous courses and programs in entrepreneurship across the country.

Jack Gill married Linda Challis on January 12, 1969, in San Francisco. They have four children: Jefferson, Jennifer, and twins Tyler (BA, 1994) and Jason (MBA, 2001). Their four children have earned eleven college degrees; all four hold MBAs. Jack and Linda's granddaughter, Montana Moore Gill, entered IU as a freshman in 2013, making IU a four-generation school for the Gill family: Linda's father, George Challis, was a 1936 graduate of Indiana University. Linda is a cousin of the famous Hoosier composer Cole Porter and of aviator Amelia Earhart. ◆

G. FREDERICK GLASS
1959–

Vice President and Director of Intercollegiate Athletics,
2009–

ATTORNEY, IU ALUMNUS, and administrator Fred Glass has been directing athletics at IU for ten years.

Born in February of 1959, G. Frederick Glass was raised in Indianapolis by his parents, George Francis Glass, a tavern owner, and Rosemary Teresa Glass, a social worker in the Indianapolis Public Schools. He has two degrees from Indiana University: a BA earned on the Bloomington campus in 1981 and a JD from the School of Law–Indianapolis in 1984 (later renamed the IU McKinney School of Law).

From 1984 to 1986, Fred Glass began his legal career clerking for United States District Court Judge Samuel Hugh Dillin (BA 1936, LLB 1938). Prior to being named IU's athletic director in 2009, Glass was a partner in the Indianapolis law firm of Baker and Daniels. Before joining Baker and Daniels, Glass worked for Indiana Governor Evan Bayh from 1989 to 1993, serving the last two and half years as chief of staff. Glass was also chairman of Indianapolis Mayor Bart Peterson's transition team from 1999 to 2000. He also served as president of the city's Capital Improvement Board from 2000 to 2007, where he successfully negotiated to keep the NFL Colts in Indianapolis and to construct Lucas Oil Stadium. He served on the organizing committees for the NCAA Final Four Tournament in 2000 and 2006 and negotiated a deal to make the city part of a permanent rotation to host NCAA Final Fours. He was also president of the City of Indianapolis's 2011 Super Bowl Bid Committee, which laid the groundwork for the city's successful bid for 2012.

Banking on Glass's reputation to get big things done, President Michael McRobbie appointed him athletic director for the IU Bloomington Athletics Department in 2009. Glass established five priorities for the department and its students, which have become the hallmark of his tenure as vice president and athletic director: (1) playing by the rules; (2) being well in mind, body, and spirit; (3) achieving academically; (4) excelling athletically; and (5) integrating with the rest of the university. In 2012 he unveiled a creed that represents IU Athletics' core values: "The Spirit of Indiana: 24 Sports, One Team." To ensure that the department meets the promise of the Spirit of Indiana, he established the IU Department of Intercollegiate Athletics Excellence Academy, a comprehensive student-athlete development program. In 2014, he unveiled the Indiana University Student-Athlete Bill of Rights. During Glass's tenure so far, there have been more than $214 million in new or renovated sports facilities; some of these include the academic center named in honor of D. Ames Shuel (1958 IU graduate), Simon-Skjodt Assembly Hall, Cook Hall, North End Zone Student-Athlete Development Center, Bart Kaufman Field, Andy Mohr Field, and the South End Zone Complex.

Fred Glass has received many honors, which include: inclusion in *The Best Lawyers in America* (Corporate Law) 2008; inclusion in Indiana Super Lawyers, 2004–2008; Brebeuf Jesuit Preparatory School President's Medal, 2007; and *Indianapolis Business Journal*'s 20 Most Influential City Leaders, 2003. In 2010, he received the Trevor R. Brown Award from the students of the *Indiana Daily Student* and the *Arbutus* for his contributions to the experiences of student journalists. In May 2012, he received the Distinguished Alumni Award from IU's Robert H. McKinney School of Law.

Fred Glass is married to Barbara Jean Lannan (BA 1980). Fred met Barbara at an IU football game, and he proposed to her in Brown County State Park after another. They have four children: Katie (BA 2008); Joe (JD from the IU McKinney School of Law, 2014); Connor (BA 2014); and George (BA 2017). ✑

GLENN A. GOERKE
1931–2015

Chancellor, IU East, 1981–1986

A LIFELONG EDUCATOR and higher education administrator, Glenn Goerke helped guide IU East through an important transition period in the early 1980s.

One of four siblings, Glenn Allen Goerke was born May 15, 1931, and grew up in Lincoln Park, Michigan, the son of Albert and Cecil (Crowl) Goerke. He attended Eastern Michigan University (EMU), earning a BA in education (1952) and an MA in administration and special education (1955). He was admitted to Phi Delta Kappa and received the Arm of Honor at EMU. While completing these degrees, he served in the U.S. Navy Reserves (1949–1957). He later earned a PhD in adult and higher education from Michigan State University (1964).

Goerke began his career teaching special needs children in the Lansing, Michigan, Public School System in 1952. He then spent eleven years in the Oak Park, Michigan, school system as a teacher and administrator. After receiving his doctorate in 1964, Goerke spent the next fourteen years in higher education in the State of Florida, where he was involved in the planning, creation, and development of Florida International University, a new state university located in Miami, where he served as vice president for community affairs and provost of the North Campus. From 1978 to 1981, Goerke served as dean of the Division of University Extension and Summer Session at the University of Rhode Island, during which time he launched the university's Providence campus.

In 1981, Goerke became the second chancellor of Indiana University East, a position he held until 1986. During those five years, Goerke led the campus as it began to transition from a two-year college to a baccalaureate-granting campus of Indiana University. The IU Board of Trustees voted to approve the change in mission in 1983. In 1986, the Indiana Commission for Higher Education also approved the change of mission and authorized the first three baccalaureate degrees for the campus. In addition, Goerke helped to further the development of cooperative programs with Earlham College and local industries. Goerke resigned from his position as chancellor in November, whereupon the Board of Trustees granted David J. Fulton, associate professor of history and political science, and director of planning and budgeting, the additional title of acting chancellor (December 1, 1986–August 14, 1987).

Goerke left Indiana University East in 1986 for the position of president of the University of Houston-Victoria (UHV) in Victoria, Texas.

During his years in Victoria, from 1989 to 1991, he also served as vice chancellor for special projects for the UH System. He left UHV in June 1991 to take the presidency of the University of Houston-Clear Lake and served there for four years. He completed his service to the University of Houston System by serving as president from 1995 through 1997, at which time the UH Board of Regents conferred upon Goerke the title of president emeritus of the University of Houston.

Glenn Goerke has been active in national and international education associations as well as in his local communities. He has been president of the National University Extension Association and has served on several committees of the National Association of State Colleges and Universities, the American Association of University Administrators, and the board of directors of the International Association of University Presidents, including as vice president of IAUP from 1996 to 1999. Goerke's involvement in his local communities includes being a member of the Richmond Area Chamber of Commerce, including serving as its president in 1985, as well as being a member of the Richmond Labor Management Council, the board of directors of the Reid Memorial Hospital Foundation, the board of directors for First National Bank of Richmond, the Richmond Symphony Orchestra, and chairman of the Indiana Arts Commission's Advisory Committee on Education.

Glenn Goerke has received numerous awards for his work and leadership in higher education and his communities. Some of those include: the National Aeronautics and Space Administration Distinguished Public Service Medal, the American Association of University Administrators Distinguished Service Award for Outstanding Leadership and Dedicated Service, the Texas Gulf Coast National Management Association Manager of the Year Award, the Victoria, and the Texas Rotary Club's Citizen of the Year award. He also received the first Breaking the Mold award given by the State of Texas Comptroller's Office for his leadership in fiscal planning and accountability at UH-Clear Lake. He was awarded an honorary Doctor of Humane Letters at the UH commencement in 1997. Goerke also holds an honorary doctorate from the University Tecnologica de Santiago, Dominican Republic.

Glenn Goerke married his wife, Joyce, in 1973. They have three children: Lynn, Jill, and Kurt. Goerke passed away November 13, 2015, in Wolfeboro, New Hampshire. ᘓ

Harry L. Gonso
1948–

Trustee, 1976–1994; 2017–

A N ATTORNEY, BOARD MEMBER, and civic leader, Harry L. Gonso is known to many Indiana University football fans as a star quarterback who led the Hoosiers to their first and only Rose Bowl appearance. His commitment to Indiana is reflected in his support for organizations and causes throughout the state and on the campuses of IU Bloomington and Indiana University–Purdue University Indianapolis (IUPUI).

Gonso, a native of Findlay, Ohio, was reared by his mother, Amy Helena Grover, a homemaker, and his father, Harry Gonso, a high school counselor. He learned the value of hard work from his father, who worked diligently to provide a modest living for a family with six children, and was inspired throughout life by his grandfather, a disabled Church of God minister. Gonso was schooled at Washington Elementary and Findlay High School before graduating from Indiana University with a BS in accounting (1970) and a JD (1973). While in law school, he served for two years as an assistant to IU Chancellor Herman B Wells.

In 1980, Gonso joined the Indianapolis law firm Ice Miller, LLP, where he became partner and leads the Life Sciences Group. His commitment to advancing Indiana's life sciences industry is also reflected in his service at IUPUI on advisory boards for the campus, the School of Science, the IU Center for Regenerative Biology and Medicine, and the Indiana Clinical and Translational Sciences Institute. In 2002, Gonso was part of a team that formed Indianapolis-based Twilight Ventures Partners, LLC, the first life sciences venture-capital firm in Indiana. He remains active on the IU Kelley School of Business Life Sciences Advisory Board, designed to nurture and support the growing field.

Gonso was elected to the IU Board of Trustees in 1976 and served for 18 years until 1994, during which time he spearheaded search committees for two former IU presidents. He is a past recipient of the IU Distinguished Alumni Service Award. He also served as vice chairman for the IU Foundation, to which he was elected in 1990. In that capacity, he helped reorganize the board and led its transition to the new structure. In 2017, he was re-appointed to the IU Board of Trustees by Governor Eric Holcomb.

Indicative of his commitment to Indiana was his service as senior counsel and chief of staff for Governor Mitch Daniels in 2005 and 2006. He also served on the boards of directors for the Community Hospital Foundation, Community Hospitals, the American College of Sports

Medicine Foundation, the Skyline Club, and Municipal Recreation, Inc., and he is a retired member of The Penrod Society and Sigma Alpha Epsilon fraternity.

An outstanding student-athlete, Gonso was named IU football team MVP, won two L. G. Balfour Awards, established the school's Total Offense Award, and was an Academic All-American. He was named a charter member of the IU Athletics Hall of Fame in 1982. He also received the Z. G. Clevenger Award in 1994. Gonso has received three Sagamore of the Wabash Awards, the highest award given in Indiana, from Governors Bowen, Orr, and Daniels.

Gonso and his wife, Lucy, are parents of Christopher, Matthew, Sara, and Ellie. He enjoys tennis, biking, golf, hiking, and Sudoku. ❧

ATTORNEY AND HIGHER EDUCATION ADMINISTRATOR James Gray served IU as president of the IU Student Association and as the fourth student to serve on the IU Board of Trustees.

Born on June 3, 1960, in Arlington, Virginia, James W. Gray graduated from Indiana University with a BS in public affairs and policy administration in 1982, and went on to earn a JD from the Indiana University McKinney School of Law in 1985. While a student, Gray was involved in Greek life and participated heavily in campus politics—he was the vice president of the Indiana University Student Association in addition to his two-year term as a trustee on the IU Board of Trustees from 1981 to 1983. His trustee service included membership on the Student Affairs Committee and the Real Estate and Legal Committee. He was vice president of Phi Kappa Psi, and was a member of the Board of Aeons, Blue Key, and the Dean of Students Advisory Board.

Gray's career has focused on the practice of law in commercial real estate development, lending, and zoning. He served three years as general counsel to Brian Properties, Inc., a Chicago area commercial real estate developer and property management firm. He then joined Duke Realty Corporation, a large real estate firm in Indianapolis, where he spent fifteen years and served as senior vice president and market officer in Cincinnati and Minneapolis/St. Paul. At Duke, he oversaw the development, construction, leasing, and management of Duke Realty's 8.5 million-square-foot office and industrial portfolios in the Twin Cities, and the 20 million-square-foot portfolio in Cincinnati. In 2003 he began an eight-year tenure as associate vice president of real estate services at Harvard University, where he was in charge of real estate and construction matters, including new development activity. He then spent a brief time as executive director for Christ Hospital in Ohio, overseeing facilities, construction, security, and real estate. From 2013 to 2014, he was the executive director of the Berkeley Student Cooperative, a historic housing cooperative providing student-run affordable and cooperative housing options to nearly 1,400 students in twenty locations around the University of California, Berkeley campus. As executive director, Gray was responsible for the overall operations of the co-op, including financial and capital affairs, and other long-range management and maintenance of assets. In June 2014, Gray joined Brandeis University as vice president of campus operations.

Gray has a long history of community involvement, having served on the executive committee of the Minneapolis Regional Chamber of Commerce, the board of directors of the Minneapolis and Boston chapters of the real estate trade group NAIOP, the board and executive committee of Downtown Cincinnati, Inc., the board of directors of the historic Findlay Market city market in Cincinnati, and the board of directors of real estate industry group CoreNet Global's New England Chapter, and as a member of the executive committee and board of the Harvard Square Business Association.

James Gray and his former wife Susan Whisler (BS 1982, MLS 1992) have two children, Joan and Steven. ᏬᏉᏞ

STUART M. GREEN
1946–

Chancellor (Interim), IU Kokomo,
2008–2010

Stuart M. Green

A N ARTIST BY TRAINING AND PROFESSION, Stuart Green spent nearly four decades bringing people together at Indiana University Kokomo and in surrounding communities.

Inspired by his fifth-grade teacher, Polly Schlimmer, Green began taking art classes at the Art Institute of Chicago when he was ten years old. He went on to earn a BFA from the Art Institute of Chicago in 1969, and an MFA from the Rochester Institute of Technology in 1970. He then spent two years working in occupational and recreation therapy and teaching fine arts courses at a community college.

In 1972, Stuart Green came to Indiana University Kokomo, beginning his academic career as assistant professor of fine arts. His areas of expertise include Michelangelo, ancient cultures, myth and art, and comparative mythology. In 1981, IUK Chancellor Hugh Thompson named Green the chairperson of the Department of Humanities. In 1982, he was appointed dean of arts and sciences, a position he held until 1998, when he was appointed vice chancellor of academic affairs. From 2008 to 2010, he served as interim chancellor of Indiana University Kokomo, appointed by President Michael McRobbie. Over the years, Green also served at various times as acting director of library services, acting dean for the School of Public and Environmental Affairs programs at IUK, chair of the School of Education, and dean of the School of Nursing. In addition, he has served as a presidential fellow and special assistant to the president of Indiana University.

In his various roles at IU Kokomo, Green established new degrees and programs to increase the collegiate opportunities available for students. His passion has been in the arts, and since first coming to Indiana University, he has worked to incorporate the arts in a variety of ways into the school's curriculum. Green developed a freshman arts course that, over the period of a semester, provided an enormous arts experience by combining visual arts, theatre, storytelling, music, and dance. During his tenure as campus leader, Green strengthened relationships with Ivy Tech Community College of Indiana and Purdue University's College of Technology, helped develop the North Central Indiana Regional Leadership Institute, and was involved in construction of a new nursing clinical simulation center.

Green also has a record of community involvement. He has been a board member of the Indiana Coalition for the Arts (1999–2010;

president 2003–2007), as well as a member of the board of advisors for the Indiana Arts Partnership, Region 4 (2004–2010). He has worked with the Kokomo Fine Arts Council (1974–1980), the Howard County Partners in Education (1997–2010), and was a member of the Dream Team of the Community Foundation of Howard County (2000–2003). He has also been on the Inventrek Technology Park board of directors (2008–2010), and part of the Greater Kokomo Economic Development Alliance (2008–2010).

After thirty-eight years of service to Indiana University Kokomo, Green retired in 2010. President Michael McRobbie presented the Distinguished Service Medal to Green at his retirement celebration. Green also received a Distinguished Hoosier Award, presented on behalf of Governor Mitch Daniels by State Senator Jim Buck, and a proclamation from Kokomo Mayor Greg Goodnight commending him for his service and declaring Monday, June 28, as Stuart M. Green Day in Kokomo.

Green is married to Janine Isaac (AS 1974); together, they have two sons, Alexander (BS 1997, MD 2001) and Joseph (BS 2001), and four grandchildren. In retirement, in addition to spending more time with family, Green has returned to his roots as a painter. ᘓ᙮

ROBIN ROY GRESS
1948–

Secretary of the Board, 1998–2014

Past secretary for the IU Board of Trustees Robin Roy Gress's professional career has included university administration and the field of communication.

Born September 26, 1948, in Van Nuys, California, Gress attended local primary and secondary schools before enrolling at the University of Oregon, where she earned a BS in journalism in 1970. She then attended the University of California, Los Angeles (UCLA) and earned an MA in architecture and urban planning in 1977.

She began her career in 1970 as an editor and reporter for the *Hartford Courant*, Connecticut's largest newspaper. She then worked for CBS Radio Network as an editor and producer from 1974 to 1975, before completing her master's degree at UCLA. Gress worked from 1978 to 1996 as a reporter and editor for the *Los Angeles Times*, a period during which the *Times* won eleven Pulitzer Prizes.

In 1996, Gress joined IU as the director of information resources for President Myles Brand. In April of 1998, Gress was appointed secretary of the IU Board of Trustees. Shortly thereafter, President Brand also appointed Gress to the post of director of ceremonies and commencement. She retired from both positions on May 31, 2014, and was succeeded as secretary by Deborah Lemon. In early 2017, Gress served as interim project manager in the Office of Marketing and Publicity at the IU Jacobs School of Music.

Gress's passions are represented by her involvement with numerous campus and community organizations. She is a member of the IU Alumni Association, the IU Friends of Music, the United Way of Monroe County, the Hoosier Salon, and the Metropolitan Opera Guild. She is a member of the Parish Council at St. Paul Catholic Center. Since 2014, she has served on the advisory council of Catholic Charities Bloomington (CCB). She was also interim director of community relations for CCB in 2015.

In recognition of her contributions to IU, the IU Foundation awarded Gress the 2008 President's Medallion. She received the E. Ross Bartley Award in 2014. Named after one of the late IU Chancellor Herman B Wells' most valued staff members, the Bartley Award is the highest staff award given by the IU president. It is given to a member of the staff who demonstrates outstanding leadership skills, service, and professional accomplishment at the local, state, or national level.

Robin Roy Gress is married to William John Gress. ❧

CORA J. GRIFFIN
1988–

Trustee, 2011–2013

D URING HER TIME AS AN UNDERGRADUATE and graduate student at Indiana University–Purdue University Indianapolis, Cora J. Griffin served as a student trustee en route to a dual MPA and JD degree.

One of four siblings, Cora Jane Griffin was born July 12, 1988, in Galveston, Indiana, to Cathy Brown and Randy Griffin. Growing up, she reaped the cultural and intellectual benefits of traveling the country during the summers as a family. After Galveston Elementary School, she attended Lewis Cass High School, where she worked on the student newspaper, updating the high school's website with news stories about students and alumni.

Griffin attended IUPUI, majored in public affairs management, and graduated with a BS in 2011. She subsequently enrolled in the dual Master of Public Affairs program in nonprofit management in the School of Public and Environmental Affairs and the Doctor of Jurisprudence program in the Indiana University Robert H. McKinney School of Law at IUPUI; she earned degrees from both programs in May 2015. During this time, she was chair of the McKinney School of Law Women's Caucus (2014–2015). In 2011, Governor Mitch Daniels appointed Griffin to the Board of Trustees of Indiana University, the nineteenth student to serve as a trustee.

Griffin has always been very involved in campus life, including serving as vice president of the Undergraduate Student Government, president of the IUPUI Student Foundation, president of the Student Activities Programming Board, president of Alpha Lambda Delta, and a campus housing residence assistant. She was an ambassador for the School of Public and Environmental Affairs and a Bepko Scholar and Fellow. During her time at IUPUI, she was actively involved in several community service projects, including as a member of the board of directors for the Indiana Chapter of the Huntington's Disease Society of America; the IUPUI Jagathon Committee, which raises money for Riley Hospital for Children; and the Alpha Lambda Delta Honor Society.

Griffin was honored as an Outstanding Woman Student Leader by the IUPUI Office for Women and the Office of Student Involvement at their annual Women's Leadership Reception in 2011. She is a recipient of the William M. Plater Civic Engagement Medallion, was twice named a Top 100 student at IUPUI, and was named a Torchbearer Award finalist by the Indiana Commission for Women.

She has worked with the Indiana General Assembly, Senate Majority from 2010 to 2011, the Indiana Bar Foundation in 2010, as well as for Indianapolis Mayor Greg Ballard from 2009–2010 and the office of Senator Richard Lugar in 2009. While interning for the Indianapolis Office of the Mayor in 2009–2010, she facilitated IUPUI's research of the Citizen Engagement Project, which seeks to provide citizens with the resources they need to work with government. The research earned first place in the competition for the IUPUI Undergraduate Research Award. Also that year, Griffin completed an internship in Washington, D.C., focusing on federal government, with the Washington Leadership Program. Her overseas experience took her to King's College in London and a study abroad program in Berlin at the Hertie School of Governance in 2010.

Since graduating in 2015, she has worked as assistant director of planned giving at Rose-Hulman Institute of Technology. ᏬᎬᏝ

Kenneth R. R. Gros Louis
1936–2017

University Chancellor, 2006–2011

Senior Vice President and Interim Chancellor,
IU Bloomington, 2004–2006

Vice President for Academic Affairs and Chancellor,
IU Bloomington, 1988–2001

Vice President and Chancellor, IU Bloomington, 1980–1988

D URING HIS DISTINGUISHED fifty-year career at Indiana University, Kenneth Gros Louis was admired for his exceptional service to the university, the state, and higher education in America. He was also revered as a speaker—in part because of his love of words and in part because of his almost encyclopedic command of the history of poetry, a deep knowledge he spent a lifetime cultivating.

The son of Albert W. and Jeannette E. (Richards) Gros Louis, Ken was born on December 18, 1936, in Nashua, New Hampshire. After attending Phillips Exeter Academy, he matriculated at Columbia University in 1955, where he pursued a broad-based liberal education, became a member of Sigma Nu Fraternity, and was elected to Phi Beta Kappa. His study of the literature of the English Renaissance, especially poetry, was refined at Columbia, where he earned both BA and MA degrees in English, the latter in 1960. While at Columbia, he also began his history of institutional service, as he served as president of the Residence Halls Association and was a member of the Senior Society of Sachems. In 1960, he enrolled in the doctoral program in English at the University of Wisconsin–Madison, continuing his study of medieval and Renaissance poetry and graduating in 1964. While at Wisconsin, he was the recipient of several academic awards, including the Knapp Fellowship in 1963–1964.

Gros Louis moved to Bloomington in the fall of 1964 to take the position of assistant professor of English and comparative literature. At IU, he advanced steadily through the academic ranks, earning tenure and the rank of associate professor in 1967 and then professor in 1973. He received the Ulysses G. Weatherly Award for Distinguished Teaching in 1970. In addition to teaching, he took on administrative duties, including associate dean of the College of Arts and Sciences (1970), chair of the Department of English (1973), and dean of the College of Arts and Sciences (1978). Throughout these years and after, he continued his scholarly engagement with British literature, particularly that of the medieval and early modern periods, publishing articles in major journals in the field such as *Speculum, Studies in English Literature,* and *The Yearbook of Comparative and General Literature.* He also authored two books: *Literary Interpretations of Biblical Narrative* (1974) and *Literary Interpretations of Biblical Narrative, Volume II* (1982). Furthermore, he served as an expert reader for numerous commercial and academic presses, evaluating manuscripts for both books and scholarly articles.

Ken Gros Louis's career as a university administrator extended in 1980 with his appointment as vice president of the Bloomington campus. Eight years later, his title was changed to vice president for academic affairs and chancellor of the Bloomington campus. Among his most significant responsibilities as vice president, Ken reviewed applications for tenure and promotion from all eight campuses of Indiana University, and he continued to hold both positions until 2001, at which point he was named chancellor emeritus. Called to serve again by President Adam Herbert, Gros Louis generously returned to serve as interim Bloomington chancellor for 2004–2006. He was appointed university chancellor in 2006, following the only other individual to serve in that position—Herman Wells (1962–2000). The Board of Trustees honored him once again by naming him university chancellor emeritus in 2011. He remained active at IU in various ways after his official retirement, including maintaining contacts with generations of students and sharing knowledge of IU's history and heritage.

Holding such positions at Indiana University means the exercise of substantial leadership on the regional and national scenes. Between 1986 and 2000, Gros Louis served as the chairman of the Committee on Institutional Cooperation (CIC). The CIC, a consortium of Big Ten schools and the University of Chicago, works to forge mutually beneficial relationships between member institutions, their faculties, and their students. During Gros Louis's tenure, the consortium's work spanned a wide variety of initiatives ranging from Courseshare, in which students from any of the member campuses can take courses offered by another school via online connection, to cooperative projects in the study of traumatic brain injury, the development of new fields such as the digital humanities, and much more. Gros Louis's leadership was instrumental in launching such programs.

Not only did Gros Louis involve himself in a number of initiatives outside the academy, but he also engaged in projects that enhanced the relationship between the campus and the community. Not long after his appointment as vice president, for example, he established a toll-free telephone line whereby any student or citizen could call him on Thursday afternoons to ask questions about the university. Some twenty years later in the wake of the economic downturn of 2008–09 and the state budget reductions to K–12 education it precipitated, Gros Louis joined other civic leaders in spearheading a fund drive for the Monroe County Community School Corporation (MCCSC). Like Herman Wells before him, Ken Gros Louis respected the relationships that exist between the university and the many constituencies it serves. There is a community beyond the Sample Gates, and he worked diligently as a citizen of it by serving on the boards of directors of the Monroe County United Way, the Blue Cross, and the MCCSC.

Among Gros Louis's many awards honoring his distinguished service are his induction into the Indiana Academy in 1991 and the Golden Deeds Award from the Northside Exchange Club of Bloomington in 2008. For his work on institutional diversity, the American Council of Education recognized him with the Reginald D. Wilson Leadership in Diversity Award in 2005. He received a Thomas Hart Benton Mural Medallion (1988), an IU President's Medallion (2006), and an honorary Doctor of Humane Letters from IUB (2001). In addition, he was honored by the Groups Program (2011), given the Mabel Award for Service for the Foundation for MCCSC (2012), presented with an Ivy Tech honorary degree (2014), received the IU GLBTAA Distinguished Alumni Award (2015), and the Bill Orwig Award (2015).

On August 28, 1965, Ken Gros Louis married fellow scholar Dolores K. Winandy, who received her PhD from Wisconsin in 1968 and who held faculty appointments in Women's Studies, Speech and Theatre, and the Honors Division at Indiana University Bloomington until her death in 1993. They had two daughters: Amy Catherine and Julie Jeannette. Gros Louis later married Diana Mallory Hawes in a ceremony at IUB's Beck Chapel in 1996. On the night of Friday, October 20, 2017, Ken Gros Louis passed away peacefully in his sleep at the age of 80. ᘓ

CAROLYN P. GUTMAN
1932–2011

Trustee, 1974–1986

TRUSTEE, CIVIC LEADER, AND EDUCATOR Carolyn Gutman earned distinction by helping to acquire 152 acres for the Fort Wayne campus, accelerating the construction of the campus library, and encouraging goodwill and collaboration between trustees at Indiana University and Purdue University.

Carolyn Prickett Gutman, daughter of Ward Delwin Prickett and Margaret Marie (Harris) Prickett, was born June 22, 1932, in Mishawaka, Indiana, where her mother served as mayor (1963–1979). From her mother, she inherited her disbelief in a glass ceiling for women. Carolyn attended grammar and high schools in Mishawaka and then entered Indiana University Bloomington, obtaining a BA in journalism in 1954 and an MS in education in 1962. While an undergraduate, Gutman was president of Alpha Phi sorority, a member of the IU Student Foundation, the *Indiana Daily Student*, and the Pleiades. Furthermore, she was one of six women chosen by the Association of Women Students to serve on the first all-student Union Board in 1953–1954. She was a residence hall counselor and the activities advisor in the Dean of Students Office.

Gutman's service to Indiana University continued when she was appointed to serve on the IU Board of Trustees by Governor Otis R. Bowen in 1974, and she was reappointed by Governor Robert D. Orr for a total of twelve consecutive years of service on the board. During her service on the board, Gutman fought to raise faculty salaries, even in disciplines that were not deemed to have high market value, in order to maintain Indiana University as a leader in higher education and to strengthen the university's ability to recruit and retain faculty. She also supported IU financially through philanthropic donations and was a member of the President's Circle. In addition, Gutman founded the Friends of IPFW, and she served for thirteen years either as vice president or president of the Indiana-Purdue Fort Wayne Foundation.

Active in both civic and educational endeavors, Carolyn Gutman served on the Board of Directors of the YWCA, Associated Churches of Fort Wayne, the Pre-School Center for Hearing Handicapped, and Big Brothers-Big Sisters of Fort Wayne; on the advisory boards of Foster Grandparents, Indiana University–Purdue University Fort Wayne (IPFW), and Fort Wayne Community Schools; on the board of trustees of Parkview Memorial Hospital and of Aldergate United Methodist Church, where she was a founding and charter member; as president of the Fort Wayne Panhellenic Council; as president of the Junior League of Fort Wayne; and as a member of the Fort Wayne bicentennial committee. Gutman was also a member of the Fort Wayne Museum of Art, Friends of Music, Hoosier Salon Patrons Association, Indianapolis Museum of Art, State Assembly Women's Club, Fort Wayne Zoological Society, Indianapolis Children's Museum, IU Alumni Association, IU Alumni Club of Fort Wayne, Well House Society, Woodburn Guild, James Whitcomb Riley Hospital Association, and Fox Island Alliance. Gutman was particularly proud of her service as the first woman chairperson of the Committee for Finance and Administration in the Northern Conference of the United Methodist Church, a committee that set the total budget for the North Indiana Conference for the United Methodist Church. She was also a certified real estate broker, appraiser, and certified environmental inspector.

Carolyn Gutman's service to her communities and to Indiana University were broadly recognized. In 1978, Gutman received the Ursa Major Award from Alpha Phi sorority, a national recognition for service and achievement in the community. She received the Ralph E. Broyles Medal from the IU Alumni Club of Allen County for unique and significant contributions to IU in Fort Wayne. For her service to Indiana University and the Fort Wayne region, she was awarded the honorary Doctor of Humane Letters from Indiana University at IPFW in 1996. Twice she was cited as a Sagamore of the Wabash.

In 1955, Carolyn married Phillip Edward Gutman (BS 1952, JD 1957). Their three children are all IU graduates: Phillip Edward Jr. (BS 1980, MBA 1982), Gretchen Kay (BA 1986, MPA 1987, JD 1997), and Kurt Alan (BS 1993). Carolyn's husband, Phillip, served as Indiana state senator from 1968 to 1976 and was president pro tempore of the Indiana Senate from 1971 to 1976. Carolyn and Phillip had six grandchildren.

Carolyn Prickett Gutman passed away on November 20, 2011, depriving Fort Wayne of one of its most valuable citizens and Indiana University of one of its most dedicated alumnae. ᑦᕦᒡ

John T. Hackett

1932–2010

Vice President for Finance and Administration,
1988–1991

A N ECONOMIST, VENTURE CAPITALIST, and educator, John T. Hackett served as the vice president for finance and administration at Indiana University from 1988–1991, bringing his internationally recognized expertise in finance to bear on the university's fiscal, financial, and administrative affairs.

The youngest son of Ruth Greer and Harry Herman Hackett, John Thomas Hackett was born in Fort Wayne on October 10, 1932. He graduated from North Manchester High School and received his BS and MBA from Indiana University in 1954 and 1958, respectively. In 1954 he married Ann Thompson of Marion, Indiana, with whom he had four children: Jane, David, Sarah, and Peter. Ann completed her BA at Indiana University in 1977. Hackett served as a first lieutenant with the United States Army from 1954 to 1958, including one year as armored recon platoon leader in the 14th Armored Calvary Unit stationed in Germany, where their daughter Jane was born. Hackett then went on to earn a PhD in finance and economics from the Ohio State University in 1961.

Hackett's career in finance administration began in 1961 with the position of research economist at the Federal Reserve Bank of Cleveland. In 1964, Hackett joined the Indiana-based Cummins Engine Company, where he worked for twenty-four years, rising to the position of executive vice president and chief financial officer, and then became a member of its board of directors. In the 1970s, Hackett served six years on the board of directors at the Federal Reserve Bank in Chicago. While at Cummins, he also served at various times on the boards of directors at Ball Corporation, Ramsburg Corporation, Meridian Insurance Corporation, and the Irwin Financial Corporation, as well as being chairman of the Indiana Secondary Market for Educational Loans and chairman for the Wabash National Corporation. He retired from Cummins in 1988 to join Indiana University.

In July of 1988, Hackett joined Indiana University as vice president of finance and administration as well as adjunct professor of economics, succeeding Edgar G. Williams as IU's chief financial officer. As vice president of finance and administration, Hackett was known for his strong commitment to keeping the university within its means while enhancing the way of life for students and faculty alike. During his tenure, he implemented a brand-new budgeting system and helped push through the Guaranteed Tuition Certificates program, which protected students from tuition inflation. Proposed by vice president John Hackett in November 1988 and approved by the Board of Trustees in December, the Indiana University Guaranteed Tuition Certificates program allowed people (e.g., students, parents, grandparents, and investors) to purchase future tuition hours at current rates for an administrative fee. Although the university sold 753 investors 39,000 credit hours at $2.8 million, the sales figures were not high enough for the program to be self-sustaining, and in 1991 the university halted the program. Hackett also restructured employee health benefits to be more fiscally responsible, which resulted in ending new enrollments in the 18-20 Retirement Plan as of January 1, 1989, and replacing it with a new retirement plan. A noted writer on economic policy, Hackett also contributed articles to numerous reviews and journals, including the *Harvard Business Review*.

Hackett was a distinguished alumnus, educator, and community volunteer. His many accomplishments and service earned him recognition, including induction into the Academy of Alumni Fellows by the Kelley School of Business Alumni Association, receipt of the Distinguished Alumni Service Award from Indiana University, and receipt of the Distinguished Alumni Award from the College of Administrative Sciences at Ohio State University. He was a member of the President's Club as well as an Indiana Academy Fellow. Hackett also volunteered his time for numerous community and public service organizations, including the Indianapolis Zoological Society, the Villages of Indiana, the Greater Bloomington Chamber of Commerce, and the Connor Prairie Pioneer Settlement. He was also a member of The Ohio State University Graduate School Council.

After retiring from IU in 1991, Hackett became managing general partner of CID Equity Partners, a venture capital firm that he had helped to establish a decade earlier. In the following years, he taught finance courses at Kent State University, Case Western Reserve University, and Franklin Pierce College. In 2004, Hackett and his wife, Ann, moved to Keene, New Hampshire, to be near their younger daughter and her family. From 2004 until his death, Hackett was an adjunct faculty member in economics and finance at Keene State College.

John T. Hackett passed away in his home in Keene, New Hampshire, on November 18, 2010. ☙

THOMAS R. HALEY III
1961–

Trustee, 1985–1987

Appointed as trustee while completing a JD in the Indiana University School of Law at Indianapolis, Thomas Haley is one of five family members to have attended IU.

Thomas Haley graduated from Seymour High School in 1980. His high school and college employment included serving as a janitor, hamburger flipper, retail sales clerk, photographer, and church organist at All Saints Episcopal Church. After graduation, he enrolled at Indiana University Bloomington, following the footsteps of his parents. His father, Thomas R. Haley II, graduated from IU in 1949 with a double major in journalism and civics, and then in 1951 with a law degree. His mother, Bette Kern, attended the IU School of Nursing, but was called home during her senior year when her brother was killed in World War II. His sister Virginia (Haley) Hinkle also attended Indiana University, graduating in 1988 with a degree in fashion merchandising. His uncle, Clifford Wiethoff, was a member of the IU national championship basketball team in 1940, and then a graduate of the IU School of Medicine.

In 1984, Thomas R. Haley III graduated from Indiana University with a double-major BA in history and journalism. During his undergraduate years, he served Indiana University as an orientation assistant, a senator in the Indiana University Student Association, member and chair of the Willkie Residence Hall Judicial Board, staff advisor to the McNutt Residence Hall Judicial Board, a General Assembly student lobbyist, and a resident assistant in McNutt Quadrangle. In the 1982–1983 school year, Haley served as co-chair of the Committee to Elect the Seymour School Board. Through its efforts, his hometown school board was approved by voters in a public referendum, to switch from an appointed to an elected school board. In 1983, Haley was a Congressional intern in Washington, D.C., for United States Representative Lee Hamilton, serving as a research assistant for the Joint Economic Committee.

Upon graduation in 1984, Haley enrolled in law school at the Indiana University School of Law at Indianapolis (later renamed the IU McKinney School of Law). In 1985 he interned for Chief U.S. Magistrate Judge Thomas J. Faulconer in U.S. District Court. On August 26, 1985, Governor Robert D. Orr appointed Haley to a two-year term as student trustee of the Indiana University Board of Trustees, just the sixth student to serve on the board. While in law school, Haley clerked for an insurance defense law firm, served as a lobbyist and law clerk for the

Hoosier State Press Association, and for two years was an associate editor of the *Indiana Law Review*. He graduated from law school in 1987. Haley was admitted to the Indiana State Bar Association and he served for two years as a judicial clerk for the Honorable James E. Noland, senior U.S. District Court judge for the Southern District of Indiana (1987–1989). He then began private legal practice with an Indianapolis law firm in the areas of insurance defense and corporate/general business/labor law litigation. In 1995 he joined the Carmel, Indiana, firm now known as Jennings Wheeler & Haley, where he continues to specialize in intermediate and complex litigation in third- and first-party claims and lawsuits. His concentration is in analysis and defense of bodily injury and property loss claims such as motor vehicle and construction site accidents, wrongful death and product liability actions, commercial litigation, uninsured/underinsured motorist claims, and arbitrations, in both state and federal trial courts and appeals courts. He has completed certification in civil mediation, and is experienced in firm management and in the training of associate attorneys.

Haley has written and spoken at continuing education seminars, and has prepared numerous articles and presentations for legal and insurance professional publications and programs. He is admitted to the U.S. Northern and Southern District Federal Courts and the Seventh Circuit Federal Court of Appeals. He is a member of the Indiana State, Indianapolis, and Seventh Circuit Bar Associations, as well as the National Society of Professional Insurance Investigators. He is a member of the Columbia Club, having achieved its twenty-five year membership award. He is a life member of the Indiana University Alumni Association. He has served as a lobbyist at the Indiana General Assembly for educational, public, and civic issues, and as a registered lobbyist for private industry (1981–1995). He has been an active member of the Indianapolis Zoological Society and the Indiana Historical Society.

Thomas Haley resides in Indianapolis and enjoys travel, writing, photography, keyboards/drums, and amateur radio. ᑳᖇᐧ

KAREN HANSON
1947–

Executive Vice President and Provost,
IU Bloomington, 2007–2012

PHILOSOPHER, EDUCATOR, AND ADMINISTRATOR Karen Hanson's career in higher education spanned thirty-six years at Indiana University before continuing at the University of Minnesota.

Karen Hanson was born on April 11, 1947, in Lincoln, Nebraska. The daughter of Lester Eugene and Gladys Diessner, she received a BA, summa cum laude, in philosophy and mathematics from the University of Minnesota in 1970. That August, she married Dennis Senchuk, also a philosopher; in 1990, their twin children Tia and Chloe (BA 2012) were born. Hanson earned both an MA and a PhD in philosophy from Harvard University in 1980. Her philosophical interests include philosophy of mind, aesthetics, American philosophy, moral philosophy, epistemology, and philosophy of language.

Karen Hanson joined the IU faculty in 1976 as a lecturer, and by 1991 had advanced to professor. From 2001 to 2012 she was a Rudy Professor, and from 1997 to 2002 was chair of the Department of Philosophy. She taught courses in gender studies, comparative literature, and American studies. During her career, Hanson served as director of graduate studies, director of undergraduate studies, undergraduate (and University Division) advisor, faculty advisor to the Philosophy Club, recording secretary, and placement officer, and served on many major university boards and committees, including as a member of the governing board of the IU Institute for Advanced Study and the IU Foundation Board of Directors. From 2002 to 2007, Hanson was dean of the Hutton Honors College; its naming for benefactor Ed Hutton was one of her hallmark achievements at IU. Hanson retired from IU in 2012 with the title Rudy Professor emeritus and with the additional title of provost emeritus.

After retiring from IU, Hanson accepted a position at the University of Minnesota as their senior vice president for academic affairs and provost, a position that expanded her academic responsibilities and brought her back to her alma mater. Since 2012, she has led the university's strategic planning and implementation efforts.

Beyond teaching and administration, Hanson has served on many academic boards and organizations, including the American Philosophical Association, the North American Society for Social Philosophy, the National Endowment for the Humanities, the American Council of Learned Societies, the Inamori Foundation, the MacArthur Prize committee, Semiotic Society of America, American Society for Aesthetics, the John Dewey Foundation, and Phi Beta Kappa. Since joining the University of Minnesota, she has been chair of the Big Ten Academic Alliance (2013–), a member of the Council for Higher Education Accreditation committee on recognition (2012–2013), chair of the Council on Academic Affairs of the Association of Public and Land-Grant Universities (APLU) and member of the executive committee (2013–), part of the Association of American Universities/Association of Research Libraries Task Force on Scholarly Communication (2014–), on the board of officers of the John Dewey Foundation (2010–2015), a gubernatorial appointee to the Midwestern Higher Education Commission (2013–) and member of the executive committee (2014–), and on the APLU Task Force on Tenure, Promotion, and Technology Transfer (2014–2015). Hanson is co-chair (with the Minnesota commissioner of health) of a collaboration between the Big Ten universities and their state health agencies to address the social determinants of health disparities.

A prolific writer, Hanson has published reviews and articles in many scholarly journals, is the author of *The Self Imagined: Philosophical Reflections on the Social Character of Psyche*, and is co-editor (with Kenneth R. Johnston, Gilbert Chaitin, and Herbert Marks) of *Romantic Revolutions: Criticism and Theory*. She has been an editor for *American Philosophical Quarterly*, *Journal of Social Philosophy*, *Notre Dame Philosophical Reviews*, *Cognitio: Revista de Filosofia*, and the Peirce Edition Project.

For her service and scholarship, Hanson received numerous awards, grants, and distinctions. IU awards include a Distinguished Scholar Award from the Office of Women's Affairs, Teaching Excellence Recognition Award, Brown Derby Award for Distinguished Teaching, and the FACET All-University Award for Distinguished Teaching. She has been the Lienemann Lecturer for Phi Beta Kappa; received the Amoco Foundation All-University Distinguished Teaching Award; won the Woodbridge Prize in Philosophy; and held a Lilly Postdoctoral Teaching Fellowship. Awards from Harvard University include fellowships in Arts and Sciences Teaching and the Graduate School of Arts and Sciences, and a nomination for the Johnsonian Prize. She won the Philip L. Quinn Prize for Service to Philosophy and Philosophers from the American Philosophical Association. IU President Michael McRobbie presented her with the President's Medal for Excellence in 2012. ❧

MICHAEL HARRIS
1956–

Chancellor, IU Kokomo, 2010–2012

Michael Harris

Educator and university administrator Michael Harris served as the sixth chancellor of Indiana University Kokomo and as a professor of public and environmental affairs, business, and education.

Born in Johannesburg, South Africa, to Taya (Katz) and Jack Harris, he moved to Israel as a child and grew up in Timorim, a commune. Harris was also a major in the Israeli Defense Forces, and was vice president for finance and marketing at Tomer Industries in Timorim. He received a BA in economics and business administration from Bar-Ilan University in 1982, an MA in public policy from Tel Aviv University in 1986, and a PhD in public policy from Indiana University in 1993. He is a graduate of the Management Development Program and the Institute for Educational Management at the Harvard Graduate School of Education.

Before coming to IU Kokomo, Harris was a faculty member at the Graduate Program on Public Policy at Tel Aviv University (1993–1994), a faculty member and administrator at Eastern Michigan University (1994–2004), vice president for academic affairs at Ferris State University (2004–2007), and provost and vice president of academic affairs and student affairs at Kettering University (2007–2010). He has also participated in the Oxford Round Table at Harris Manchester College of the University of Oxford.

While chancellor at IU Kokomo, Harris initiated new academic programs and degrees, including the introduction of the campus's first bachelor of fine arts degree and a student success program. He partnered with local business and government to enhance economic development opportunities in the City of Kokomo. Through his efforts a new state-of-the-art nursing simulation lab was established, record fundraising was achieved for the campus, and enrollment increased to the largest freshman class in IUK history and the largest number of full-time students at 3,700. Harris helped establish new club sports and improved facilities for basketball.

After leaving IU, Harris was appointed dean of the College of Public Service and Urban Affairs at Tennessee State University in Nashville in May 2013.

Harris has been the recipient of the Notable Alumni award from Tel Aviv University, a Best in Class distinction by the Kern Family Foundation, the Golden Medallion Award from Eastern Michigan University, recognition for Excellence in Teaching from the American

Political Science Association, a Distinguished Faculty Award from the Michigan Association of Governing Boards, and recognition by the Department of the Army for outstanding support of the United States Army R.O.T.C. cadre and cadets at Eastern Michigan. In 2003, he received an honorary doctorate in educational administration from Ave Maria College. The *Kokomo Perspective* named Harris its 2011 Person of the Year. And in 2012, Maariv selected Harris as one of the "10 Most Successful Israelis in 10 Different Fields in the World." He has also been a senior fellow with the American Association of State Colleges and Universities, as well as a fellow with The Levin Institute at SUNY.

He and his wife, Tali, have three sons: Ronen, Asaf, and Amit. ❧

Thomas C. Healy

1944–

Vice President for Government Relations,
2004–2007

A LIFELONG EDUCATOR and higher education administrator, Thomas Healy came to IU as vice president for government relations at the behest of President Adam Herbert.

Thomas Clair Healy was born in Preston, Minnesota, in 1944. After earning both a BS in elementary education and an MS in school administration from Winona State University, Healy went on to receive a PhD from the University of Maryland in 1972.

Before coming to Indiana University, Healy worked in higher education for over thirty-five years. Much of this work experience came during his twenty-six-year tenure at the University of North Florida, where he held numerous positions. He served as a charter member of the faculty for seven years, founded and became the first director of the Downtown Center in 1978, and continued that responsibility when he became the dean of continuing education and external affairs in 1979, a position he held until 1983. In the following years, Healy held assistant and associate vice president positions in academic affairs and university relations. He also was interim vice president for student affairs, university relations, and administration and finance and served five years as athletic director. Some of his jobs overlapped with his duties as vice president for government affairs. From 1998 to 2001, Healy was the vice chancellor for government affairs for the State University System of Florida. His office was responsible for coordinating the lobbying efforts of the nine state universities in Florida and in Washington, D.C. This cooperative effort, aided by the opening of an office in D.C., resulted in an additional $125 million in funds annually for Florida's higher education institutions. He then spent three years as assistant to the president for government relations at Florida Gulf Coast University.

The Indiana University Board of Trustees confirmed the appointment of Thomas C. Healy to the newly established position of vice president for government relations in April 2004. President Herbert recommended the appointment and said the position was designed to more effectively lead, manage, and coordinate the university's governmental efforts at the state and federal levels. Healy combined the offices of state relations, federal relations, and Hoosiers for Higher Education into a new office of government relations and hired an experienced director for each area. Together, the staff developed a new strategic plan for all government contacts.

Healy has served on numerous community and state boards and committees, including the Jacksonville (Florida) Chamber of Commerce, the Florida State Institute of Government Police Board, the Florida Engineering Education Delivery System, and the Southwest Florida Legislative Issues Group. He has also been a member of the National Association of Intercollegiate Athletics, the Athletic Directors Association, Phi Delta Kappa, and the National University Continuing Education Association. Since 2014, he has served as chairman of the board of the Tournament Players Championship Village, which partners with the Eisenhower Center of Ann Arbor, Michigan, to provide residential treatment for military personnel, first responders, and retired NFL players who have suffered post-traumatic stress disorder and brain and other related injuries.

Healy received an alumni award for Outstanding Leader in Education in 2005 from the University of Maryland. In 2011, Healy was one of three graduates to be recognized as distinguished alumni by Winona State University. He was the 2014 recipient of the Spring Valley, Minnesota, High School Wall of Honor Award, recognizing graduates who have represented the school and community in an exemplary manner (after consolidation, the school is now known as Kingsland High School). He was a fellow at the Institute for Educational Management at Harvard University in 1984.

Healy and his wife, Jan, have two sons, Mark and Brent. In 2007 Healy retired, and the couple returned to Jacksonville, Florida, to spend more time with their granddaughter, travel the world a bit, and play a lot of golf. ᔕ

Adam W. Herbert

1943–

President, Indiana University, 2003–2007

THE SEVENTEENTH PRESIDENT of Indiana University, Adam W. Herbert, who led IU from 2003 to 2007, was born in Muskogee, Oklahoma. He attended the University of Southern California, receiving a BA in political science in 1966 and an MA in public administration in 1968. He then earned a PhD in urban affairs and public administration from the University of Pittsburgh in 1971.

Herbert's career has included roles in public administration as well as in education, roles that seemed to blend later in his career. As an educator, Herbert began teaching in 1971 at the University of Southern California as a faculty member in the School of Public Administration and the Center for Urban Affairs. In 1972, he was appointed as chair of the Urban Affairs Program and associate professor of urban affairs at Virginia Polytechnic Institute and State University (Virginia Tech), where he was the recipient of a Teaching Learning Grant (1974) as well as an Excellence in Teaching Award. In 1974–1975, Herbert was a White House Fellow in the Nixon and Ford Administrations, where he was a special assistant to the U.S. secretary of health, education, and welfare. In 1975, he worked as a special assistant to the U.S. undersecretary of housing and urban development, and subsequently served as director of research for the Joint Center for Political Studies in Washington, D.C.

After a brief return to Virginia Tech, Herbert joined Florida International University in 1979 as professor of public administration, where he held various leadership posts including dean of the School of Public Affairs and Services as well as vice president and chief executive officer of the North Miami campus. Afterward, he was appointed president of the University of North Florida, a position he held from 1989 to 1998 before becoming chancellor for the State University System of Florida from 1998 to 2001, the first African American to hold both positions. During this period, Herbert developed ties to the Florida political establishment, leading Governor-Elect Jeb Bush's gubernatorial transition team in 1998 and later co-chairing Governor Bush's Reading Priority Transition Team for Florida in 2002.

Throughout his career, Herbert has also held various high-level positions in professional organizations and committees. Some examples include: election to the National Academy of Public Administration and two terms on its board of directors; numerous committees of the American Society for Public Administration; president of the National

Association of Schools of Public Affairs and Administration; committees of the Conference of Minority Public Administrators; chairman of the Division II President's Council of the National Collegiate Athletic Association and a member of the NCAA Executive Committee; and the Knight Commission on Intercollegiate Athletics.

Appointed president of Indiana University in 2003, Herbert was the first African American to hold that position. Herbert committed himself to enlarging the school's racial and international diversity. He accompanied eleven other university presidents on a diplomatic mission to Japan, Korea, and China with the U.S. Secretary of Education Margaret Spellings and Deputy Undersecretary of State Dina Habib Powell in order to foster relations and to invite the countries to send students to study abroad in the United States. In addition, he began and oversaw the Life Sciences Strategic Plan, improved relations with the Indiana General Assembly as well as with Ivy Tech Community College, and built several athletic fields, breaking ground on brand new basketball and football facilities. He resigned as president in 2007, becoming president emeritus. In 2008, he officially retired from the faculty as professor emeritus of political science and of public and environmental affairs.

Adam Herbert's wife, Karen, represented the university as a speaker and participant in higher education organizations as well as overseeing the operations and staffing associated with the presidential residences, in addition to hosting university-related functions. Prior to her time at IU, Karen had a career in telecommunications management as well as a history of fundraising for community foundations and public libraries, philanthropic endeavors that she continued while at IU. This included serving as an important role model for women of color on campus, and advocating for Big Brothers Big Sisters. An artist and avid collector of paintings, she sponsored the restoration of John Edward Bundy's *View from Bay* (1902), a painting in the Hoosier Salon style, which was exhibited at the IU Art Museum (later renamed the Eskenazi Museum of Art) in 2004, and later housed in the sunroom of Bryan House.

Upon retirement in 2007, the Herberts returned to Jacksonville, Florida. ᘏ

DEAN A. HERTZLER II
1976–

Trustee, 1999–2001

PEDIATRIC NEUROSURGEON and former student leader at IUPUI, Dean Hertzler was the thirteenth student to serve on the Indiana University Board of Trustees.

Dean Allen Hertzler II was born in Elkhart, Indiana, in 1976 to Janet Arlene (Gutwein) and Dean Allen Hertzler, a nurse practitioner and a pastor, respectively. From 1994 to 1995, he worked for the Air Land Emergency Resource Team (ALERT) as an emergency medical technician, assisting in land search and rescue, underwater search and recovery, firefighting, and construction. Hertzler learned the importance of responsibility and taking on leadership roles, characteristics he carried into his academic and professional careers.

Appointed to the Board of Trustees by Indiana Governor Frank O'Bannon, Dean Hertzler II served IU as a trustee from 1999 to 2001 while he was an undergraduate earning a BS in biology with minors in chemistry and medical humanities at Indiana University–Purdue University Indianapolis (IUPUI). Hertzler graduated with distinction, twice being awarded the Most Outstanding Undergraduate Male Student award, receiving the Charles O. McGaughey Leadership Award, the William L. Garrett Most Outstanding Student in Activities Award, and the Outstanding Academic Achievement in Biology award. While an undergraduate, Hertzler served in student leadership roles at IUPUI, including as vice president of the IUPUI Student Foundation, a member of the steering committee and the executive committee of the IUPUI Student Foundation, senator in the IUPUI Undergraduate Student Assembly, and member and president of the School of Science Undergraduate Student Council.

Hertzler enrolled at the IU School of Medicine, where he was the assistant editor for *Iatrogenesis* and a co-chair of the Ethics at Lunch committee. He completed his MD in 2005. By the time of his graduation, Hertzler had served on numerous boards and committees at the university, including the Purdue University Strategic Plan Task Force for IUPUI, the Student Trustee Search and Screen Committee, the Campus Community Committee, the Facilities Committee Board of Advisors, the Dean's Advisory Council for the School of Science, and the Technology Committee for the School of Science. Additionally, he was a research, laboratory, and teaching assistant.

Following his medical education, Hertzler completed a residency in neurosurgery at the University of Cincinnati, and was a fellow in pediatric neurosurgery at Primary Children's Hospital in Salt Lake City, Utah, from 2011 to 2012. He then took a position as pediatric neurosurgeon at Joe DiMaggio Children's Hospital in Hollywood, Florida.

Hertzler has been the recipient of numerous awards, grants, and scholarships, including the Indiana University School of Medicine Dean's Council Scholarship, the USA Group Scholarship, the School of Science Dean's Scholarship from IUPUI, and the School of Sciences Department of Biology Richard O. McCracken Scholarship. He was awarded first place in the Undergraduate Research Symposium from the School of Science and was named to the Scholar's List. During his residency training, he was the recipient of the Ellen and Stewart B. Dunsker, MD, Award for Clinical Research. He was also a Slemenda Scholar in Eldoret, Kenya.

In 2005, Dean Hertzler II was married to Senait Hagdu Araia. Together, they have four children: Hannah, Levi, Benjamin, and Theodore. ↶

JAY L. HESS
1960–

Executive Vice President for University
Clinical Affairs, 2018–

Vice President for University Clinical Affairs,
2013–2018

A LONGTIME PROFESSOR OF PATHOLOGY, Jay Hess has become a leader in medical higher education at Indiana University. Jay Hess was born in North Tarrytown, New York, on May 14, 1960, to Geraldine L. Frymire, an artist and administrative assistant, and Lowell F. Hess, an artist. Both of his parents, as artists, put a tremendous value on creativity, which served as a constant source of inspiration. His father was the chief artist for *Collier's* magazine and did illustrations for various other publications, such as *Boys' Life*, Golden Books, Time Life books and magazines, and *Reader's Digest*. His mother suffered from breast cancer for many years when he was growing up, and passed away when he was in college. That was part of his inspiration for pursuing a medical career and, in particular, cancer research.

Hess grew up in Connecticut, attending public schools in Southport and Fairfield before going to university. He attended Johns Hopkins University (1978–1982), earning a BA in biophysics. He then entered the Johns Hopkins University School of Medicine (1982–1989), earning an MD and a PhD. He completed residency training in anatomic pathology and fellowships in hematopathology and surgical pathology at Brigham and Women's Hospital. As a student, Hess was active in the Glee Club and the Physics Club. He was a member of the National Honor Society, a National Merit Scholar, elected to Phi Beta Kappa (1989), elected to the Alpha Omega Alpha Honor Medical Society (2004), held a Howard Hughes Research Fellowship at Johns Hopkins, and participated in the NIH Medical Scientist Training Program (1982–1989). Hess returned to school twice in mid-career, earning a Certificate in Management from the Wharton School of the University of Pennsylvania (2001–2002) and completing an MHSA at the University of Michigan School of Public Health (2010–2012).

Hess began his professional career at the Washington University School of Medicine in St. Louis, Missouri, as assistant professor of pathology (1993–1999). He then moved to the University of Pennsylvania School of Medicine, Philadelphia, Pennsylvania, where he taught as a lecturer in pathology and laboratory medicine (1999–2000), associate professor (2000–2004), and then professor (2004–2005), as well as director of hematopathology. After six years at Penn, Hess was recruited to the University of Michigan Medical School in Ann Arbor, Michigan, where he was appointed Carl V. Weller Professor and Chair of

Pathology (2005–2013) and to the additional post of professor of internal medicine (2012–2013). Although Hess moved to Indiana University in 2013, he maintained ties with Michigan, where he continues to serve as adjunct professor of pathology (2013–) in the Medical School and as adjunct professor of health management and policy (2016–) in the School of Public Health.

Arriving at Indiana University in 2013, Jay Hess serves in multiple positions. He is executive vice president for university clinical affairs, Walter J. Daly Professor of Pathology and Laboratory Medicine, dean of the Indiana University School of Medicine, adjunct professor of health policy and management at the Richard M. Fairbanks School of Public Health, and director of the Indiana Statewide Medical Education System. Between 2013 and 2017, Hess increased funding to the School of Medicine by over $70 million annually, raised more than $450 million as part of For All: The Indiana University Bicentennial Campaign, increased integration and alignment of the IU School of Medicine with IU Health, helped launch the IU Interprofessional Practice and Education Center (2014), led the IU School of Medicine through reaccreditation (2016–2017), and led the school through implementation of a new curriculum across nine campuses, including the new campus in Evansville (2016). He has also been involved in planning the Regional Academic Health Center, a new medical campus located at IU Bloomington.

Beyond IU, Hess serves on the editorial boards of a number of journals, such as the *American Journal of Clinical Pathology* (1996–2016) and the *American Journal of Blood* (2011–). He has served on numerous scientific review committees, such as the NIH Cancer and Molecular Pathobiology Study Section (2001–2005) and the Lymphoma and Leukemia Society SCOR Review Committee (2012–). He is a member of the American Society of Clinical Investigation. He is on the board of directors at BioCrossroads (a consortium of Indiana business and academic leaders), the board of directors at Riley Children's Foundation (Grants Committee, 2013–), the board of directors for the Indiana Health Information Exchange (2013–), board of directors at the Regenstrief Institute (Governance Committee, 2013–; Audit Committee, 2014–), board of directors for IU Health (chair of Research and Education Committee, 2013–), and board of directors for the IU Health North Hospital (2017–).

Over the years, Hess has garnered several honors and awards. He was elected to the John Morgan Society (1999), held the Morton F. Mason Lectureship at the University of Texas Southwestern (2003), was elected to American Society of Clinical Investigation (2004), elected to the Pluto Society (2006), was awarded the Ramzi S. Cotran Lectureship by the New England Society of Pathologists (2009), and won the University of Michigan Health System's Making a Difference Award (2011–2013). Hess also was named the 2014 Translating Research into Practice Scholar by Indiana University and was a distinguished lecturer at Beth Israel Deaconess Medical Center/Harvard Medical School (2016).

Jay Hess and his wife, Robin, were married September 15, 1984, and together they have two children: Andrew L. Hess and Wren Hess. ⌒❧

EMITA BRADY HILL
1936–

Chancellor, IU Kokomo, 1991–1999

$\mathbf{A}$ HUMANITIES SCHOLAR and an experienced administrator, Emita Hill was IU Kokomo's fifth chancellor.

The youngest of five sisters—all of whom earned advanced degrees— Emita Hill was born on January 31, 1936, in Baltimore, Maryland. Her interest in the study of foreign languages at a young age, encouraged by her parents and a dedicated high school French teacher, developed within her a passion for travel and for the literature and music of other cultures. As an undergraduate at Cornell University, Hill majored in French but also studied German and Italian languages and literatures, as well as music theory and performance. After graduating Phi Beta Kappa from Cornell, she traveled to France to study literature at the Sorbonne and to study viola with Léon Pascal and organ with the late Jean Langlais. Following the yearlong sojourn in France, Hill continued her studies at Middlebury College, where she earned an MA in 1958 before beginning her studies at Harvard University, where she graduated with a PhD in romance languages in 1967.

Hill taught at Western Reserve University in Cleveland from 1967 until 1969. After a brief stint as a visiting lecturer at Columbia University's graduate school, she joined the Department of Romance Languages at Lehman College, CUNY, in 1970 as a professor of French literature and, though an untenured assistant professor, as chair of romance languages. Later she became associate provost, and then vice president for institutional advancement. At Lehman, she received grants from the National Endowment for the Humanities to initiate a number of large interdisciplinary projects, including the City and the Humanities program and the Bronx Regional History project, both of which still exist on Lehman's campus thirty years later. She also oversaw the development of a program specifically designed for deaf and hearing-impaired students, which was the first of its kind at a four-year liberal arts college in the East. Hill eventually left Lehman in 1991 to become the chancellor of Indiana University Kokomo.

Indiana University President Thomas Ehrlich appointed Emita Hill as the fifth chancellor of Indiana University Kokomo in April of 1991, relieving acting chancellor Arthur C. Gentile (August 1990–April 1991), and holding the position until her retirement in 1999. She spent the next nine years as Kokomo's chancellor, encouraging the growth of programs in the humanities, successfully raising funds for a new library and an art gallery, and developing community programs and international exchange programs. On campus, Hill is credited with encouraging cultural, social, and racial diversity, spurring creation of the IU Kokomo Art Gallery and the annual Enhancing Minority Attainment conference. In 1995, she oversaw the opening of a new 48,360-square-foot library, as well as Kresge Auditorium, Alumni Hall, and the Art Gallery. Before retiring, she also oversaw the funding and architectural plans for a new science building on the IUK campus. The Emita B. Hill Scholarship fund for study abroad at IU Kokomo is awarded annually in her honor.

In June of 1994, President Ehrlich awarded Hill the Thomas Hart Benton Mural Medallion for her outstanding service and support to the university. Following his appointment as president of IU in 1994, Myles Brand acted to expand several administrators' roles, including Hill's role as chancellor. Hill's additional title was chancellor liaison, office of the president, a role in which she was responsible for coordinating the efforts of regional campus administrators and IU's central administration. In this position, and in her role as chancellor, Hill worked to ensure that the regional campuses were fully developed liberal arts and professional campuses.

After her retirement from Indiana University, Hill continued her service to higher education by participating in three ongoing international university development projects in Poland, in Kyrgyzstan, and in Macedonia through the Indiana Consortium for International Programs. She served as trustee of Tetovo University in Macedonia for several years and of American University Central Asia (AUCA) in Kyrgyzstan for twelve years. She continued her relationship with AUCA as executive director of the AUCA Foundation (2012–2015) and remains a board member. She also took part in a number of consulting visits to universities in Eastern Europe under the auspices of the Salzburg Seminar. She was a member of the International Women's Forum, the International Association of University Presidents, and the New York Women's Forum (where she has been chair of the Awards Committee since 2010). In 2015, Texas Tech University Press published Hill's labor of love, *Bronx Faces and Voices: Sixteen Stories of Courage and Community*, a book based on her research on the Bronx during her years at Lehman. She is presently at work on two additional projects: a regional oral history of women in local food movements in Northwest Michigan (accepted for publication by Wayne State University Press), and an oral history of ballroom dancers, to be archived by the New York Public Library Performing Arts Division.

Hill married William Speed Hill in 1960. They divorced in 1980. He died in 2007. Their three children are Julie Beck, a nurse practitioner in oncology; Christopher Hill, a professor of biology and animal behavior; and Madeleine Vedel, trained as a specialist in East Asia, fluent in Japanese and French, and presently a culinary expert managing a goat farm and producing and marketing French-style goat cheeses. ᴄ𝕚𝕃

GLENN W. IRWIN JR.
1920–2012

Vice President and Chancellor,
IUPUI, 1973–1986

F REQUENTLY DESCRIBED AS "HIGH CLASS, LOW KEY," Glenn Ward Irwin Jr. was vice president emeritus, chancellor emeritus of IUPUI, and dean emeritus of the IU School of Medicine (IUSM). While serving as dean of medicine in the 1960s, Irwin led the creation of a statewide medical education program, and while chancellor and vice president in the 1970s and 1980s, he drove the growth of programs and facilities at the Indianapolis campus.

Irwin was born in Roachdale, Indiana, in 1920 and attended Indiana University, where he earned a BS in 1942. He went on to graduate from the IU School of Medicine in the spring 1944 class, one of the school's two wartime classes that year, which was the result of the school's effort to produce more doctors to serve the troops injured in the war. After serving at the Schofield Barracks Hospital in Hawaii, he joined the Indiana University faculty at the medical school in 1950, rising through the ranks to become a professor in 1961 and then dean in 1965.

As dean of the IUSM from 1965 to 1973, Irwin oversaw the school's growth and played a significant role in the expansion and coordination of medical education across Indiana. Irwin began the drive to build Indiana University Hospital in June 1965, which was the first adult hospital built by IU since Coleman Hospital for Women opened in 1927. Medical education was a key focus for Irwin and the school during his tenure. In the 1960s, under Irwin's direction, IUSM developed the Indiana Plan for a coordinated statewide system of undergraduate, graduate, and continuing medical education. Conceptualized to create "a medical school without walls, both in space and in time," the plan established seven new medical campuses beyond Indianapolis and the Bloomington program. The plan called for the first two years of medical education to be taught in collaboration with basic science faculty at IU Bloomington, the University of Notre Dame, Ball State University, Indiana State University, the University of Evansville, and Purdue University. This was the first comprehensive program to use all of the resources for medical education within an entire state, and to develop an integrated system of medical education that served physicians as well as medical students anywhere within that state's borders.

In 1973, Irwin was appointed vice president and chancellor of IUPUI. In this role, Irwin oversaw the growth of the campus's academic programs and gave particular attention to its physical development at a time of rapid expansion. The campus underwent a transformation that brought continued dramatic growth in subsequent decades. Work progressed to enhance and expand Riley Hospital for Children (Phase III, 1986) and IU Hospital (Phase II, 1975), and both the Regenstrief Institute and the Ronald McDonald House opened, adding both research space and a home away from home for families with children being cared for at Riley Hospital. In partnership with the city of Indianapolis, IUPUI added a sports complex that included a natatorium, an attached physical education building, and a track and field stadium. To improve access to Wishard Hospital and the campus, Lockefield Gardens was partially razed and new apartments were added for university students and residents.

Under Irwin's leadership, IUPUI's visibility and prestige as an academic institution increased. Enrollment grew from fewer than 17,000 students to more than 23,000; full-time faculty increased from approximately 800 to more than 1,300; and the operating budget of the campus increased from $97 million to $409 million. Irwin's vision and effort helped IUPUI establish a reputation as a leader among urban universities, offering undergraduate and graduate degrees in sciences and liberal arts as well as business and technology. Irwin retired in 1986 with the title chancellor emeritus.

Indiana University recognized Irwin's distinguished contributions many times, with the 1972 School of Medicine Distinguished Alumni Award, the 1986 School of Dentistry Distinguished Service Award, an honorary doctorate in 1986, the Maynard K. Hine Medal in 1992, the Distinguished Alumni Service Award in 1995, and the President's Medal for Excellence in 2012. He also received three Sagamore of the Wabash citations and an honorary degree from Marian University.

In retirement, Irwin continued to serve the community as a member of the boards of the Eiteljorg Museum of Western Art and the American Indian, the YMCA of Greater Indianapolis, the American Fund for Dental Health, the Greater Indianapolis Progress Committee, the Indianapolis Center for Advanced Research, the Indianapolis Chamber of Commerce, the United Way, and the Riley Children's Foundation.

Irwin passed away August 23, 2012, preceded by his wife, Marianna Ashby, and survived by three children and seven grandchildren. ❧

JORGE V. JOSÉ
1949–

Vice President for Research, 2010–2015

Professor, scientist, and administrator Jorge José joined Indiana University as vice president for research in August 2010. A native of Mexico City, Jorge V. José received a BS (1971), MS (1973), and Doctor of Science (1976) degrees in physics from the National Autonomous University of Mexico (UNAM). He was trained as a theoretical condensed matter physicist, and his doctoral work was guided by the distinguished L. P. Kadanoff of the University of Chicago. He held research associate positions at UNAM (1972–1974) and Brown University (1974–1976) before his appointment as assistant research professor at Brown (1976–1977) and Rutgers University (1979–1980). He also held a postdoctoral appointment at the University of Chicago and was a visiting fellow at Kyoto University in Japan.

In 1980, José accepted a position at Northeastern University as assistant professor, beginning a twenty-five-year tenure that saw him promoted to associate professor in 1984, professor in 1988, and Matthews University Distinguished Professor in 1996, a position he held until 2005. At Northeastern, José was the director and founder of the Center for Interdisciplinary Research on Complex Systems (CIRCS) as well as the chair of the Department of Physics in 2003. In 2005, José became vice president for research at the State University of New York at Buffalo, and held academic appointments in physics, physiology, and biophysics there until 2010. At SUNY Buffalo, he is credited with increasing research expenditures by 30 percent, to over $330 million. Additionally, José has been a visiting professor at the Institut Laue–Langevin in Grenoble, France, and at Saclay in Paris, and he has spent sabbatical leaves at the Institute for Theoretical Physics at Utrecht University in the Netherlands as well as the Salk Institute for Biological Studies in La Jolla, California.

In 2010, José was appointed vice president for research at Indiana University and the James H. Rudy Professor of Physics, with additional appointments in integrative and cellular physiology and medicine. In his administrative role at IU, José coordinated and oversaw all areas related to research on IU's eight campuses. In the first three years of his tenure, he reorganized and consolidated research and compliance units including the office of research administration, the office of ethics education and policies, and the Indiana Clinical and Translational Sciences Institute. He initiated a $1 million annual Indiana University

Collaborative Research Grants program and rejuvenated the $1 million annual New Frontiers in the Arts and Humanities seed funding program. José was active on university committees including the KUALI/ COEUS grant submission and management program implementation, the IU Public Health Coordinating Council, and the New Academic Directions Committee, and served as a board member for IU Research and Technology Corporation.

After stepping down from the position of vice president for research in 2015, José returned to teaching and research. He continued to hold the position of James H. Rudy Professor of Physics and the position of adjunct professor of integrative and cellular physiology at the IU School of Medicine (IUSM). He has also been an active member of the Stark Neuroscience Institute at IUSM (2015–), a visiting professor in the Center for Interdisciplinary Research at Northeastern University in Boston (2015), a visiting scientist at the Salk Institute for Biological Sciences in La Jolla, California (2016–), and a Chinese Academy of Sciences President's International Fellow at the Institute of Theoretical Physics and at the Kavli Beijing 2016 Chinese Academy of Sciences Institute of Neuroscience (2016–). He is the author and co-author of more than 145 publications, has given over 200 talks in more than 22 countries, has supervised 11 PhD students and 13 postdoctoral fellows, and has received over $20 million in research funding.

José has been recognized with several honors and awards. He was named a fellow of the American Physical Society in 1997, a corresponding member of the Mexican Academy of Sciences in 1999, a fellow of the New York Academy of Sciences in 2006, a fellow of the American Association for the Advancement of Science in 2007, and was the inaugural James Frank Fellow at the James Frank Institute at the University of Chicago. He received the Manuel Sandoval-Vallarta award from the Universidad Metropolitana de Mexico in 2004, the Chercheur Etranger D'Haut Niveau et de Renommée Internationale from the French government from 2002 to 2007, and the Phi Beta Delta Medallion from Northeastern University in 1998. In 2016 he received the Chinese Academy of Sciences President's International Fellow Initiative Award.

José has served on a wide range of organizations, including as a NYSGrid Council Member (2007–2010), a board member of the Calspan-University at Buffalo Research Center (CUBRC) (2007–2010), vice chair of the committee for the Nicholas Metropolis Award for Outstanding Doctoral Thesis Work in Computational Physics of the American Physical Society (2007–2009), board member of the Great Lakes Consortium (2005–2010), senior research officer of the Association of American Universities (AAU) (2005–2013), board member of the New York Structural Biology Center (2005–2010), and a member of the External Advisory Board of the NSF–CREST Center for Mesoscopic Modeling and Simulation for the president of the City University of New York (2002–2007). He was also a member of the New England Board of Higher Education Minority Mentor Program for students who are underrepresented in science, technology, engineering, and mathematics, particularly African Americans, Hispanics, and Native Americans (2001–2005). He served as secretary-treasurer of the International Physics Group (now FORUM) in the American Physical Society (1990–1994). He has been a referee for the National Science Foundation, the Department of Energy, the National Institutes of Health, and the Department of Defense in the United States; Conicet (Argentina), Conycit (Chile), Conacyt (Mexico), and DyiCyt (Spain); as well as an advisor for Houghton Mifflin Publications for high school physics education. ᘓ

Jann L. Joseph

1962–

Chancellor (Interim), IU South Bend, 2018–

A SPECIALIST IN PLANT PATHOLOGY and a lifelong educator, Jann Joseph spent her career working to increase educational opportunities and student success in the West Indies, Michigan, and Indiana. Born in 1962 in Princes Town in Trinidad, West Indies, as the youngest of five siblings, Jann Luciana Joseph was raised by her mother, Sybil, a housewife, and her father, Fred Pantor, a tailor. Although neither parent completed elementary school, they valued and understood the power of education to transform lives for generations. With their encouragement and sacrifices, Jann not only attended the Princes Town Roman Catholic Elementary School and St. Stephens College secondary school, but graduated from the University of the West Indies at St. Augustine with a BS in agriculture (1984) and an MPhil in plant science (1989). She then graduated from the University of Wisconsin–Madison with a PhD in curriculum and instruction for science education (1998). Jann Joseph credits her mother, in particular, for insisting that she attend college, recalling that Sybil read a lot and wanted more for her children, especially for her two daughters; education and learning were everything in their family. Joseph remains forever grateful to her parents for doing the impossible and giving her an education, and this feeling inspired her to serve in higher education and pay it forward.

Jann Joseph's career in education began as a graduate student in St. Augustine when she was a teaching assistant for various biology courses at the University of the West Indies from 1985 to 1989. After graduation in 1989, she began teaching with the Ministry of Education for the Government of Trinidad and Tobago, where she also served as Agricultural Science Department chair from 1990 to 1992. During her PhD program at UW–Madison (1994–1998), she held various teaching and research positions and served as program coordinator of Wisconsin Fast Plants in the Department of Plant Pathology. Her first full-time faculty appointment came in 1998 at Grand Valley State University (GVSU) in Michigan, where she advanced through the ranks from assistant professor to professor in the Department of Biology—Science Education from 1998 to 2011. While at GVSU, Joseph served as associate dean in the College of Liberal Arts and Sciences from 2006 to 2011. She then took an appointment as dean of the College of Education (COE) at Eastern Michigan University (EMU) in Ypsilanti, Michigan, a post she held from 2011 to 2014. During her tenure at EMU, Joseph led the development and implementation of the COE's first strategic plan, and she created the Office of Urban, Community, and International Outreach (OUCIO) among other accomplishments.

Indiana University hired Joseph in 2014 as executive vice chancellor for academic affairs (Division of Student Engagement and Success) at IU South Bend, a position she held until 2018, when she became interim chancellor of IUSB. In her role as executive vice chancellor, Joseph was responsible for budget planning and developing a long-term sustainable economic model that secures the viability of campus operations. Among her many accomplishments, she reallocated resources to fund and fully support the campus Titan Success Center to offer "intrusive" advising and coaching for more than 40 percent of newly admitted students; increased IUSB's contribution to IU Online Class Connect (IUOCC) from 3 courses in fall 2014 to 37 in Spring 2018; developed a base-funded budget model to support key programs for minority, first generation, and low-income students including a summer leadership program; revitalized faculty shared governance and established faculty taskforces to address key campus initiatives including the Reimaging First Year (IUSB CARES) project, General Education Program revision, the Carnegie Engaged Campus initiative and Center for Research and Scholarship; increased funding for the University Center for Excellence in Teaching (UCET) to provide professional development for associate faculty (adjuncts) and increased funding for lecturers and tenure/tenure track professors. Joseph also engaged in proposal development, donor cultivation, and solicitation for major gifts including $5.8 million to name the Vera D. Dwyer College of Health Sciences and $1.6 million for a chair of palliative care. As interim chancellor, Joseph is working closely with the other regional campus chancellors to advance the goals of *Blueprint 2.0*, the bicentennial strategic plan for IU regional campus collaboration.

Beyond Indiana University, Joseph has served in several professional and civic organizations. Some of her professional service includes serving as campus leader of the Center for Regional Campus Excellence (CRCE), campus representative of the IU Academic Leadership Council (ALC), campus liaison for the Higher Learning Commission, chair of the Michigan Council of Deans of Colleges of Education, executive board member of the Michigan Association for Colleges of Teacher Education

(MACTE), member of the MI–ACE Women of Color Committee, member of the Council of Colleges of Arts and Sciences Committee on Associate/Assistant Deans, member of the Detroit Schools Higher Education Consortium, and chair of the Content Advisory Committee of the Michigan Test for Teacher Certification—Integrated Science, among many others. Her civic engagement has included serving as board member in the South Bend Regional Chamber of Commerce, board member of the St. Joseph County Historical Society, president of the South Bend Chapter of The Links Inc., member of the Ypsilanti 20 Club (town and gown group), volunteer with Dress for Success, and volunteer leader for the American Heart Association, among other organizations.

Jann and Edwin Joseph (PhD 2002) married March 5, 1982. Together they raised three children: Kwasi, Kendell, and Kheran. Edwin, a professor of sustainability at IU South Bend, passed away in July 2018 after a long battle with cancer, and he is remembered by Jann as a champion for women who empowered and supported her throughout a long and beautiful union. ॐ

EMERSON KAMPEN
1928–1995

Trustee, 1983–1989

BUSINESSMAN AND PHILANTHROPIST Emerson Kampen remained a Midwesterner with a hands-on work ethic his entire life, from running Great Lakes Chemical Corporation to serving as a trustee at IU.

Born in Kalamazoo, Michigan, on March 12, 1928, Emerson Kampen was the only one of his parents' nine children to earn a college degree (BS chemical engineering, University of Michigan, 1951). Fresh out of college, he took a job with a small oil and gas exploration company in central Michigan, then known as Great Lakes Oil and Chemical Company. Over the next forty years, Kampen would rise to be chairman, president, and chief executive officer of the company. Under his leadership and innovation, Great Lakes Chemical Corporation grew to become the world's leading manufacturer of bromide and brominated chemicals and furfural derivatives, used in applications such as flame retardants, oil and gas well completion fluids, water sanitizers, and other specialty applications. Employing just fourteen people in 1951, the company grew to more than 6,000 employees by the late 1980s, with sales of more than $250 million.

While at Great Lakes, Kampen wandered the deserted oil well ponds of south-central Arkansas in 1958, testing the fluid in search of just the right combination of minerals to produce bromide. The find proved to be a catalyst of the company's forty years of growth. As he rose through the ranks of the company, (chemical engineer 1951–1957; plant manager 1957–1962; vice president 1962–1967; senior vice president 1968; executive vice president 1969–1971; and president 1971–1994), Kampen aimed for perfection by following three simple rules of business success: work hard, look for opportunities in *every* situation, and accept nothing short of your objectives. One objective he sought and achieved during the 1960s was to relocate the company to a place that would provide access to academic resources and personnel that would help the company continue to grow. With this in mind, the company moved to West Lafayette, Indiana, and Kampen began a relationship with the Indiana higher education system that would last the rest of his life. The only period as an adult when he was not associated with Great Lakes was a seven-month stint in 1953 that he spent as a captain in the United States Air Force Research and Development Command.

During his years in Indiana, Kampen served on innumerable boards, including: Lafayette Life Insurance, Co.; Lafayette National Bank;

Purdue Research Foundation; Junior Achievement of Greater Lafayette, Inc.; Indiana Chamber of Commerce; Lafayette Symphony Foundation; and the Lafayette Art Association Foundation, Inc. He was a fellow of the American Institute of Chemists, a director of the American Industrial Health Council, and director of the National Association of Manufacturers. Kampen received the *Wall Street Transcript*'s bronze medal award in 1980 and 1986, and the publication's gold award three times (1983, 1984, and 1985). The 1984 award was presented for his "aggressive and determined leadership." Among his other awards were *Indiana Business Magazine*'s Industrialist of the Year (1991), the Chemists' Club Winthrop-Sears Medal (1993), and the Kavaler Award, which is awarded for outstanding performance by a chief executive officer in the chemical industry (1992).

Appointed a trustee of Indiana University in 1983 by Governor Robert D. Orr, who also awarded him a Sagamore of the Wabash, Kampen served until 1989. From 1990 until 1995, he served as a member of the board of directors of the Indiana University Foundation. Kampen was also a trustee at Ashland College in Ohio. As a longtime resident of West Lafayette, Kampen had a long relationship with Purdue University, serving on the dean's advisory council of the School of Management and of the Graduate School of Management. He was appointed a trustee of Purdue in 1990, serving until his death on June 8, 1995, in Lafayette, Indiana. Kampen was an avid supporter of Purdue athletics and a recreational golfer; a statue of him can be found overlooking the first tee at Purdue's Kampen Golf Course.

In 1951, the same year that he joined Great Lakes, Kampen married Barbara Frances Spitters; the couple had seven children. ᵕᕈᕈ

EDGAR F. KETTLER
1923–2011

Trustee, 1986–1989

USINESSMAN AND PHILANTHROPIST Edgar Kettler was a dedicated supporter of higher education in Indiana, following in the footsteps of his father.

Edgar F. Kettler was born in Fort Wayne, Indiana, on February 10, 1923, to Margery Pickard, a homemaker, and Alfred W. Kettler, the president and CEO of Indiana Construction Company. Alfred was a powerful role model to his son Edgar, especially because of his role in higher education: Alfred was one of the founders of Indiana University–Purdue University Fort Wayne (IPFW), served on the Purdue University Board of Trustees for eighteen years, received an honorary doctorate degree, and had the administration building at IPFW, Kettler Hall, named in his honor. Throughout his life, Edgar remained deeply inspired by his father's accomplishments, which reflected in his own dedication to higher education in Indiana.

Growing up in Fort Wayne, Edgar Kettler graduated from South Side High School and attended Carleton College in Minnesota from 1941 to 1942. He left college to join the Army Air Corps, where he served for three years with the 8th Air Force in England; he was honorably discharged as a first lieutenant and received recognition for combat flight duty. Kettler then returned to school, completing a BS in business from Indiana University in 1948. He was a member of Phi Gamma Delta, where he was president of his fraternity pledge class. He was also a member of Delta Sigma Pi honorary society.

From 1950 to 1995, Edgar Kettler was the president and CEO of the Fort Wayne Storage Company, an agent of Allied Van Lines, during which time he also served as the president of Indiana Household Movers and Warehousemen, Inc., and of the National Moving and Storage Association.

Kettler was appointed to the Board of Trustees in 1986 by Indiana Governor Robert Orr and served on the board for three years. Even before becoming trustee, Kettler devoted much of his time to giving back to the university. He was the president of the IU Allen County Alumni Association, a founder of the Varsity Club, and served two terms on the Executive Council of the Alumni Association. In addition, he was president of the National IU Alumni Association, co-chairman of the national fundraising campaign for the class of 1948, cabinet member for the Campaign for Indiana, president of the Indiana-Purdue Fort Wayne

Foundation, a member of the IPFW Community Advisory Council, and a member of IU Football's 12th Man Club.

Throughout his life, Kettler maintained an active interest in local, state, and national public service organizations. He served on the Governor's Personal Advisory Committee and the State Student Assistance Commission of Indiana. His civic involvement included Mad Anthony's (charter member), the Kiwanis Club of Downtown Fort Wayne (38-year member), the Friars Club (president), the Fort Wayne Fine Arts Foundation (board member), the Fort Wayne Civic Theater (president), the Allen County Memorial Coliseum (member and chairman of the board of trustees), the Good Roads Committee, and the Veterans of Foreign Wars. He was also an Elder at First Presbyterian Church and a superintendent of First Presbyterian Sunday School. Kettler served over thirty years on the Allen County Republican Central Committee (treasurer). He attended several Republican National Conventions as an elected delegate and alternate, and many Indiana Republican Conventions as an elected delegate.

Kettler was recognized for his many contributions to the State of Indiana and to the communities he served. He received a Sagamore of the Wabash, was commissioned as a Kentucky Colonel, and was honored with several alumni awards, including the South Side High School Distinguished Alumni Award, the IU Allen County Club Distinguished Alumni Award, the Ralph E. Broyles Medal from the IU Alumni Association (1987), and the Indiana University Distinguished Alumni Service Award (2002)—the highest honor bestowed upon IU alumni.

Edgar Kettler met his future wife, Mary Burgman (BS 1947), on the IU Bloomington campus, where she was affiliated with Alpha Chi Omega. Together they had three children: Linnea Brunk, Carol (BS 1972, MS 1974), and Gregory (attended IU, affiliated with Phi Gamma Delta). At the time of Edgar's passing on June 3, 2011, he and Mary had five grandchildren and two great-grandchildren. Granddaughter Andrea received a BS from IU in 1999 and was affiliated with Kappa Kappa Gamma. ᐅ

ARTHUR D. KING
1986–

Trustee, 2007–2009

An INVESTMENT BANKER AND A FORMER STUDENT LEADER at IU Bloomington, A. D. King was the seventeenth student to serve on the IU Board of Trustees.

Born April 30, 1986, in Columbus, Indiana, to Peter (BA 1976) and Catherine King, Arthur Daniel "A. D." King graduated from Columbus North High School in 2005, where he was student body president and quarterback of the football team. He inherited his passion for Indiana University and IU athletics from his parents and grandparents, who started bringing him to IU football games when he was in a stroller. A. D. and his sister Sarah King (BA 2005) followed in their footsteps by enrolling at Indiana University, while their younger sister Mary Claire chose Syracuse University.

At IU, King majored in finance in the Kelley School of Business and minored in classical studies, earning a BS with distinction in 2009. He was a member of the Hutton Honors College, the Mitte Honors Business Program, and the Investment Banking Workshop. In conjunction with his studies, King traveled to India with the Kelley School of Business to visit businesses in the manufacturing and service industries. He also completed a three-month internship with Spraylat Corporation in Shanghai, China. His list of student activities included the Phi Gamma Delta Fraternity (rush chairman), the fraternity's Little 500 bike team (three-year rider), and the Board of Aeons (three-year member). For his involvement and leadership, King received the Elvis J. Stahr Senior Recognition Award in 2009.

A. D. King was appointed as the seventeenth student trustee by Governor Mitch Daniels in July 2007 and served until 2009. While on the board, he served on the Academic Affairs, Facilities, and Finance and Audit Committees.

Upon graduation, A. D. King joined the Investment Banking Division of Bank of America Merrill Lynch (2009–2018) and in 2018 became vice president at Crescent Capital Group LP.

Although he resides in New York City, he visits Bloomington as often as he can and still enjoys spending time with friends and fraternity brothers, keeping up with world events and politics, and watching college football and basketball. ⌒𝔰𝔳

LESTER C. LAMON
1942–

Chancellor (Interim), IU South Bend,
1995–1997

PROFESSOR OF HISTORY AND ADMINISTRATOR at Indiana University South Bend Lester C. Lamon served the university in multiple capacities for thirty-five years, from 1971 until his retirement in 2006.

Born October 12, 1942, in Maryville, Tennessee, Lester Crawford Lamon grew up on a small farm in rural East Tennessee. He was the oldest of three children born to Howard F. and Ruth Crawford Lamon, both natives of Maryville, Tennessee, and graduates of Maryville College. Lester Lamon matriculated to Vanderbilt University and earned a BA in 1964 followed by an MAT in 1965. In 1965, he was hired as a history teacher and assistant basketball coach at Oak Ridge High School in Oak Ridge, Tennessee. This school system was the first public system integrated in the South, the result of a January 1955 directive by the Atomic Energy Commission due to the construction and presence of large atomic energy research facilities in the town. Lamon then earned a PhD in history from the University of North Carolina (UNC) in 1971.

After graduating from UNC, Lamon began his academic career as a professor of history at Indiana University South Bend (1971–2006), during which time he held several key administrative positions. Lamon has been the dean for the Division of Arts and Sciences (1981–1989), the vice chancellor for academic affairs (1989–1995, 1997–1998), the interim chancellor (1995–1997), and the director of the Civil Rights Heritage Center (2000–2006). In addition, he has spearheaded several unique and opportunistic projects for students and community members alike. In 2000, he organized a Freedom Summer Tour Course in which students and community members retraced the routes of the Civil Rights Movement, met with Movement veterans, and studied the success and impact of the Movement. From 1978 to 1979 Lamon was the Leverhulme Visiting Fellow at the New University of Ulster in Coleraine, Northern Ireland. He later was visiting professor at the University of Ulster in 2006. Lamon retired from IU at the end of 2006 with the title professor emeritus of history.

Lester Lamon devoted much of his professional life to studying civil rights history and related issues. He is a widely-known scholar in the area of African American history and has worked as a consultant to related organizations throughout the United States. He is the author of three books and has published countless articles and reviews in and outside of the United States. He has presented his work in four countries and has worked as a referee and manuscript reader for ten different academic presses and professional journals. Lamon was instrumental in the development of the Oral History Project, a collaborative effort of the Civil Rights Heritage Center and the Northern Indiana Center for History. Additionally, he has given expert witness testimony in high-profile cases for the NAACP and the ACLU.

For his scholarship, Lamon has received numerous grants, fellowships, and awards from the National Endowment for the Humanities, the American Philosophical Society, the American Council of Learned Societies, Indiana University, and the University of Ulster. He received the AMOCO Distinguished Teaching Award from Indiana University in 1981, an award given once a year to a single recipient chosen among all current Indiana University faculty. He was also the recipient of the Black History Award at IUSB in 2002, and the IUSB Student Government Outstanding Service to the Students Award in 1996. In 2002, he received the IUSB Student Government Vision Award. Outside of Indiana University, he has received the prestigious Sagamore of the Wabash award (1997), the Martin Luther King Jr. Community Service Award (2001), the Merle Blue Humanitarian Award (2001), the Northern Indiana Center for History Black History Award (2002), the Community Service Visionary Award of the Urban League of St. Joseph County (2002), the Eldon Lundquist Award (2003), and in 2004 was inducted into the South Bend Community Hall of Fame. In 2006, he was the recipient of an honorary associate of science degree from Ivy Tech State College.

Lamon has volunteered his time with local and statewide organizations, including the Indiana Humanities Council, the Scholarship Foundation of St. Joseph County, the Michiana Arts and Sciences Council, the Northern Indiana Center for History, the Northern Indiana Historical Society Foundation, and Project Future.

Lester Lamon and his wife, Elizabeth, have two children: Ward and Katherine. ❧

DEBORAH A. LEMON
1954–

Secretary of the Board, 2014–

Deborah A. Lemon

Alumna and civic leader Debbie Lemon has been part of IU's administration for over fourteen years.

Born in January 1954 in Bloomington, Indiana, to LaDonna Newton and Forest G. Lemon, who co-owned a small retail business, Deborah A. "Debbie" Lemon grew up in Bloomington, where she assisted in managing the family business while in high school. Her family has ties to both the city and the university, with cousin Tom Lemon having been a mayor of Bloomington in the 1950s and her grandfather having painted the interior of IU Auditorium when it was built. Her father was a first-generation IU student, in whose footsteps she followed by also enrolling at IU Bloomington, earning a BS in marketing management and small business entrepreneurship from the IU Kelley School of Business (1976). While an undergraduate, she was a sister in the Delta Delta Delta sorority, participated in the first dance marathon (pre-IUDM), and was on the Mini-Trike Committee of the IU Student Foundation (IUSF) and a rider in the Mini 500. She was also elected to Beta Gamma Sigma honor society.

Lemon supported herself in college by working at Burkhart Floor Covering (1970–1976). After graduation, she took a job at American Hospital Supply Corporation (1976–1983), where she was the top regional sales representative in 1981. She then worked at the Bloomington/Monroe County Convention and Visitors Bureau (1987–1991). In 2004 Lemon joined Indiana University as director of Hoosiers for Higher Education (2004–2010). She then served as deputy executive director of the IU Alumni Association (2010–2013). In 2013 she was appointed secretary of the Indiana University Board of Trustees. She has also been a member of the Arbutus Society since 2016.

A member of various community and civic organizations, Debbie Lemon has served as a leader in many of them. Some of these have included the Bloomington Parks Foundation (1990–; president, 2017–), IUSF Board of Associates (1986–), Hoosiers Outrun Cancer (steering committee, 2000–2013), Bloomington Hospital Foundation (2000–2011; president, 2009–2011), and Bloomington Hospital Board (1992–2000; president 1998–2000). She has also served in the following organizations: American Red Cross of Monroe County (president), Girls Incorporated of Monroe County, Local Council of Women, Colloquium for Women of Indiana University (co-chair), Salvation Army Kettle

Kick-Off (chair), Bloomington Country Club (president of the board). Debbie Lemon's work has been recognized with several awards. These have included the Women Excel Bloomington (WEB) Award, presented by the Bloomington Chamber of Commerce (2017); the Agape Award, presented by the Local Council of Women (2001); the Distinguished Leadership Award, presented by Leadership Bloomington-Monroe County (1988); Exceptional Management Services Volunteer Award, presented by the American Red Cross (1992); and being named Outstanding Board Member by the Bloomington Volunteer Network (1995).

From 1983 to 2005 Lemon was married to William Sibbitt Jr. ᑲᑋᒷ

CLARENCE W. LONG
1917–2009

Trustee, 1975–1984

THE DAY HE ENTERED COLLEGE was the beginning of Clarence W. Long's relationship with Indiana University, which continued for more than fifty years and included three consecutive terms as a trustee.

Clarence W. Long was born on April 17, 1917, in Hartford City, Indiana, to Alice Weschke and Adam Long. He earned his BS in business from Indiana University in 1939. As a student, he engaged in a broad range of activities including the Beta Alpha Psi accounting and business information fraternity, Alpha Kappa Psi business fraternity, Delta Chi fraternity (where he served as social chairman), and the IU football team (as its senior manager).

A certified public accountant, Clarence Long worked for the accounting firm of Ernst & Whinney (renamed Ernst and Young) from 1939 until 1978. He became a partner in the prestigious firm in 1954 and led the Indianapolis office until his retirement. Long's career in Indianapolis oversaw the firm's rapid expansion into the largest international accounting firm practicing in Indiana. His operating philosophy was one of work, perseverance, high-quality effort, and active community involvement. He enthusiastically volunteered his time for youth, education, the arts, and the business community.

Clarence Long was appointed to the Indiana University Board of Trustees for three consecutive terms from 1975 to 1984, serving four years as vice president of the board. He was highly involved in IU's fiscal operations, and he also chaired the trustee committee that was instrumental in improving communication and rapport between the administration and the faculty. He was a leader in the university's extensive building and renovation programs during the 1980s, insisting on the highest standards of architectural design, aesthetics, and construction. In addition to his service as a trustee, Long served on the Kelley School of Business Dean's Advisory Council, the IU Art Museum (now Eskenazi Museum of Art) Board of Directors, and the IUPUI Board of Advisors.

In recognition of his dedicated service to IU and his professional distinction, Long was inducted into the Kelley School of Business Academy of Alumni Fellows in 1975, received the Distinguished Alumni Service Award from Indiana University in 1990, the Z. G. Clevenger Award in 1991, and was a member of the football team's honorary 12th Man Club.

Long's public service work included organizing the Junior Achievement Program of Indianapolis in 1957 and serving on its board of directors from 1957 to 1967. He served on the boards of the United Way of Indianapolis (1966–1978) and the Indiana Division of Natural Resources (1980). He served more than twenty years for the Indianapolis Museum of Art (beginning in 1964) and was a renowned art lover and collector. He was also affiliated with the Downtown Indianapolis Indiana State Chamber of Commerce, Jenn Foundation, Indiana Legal Foundation, Community Service National Institutes of Health, United Way of America, United Fund of Greater Indianapolis, Indianapolis Hospital Development Association, American Institute of CPAs, Indiana Association of CPAs, National Association of Accountants, Woodstock Club, Columbia Club, and the Royal Poinciana Golf Club of Naples, Florida.

Clarence Long was married for sixty-nine years to his wife, Mildred. He was a proud father, grandfather, and great-grandfather. The Longs traveled widely after their respective retirements, and Clarence loved to fish, hunt, and golf. They divided their time between their home in Indianapolis, their farm in Brown County, and their beach house in Naples, Florida. Together, they endowed the Clarence W. and Mildred Long Art Purchase Fund at Indiana University. After Clarence suffered a debilitating stroke in 2006, the Long family established and funded the Clarence and Mildred Long Lectureship in Stroke at the Indiana University School of Medicine. After a long and distinguished career as an accountant and public servant, Clarence William Long passed away on July 4, 2009, at the age of 92. ᐊᔑᑊ

WILLIAM J. LOWE
1950–

Chancellor, IU Northwest, 2010–

PROFESSOR OF HISTORY and university administrator William J. "Bill" Lowe has built a forty-year career in higher education at institutions across the Northeast and Midwest.

Born in 1950 in Brooklyn, New York, to Julia and John P. Lowe Sr., an office worker and police officer, respectively, William Lowe was the oldest of seven siblings. He found inspiration in his parents as well as his maternal uncle, who was a behavioral neuroscientist working for the U.S. Army, NASA, and the Johns Hopkins University School of Medicine (among his achievements: training monkeys for space flight). His father, who was a chief in the New York City Police Department, attended the City University of New York part time, at the same time that Lowe was an undergraduate. His father completed a BA and an MA, providing Lowe with inspiration and insight into the experience of adult learners in the college setting. Lowe received his BA in history from Michigan State University and a PhD in modern history from Trinity College in Dublin, Ireland, as a Fulbright Scholar.

Lowe began his career in higher education as an assistant director of admissions at Lake Erie College (1976–1977) before becoming assistant professor of history (1977–1979) and assistant director for alternative and continuing education (1977–1979). Lowe then went to the State University of New York College at Cortland to work as director of continuing and graduate education (1979–1984), after which he moved to Chicago State University to work as dean of graduate studies and professor of history (1984–1991). He then served as dean for the College of Liberal Arts and professor of history at the University of Detroit Mercy (1991–1997) and as vice president for academic affairs and professor of history at the College of Saint Rose (1997–2003). Next, Lowe moved to Metropolitan State University (St. Paul, Minnesota), where he held the positions of professor of history, provost and vice president of academic affairs (2003–2010), and interim president (2007–2008).

In 2010, William Lowe became professor of history and chancellor of Indiana University Northwest. As chancellor, Lowe is in charge of academic leadership and planning on the campus and is highly engaged in the Northwest Indiana community. Some of the highlights of his leadership so far include: the continuing Campus Conversation on Diversity, Equity, and Inclusion to promote an inclusive environment for the different people and cultures who learn, work, and collaborate on IU's most diverse campus; a commitment to the steady expansion of online learning programming; three comprehensive planning exercises (2011, 2015, 2016–2017; reviewed annually) resulting in the adaptable *IU Northwest Strategic Priorities and Objectives, 2015–2020*, which are aligned with Indiana University Bicentennial planning; and construction of a new 126,000-square-foot, $45 million academic partnership building that serves the educational needs of both IU Northwest and Ivy Tech–Northwest students, which opened in 2017. Lowe is a life member of the IU Alumni Association and has worked on the search and screen committees for the chancellorships at IU South Bend and IU Kokomo.

William Lowe has been professionally affiliated with the American Association of State Colleges and Universities (AASCU), the Higher Learning Commission of the North Central Association, the Middle States Association Commission of Higher Education, Wayne State University, the National Endowment for the Humanities, the Association of American Colleges and Universities, the Chicago Academic Alliance, and the American Association for Higher Education.

Lowe has volunteered for numerous community and professional organizations, including the Urban League of Northwest Indiana, South Shore Arts, the Methodist Hospital Foundation, the YWCA of Northwest Indiana, the Northwest Indiana Quality of Life Council, the Minnesota Sinfonia, the Friends of the Ramsey County Workforce Investment Board of Washington County (Minnesota), WMHT-FM radio station (New York), RISE (Radio Information Service for the Print Disabled), the American Conference for Irish Studies, Michigan State University Arts and Letters Alumni Association, and School District No. 97 in Oak Park, Illinois. He served as co-chair of the board of directors for One Region: Improving the Quality of Life of Northwest Indiana (2012–2014). He is on the managing board of the Northwest Indiana Forum and represents Indiana on the executive board of the Alliance for Regional Development (Illinois, Indiana, Wisconsin).

Lowe received a Phi Delta Kappa Educator of the Year Award and is the namesake of William J. Lowe Day in Saint Paul, Minnesota. He was also the recipient of a 2013 Urban League of Northwest Indiana Diversity and Inclusion Community Relations Award.

He is married to Pamela Lowe. Together they have two children, Siobhan and Sean. ᐟᔓᕽ

DONALD S. LUKES
1975–

University Treasurer, 2015–

A N ACCOUNTANT AND CIVIC LEADER, Donald Lukes began strengthening IU's finances in 2014.

Donald S. Lukes was born in 1975 in Trenton, New Jersey, to Vivian and George Lukes. His father, George, was a metallurgist and steel industry executive. His grandfather, George Lukes Sr., was a meteorologist involved in forecasting weather for the U.S. invasion of Normandy (D-Day) during the Second World War, and also served in the Eisenhower and Kennedy Administrations. Donald S. Lukes grew up in New Jersey and Indiana, graduating from Valparaiso High School in Indiana, in 1993. He attended IU Bloomington's Kelley School of Business, earning a BS in accounting (1997), followed later by an MBA in finance and strategic management (2003). While a student at IU, Lukes was active in the Student Alumni Association, served as a volunteer income tax advisor, and was a member of Beta Alpha Psi.

Beginning his career in accounting and finance, Lukes worked as an auditor at PricewaterhouseCoopers, LLP (1997-2001), before taking a position as manager of financial planning and analysis at Praxair Surface Technologies (2003–2004). Lukes then spent ten years (2004–2014) at Citizens Energy Group in a variety of positions: manager, financial analysis (2004–2007); manager, business development (2007–2011); and director, treasury (2011–2014). While at Citizens, he led financing for the acquisition of City of Indianapolis Water and Wastewater assets in 2011, which at the time was one of the largest municipal utility acquisitions in U.S. history. Lukes also led financing for Citizens' acquisition of Westfield, Indiana's water and wastewater assets, in 2014.

In 2014, Lukes joined Indiana University as associate vice president and associate treasurer (2014–2015) before succeeding MaryFrances McCourt as university treasurer in 2015. In these roles, Lukes helped complete the first Green Bond issuance for Indiana University (2014). This was the first such issuance in the Big Ten, and only the second for any public university in the country. Under Lukes' guidance, IU achieved the AAA bond rating from Standard & Poors in February 2016. IU is one of only seven public universities with two such bond ratings (having received its first Aaa rating from Moody's in 2010). Since joining IU, Lukes has also been an active member of various university committees and organizations, including: treasurer of the Indiana University Building Corporation (2014–), the Operating Funds Investment

Committee (2014–), the Financial Systems Steering Committee (2015–), the Enterprise Risk Management Advisory Committee (2015–), the Information Security and Privacy Council (2015–), the Compliance Advisory Committee (2016–), Old Crescent Insurance Company's board of directors (2014), and the For All Bicentennial Campaign Steering Committee (2016–).

Beyond IU, Donald Lukes has been involved in various civic activities. Some of these include serving as president and treasurer of the King Park Area Development Corporation (2010–2014); volunteering with the Indiana Sports Corporation, for which he served on the local organizing committees for Big Ten basketball (2004–2016) and Super Bowl XLVI (2011–2012); and serving as a board member of the Bloomington Hospital Foundation (2016–). He was recognized by the Indiana Sports Corporation as Volunteer of the Year (2009–2010). He has also been recognized as a Certified Public Accountant (CPA) and member of the American Institute of Public Accountant and Indiana CPA Society, having achieved his CPA License in 2000. He has also been a Chartered Global Management Accountant since 2011.

Donald Lukes married his wife, Nicole, in 1999, and they have two children: Steven and Nathan. Nicole is a leukemia survivor. She was diagnosed during her sophomore year at IU. She missed one semester while undergoing chemotherapy and graduated from the Kelley School of Business in four and a half years, in December 1996. Since then she has raised money participating in dozens of events for the Leukemia and Lymphoma Society's (LLS) Team in Training. She has completed many marathons, bike rides, and triathlons, raising over $50,000. In addition, Nicole and Don completed a 100-mile bike ride in Lake Tahoe in 2009, raising over $10,000 for LLS. ᏬᏝ

P. A. MACK JR.
1930–

Trustee, 1992–1998

A BANKER AND PHILANTHROPIST, P. A. Mack Jr. has supported Indiana's higher education statewide, including as an IU trustee, as chairman for the Indiana Commission for Higher Education, and as founder of IU's Mack Center for Inquiry in Teaching and Learning.

P. A. Mack Jr. was born September 8, 1930, in Chicago, Illinois, to Elizabeth Crabb Mack, a homemaker, and Pierpont Askren Mack Sr., an engineer and manager. P. A. Mack Jr. was inspired by his maternal grandmother, Edna Crabb, and by many excellent teachers throughout his education. After the family moved to Missouri, he attended Bristol Elementary School and Webster Groves High School. For college, he attended Purdue University, earning a BS in agriculture (1952), followed by Indiana University, where he earned an MBA in management (1955). At Purdue, Mack was the baseball manager and was active in the P-Man's Club and Alpha Tau Omega Fraternity.

Professionally, Mack held key executive positions for banks across the Midwest, beginning with the Harris Trust & Savings Bank (1958–1968) and the Continental Illinois Bank (1968–1971). He was the executive director of the Bayh for President Campaign Committee, and then the chief of staff to United States Senator Birch Bayh from 1971 to 1979. Mack then became vice chairman of the National Credit Union Administration Board (1979–1987) followed by president of the AARP Federal Credit Union (1987–1990). He has also worked as a consultant for the AARP and served as chairman for the Indiana Commission for Higher Education. He is the owner and manager of Mack Farms in Illinois. During his professional career, Mack completed specialized banking courses at Washington University, the American Institute of Banking, Iowa State University, the University of Wisconsin, and the Program for Senior Managers in Government at Harvard University. He also taught management courses at DePaul University and the American Institute of Banking.

P. A. Mack Jr. has supported IU quite extensively over the years. He was appointed by Indiana Governor Evan Bayh to two terms on the Indiana University Board of Trustees (1992–1998). While serving on the Board of Trustees, Mack was vice chairman of the Presidential Search Committee, chairman of the Joint Committee on Learning, and a member of the Supervisory Committee. In addition, he served as chairman of the board of directors of the IU Credit Union, a member of the Hoosiers for Higher Education Steering Committee, a board member of Clarian Health Partners (now IU Health), the first chairman of the national board of visitors for the Center on Philanthropy (now the Lilly Family School of Philanthropy), a member of the Kelley School of Business Dean's Council, and a member of the IU Foundation Board of Directors. He also served as a member of the board of advisors at IUPUI, IU Southeast, and IU South Bend. In 2003, Mack endowed the formation of the Mack Center for Inquiry in Teaching and Learning at Indiana University, in conjunction with the Faculty Colloquium on Excellence in Teaching (FACET; now Faculty Academy on Excellence in Teaching). In 2007, he established a fellowship to assist students pursuing doctoral degrees at the Center on Philanthropy. In 2017, he endowed the Jon Vickers Film Scoring Award, to be awarded annually through a film scoring competition to a student from the Jacobs School of Music.

Mack's contributions to the university and to the state have been recognized with many awards and honors. In 1999, FACET initiated the P. A. Mack Award for Distinguished Service to Teaching and named Mack as its first recipient. In 2008, he was named an honorary member of the Alliance of Distinguished and Titled Professors, and he also received the Henry R. Besch Jr. Promotion of Excellence Award. To have been recognized with three awards given by the IU faculty speaks to Mack's devotion to excellence in teaching. In recognition of his lifetime of service to the university, in 2002 he was awarded an honorary Doctor of Humane Letters from Indiana University. He was twice named a Sagamore of the Wabash (1993 and 2004). In recognition of his support of scholarships for non-revenue sports coaches, he received the Spirit of Philanthropy Award from the Center on Philanthropy (2008) followed by the Partners in Philanthropy Keystone Award (2010).

Mack married Marian von Lackum (1932–2001) on December 27, 1958, and they had three children: Emily, Kathryn (McDonald), and Jonathan. When he is not cheering on the Hoosiers in every sport he can attend, he enjoys opera, cycling, art, music, theatre, travel, photography, and reading. ⌘

EDWIN C. MARSHALL
1946–

Vice President for Diversity, Equity,
and Multicultural Affairs, 2007–2013

PROFESSOR AND ADMINISTRATOR Edwin Marshall's relationship with Indiana University has spanned over fifty years, from his time as an undergraduate to his continued involvement in the School of Optometry. Originally from Albany, Georgia, Edwin Cochran Marshall grew up in Newark, New Jersey, the son of a schoolteacher and a bus driver. He came to Indiana University to study zoology, earning a BA in 1968. He continued his studies at IU, earning a BS in optometry (1970) en route to a Doctor of Optometry degree (1971). After working for a few years, he earned an MS in visual science and physiological optics (1979) from IU, followed by an MPH in health policy and administration (1982) from the School of Public Health at the University of North Carolina, Chapel Hill. He is a lifetime member of the Kappa Alpha Psi fraternity.

Marshall has held many academic appointments at Indiana University. He began in the School of Optometry in 1971 as a clinical associate, during which time Marshall founded and acted as director of the IU School of Optometry's first off-campus clinic, a facility designed to meet the vision and eye care needs of the community's underserved population. Marshall rose steadily in rank from lecturer (1971–1973) and assistant professor (1973–1977) to associate professor with tenure (1977–1992) and professor of optometry (1992–2013). He also held appointments in the Program in Vision Science within the Indiana University Graduate School (1983–2013). He was adjunct professor of public health at the IU School of Medicine in Indianapolis (1998–2013) and for the IU Richard M. Fairbanks School of Public Health in Indianapolis (2012–2013). He has been an honorary faculty member at Cebu Doctor's College in Cebu City, Philippines, and an external examiner at the Universiti Kebangsaan Malaysia in Kuala Lumpur.

Marshall's administrative appointments at Indiana University include chair of the Department of Clinical Sciences (1983–1992), associate dean for academic affairs (1992–2003), and associate dean for academic affairs and student administration (2003–2007) for the School of Optometry. Indiana University President Michael McRobbie appointed Marshall vice president for diversity, equity, and multicultural affairs in 2007. His responsibilities included diversity efforts on all IU campuses and specific oversight for the diversity and equity programs and initiatives at IU Bloomington. In addition, Vice President Marshall oversaw the development of IU's two independent schools of public health from concept through their accreditation applications. Marshall retired in 2013 with the titles of professor emeritus of optometry and of public health, IU Bloomington and IUPUI.

Marshall has served professionally for a variety of other organizations over the years. These have included the National Optometric Association (executive director 1981–1989 and 1993–2009), the World Council of Optometry (2006–2008), the Joint Committee of Danish Optometrists and the Department of Optometry at the Frederiksberg Tekniske Skole in Copenhagen (1984), the International Federation of Asian and Pacific Associations of Optometrists (1982), the Inter American University of Puerto Rico (1982, 1996–1997), the International Optometric Association and Optical League in London (1980–1996), and the Indian Optometric Association in New Delhi (1975–1976). Even in retirement, Marshall has served on numerous boards, ranging from the Kentucky College of Optometry Advisory Board (2015–) to the Public Health and Prevention Editorial Advisory Board of Medscape, WebMD LLC (2010–).

Marshall has had an extensive record of civic engagement, volunteering his time with countless federal, state, and community-based organizations. He has been a member of the National Advisory Council on Health Professions Education, vice chair of the Indiana Public Health Institute, chair of the Executive Board of the American Public Health Association, chair of *The Nation's Health* Editorial Advisory Committee, chair of the National Commission on Vision and Health, president of the National Optometric Association, and co-chair of the Indiana Interagency State Council on Black and Minority Health, in addition to working with numerous other public service institutes. He was the founding chair of the Minority Health Advisory Committee of the Indiana State Department of Health and has served for over twenty years as an optometric representative on the National Institutes of Health's National High Blood Pressure Education Program Coordinating Committee. He also has served on the National Institutes of Health's National Eye Health Education Program Planning Committee and as chair of its Health Disparities Task Force. In 2017, Marshall served on an expert panel for the Vision Health Initiative Strategic Plan of the Centers for Disease Control and Prevention.

Marshall has been the recipient of numerous local, statewide, and national honors, fellowships, and awards. He is a member of the

Delta Omega National Public Health Honor Society, a Distinguished Practitioner in the National Academies of Practice, a former U.S. Public Health Service Primary Care Policy Fellow and has been awarded the Tony and Mary Hulman Health Achievement Award in Public Health and Preventative Medicine from the Indiana Public Health Foundation. In addition, he has received the State Health Commissioner Award of Excellence in Public Health, the Distinguished Service Award from the Vision Care Section of the American Public Health Association, the Distinguished Hoosier Award from the Office of the Governor, the Indiana Optometrist of the Year Award from the Indiana Optometric Association, the National Optometrist of the Year Award from the American Optometric Association, and the Person of Vision Award from Prevent Blindness Indiana. In 2009, he was inducted into the National Optometry Hall of Fame. Marshall's latest awards include: Distinguished Leadership Award, African Studies Program, Indiana University (2011); President's Medal for Excellence, Indiana University (2013); Founding Dean's Medallion, School of Public Health-Bloomington, Indiana University (2015). In 2013, Marshall was nominated as a White House Champion of Change for Public Health and Prevention.

He has twin daughters, Erin and Erika. ᑤ

MaryFrances Moriarty McCourt

1961–

Senior Vice President and Chief Financial Officer,
2013–2016

University Treasurer, 2005–2015

S KILLED FINANCIAL MANAGER MaryFrances McCourt guided IU safely through a turbulent economic period in U.S. history.

Born June 1, 1961, in Boston, Massachusetts, MaryFrances Moriarty McCourt attended school in New Jersey and Ohio. Her mother worked as a realtor and her father as a senior executive in chemical sales. She credits her parents and grandparents with teaching her the value of hard work. She attended college at Duke University, graduating not only on the Dean's List and magna cum laude with a BA in economics, but also with the experience of a summer studying abroad in Oxford, England, made available through a competitive scholarship program.

MaryFrances left North Carolina newly married to Michael Patrick McCourt and began working for Hester & Fleming in Ohio. After a year of learning financial justification in energy management, she accepted an offer with Brady and Company to work in personal financial planning before moving to Dexter Water Management Systems, Inc. Her strong work ethic enabled her to advance in rank from budget analyst, to financial analyst, to senior financial analyst. McCourt was then hired at Agilysys, Inc., a multibillion-dollar distributor and premier reseller of enterprise computer technology solutions. There she held various positions in strategic planning, financial analysis, and treasury management with particular focus on operational efficiency, business planning (including acquisitions, divestitures, and new business modeling), as well as customer, vendor, and product line profitability analyses and balance sheet management. Settling in Cleveland, Ohio, with two children, she began a fourteen-year career that established her leadership in financial management. During her tenure at Agilysys, she served as director of planning, director of treasury, and eventually assistant treasurer. McCourt led a budget system design team that developed and implemented a corporate-wide financial system in less than two months. In 1999, she returned to school to pursue an MBA at Case Western Reserve University.

In 2005, McCourt was appointed university treasurer at IU, her first position in higher education. As treasurer, her responsibilities included investing over $1.8 billion in university assets and managing over $950 million in debt. She established a goal of delivering increased financial resources for the university within appropriate risk parameters. She developed new policies and guidelines to strengthen the capital finance framework at IU and structured a new Consolidated Revenue Indenture to modernize the operating framework within which IU issues debt. Her work at Indiana University was characterized by streamlined business processes, enabling technology, increased governance, and the delivery of financial analysis and forecasting tools. Of particular note was her work in managing Indiana University through the 2008 financial crisis and the recalibration of its bond rating to Aaa by Moody's Investor Services, making IU one of only eight Aaa-rated public universities in the United States. Her collaboration with Vice President and Chief Financial Officer Neil Theobald created IU's MoneySmarts Program, a student financial literacy initiative that won several national awards and recognition by the Department of Education and the Secretary of the Treasury. This program led to a $70 million (17 percent) decrease in student loans over its first four years.

When Theobald left IU in December 2012, McCourt was given the additional role of interim chief financial officer (CFO), becoming vice president and CFO (2013–2014) and then senior vice president and CFO (2014–2016). In this position, she played an integral role in achieving the lowest tuition increase—1.75 percent—in thirty years through diligent modeling and budgeting. In 2015, she stepped down as university treasurer, handing that role to Donald S. Lukes. In 2016, she resigned as CFO to become vice president of finance and treasurer at the University of Pennsylvania.

Recent civic activities include serving on the Penn Club of New York board (2016–), the Penn Praxis board (2016–), the NACUBO Research Council (2013–), the Community Foundation of Bloomington and Monroe County (2008–2016; chair 2011 and 2012; executive and finance committees 2008–2016), and the school commission of the St. Charles Church and School (executive and finance committees 2009–2014).

Recent honors include receiving the Indiana University President's Medal (2016), the Bloomington Women Excel Award (2015), and the *Indianapolis Business Journal* CFO of the Year Award (2014).

McCourt has developed a personal mission statement that summarizes the way she approaches life and explains her professional success: *To Learn, To Teach; To Add Value, To Be Valued; To Drive Change, To Accept Change; To Show Respect, To Be Respected.*

ROBERT H. MCKINNEY
1925–

Trustee, 1989–1998

A SUCCESSFUL LAWYER, business executive, and public servant, Robert H. McKinney not only served as a trustee long after graduating from Indiana University School of Law–Bloomington (now the IU Maurer School of Law) but also left a legacy to support future legal scholars.

Robert McKinney was born in Indianapolis in 1925, the son of E. Kirk and Irene H. McKinney. During the Great Depression, E. Kirk McKinney was manager of the Indianapolis office of the Reconstruction Finance Corporation, which helped struggling homeowners avoid foreclosure. Through his father's example, Robert McKinney was exposed at an early age to the importance of supporting people in need of assistance. McKinney graduated from Shortridge High School in 1942 and from the United States Naval Academy at Annapolis in 1946. He served in the Navy for three years in the Pacific Theater following his graduation from Annapolis and for two years in the Pacific during the Korean War. In 1952, McKinney earned a JD from the Indiana University School of Law in Bloomington.

McKinney joined the Indianapolis firm McHale, Cook, Welch & McKinney in 1953. Ten years later, he was one of the founders of the firm now known as Bose McKinney & Evans LLP, where he was a partner until his retirement in 1992. He has also played a leadership role in several businesses, including founding and serving as chairman and CEO of three companies: First Indiana Corporation from 1961 to 2005; Jefferson Corporation, the holding company for Jefferson National Life Insurance Company, from 1961 to 1986; and The Somerset Group, Inc., a diversified business holding company, until its merger with First Indiana in 2000. First Indiana Corporation was the holding company for First Indiana Bank (now BMO Harris Bank), the largest publicly owned bank in Indianapolis.

McKinney left the private sector in 1977 to serve in the administration of President Jimmy Carter as chairman of several regulatory agencies governing the housing finance industry, including serving as chairman of the Federal Home Loan Bank Board, the Federal Savings and Loan Insurance Corporation, the Federal Home Loan Mortgage Corporation, and the Board of the Federal National Mortgage Association (Fannie Mae). While in Washington, he pushed the banking industry toward community investment and implemented regulations that reduced interest rate risk in the housing finance sector. McKinney returned to his legal and business interests in Indianapolis in 1979.

A civic leader for many years, McKinney was a co-founder of LYNX Capital Corp., Greater Indianapolis Progress Committee, and the Minority Task Force of Indianapolis. He has served on the board of directors of the Indianapolis Neighborhood Housing Partnership, the Indiana and Indianapolis Chamber of Commerce, Marian University, the Capital Improvement Board, the United States Naval Academy Foundation, and the Indiana Symphony Society. A passionate environmentalist, he also served on the board of the Sierra Club Foundation. He was appointed by United States Senator Evan Bayh to the Naval and Merchant Marine Academy Selection Committee. McKinney's involvement in national politics dates back to 1960, when he chaired the Indiana Kennedy for President Committee; he also served as the chairman for the Indiana campaigns of presidential candidates Robert F. Kennedy, Edmund Muskie, Jimmy Carter, and Walter Mondale.

McKinney has served IU and supported its mission in many ways. In 1989, he was appointed to the IU Board of Trustees and served until 1998, including as president of the board (1993–1994). He also served as chairman of the board of advisors of Indiana University–Purdue University Indianapolis and as a director of Indiana University Health (formerly Clarian Health Partners) and Community Hospital. He also serves on the board of directors of the IU Foundation (1992–). In 2011, McKinney made a $24 million gift to the IU School of Law at Indianapolis, which was renamed the IU Robert H. McKinney School of Law in his honor. The largest gift in the school's history, it provides funding for five endowed chairs to attract and retain nationally recognized scholar-teachers to the faculty. The gift also created a $17.5 million endowment to fund McKinney Family Scholarships for outstanding students. At the naming announcement, McKinney linked his gift to the importance his parents placed on education and giving back to the community through public service.

McKinney received several recognition awards for his service to the State of Indiana and his community. He is the recipient of honorary doctorates of law from Marian University (1976) and Butler University (1981) and an honorary Doctor of Humane Letters from Indiana University (2018). He is the 1994 recipient of the Junior Achievement Central

Indiana Business Hall of Fame Award, a 1995 recipient of the Hoosier Heritage Award, a 1999 recipient of the Indiana University Academy of Law Fellows Award, and the 2000 recipient of the Indianapolis Archdiocese Spirit of Service Award. He is also a Master Knight of the Sovereign Military Order of Malta.

In 1951 McKinney married Arlene A. (Skip) Allsopp, and they spent fifty-nine years together until her passing in 2010. McKinney counts his marriage to Skip and his family of five children and five grandchildren among his proudest accomplishments. ᘔ

MICHAEL A. MCROBBIE
1950–

President, 2007–

Provost and Vice President for Academic Affairs,
Bloomington, (Interim), 2006–2007

Vice President for Research, 2003–2007

Vice President for Information Technology and CIO,
1997–2007

Michael A. McRobbie

Michael A. McRobbie

SERVICE IN THREE VICE PRESIDENTIAL PORTFOLIOS over ten years and an academic background that straddled the sciences and the humanities prepared Michael McRobbie well for the IU presidency.

Michael McRobbie was born October 10, 1950, in Melbourne, Victoria, Australia, to parents Joyce and Alexander McRobbie, who was an immigrant to Australia from Scotland. McRobbie cites his mother, a physiotherapist, as a formative influence while he was growing up and credits her and his maternal grandmother, Grace Gair, for instilling in him "a love of all the great arts of civilization." He also admired his maternal grandfather, Richard Leslie Gair, a businessman and philanthropist who served in the Australian Army in the First World War, fighting in the Hundred Days Offensive that ended the war. His paternal grandfather served in the British Army in the same war.

His mother worked hard to raise him and his siblings in what was then the small beachside resort of Surfers Paradise in the area of Queensland known as the Gold Coast (now a major city). McRobbie attended Surfers Paradise State School and Miami State High School. He received a BA with first class honors in philosophy from the University of Queensland in 1974 and a PhD in mathematical logic from the Institute of Advanced Study at the Australian National University (ANU) in 1979.

McRobbie held postdoctoral appointments at Latrobe University (1979–1981) and the University of Melbourne (1981–1983) in Victoria, where his research interests turned to artificial intelligence and computer science. He returned to ANU in 1983 and held a variety of academic and senior administrative positions there, serving as a professor of information science from 1990 to 1996. At ANU he founded and led research centers in various areas including artificial intelligence, information science and high-performance computing, and communications. He worked extensively internationally, especially in Japan, where he coordinated a large-scale collaboration between ANU and the major computer company Fujitsu. He also co-founded the Asia Pacific Advanced Network (APAN) which involved the development of high-performance Internet connectivity in and between countries in the Asia Pacific.

McRobbie joined IU in 1997 as the university's first vice president for information technology and chief information officer (VPIT and CIO) with responsibility for IT on all IU campuses. In this role he carried out a

254

comprehensive reorganization of IT and led the development of IU's first IT strategic plan. He conceived and led major initiatives in the modernization and systemization of IU's IT infrastructure in a way that would be financially sustainable; and in supercomputing (the acquisition of supercomputer systems including Big Red 1, 2, and 200); massive data storage; replacement of IU's administrative systems; and state, national, and international high performance research and education networks (I-Light and its successors, Internet2, TransPAC) as well as the Global Network Operations Center. He expanded IU's capabilities in cybersecurity and established the Center for Applied Cybersecurity Research and the Research and Education Networking Information Sharing and Analysis Center (REN-ISAC), which is the only ISAC nationally in higher education. In 1999 and 2000, McRobbie worked with then-President Myles Brand to establish the IU School of Informatics (now the School of Informatics, Computing, and Engineering at IUB, and the School of Informatics and Computing at IUPUI). In 1999 he was principal investigator on a $30 million grant from the Lilly Endowment to establish IU's Pervasive Technology Laboratories.

In 2003 he was appointed vice president for research (VPR) in addition to his roles as VPIT and CIO. As VPR, his focus was on increasing IU's externally funded research, improving research administration, expanding and modernizing research infrastructure, rationalizing IU's centers and institutes, and addressing IU's severe research space shortage. Notable achievements were securing a $53 million grant in 2004 from the Lilly Endowment to establish the Metabolomics and Cytomics Initiative (METACyt) to expand life sciences research at IUB, and establishing the New Frontiers in the Arts and Humanities Program, initially also funded by the Lilly Endowment, which invests $1 million annually in the arts and humanities.

In 2006, he became interim provost and vice president of academic affairs for IU Bloomington in addition to his other roles. In this position, he focused on renewing and defending liberal arts education at IUB, developing recruitment strategies and increasing financial aid to improve the quality and diversity of the student body, and developing a strategic approach to IU's international engagement.

In March 2007, McRobbie became the eighteenth president of Indiana University. His presidency has seen major academic restructuring and expansion with the creation of ten new schools including the Richard M. Fairbanks School of Public Health, the Lilly Family School of Philanthropy, and the School of Health and Human Sciences at IUPUI and the School of Public Health, the Hamilton Lugar School of Global and International Studies, the Media School, and the School of Art, Architecture, and Design at IUB; the establishment of IU Online; the introduction of degrees and programs in engineering and architecture; and the start of efforts to revitalize IU's extensive collections. He oversaw a major building program in excess of $2.5 billion based on master plans developed for all campuses, resulting in construction or renovation of over 100 major facilities. During his presidency, IU has reinvigorated its global engagement, with twice as many students studying abroad, alumni chapters in more than fifty countries, and the establishment of Global Gateway Offices in Bangkok, Beijing, Berlin, Mexico City, and New Delhi. He also oversaw completion of the $1.1 billion IUB Matching the Promise campaign (in 2010), the $1.4 billion IUPUI Impact campaign (in 2013), and the launch of the $3 billion Bicentennial campaign, IU's first university-wide campaign and its largest. Most of these initiatives are components of the IU Bicentennial Strategic Plan approved by the Trustees in 2014, whose development McRobbie oversaw.

McRobbie is a member of numerous outside committees and organizations including serving as 2019–2020 chair of the Association of American Universities, vice chair of the board of directors of Indiana University Health, and member and previous chair of the board of the Big Ten athletics conference. He served as co-chair of the National Academies Committee on the Future of Voting, chair of the Board of Trustees of Internet2, and member of the National Security Higher Education Advisory Board.

McRobbie holds faculty appointments in computer science, philosophy, cognitive science, informatics, and computer technology, and has been an active researcher in artificial intelligence, information technology, and logic. He was principal investigator on many major grants, published a number of books and articles, and served on numerous editorial boards and conference committees.

McRobbie was named a Sagamore of the Wabash twice, by Indiana Governor Mitch Daniels in 2007 and by Governor Eric Holcomb in 2017. In 2010, he was made an Officer of the Order of Australia, Australia's national honors system. He received honorary doctorates from the University of Queensland (2007), Sung Kyun Kwan University in Korea (2008), Australian National University (2010), South East European University in Macedonia (2011), and Griffith University in Australia (2014). The Australian National University named him Alumnus of the Year in 2015, and he is an honorary fellow of the Australian Academy of Humanities and a fellow of the American Academy of Arts and Sciences. He has received the Bicentenary Medal of the University of Warsaw in Poland and the Prince Naradhip Bongsprabandha Plaque for service to international education from the National Institute for Development Administration in Thailand. In 2016 he was appointed to the Council on Foreign Relations, received the International Center's International Citizen of the Year award for his contributions to the globalization of Indiana, and received the Anti-Defamation League's Man of Achievement Award.

Michael McRobbie is married to Laurie Burns McRobbie (MA in philanthropic studies, IU Lilly Family School of Philanthropy, 2016). Laurie worked as a technology executive in higher education, at the University of Michigan, and with the national next-generation internet university consortium, Internet2. She is an adjunct faculty member in IU's School of Informatics, Computing, and Engineering, where she helped found the ServeIT service-learning clinic and helped establish the Center of Excellence for Women in Technology. She is also adjunct faculty in the Lilly Family School of Philanthropy and founded the Women's Philanthropy Leadership Council at the IU Foundation. Laurie serves on the boards of the Community Foundation of Bloomington and Monroe Country, the Riley Hospital for Children Endowment, and the Indiana Conference for Women, and was appointed by Governor Eric Holcomb to the Indiana Arts Commission in 2017. She has received the Woman of the Year award of the City of Bloomington's Commission on the Status of Women and the Woman of Character award from the Girl Scouts of Central Indiana. Michael and Laurie were both widowed in 2003 and were married in 2005. They have six children—three each by their first marriages: Carol, Josephine, Charlie, Lucien, Margaret, and Arabella.

McRobbie became a United States citizen in 2010 and now holds dual American and Australian citizenship. ᕙ

PEGGY GORDON ELLIOTT MILLER
1937–

Chancellor, IU Northwest, 1984–1992
Acting Chancellor, IU Northwest, 1983–1984

OLLOWING IN THE FOOTSTEPS of pioneering women in her family—
one grandmother rode with the Frontier Nursing Service and her
other grandmother helped establish a church—Peggy Miller became the
first woman chancellor of not only IU Northwest, but of any of Indiana
University's campuses.

Born May 27, 1937, and raised in western Kentucky by Mary Ann
Renfro and Herbert Hunt Gordon, a nurse and contractor, respectively,
Peggy Miller took on leadership roles at school and within her church
from a young age. She attended Longfellow School and Mayfield High
School, both public schools in Mayfield, Kentucky, before enrolling at
Transylvania University, receiving a BA in English (1959). She earned an
MS in English and secondary education from Northwestern University
(1964) and then in 1975 earned an EdD in secondary education, reading,
and Afro American literature from Indiana University.

Miller was an active college student, serving as a member and officer of Chi Omega sorority, as a member and officer of student government, as well as president of the International Relations Club and of
the Student Christian Association. She was also director for the Campus
Affairs Commission and chairperson for campus events including
Parent's Day, Campus Carnival, and Brotherhood Week. She was named
Outstanding Freshman, Outstanding Junior, and Outstanding Graduate
in Field. She was a Lampus Academic Honorary, a Crimson Beauty, and
a University Mountain Laurel Representative.

Miller has had a long and distinguished career in both education and
university administration. She joined the faculty of Indiana University
Northwest in 1965, teaching in the fields of English and education.
From 1981 to 1983, she was the executive assistant to the chancellor at
IU Northwest, and acting chancellor the following year. She served as
IUN's chancellor from 1984 to 1992, the first woman to lead any campus of Indiana University. She worked to increase enrollment; secured
funding for academic programs, student support, and facilities (from
both public and private sources); increased sponsored research; refocused campus efforts toward diversity; initiated international engagement for the campus; established university economic development
activity in the region; and completed long-term comprehensive academic and physical planning. She was responsible for establishing the
Valedictorian Scholarship Program and the World Affairs Program, and

for securing a United States Army ROTC affiliation for the campus. She created the Urban Teacher Education Program, securing financial support from the Lilly Endowment. Additionally, she was the host of *Your Indiana University*, a television program aimed at keeping students and community members informed on university matters, which aired more than 175 episodes. Miller resigned as chancellor in 1992, whereupon the Board of Trustees appointed IUN Vice Chancellor for Academic Affairs Lloyd A. Rowe as acting chancellor (August 1992–April 1993).

After Miller left IUN, she held a variety of leadership positions in higher education. In 1992 she became president of the University of Akron, a position she held until 1996. At Akron, she was also the Harrington Distinguished Chair in Education and the Charles G. Herbrick Chair in Leadership. She is credited with enhancing the honors college, increasing endowed chairs and scholarships, and creating a faculty senate. During her tenure at Akron, she was invited by the American Council on Education to write their first book about the importance of urban and metropolitan universities. Published in 1994, her *Urban Campus: Educating a New Majority for a New Century* introduced scholars and practitioners to this important and growing sector of American higher education. Next, she served as acting vice president for academic and international programs for the American Association of State Colleges and Universities from 1996 to 1997, and from 1998 to 2006, she served as the president of South Dakota State University. At SDSU, Miller created an honors college and a comprehensive scholarship program called the Jack Rabbit Guarantee Program, founded the privately funded Innovation Campus (the first research park in the state), and transitioned the athletics program from NCAA Division II to Division I. In 2010, Miller began an interim position as dean of the Graduate School at Texas Tech University (TTU). Under Miller's leadership, the TTU Graduate School earned National Research Institute Fund eligibility. She then served as vice provost for extended and distance education until 2014, and then served as director and special assistant to the provost for Remnant Trust (2014–). She also established the Peggy Gordon Miller Graduate Fellowship.

In addition to her institutional responsibilities, Peggy Miller has been active in professional and civic organizations. In 1991 she was selected as the first national chairman of the Coalition of Urban and

Metropolitan Universities. In addition, she has been a member of the National Competitiveness Council, the Value Added Finance Authority of South Dakota, *New York Times* Women in Education Advisory Board, and has served on the board of directors for Gary National Bank, Bank One Akron, and First National Bank of Brookings, South Dakota. She also served on the boards of directors for the Lubrizol Corporation, A. Schulman Corporation, National Invention Center, Indiana Vocational and Technical Education Commission, Boys and Girls Club of Northwest Indiana, Methodist Hospital of Northwest Indiana, Symphony Groups in Northwest Indiana and Ohio, Ohio Supercomputer Center, the Ohio Aerospace Institute, and the American Council on Education. She has been a general chairman for the United Way and for the NAACP and was a higher education representative to the United States Army War College National Civilian Seminar.

For her accomplishments and service, Miller has been recognized with many honors and awards. She has received the Distinguished Alumna Award from Northwestern University, Distinguished Alumni Service Award from Indiana University, the Distinguished Service Award from South Dakota State University, the Thomas Hart Benton Mural Medallion from Indiana University President Tom Ehrlich, the ORT Award for Woman of the Year, the NAACP Golden Heritage Award, the Sagamore of the Wabash, and an Indiana Governor's Citation for Leadership. She was the first Athena Award recipient from the Gary, Indiana, Chamber of Commerce, and was named an Honorary Alumna by the University of Akron. In 2005, she was given the Freedom Award from both the State of South Dakota and the National EDGAR Association for the leadership taken at South Dakota State University during the mobilization of the National Guard and the Army Reserve in the Iraq War. She is also the recipient of three honorary degrees: a Doctor of Humane Letters from Transylvania University, a Doctor of Public Service from South Dakota State University, and a Doctor of Philosophy from Chungnam National University in Korea.

In 1961, Peggy Gordon married Scott Vandling Elliott Jr. and they have two children: Scott Vandling Elliott III, a graduate of Wabash College, and Anne Gordon Elliott (BGS 1993; d. 2014). In 2001, she married Robert Lawrence Miller (d. 2010), retired chairman of Centron Corporation and an alumnus of South Dakota State University. ॐ

STEVEN A. MILLER
1948–

University Treasurer, 1991–2004

A NATIVE HOOSIER, Steven Miller began a relationship with IU as an undergraduate and later continued as treasurer of Indiana University, in between which he had a successful career in finance.

Steven Alan Miller was born at Methodist Hospital in Indianapolis to Robert Jack and Ruth Elizabeth (Gasaway) Miller, a postal worker and nurse, respectively. He was schooled in Perry Township before graduating from Southport High School. He attended Indiana University, receiving a BS in business in 1970 and an MBA in 1974. He was a member of the Theta Chi Fraternity and the Army ROTC. Miller served as a United States Army artillery officer, adding to a rich tradition of service within his family: his father was an aviator in World War II, and his great-great-grandfather, Benjamin Mabrey, served with the 82nd Indiana Volunteers in the Civil War, fighting in battles such as Chickamauga, Missionary Ridge, and the Siege of Atlanta.

Before joining the staff of Indiana University, Steven Miller was assistant vice president at Aetna Capital Management, Inc., an investment advisory subsidiary of Aetna Life & Casualty, and he held various treasury management and investment positions at The Upjohn Company and the National Bank of Detroit. In addition, Miller was on the City of Kalamazoo Pension Committee from 1981 to 1983.

Steven Miller was elected treasurer of Indiana University by the Board of Trustees in 1991, a position that he held until 2004. As treasurer, Miller is credited with forging strong relations with the trustees, providing crucial advice and counsel on key investments and important bonding issues, and enhancing the university's investment management and debt financing strategies. He was responsible for over $1 billion worth of bond issuance to refinance debt and build new facilities, started the first commercial paper (short-term unsecured promissory note) program to finance current operations, and secured Attorney General Opinion streamlining management of operating funds. In addition to serving as treasurer of the university, Miller served on the Investment Committee for the Indiana University Foundation and on the Committee for Investments for Clarian Health Partners, Inc. (now IU Health), and was chairman of the investment committee for the board of trustees of the Indiana Public Employees Retirement Fund, a position he was appointed to by the governor. He was also an original member of the advisory board of the Indiana Future Fund I, a venture capital fund focused on developing the life sciences industry in Indiana. Despite retirement, he continues to serve on the investment subcommittee of IU Health.

After leaving Indiana University, Miller worked as senior vice president and practice leader of Northern Trust Asset Management in Chicago (2005–2015). Before retiring, he led Northern Trust's Manager of Managers practice for U.S. institutional investors who chose to outsource their investment programs.

He is a two-time recipient of the Thomas Hart Benton Mural Medallion (1994, 2004) and also received the IU Foundation President's Medallion (2004) and the Sagamore of the Wabash presented by Indiana Governor Joseph E. Kernan (2004). He has done volunteer work for the VA Hospital in Murfreesboro, Tennessee, as well as the Nashville chapter of the American Red Cross.

He married Blanca Narcio Miller on April 15, 1978. They have three children, all of whom are IU alumni: Andrew (BS 2002), Alicea (BS 2005), and Evan (BFA 2008). ᑫ

MICHAEL J. MIRRO
1949–

Trustee, 2014–

As a physician, clinical professor, and researcher, Michael J. Mirro, MD, has maintained an association with Indiana University that spans his days as a graduate student at the School of Medicine to his time as a trustee.

Michael Joseph Mirro was born February 16, 1949, in Gary, Indiana, to Cecilia Dolores and John Anthony Mirro, a clinical nurse and a physician, respectively. His grandparents both independently emigrated from Southern Italy in late 1890, meeting in Chicago and marrying. His father, the oldest of eight, was the only child to attend college, graduating from the University of Illinois School of Medicine (1938). He practiced medicine in rural Lowell, Indiana, where he was the sole primary care physician, and he later served as Lake County health commissioner. Michael Mirro was the middle of five siblings, all raised in Lowell. Being raised in a family of practicing medical professionals greatly influenced his future, starting at age three when he developed acute epiglottitis— his mother (an RN) rushed him to the closest emergency room (thirty-five miles away), where he underwent an emergency tracheotomy. At age seven, he witnessed his father attempting to resuscitate a neighbor who suffered a fatal cardiac arrest. Mirro attended Catholic schools through ninth grade and finished high school at Andrean High School in Merrillville, Indiana, in 1967. He matriculated at Loyola University in Chicago, Illinois (pre-med, 1967–1970), and then earned an MD from Indiana University School of Medicine in 1974. While an undergraduate student, Mirro was a member of the Loyola University track team (1967–1968), the golf team (1969–1970), and president of Alpha Delta Gamma Fraternity (1969). His postgraduate education was completed at Indiana University Medical Center from 1974 to 1979.

Professionally, Mirro's work has been primarily that of a research scientist (basic and clinical) and that of a physician (clinical cardiac electrophysiologist). He has held several academic appointments, beginning at University of Iowa Hospitals and Clinics as instructor of medicine (1979–1980) and then assistant professor of medicine (1980–1982). He then returned to Indiana University School of Medicine, where he served as clinical assistant professor of medicine (1982–1992), clinical associate professor of medicine (1992–1997), and then clinical professor of medicine (1998–). From 1981 to 2014 he practiced cardiology in private practice at Fort Wayne Cardiology. During these years he also conducted clinical research in Fort Wayne at Parkview Hospital Randallia, Parkview Regional Medical Center, and the Parkview Research Center, as well as the Wabash County Hospital in Wabash, Indiana. His clinical work has focused on cardiac implantable electronic devices (CIED) and clinical investigation into new and advanced technology to enhance CIED function. Since 2014 he has served as senior vice president and chief academic-research officer of Parkview Health System.

In addition to his clinical work, Mirro has been a leader on a national level in the field of cardiology and as an advocate for reimbursement of cardiac technologies, having served as a member of the board of trustees of the American College of Cardiology (ACC) from 2003 to 2009 and having served as the co-chair of the ACC Advocacy Committee from 2002 to 2004. He has also served on the Health Policy Committee and the Quality Improvement Sub-Committee of the Heart Rhythm Society. Furthermore, Mirro testified before the U.S. Senate Health, Education, Labor, and Pension Committee on Health Information Technology and Interoperability of Data in 2016.

Beyond his professional activities, Mirro has been involved in many civic organizations. These have ranged from serving on committees and as chairman of the board of trustees for the Fort Wayne Medical Society (1990–2003) to serving on the advisory board of Big Brothers/Big Sisters (1990–1995) to being a member of the YMCA's Medical Advisory Committee (1991–1995) and Metro Board of Trustees (1993–1995). He has also served on the Northeast Indiana Regional Corporate Council (1998–2003) and the Northeast Indiana Innovation Center (chairman, 1999–2002; board member and Executive Committee member, 2016–).

Mirro has served IU in a variety of roles over the past two decades. In 2014, he was appointed to the Indiana University Board of Trustees by Indiana Governor Mike Pence and reappointed by Governor Eric Holcomb in 2017. He has served on the Indiana University School of Informatics Dean's Advisory Council (1999–), helping to establish the first school. Previous service to IU includes being a member of the Indiana University Hospitals Board (1994–1995), the IU School of Medicine Fort Wayne Community Advisory Board (Chairman 1993–), and the IU Research Technology Center Presidents Cabinet (1999–2002).

Among the honors and awards that Michael Mirro has received are the National Institutes of Health (NIH) Individual Fellowship Award

(1978–1979), Sagamore of the Wabash (awarded by Indiana Governor Frank O'Bannon in 1999), Doctor of Science honorary degree (Indiana University, 2003), Order of William Harvey (ACC, 2003), and the Distinguished Hoosier Award (2005).

In 1971, Michael Mirro married Jeanne Ellen Behnke of Hobart, Indiana, an educator, community volunteer, and philanthropist. Together they have three children: Emily, Katherine, and Megan. ❧

ANDREW F. MOHR
1961–

Trustee, 2014–2017

E NTREPRENEUR, PHILANTHROPIST, AND IU ALUMNUS Andy Mohr has been a supporter of Indianapolis-area schools and of Indiana University, serving one term as trustee.

Andrew Mohr was born in Brownsburg, Indiana, in 1961 and grew up in Indianapolis and Brownsburg. His father was an industrial pattern maker and his mother was a homemaker. Mohr graduated from Cardinal Ritter High School and went on to earn a BS in public affairs from the School of Public and Environmental Affairs at IU Bloomington (1983). To pay for his undergraduate education, Mohr held various jobs, the most significant of which was at a small Ford dealership in Brownsburg during the summer between his junior and senior years.

After graduation, Mohr worked for a brief time in industrial sales in Cincinnati, Ohio, before returning to central Indiana to work in a series of sales and finance jobs at local automotive dealerships, where he rose from a salesman to a finance manager to a sales manager. In 1991 he was hired as the general manager of a struggling Chevy/Buick dealership in Greencastle, Indiana, which he returned to profitability and subsequently purchased in 1993. That year he founded Andy Mohr Automotive Group, which has become one of the largest automobile and truck dealership groups in Indiana. As of 2017, he was the company's chief executive officer. In 2015, he was named the Indiana TIME Dealer of the Year.

In 2012, IU Athletics announced it was officially naming its new softball facility Andy Mohr Field in honor of a major gift from Mohr, who has been a longtime supporter of the IU Varsity Club and of intercollegiate athletics at the university. He is a member of the 1820 Society and of the President's Circle at the IU Foundation. Mohr has also been active in professional, civic, and philanthropic organizations. He is a member of the United Way of Central Indiana's board of directors, and he chaired the capital campaign for the United Way of Central Indiana's 2013–2014 community campaign. In 2014, Mohr was appointed by Governor Mike Pence to the Indiana University Board of Trustees for a single term.

Andrew Mohr resides in Indianapolis with his wife, Lorna, a fellow IU graduate (BS in public affairs, SPEA, 1983), and their two children: Andrew (BS 2017) and Samuel. ᴄᴤᴅ

JAMES THOMAS MORRIS
1943–

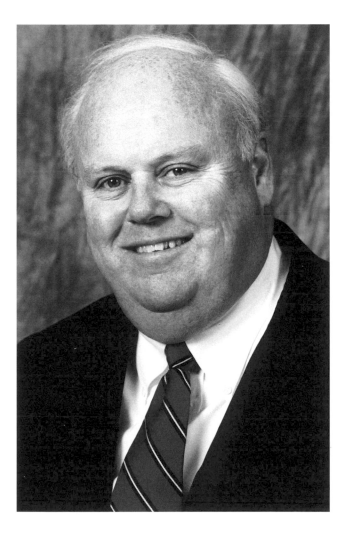

Trustee, 1996–2002; 2013–

A BUSINESS AND CIVIC LEADER AS WELL AS PHILANTHROPIST, James T. Morris has been a transformational figure in the histories of Indiana University, the City of Indianapolis, and the State of Indiana. Born in Terre Haute to a small business owner father and university administrator mother, James Morris grew up an active member of the Boy Scouts, eventually attaining the rank of Eagle Scout. He graduated from Indiana University in 1965 with a BA in government followed by an MBA from Butler University.

Morris worked as former Indianapolis Mayor Richard G. Lugar's chief of staff from 1967 to 1973. In this role, Morris helped implement Lugar's "UNIGOV" plan, which consolidated city and county governments to more efficiently serve the citizens of Indianapolis. Morris's efforts also helped transform Indianapolis from being a fairly nondescript "rust belt" state capital to being widely recognized as the "Amateur Sports Capital of the World." Numerous infrastructure upgrades, capital improvements, and public/private partnerships occurred as a result of his leadership in the Mayor's Office. After leaving the Mayor's Office, Morris continued to fuel Indianapolis's renaissance while working at the Lilly Endowment from 1973 to 1989, beginning as its director of community development, and advancing to vice president, executive vice president, and then president from 1984 to 1989. Morris administered the endowment's multimillion-dollar grantmaking program. Those grants revitalized Indianapolis's downtown through public-private partnerships and provided capital funding for numerous community venues. Morris then served as chairman and chief executive officer for IWC Resources Corporation and Indianapolis Water Company from 1989 to 2002. In this role, he developed strategic growth initiatives through acquisitions and mergers. Morris next led the United Nations World Food Programme (WFP) as its tenth executive director (2002–2007). In that capacity, he visited over eighty countries, spoke to most of the parliaments and congresses in the world, and spearheaded efforts to alleviate famine and suffering among the world's hungry poor. His efforts fed victims of tsunamis and earthquakes, as well as the needy, in politically tumultuous areas such as Darfur, Iraq, North Korea, and Niger. Beginning in 2008, Morris became president of Pacers Sports & Entertainment, helping to lead the resurgence of the once-struggling basketball franchise, before becoming the organization's vice chairman.

James Morris has long been a supporter of Indiana University. He was elected to the IU Board of Trustees and served from 1996 to 2002, serving as chairman of the board in 2001. In 2013, Morris returned to the board when he was appointed by Governor Mike Pence, and reappointed in 2016, when he again became chairman (2016–2017). He has also served as a director of the IU Foundation.

Morris has contributed to the local, state, and world community as a philanthropist and humanitarian. Some of the organizations he has been part of include the United States Olympic Committee (as treasurer and chairman of the Audit and Ethics Committee), the NCAA Foundation (chairman), the United Way of Central Indiana, the American Red Cross (member of the Board of Governors), the Boy Scouts (National Advisory Board), chair of the board for Riley Children's Foundation, and treasurer of the U.S. Gymnastics Federation.

Over the years, Morris has earned numerous awards for his service. From Indiana University, some of these include the College of Arts and Sciences Distinguished Alumni Award (2005), the Kelley School of Business Academy of Alumni Fellows (inducted 2001), the Distinguished Alumni Service Award (1991), the IUPUI Spirit of Philanthropy Award (1995; 2003), and the Herman B Wells Visionary Award (2011). He also received the Michael A. Carroll Award for Outstanding Community Service from the *Indianapolis Business Journal* (1993), Charles L. Whistler Award from the Greater Indianapolis Progress Committee (1993), Indiana Black Expo's Spirit of Freedom Award (2005), multiple Sagamore of the Wabash Awards from Indiana governors, the Mitch Daniels Leadership Award (2015), the George M. Steinbrenner III Sport Leadership Award for his commitment and contributions to the Olympic and Paralympic movements (2016), and the Presidential Lifetime Achievement Award (2016), recognizing Morris's tireless devotion to volunteering and community service. He has also received sixteen honorary degrees in recognition of his service and distinction.

Married to his wife, Jacqueline Harrell Morris (BS 1965), for over fifty years, Jim Morris is the father of three children, all of whom are IU graduates, and the grandfather of eight.

Thomas A. Morrison
1963–

Vice President for Capital Planning
and Facilities, 2009–

VICE PRESIDENT Tom Morrison's footprints in Indiana higher education crisscross the state, reflecting his effective work as a university liaison to government agencies and legislature, securing funding for and overseeing the completion of major facilities projects at both Ball State University and Indiana University.

Born in 1963, Tom Morrison earned a BA from the University of Denver, an MA from the University of Maryland, and a PhD in higher education administration from Ball State University.

Early in his career, Morrison was assistant director for intramural-recreational sports and facilities manager for intercollegiate athletics at the University of Virginia. He then moved to Ball State University, where he worked for seventeen years, most notably in the position of associate vice president for business affairs and as the interim chief financial and administrative officer (2007–2008). In addition to representing Ball State in several legislative sessions, Morrison held responsibility for facilities management and strategic planning, development of capital budgets, government relations, auxiliary services, and human resources. He was involved in projects that included the Art and Journalism Building, the Music Instruction Building, the Letterman Communication Media Building, the boiler and chiller plant renovation, and the central campus renovation project. He also was instrumental in procuring several federally funded projects, including the McKinley/Riverside Avenue reconstruction project.

In 2008, Tom Morrison came to Indiana University as the associate vice president for public affairs and state relations, serving as a liaison to state and federal agencies for capital-related items. In July 2009, Morrison was appointed by President McRobbie to the position of vice president for capital planning and facilities. In this position, Morrison serves as IU's chief capital, facilities, planning, and real estate officer overseeing all facility-related operations, acquisitions, and capital projects, as well as continuing to serve as a liaison to state and federal agencies for all capital-related items. Morrison has overseen the planning and construction of numerous new major capital and renovation projects on every IU campus—projects that total in excess of $1 billion dollars of capital construction and renovation. A few of the highlights include: IUB Cyberinfrastructure Building, IUB Cinema and Theater, IUB Global and International Studies Building, IUB Simon Skjodt Assembly Hall,

IU School of Medicine Walther Hall, IUPUI Science and Engineering Laboratory Building, IU School of Medicine Neurosciences Research Building, IU Natatorium, IUE Student Activities and Events Center, IUK Main Building, IUN Arts and Sciences Building, IUSB Harper Hall, and IUSB Education and Arts Building, among others.

Morrison has served Indiana University and the community on a variety of committees and organization boards, including the President's Cabinet, the IU Naming Committee (co-chair, 2009–), the IU Building Corporation Board of Directors (2009–), and the Enterprise Risk Management Committee (2012–). Broader civic engagement includes serving on the board of directors for the Community Foundation of Bloomington and Monroe County (CFBMC) and for the Bloomington Hospital Foundation, as well as on the IU Health Bloomington board and the Indiana Sports Corp board of directors. Morrison has also represented Indiana University regionally, nationally, and internationally as a member of the Big Ten Business Officers (2009–), the Education Advisory Board (2015–), the Society for College and University Planning (2009–), and the Green Campus Study—Higher Education and Corporate Industry (Switzerland, 2012).

Morrison has been recognized for his work with two Outstanding Preservation Project Awards—in 2015 for the restoration of McNutt House at 712 E. Eighth Street and a house at 809 E. Ninth Street, and in 2016 for the relocation of five houses in University Courts Neighborhood (E. Eighth Street area)—which he received on behalf of the IU Real Estate Department. In 2002, he received the National Recreational Sports Association National Service Award.

In his spare time, Morrison serves as a technical race official for the Indycar Series and for the Indianapolis 500. He and his wife, Kathryn, have three children: John Paul, Marikate, and Erin (1998–2012). ᐸᔑᐳ

JOSEPH R. MOTHERWELL
1958–

Trustee, 1987–1989

A PRACTICING ATTORNEY and a former student leader at IPFW, Joseph Motherwell was the seventh student appointed to the Indiana University Board of Trustees.

Joseph R. Motherwell was born on November 6, 1958, to Richard J. and Marjorie M. Motherwell, both of whom attended Indiana University. He grew up in Fort Wayne, Indiana, along with his sister, Christine (BA in home economics, 1975).

Joseph Motherwell first enrolled as a part-time student on the Fort Wayne campus. He quickly became involved in student governance, serving as an IPFW student government member from 1981 to 1983 and as student body president from 1985 to 1987. During his tenure as student body president, he served on the IPFW chancellor search and screen committee that recommended the appointment of Chancellor Joanne B. Lantz. He was a member of the Business Student Advisory Board, the Task Force on Strategic Planning, and the 1966 Leadership Fort Wayne program. While in school, he was a regional manager and merchandise advisor for a national clothing store. Motherwell earned a BS in business with a major in finance in 1987 with nearly enough credits for a second major in biology.

Upon completing his undergraduate degree, Motherwell enrolled in the School of Law–Indianapolis (later renamed the IU McKinney School of Law), where he was the recipient of the Peters Scholarship. In 1987, he was appointed by Governor Robert D. Orr to succeed Thomas Haley III as student trustee for a two-year term. As a member of the Board of Trustees, Motherwell served on the Student Affairs Committee, Real Estate and Legal Committee, Hospitals Committee, the Natatorium and track/field advisory board, and was the trustee representative to IU Kokomo and IUPUI. He also served as a member of the IUPUI Board of Advisors from 1987 to 1990. Motherwell earned a JD in 1991 and was admitted to the Indiana Bar in 1992. ᔕ

JOHN D. MULHOLLAND
1927–

University Treasurer, Indiana University,
1974–1991

ACCOUNTANT AND CIVIC LEADER John Mulholland served IU and the community in a variety of roles with dedication and distinction. Born in Rochester, New York, in 1927, John D. "Jack" Mulholland was drafted into the United States Infantry, where he played in an Army Band. After his term with the Army, Mulholland attended Clarkson College of Technology in Potsdam, New York, and received a BA in business administration in 1950. He then went to the University of Michigan, where he earned an MBA in 1951, specializing in accounting.

Mulholland began his accounting career at Arthur Andersen Co. in New York City (1951–1956), after which he spent one year as assistant to the controller of H.C. Huber Construction Company, Inc. (1956–1957). In 1957, he moved with his family to Rochester, New York, where he worked as an internal auditor for General Dynamics (1957–1961). During this period, he became a CPA (1958). From 1961 to 1965, Mulholland was the manager of general accounting for Mead Johnson & Company in Evansville, Indiana, becoming controller (1965–1968) and then vice president of Mead Johnson Operating Division (1968–1969). He then accepted a position in Honolulu at Theo. H. Davies & Co., Ltd. as vice president and controller (1969–1972).

Indiana University hired Mulholland in 1972 as assistant vice president for financial affairs. In 1974, he was named treasurer of the university, a position he held until retirement in 1991. His tenure is remembered for his development of IU as a model of fiscal responsibility. After stepping down as treasurer, Mulholland continued to provide counsel and guidance as senior advisor to the Office of the Vice President for Finance and Administration from 1991 to 1992, when he officially retired. While a dedicated member of the Indiana University administration, Mulholland also taught accounting courses, and worked to extend his service beyond the professional level, serving with numerous university, community, and alumni groups. He was president of the Indiana University Theatre Circle, president of the University Club, president of the Central Association of College and University Business Officers (1983), as well as president of the National Association of College and University Business Officers (1989).

Mulholland served beyond Indiana University in several professional and civic organizations. He was a member of the American Institute of CPAs and the National Association of Accountants. He was elected to the board of directors of the Greater Bloomington Chamber of Commerce and was on the board of directors for both Big Brothers Big Sisters of Monroe County and Habitat for Humanity. Following retirement from IU, he became the first executive director of the Community Foundation in Bloomington, serving in this position for six years, followed by six years on their board of directors. He also served for six years as treasurer of Meals on Wheels in Bloomington and for one year as president of the Meadowood Residents Council.

Mulholland's leadership and service have been recognized with several awards and honors. In 1963, Mulholland received the Mead Johnson & Company President's Award, and the National Association of Business Officers awarded him their most prestigious honor, the Distinguished Business Officer Award. In 1999, IU President Myles Brand presented to Mulholland the E. Ross Bartley Award, the highest award an IU president can bestow on a staff member in recognition of their dedicated service and professional distinction.

John Mulholland married Patricia Walker on December 27, 1954, in Potsdam, New York. Patricia earned an MA in education counseling and guidance from IU in 1977. Together they had three children: Gail M. Ringwalt (BS 1978, MS 1984, EdD 2013), Joyce M. St Clair (BA 1981, MBA University of Chicago), and Wendy W. Moyle (BS 1983, MBA Northwestern University). ◈

CHARLIE NELMS
1946–

Vice President for Institutional Development
and Student Affairs, 2003–2007

Vice President for Student Development
and Diversity, 1999–2003

Chancellor, IU East, 1987–1994

$\bigvee$ ICE PRESIDENT Charlie Nelms' career in higher education spans more than forty years and positions at institutions in five states, as well as consultant work, motivational speaking, and leadership in areas ranging from student access and retention to institutional effectiveness and strategic planning.

Charlie Nelms was raised along with his ten siblings by their parents, Eddie and Carrie Nelms, on a forty-acre farm near Crawfordsville, Arkansas. Even though neither of his parents graduated elementary school, they encouraged all of their children to seek an education. Charlie Nelms' entry to a life in higher education began at the University of Arkansas at Pine Bluff, where he received a BS in agronomy and chemistry in 1968. Following graduation, he served as ombudsman for student affairs at his alma mater from 1968 to 1970. Charlie Nelms' first taste of Indiana University came soon after, as he earned an MS in higher education and student affairs (1971), and his EdD in higher education administration (1977).

Immediately after earning his master's degree in student affairs, Nelms served as lecturer and counselor at Lehman College of the City University of New York (1971–1973), which was followed with a position as assistant professor of education and associate dean for student development at Earlham College in Richmond, Indiana. He then spent one year as associate director for the Center of Human Development and Educational Services and assistant professor of education at the University of Arkansas at Pine Bluff. In 1978, Nelms returned to Indiana University as an assistant professor of education and associate dean for academic affairs, in which capacity he served for six years at Indiana University Northwest in Gary, Indiana. In 1984, he accepted the position of vice president for student services at Sinclair Community College in Dayton, Ohio (1984–1987).

Indiana University called on Nelms to return as chancellor of IU East in 1987. Nelms was the youngest person and the first African American to serve as chancellor of an Indiana University campus. Under his leadership, IU East was the fastest-growing college in the State of Indiana. During his tenure as chancellor from 1987 to 1994, Nelms oversaw the university's first accreditation as a comprehensive four-year campus, the launching of several new degree programs and other initiatives such as chartering of the IU East Alumni Association, the dedication of a new campus building, the opening of an off-campus site in Connersville, and a 52 percent increase in enrollment. Under Nelms's leadership enrollment surpassed 2,000 students for the first time.

In 1994, Nelms left IU to pursue a challenge elsewhere, this time as chancellor at the University of Michigan–Flint (1994–1998), where he and his leadership team resolved a campus budget deficit and increased enrollment by 6 percent, developed a comprehensive academic plan, secured more than $75 million in private gifts for the university, and established outreach centers and alliances with school districts, business, and industry to improve education and quality of life in the underserved areas of mid-Michigan.

In 1998, Nelms was again drawn to Indiana University, hand-picked by IU President Myles Brand to serve as special assistant to the president and professor of education with tenure. In 1999, he became vice president for student development and diversity and vice chancellor for academic support and diversity, while dropping the titles of interim vice chancellor for student life and diversity (IUPUI) and special assistant to the president. In December 2003, IU President Adam Herbert expanded Nelms' responsibilities, appointing him vice president for institutional development and student affairs (2003–2007) and professor of educational leadership and policy studies in the School of Education. Nelms retired from IU effective July 31, 2007, with the title professor emeritus of education.

Upon retirement from Indiana University in 2007, Charlie Nelms was appointed chancellor of North Carolina Central University in Durham, North Carolina. He retired from that position after five years to devote his time to working with HBCUs (historically black colleges and universities) and other minority-serving institutions to increase student retention and graduation rates. As of 2017, Nelms serves as a senior scholar with the American Association of State Colleges and Universities, senior consultant for the Association of Governing Boards, Center Scholar with the Indiana University Center for Postsecondary Research, as a consultant to the United Negro College Fund, and to major foundations, including the Lilly Endowment. Nelms has been a contributing writer to *The Huffington Post*, *HBCU Life Style*, and a frequent guest on the *HBCU Radio Nation* broadcast. He is the founder of the nonprofit organization Destination Graduation.

Nelms has been consistently recognized for his talents and accomplishments. He is recipient from Indiana University of the Thomas Hart Benton Mural Medallion (1994), the Distinguished Alumni Service Award (1996), and the Indiana University President's Medal (2007). He is also recipient of the University of Michigan President's Medallion (1996), the distinguished alumni award from the Indiana University School of Education (1999), and outstanding service awards from the National Association of Student Personnel Administration (1990), the City of Bloomington Dr. Martin Luther King Jr. Legacy Award (2007), and the Distinguished Service Award from *Negro Education Review* (1990). In 2012, President Barack Obama honored Charlie Nelms with the MLK Drum Major for Service Award for helping address the pressing needs in our communities around the nation. He has served as an American Council on Education Fellow, Ford Foundation Fellow, and is recipient of the Benjamin Hooks Award, the State of Indiana Sagamore of the Wabash (1994), Indiana's Distinguished Hoosier Award (2007), and the American Association of Blacks in Higher Education Delaney Distinguished Leadership Award (2013), among others. In addition, he has received honorary degrees from Earlham College (Doctor of Laws 1993) and the University of Arkansas at Pine Bluff (Doctor of Humane Letters 2001).

Active in professional, civic, and higher education organizations, Nelms has served on the board of advisors for the Center on Philanthropy at Indiana University (now the IU Lilly Family School of Philanthropy) and the National Advisory Board of the National Survey of Student Engagement, and has chaired the American Council on Education Commission for Leadership Development. He has also served as chair of the Higher Learning Commission Board of Trustees, a member of the NCAA Sports Wagering Task Force, founder and member of the executive steering committee for the Millennium Leadership Initiative, and the Kinsey Institute Board of Advisors, among others. He serves as a member of the board of trustees of the Charles Stewart Mott Foundation.

Nelms has published widely, including the book *Lessons Taught, Lessons Learned* (2004) and the policy directive *A Call to Action* (2011), which was intended to spur a national dialogue concerning the revitalization of HBCUs as an important sector of American higher education. His recent books include *Having My Say: Reflections of a Black*

Baby Boomer (2018), and his memoir *From Cotton Fields to University Leadership: All Eyes on Charlie* (2019, IU Press). All proceeds from the sale of his books are donated to support scholarships for students attending HBCUs. He has also published numerous essays and articles in scholarly journals such as *Southern Indiana Review* and *Synthesis*, as well as in book-length collections including *Black Men and the Culture of Education* and *On the Inside Looking Out: Observations from African American Administrators in Predominantly White Colleges and Universities.*

Charlie Nelms and his spouse, Jeanetta Sherrod Nelms, reside in Bloomington, Indiana, and they have one child, Rashad Nelms. Through their philanthropic endeavors, more than twenty students at five different universities receive scholarships annually.

PETER L. OBREMSKEY
1936–

Trustee, 1998–2004

Peter L. Obremskey

ATTORNEY AND INDIANA BASKETBALL HALL OF FAMER Peter Obremskey has strong ties to IU from his time as a student through his time on the IU Board of Trustees and IUPUI Board of Advisors.

Peter Obremskey was born in New York City, and may have inherited his determination and tenacity from his city roots. A graduate of Jeffersonville High School, he was the leading scorer for the 1953 Jeffersonville basketball team and the 1954 Indiana All-Stars. He was a three-year starter for Jeffersonville and also ran track and played baseball before accepting an athletic scholarship from IU basketball head coach Branch McCracken. He was a three-year regular, two-year starter, and captain for the Hoosiers, who were 1957 Big Ten co-champs and 1958 outright league champions. Obremskey played 546 games for the Hoosiers while also competing in baseball and serving as a member of the Student Athletic Committee. He was a member of the Arnold Air Society (Air Force ROTC), the IU Student Foundation, and the Phi Gamma Delta fraternity (and rode for the house Little 500 team). He earned a BS in business in 1958. After graduation, McCracken asked Obremskey to help coach and to scout for him, which facilitated his receiving an IU law degree in 1961. Obremskey's love for IU spread through his family as both of his younger brothers, Michael (BS 1961, OD 1963) and Steve (BS 1965), followed him to IU for their education.

From 1961 to 1964, Obremskey was a United States Air Force Judge Advocate and played on the Air Force basketball team. He has been affiliated with the law firm of Parr, Richey, Obremskey & Morton in Lebanon, Indiana, since 1964, first as an associate and later as partner. He practices in the areas of personal injury, products liability, medical malpractice, and civil litigation. In addition to practicing in Indiana state courts, Obremskey is admitted to practice before the U.S. Supreme Court, U.S. Court of Appeals, Second and Seventh Circuit Courts, U.S. District Court, Northern and Southern District of Indiana, and the U.S. Court of Military Appeals.

Obremskey's professional and community service is broad. He has served as president of the Indiana Trial Lawyers Association and on the association's board as director emeritus; as Boone County Bar Association president; on the Indiana State Bar Association Board of Managers; and on the Indiana Judicial Nomination and Qualifications Committee. He has been on the board of directors for the YMCA and the Boy's Club, as well a member of the Indiana Civil Court Study Commission, Kent Frandsen Scholarship Fund Drive and Steering Committee, and Lebanon Chamber of Commerce (president in 1969). He has been a member of the American Legion, the Elks Club, and the Boone County Sheriff's Merit Board.

Obremskey was appointed to two terms on the IU Board of Trustees (1998–2004), where he brought his booming voice and high expectations for academic principles for the betterment of Indiana University. He worked diligently to improve communications between the trustees and the faculty. As chair of the trustees' Policy Committee (2002–2003), Obremskey worked closely with the University Faculty Council as they overhauled the Master Course Inventory in order to facilitate intercampus transfers (ICTs), producing a policy that ensured identically numbered courses would transfer seamlessly between campuses, as well as a procedure to facilitate intercampus cooperation and knowledge-sharing when one campus desired to offer a course hitherto offered only on another campus.

Obremskey has been widely recognized for his service. The Indiana Trial Lawyers Association awarded him the Lifetime Achievement Award in 2005. He was also selected one of the Top Ten Attorneys by Best Lawyers in Indiana. He is a fellow of the American College of Trial Lawyers, the International Society of Barristers, the Indiana Bar Foundation, and the American Bar Foundation. He was inducted into the Indiana Basketball Hall of Fame in 1992 and has received the Z. G. Clevenger Award from IU Athletics. He is a life member of the IU Alumni Association and a member of the I-Men's Association, the Well House Society, Hoosier Hundred, Hoosiers for Higher Education, the Varsity Club Board of Directors, and the IUPUI Board of Advisors.

He and his wife, Sandra (BS 1958, MS 1991), have four children: Stasia Ann, William, Jennifer (BS 1987), and Katherine (BA 1991). As a student, Sandra was on the *Arbutus* staff and was a member of the IU Student Foundation, IU Student Association, Delta Gamma (which awarded her the Oxford Award), and the Mortar Board honorary society. She served on the board of the Indiana Society to Prevent Blindness, the Indianapolis 500 Festival Inc., Hoosier Counsel of Girl Scouts of America, Indianapolis Symphony Women's Committee, Witham Hospital Foundation, and the Lebanon Educational Foundation. ♋

PATRICK O. O'MEARA
1938–

Vice President for International Affairs,
2007–2011

A SCHOLAR OF AFRICAN STUDIES and higher education leader, Patrick O'Meara served IU for over forty years, strengthening its international relations and programs.

O'Meara's accomplishments are rooted in scholarship and teaching. Born in Cape Town, South Africa, and educated through to his BA in 1960 at the University of Cape Town, Patrick O'Meara attended Indiana University for graduate school, completing an MA (1966) and a PhD (1970) in political science.

After graduation in 1970, he joined the Bloomington faculty. He served as director of African Studies (1972–1993), dean for international programs (1993–2007), and vice president for international affairs (2007–2011). Throughout his tenure at IU, O'Meara was instrumental in elevating International Programs from a dean's to a vice president's office. In 2011, the offices he developed oversaw study abroad programs for more than 2,200 students, supervised exchanges with more than 200 institutions abroad, and served nearly 5,000 international students and 1,000 visiting scholars. O'Meara did not merely represent IU's international aspirations and activities with sophistication, grace, and nicely timed humor, he built on the legacy of Herman B Wells to enrich the international understanding and experience of IU faculty, staff, and students and to raise the global stature of the university. In June 2011, after more than forty years of service to Indiana University, Patrick O'Meara retired with the titles vice president emeritus of international affairs, professor emeritus of public and environmental affairs, and professor emeritus of political science.

Despite retiring from those positions, O'Meara continued to serve Indiana University, being immediately appointed as chair of the Center for International Education and Development Assistance (now the Office of International Development), which he helped establish in 1995, and which focused on IU's engagement and involvement in international institution building. President McRobbie also tapped O'Meara to serve as special advisor to the president with the responsibility for assisting in hosting visits by luminaries from all over the country and the world. Beginning in 2017, O'Meara continued to serve past retirement in both capacities and has undertaken the publication of texts about the history of IU's international engagement.

O'Meara was also a leader beyond IU. For twenty-five years, he directed a scholarship program funded by Spain's La Caixa Bank. He has been described as a consummate diplomat-in-action who moved deftly among government leaders, corporate executives, faculty from many disciplines, and students from all economic strata. For his IU colleagues, he was a knowing, enrapturing guide to the cultural treasures of many cities. Due to his administrative acumen and his expertise on African politics in general (and South African politics in particular), he has testified before Congress and consulted for universities in the United States and abroad. His publications range from *Rhodesia: Racial Conflict or Coexistence* (1975) and *International Politics in Southern Africa* (1982) to *Globalization and the Challenges of a New Century* (2000) and *Africa*, 4th edition, with John Hanson and Maria Grosz-Ngaté (2013).

For service to his field, to IU, and to institutions abroad, O'Meara received many honors including: the IU President's Medal for Excellence Award and the Thomas Hart Benton Mural Medallion; The Founder's (Casey) Award for Distinguished Achievement in Higher Education Planning; the Higher Education Prize from the Goldman Sachs Foundation; the Cross of Saint George Award from Catalonia; the Warsaw University Medal; the Amicus Poloniae from the Embassy of Poland; the Gold Cross of Merit of the Republic of Hungary; and an honorary doctorate from the National Institute of Development in Thailand. ⟋

DANILO ORESCANIN
1932–1999

Vice President for University Relations,
1983–1988

Chancellor, IU Northwest,
1975–1983

V ICE PRESIDENT Danilo Orescanin's forty-year relationship with
Indiana University began in the early 1950s at graduate school and
later continued not only as a professor but also as one of IU's most versa-
tile administrators, in which capacity he enhanced the university's academic excellence, international programs, and community partnerships
across the state.

Danilo Orescanin was born in Mingo Junction, Ohio, on April 7,
1932, the son of Nellie Kukich and George Orescanin, who had immigrated to the United States from Serbia at the age of nineteen. Orescanin
earned a BS from West Virginia University in 1953. He then spent a year
in the United States Army as a corporal in Military Police while he was
at Indiana University completing an MBA (1954), before continuing to
earn a DBA (1960). He married Kathleen Virginia Wolfe in 1954, and
they had two children: Danilo II (BA 1978) and Lori (BS 1981).

Orescanin's career as an educational administrator began during his
time in graduate school where, after several teaching appointments, he
served as the administrative assistant to the business school dean from
1959 to 1960. He then served as assistant professor of business and
assistant coordinator of evening and summer schools at the University
of South Florida from 1960 to 1963. He returned to IU as assistant professor of business administration and assistant dean in the Division of
University Extension from 1963 to 1965. He returned to full-time teaching from 1965 to 1968, which included a year as resident advisor for
the IU program at the University of Dacca in East Pakistan. Returning
from Pakistan, Orescanin was appointed assistant dean of research
and advanced studies from 1967 to 1968, associate dean from 1968 to
1969, and assistant to the president from 1969 to 1972. He left IU for
three years to serve at Southern Illinois University as vice president for
administration and campus treasurer, executive vice president, and professor of business administration. Those experiences helped to prepare
him for two later roles at Indiana University.

In 1975, Orescanin was called back to Indiana University to become
chancellor of IU Northwest in Gary, Indiana. During his tenure in Gary,
Orescanin worked to improve the financial and physical state of the campus and to improve the image of the campus in the surrounding communities. He oversaw the opening of Hawthorn Hall and the groundbreak-
ing for the Library Conference Center on campus. He was involved in

numerous community organizations, and in 1979 he received a national award for outstanding contributions and service by the Association of Teacher Educators, the first time the award was given to a non-education faculty member.

Orescanin's final administrative post at IU was as vice president for university relations from 1983 to 1988. In this capacity, he oversaw the News Bureau, and the offices of University Publications, Community Relations, and Special Events, as well as the offices of University Relations at all campuses. He expanded the staff and developed a statewide image for IU. He launched a "Speakers Team" project to invite faculty experts to visit with community groups around the state. He served as vice president until 1988, when he returned to teaching management and business policy classes in the business school. When he retired in 1992, he was given the Otteson Undergraduate Teaching Excellence Award and the title of professor emeritus of business administration from the Kelley School of Business Indianapolis.

Orescanin authored numerous research articles in business journals and was involved in civic affairs including board service on the Gary Chamber of Commerce, Lake County Mental Health Association, United Way, and the American Red Cross, among many others. He served as the United States delegate to the International Seminar on "The University Today" in Yugoslavia in 1964, was a member of a Venezuelan survey team in 1979, and an AID program advisory committee in East Pakistan in 1970.

Danilo Orescanin passed away May 22, 1999, at the age of 67 in Tampa, Florida. The Danilo Orescanin Memorial Scholarship at IU Northwest was established to honor his contributions to Indiana University and to the pursuit of educational excellence in Indiana, the Midwest, and around the world. ✧

Frank D. Otte
1970–

Trustee, 1995–1997

A STRONG SUPPORTER OF INDIANA UNIVERSITY since his days as a student, attorney Frank Otte's service to the university includes a term on the IU Board of Trustees and on the Indiana University Alumni Association (IUAA) Executive Council.

Born October 26, 1970, in Indianapolis, Frank D. Otte was reared by parents Sally Wilson and Frank J. Otte (BS 1960; JD 1966), an attorney and federal bankruptcy judge. He and his two sisters, Claire (Otte) Becker (BS 1997; MS 2002) and Sarah (Otte) Graber (BA 1994) were raised in Indianapolis. He attended Immaculate Heart of Mary Indianapolis and Cathedral High School before enrolling at IU Bloomington. Otte received a BS in environmental science in 1993 and a JD in 1997 from the IU School of Law–Bloomington (later renamed the Maurer School of Law). While earning his degrees, Otte was involved in student leadership, holding memberships with Phi Gamma Delta, Off–Campus Student Union, the Student Alumni Council, and the Student Athletic Board. Every summer, he followed in his father's footsteps by working with a herd of more than 3,500 cattle at Valley Garden Ranch, a 9,000-acre spread in Ennis, Montana.

While a student at the law school, Frank Otte was appointed in 1995 by Indiana Governor Evan Bayh to a two-year term on the Board of Trustees at Indiana University, only the eleventh student to hold that position. Otte was the trustee liaison to IUPUI, where he served on its Board of Advisors. In addition to his student positions and his work with the Board of Trustees, Otte has served Indiana University in a variety of ways. He has twice been on the IU Alumni Association CEO search committee, has been on the IUAA's Executive Council, has been treasurer for the IUAA, and is a member of the IUAA and the Varsity Club. Additionally, he has been a member of the Well House Society.

Professionally, Otte is an experienced private attorney, admitted to practice law in the states of Indiana and Montana. He is a member of the Indianapolis, Indiana, and Montana State Bar Associations. Initially, Otte worked with McHale, Cook & Welch before starting a solo practice in 2000. Since 2004 he has worked in Indianapolis with the law firm Clark, Quinn, Moses, Scott & Grahn, eventually becoming partner. Otte's general business litigation practice is focused on providing efficient and cost-effective representation for family and closely held businesses in matters including landlord-tenant disputes, contracts, mechanics liens, collection, and general corporate matters. In addition to his general litigation practice, Otte regularly assists clients in the areas of family law, estate planning, probate, and real estate. He also provides advice and counsel to numerous small businesses handling day-to-day issues that confront the small business owner.

Frank Otte is a member of Immaculate Heart of Mary Church in Indianapolis and is active in the Indianapolis-based Boy Scout Troop 174, serving as scoutmaster since 2008. In 2007, Otte married Julie Lynn (PhD 2008), an Indiana University School of Nursing associate professor. Together, they have three daughters: Sally Gayle, Helen Marie, and Jane. Spending as much time outdoors as possible, Otte pursues hobbies including bird hunting, fly fishing, and working on a family farm in Morgan County, Indiana. ✍

JUDITH G. PALMER
1948–

Vice President and Chief Financial Officer,
Indiana University, 1994–2007

Vice President for Planning and Finance Management,
1991–1994

Vice President for Planning, 1986–1991

VICE PRESIDENT AND CFO Judith G. Palmer's career was full of firsts: she was the first woman vice president of IU, the first woman state budget director for Indiana, the first woman on the Indianapolis Columbia Club Board of Directors, and the first woman president of the Columbia Club. She served under five different IU presidents from 1985 until her retirement in 2017.

Judith G. Palmer joined IU in 1985 and was appointed to the position of vice president in 1986 by President John W. Ryan. However, her affinity for IU began much earlier in life. The only child of Mr. and Mrs. William T. Palmer, she and her parents often visited IU as a family and attended IU football games. In the summer of 1965, having just completed her junior year of high school in Montgomery, Indiana, Palmer was selected to participate in an IU accelerated learning program for students entering their senior year. During the course of that summer program, she gained early admittance to IU and was awarded her high school diploma without returning to complete her senior year.

In college, Palmer's interest in public service and politics led her to participate in political campaigns both at the state and congressional levels. She served as campaign communication coordinator during the 1968 gubernatorial campaign. Upon the advice and support of her IU professors and mentors, she decided to accept an appointment on the governor's staff serving in the State Budget Agency and earned a BA in government with a minor in economics in 1970 without returning to the Bloomington campus. Following graduation, Palmer entered the evening division of the Indiana University School of Law–Indianapolis (now the McKinney School of Law). She continued to work full time in the State Budget Agency, worked for several political campaigns, expanded her public service interests through local civic organizations, and helped launch a law school newspaper before graduating cum laude with a JD in 1974.

Following her graduation from law school, Palmer continued her career in state government. Between 1969 and 1985, she served Governors Edgar D. Whitcomb, Otis R. Bowen, and Robert D. Orr in the roles of senior budget analyst, executive assistant to the governor, and Indiana state budget director. Among other accomplishments, Palmer managed the state's finances during a difficult fiscal recession in the early 1980s which threatened the continuation of the state's popular property tax relief program. The actions taken to increase state revenue during that period helped set the financial foundation for the development of "The Indiana A+ Plan" education program, which Governor Orr eventually signed into law in 1987.

Palmer left state government for Indiana University in 1985, becoming special assistant to President John W. Ryan and a part-time associate professor in the School of Public and Environmental Affairs. She held this position for just over one year before being promoted to the position of vice president for planning, a position newly created by the IU Board of Trustees in 1986. In this position, Palmer coordinated surveys and analyses to create plans for the general development of IU's eight-campus system. In 1991, President Tom Ehrlich expanded her responsibilities to include financial operations for the university, and her title was changed to vice president for planning and finance management. Then in 1994, upon Myles Brand's appointment as president, he changed her title to vice president and chief financial officer to emphasize the overall financial responsibilities of the position, which she held until June 2007. During this period, she participated in activities related to the establishment of what is now known as IU Health, a partnership between Methodist Hospital in Indianapolis and Indiana University through its IU School of Medicine and hospitals.

In 2007, after twenty years of responsibility for the university's finances, Palmer stepped down and took a six-month leave of absence before assuming the directorship of IU's Office of Legislative and Policy Analysis. In this position, created by newly appointed President Michael McRobbie, Palmer was tasked with reviewing state laws related to Indiana University in an effort to develop a prioritized agenda for legislative initiatives. In addition, she helped establish a process and office to coordinate official university policies. During this time, she also assisted with the development of the *Blueprint for Student Attainment* for IU's regional campuses, an effort that took her back to her early days in planning activities for IU. She continued to lead the Office of Legislative and Policy Analysis until her official retirement in September of 2012.

Since her retirement, Palmer has kept busy as a consultant on higher education finance and strategic planning issues. In May 2017, she was elected chairman of the Indiana Farmers Mutual Insurance Company Board of Directors.

Judith Palmer's awards and honors include the Indiana University President's Medal for Excellence awarded by President McRobbie (2007), the Thomas Hart Benton Mural Medallion awarded by President Tom Ehrlich (1988, 1994), as well as two Sagamore of the Wabash Awards awarded by Governor Bowen (1977) and Governor Orr (1985). She has also been named Indiana's Outstanding Young Woman (1978), one of the Ten Outstanding Young Women of America (1978), and a Distinguished Fellow of the Indianapolis Bar Foundation (1988). ❧

SUSAN PARRISH
1947–

Secretary of the Board, 1990–1998

I N A DIVERSE CAREER, Susan Parrish's service to IU touched five decades and four administrative units.

Julia Susan Parrish was born June 25, 1947, to Reba Jo Waldrop and James Multon Parrish Sr. in Marietta, Georgia, a small town with a Lockheed plant on the outskirts of Atlanta. Her mother was an administrative assistant and her father owned a tariff bureau. Growing up, she was influenced by her grandfather, William Allison Parrish, who was a self-educated, wise, and kind man, as well as by her aunt, Julia Beth Parrish Sadler, who always urged Susan to get as much education as possible. She attended West Georgia College, studied abroad in Mexico, and earned a BA (1971). As an undergraduate, she played on the women's volleyball team and in various intramural sports.

Upon graduating, Parrish joined the Peace Corps and served two years in Ethiopia (1971–1973), where she worked with the vocational education group to help students who could not get into college develop life skills outside the education system. When she returned to the United States, she joined Lincoln Life Insurance Company in Fort Wayne as a computer programmer (1973–1976). She then moved to Bloomington, Indiana, with her partner, Thomas Paul Shafer, so that he could study theatre at IU. She took a position at the university's office of data systems and services (now University Information Technology Services), working primarily on the System 2000 student records project (1976–1978). She then worked for Professor Morton Marcus in the Division of Research (now the Center for Business Research) from 1978 to 1985, while taking courses in marketing and management. When her husband graduated and took a job at a college in Florida, she worked as director of store systems at Scotty's Home Improvement Centers (1985–1989), before the couple returned to IU Bloomington. Once back at IU, she worked for Janet Shirley in the Trustees office. In 1990, Richard Stoner appointed her secretary of the Board of Trustees (1990–1998). Next, she joined the University Budget Office, where she worked until retirement in 2014.

For her meritorious service to Indiana University, IU President Thomas Ehrlich presented Susan Parrish with the Thomas Hart Benton Mural Medallion in 1994.

In 1977, Julia Susan Parrish married Thomas Paul Shafer (MA 1981), who performed in theatre and drama productions at IU. Together they have one son, Joseph Parrish Shafer. ᘉ

SANDRA R. PATTERSON-RANDLES
1948–

Chancellor, IU Southeast,
2002–2013

A FTER A TWENTY-YEAR CAREER IN HIGHER EDUCATION, Sandra R. Patterson-Randles became the first woman to serve as chancellor of Indiana University Southeast, strengthening the university and leaving a lasting legacy.

Sandra Reindl Patterson-Randles was born February 27, 1948, in Chicago, Illinois, and knows a thing or two about succeeding—no matter the odds. She is the oldest of seven children. When she was 17, her family's house and father's business were destroyed in a tornado in northern Illinois, which killed six of her neighbors and destroyed more than 250 homes. Patterson-Randles cites her maternal grandfather, Gus, as having a major influence on her; at the time of his retirement, despite only having a sixth-grade education, he was the head of the entire Northeastern U.S. inventory operations for a major U.S. corporation. Her aunt Gladys was equally influential, having beaten the odds after being severely injured in a car accident and proving wrong the doctors who had said she would never walk again.

Patterson-Randles was the first member of her family to receive a college degree. She earned a BA in classical languages and literatures from the University of Colorado Boulder in 1970. From 1970 to 1972, she taught at Royalton-Hartland High School. She then went to graduate school at the University of Kentucky, earning an MA in classical languages and literatures (1974), an MA in English (1977), and a PhD in English (1982). While a graduate student, she worked as a graduate teaching assistant and an instructor.

From 1983 to 1987, Patterson-Randles launched her career in higher education as an assistant professor of liberal studies and English and writing facilitator at Kentucky State University, where she also worked as an academic program developer. She then taught for a year at Boston College as assistant professor of humanities and cross-disciplinary writing. From 1988 to 1998, she was professor of English and general studies at Western State College and was chair of the Department of Modern Languages for the duration of her tenure, as well as chair of the university's Task Force on Diversity. In the summer of 1990, she participated in the administrative-faculty exchange at the University of Colorado Boulder. From 1998 to 2002, she was vice president for academic affairs at the University of Pittsburgh.

Patterson-Randles came to Indiana University in 2002 as the fourth chancellor of IU Southeast. Her legacy includes leading the campus's Strategic Planning Committee, which was responsible for developing its first comprehensive and long-range strategic plan. She spearheaded the development of an enrollment management strategy, and hired experienced leaders to create a collaborative senior administrative team. She enhanced facilities at IU Southeast in many ways, including opening a new Graduate Center and building a state-of-the-art library. She stepped down as chancellor in 2013, took a one-year sabbatical, and returned to teaching as professor of English (2014–).

Patterson-Randles' list of awards is testament to her success: a National Endowment for the Humanities Postdoctoral Fellowship (1984), a Presidential Commendation for Excellence in Teaching (1984), a Harvard University grant for a management development program (1995), an alumni award for excellence from Western State College (1997), a fellowship from the Pennsylvania Education Policy and Leadership Center (2001–2002), a Southern Indiana Community Leadership Award (2002), an ASPIRE outstanding educator/administrator award in diversity (2002), a recognition for service from the Indiana General Assembly (2007), and a Governor's Distinguished Hoosier Award for "significant contributions to our communities" (2007). Upon retiring as chancellor in 2013, she was named chancellor emerita, named a Sagamore of the Wabash, and received the IU President's Medal for sustained excellence in service, achievement, and leadership.

Patterson-Randles has been a member of the American Association of State Colleges and Universities; a trustee of the American Cancer Biorepository; a member of the American Council on Education; chair and member of the board of directors for the Indiana Campus Compact; and a member of the board of directors and secretary treasurer for the Kentuckiana Metroversity. She was on the board of directors for the Backside Learning Center at Churchill Downs (2010–2015; president 2013–2015). In addition, she has been involved with Leadership Louisville, Leadership Southern Indiana, Louisville Science Center, New Albany-Floyd County School Corporation, One Southern Indiana, and 20/20 Southern Indiana Visioning Project, among many others.

Sandra Patterson-Randles married Jeff Randles on a cattle farm in Gunnison, Colorado, in 1992. She currently lives on a horse farm and is an avid equestrian. ⟡

NASSER H. PAYDAR
1956–

Executive Vice President and Chancellor,
IUPUI, 2015–

Chancellor, IU East, 2007–2012

THROUGHOUT HIS MORE THAN THIRTY-YEAR CAREER at Indiana University, Nasser Paydar has built a reputation for data-driven decision making, creative problem solving, and healthy debate by applying his training as an engineer to his administrative practice.

Born in Tehran, Iran, to Houssain and Pouran Hamed Paydar, Nasser came to the United States to study mechanical engineering at Syracuse University, where he earned a BS (1979), MS (1981), and PhD (1985). Paydar's interest in a career in teaching and research was piqued in 1979 when he worked as a teaching associate at Syracuse University. After graduation in 1985, he joined Indiana University as a professor and has remained ever since.

Paydar's career in higher education began at IUPUI in 1985, when he joined the Department of Mechanical Engineering as assistant professor. From 1989 to 2003, he took on additional duties including chairman of the Department of Mechanical Engineering (1989–1996), associate dean for graduate programs (1995–1996), associate dean for academic programs (1996–2001), and executive associate dean for academic programs (2001–2003). He has been the principal investigator on eighteen grants totaling more than $1.3 million in funding and is widely published in engineering journals.

From 2003 to 2007, Paydar served as vice chancellor and dean, Indiana University–Purdue University Columbus (IUPUC), where he led the Columbus Center to unprecedented growth and success. IUPUC experienced significant enrollment growth, had the largest fundraising campaign in its history, and received its first major state appropriation. Known for his ability to foster new partnerships, Paydar led the creation of a seamless education system for south central Indiana by collaborating with Ivy Tech Community College, the Community Education Coalition, and local business leaders.

On the basis of these earlier successes, in 2007 Paydar was appointed interim chancellor of Indiana University East before being hired permanently in 2009 and serving as chancellor until 2012. Paydar led a transformation of mission and image at IU East, leading it to become an institution of choice for high school students in eastern Indiana as well as a leading provider of online undergraduate programs. Student enrollment grew by 85 percent during Paydar's tenure, with the campus's new strategic approach to recruiting, retaining, and graduating more students who would, in turn, shape and lead IU East's service region. In addition to record enrollment, Paydar brought more than twenty new bachelor's and master's degree programs to IU East. In 2008, IU East became the first state university campus in Indiana to discontinue all associate degree programs and remedial courses, partnering with Ivy Tech to create an affordable and accessible higher education system for area residents. Under Paydar, IU East's new model for higher education received both statewide and national recognition.

In 2012, Paydar's experience and talent were tapped to help lead IUPUI, first as executive vice chancellor and chief academic officer (2012–2015) and then as chancellor of IUPUI and executive vice president of Indiana University (2015–). One of his major accomplishments during this period was to lead IUPUI in a comprehensive and inclusive strategic planning process ("Our Commitment to Indiana and Beyond"), aligned with IU's Bicentennial Strategic Plan. During his time as chancellor, he has worked toward increasing diversity, campus beautification, and student engagement and retention. Toward this end, in the spring of 2016 he launched the Welcoming Campus Initiative, powered by a $1 million innovation fund that enables faculty, staff, and student leaders to launch a variety of projects each year, ranging from summer camps for children to mentoring programs, from 3D campus maps to public art projects. In addition, he has worked to strengthen IUPUI's international partnerships, such as by leading delegations to Malaysia, Mexico, Saudi Arabia, and Thailand to meet with officials from various higher education institutions and strengthen alumni networks.

Paydar holds or has held memberships in several scientific and professional societies, including the American Society of Mechanical Engineers and the American Society of Engineering Education, and has served on numerous committees at IUPUI, including the Scholarship Committee, the Fellowship Subcommittee, the Ethics in Research Committee, the Council on Undergraduate Learning, the Graduate Affairs Committee, and the International Affairs Program and Recruitment Committee. In 2014, he was elected to the board of directors of the National Association of Chief Academic Officers and, in 2015, he was elected to the board of directors of the American Association of State Colleges and Universities.

Paydar has also been active in several civic organizations over the years, including the board of directors of the Wayne County, Indiana,

Chamber of Commerce (2010–2012); board of directors of Indiana Campus Compact (2015–); board of directors of the Indianapolis Chamber of Commerce (2015–); board of directors of Greater Indianapolis Progress Committee (2015–); board of directors of United Way of Central Indiana (2016–); board of directors of Ascend Indiana (2017–); vice president of the Economic Club of Indiana (2017–2018); president of the Economic Club of Indiana (2018–2019); and the 500 Festival Board of Directors (2018).

Among Paydar's many awards and recognitions are: the Wisner-Stoelk Outstanding Faculty Award (1988), consecutive IUPUI Outstanding Teacher Awards, as well as the Abraham M. Max Distinguished Professor Award (1994) and the Doris H. Merritt Outstanding Leadership Award (2000). He was the 2010 recipient of the Circle of Leadership Service Award at IUPUC and the 2014 IUPUI Administrator of the Year as selected by the Undergraduate Student Government.

Nasser Paydar married his wife, Niloo, in 1979. They have two sons, Omeed and Naveed. ♋

KENNETH L. PERRIN
1937–2018

Chancellor, IU South Bend,
1997–2002

As the fourth chancellor of IU South Bend, Kenneth L. Perrin often referred to IUSB as the "People's University" and oversaw an expansion of campus buildings, an increase in student enrollment, and the campus's first capital campaign.

Kenneth L. Perrin was born in Los Angeles to Lois (Bowen) Perrin, a homemaker, and Freeman Perrin, a pharmacist. He attended public school in Alhambra, California, before earning a BA in psychology from Occidental College in Los Angeles (1958), where he was the senior class president and a member of the Senior Honor Society (now Mortar Board, National College Senior Honor Society). He attended California State University, Long Beach, where he earned an MA in speech pathology in 1964. He then taught from 1965 to 1967 at the University of the Pacific as assistant professor of speech pathology while working toward a PhD in speech and hearing sciences from Stanford University Medical School, graduating in 1969.

After receiving his doctorate, Perrin became associate professor and also directed the Division of Speech and Hearing Sciences at the University of the Pacific. From 1971 to 1977, Perrin was professor of communicative disorders, chairman of the Department of Communicative Disorders, and also director of the Speech, Hearing, and Language Center. In 1977, he became director of the Education and Scientific Programs for the American Speech-Language-Hearing Association. From 1980 to 1991, he served as dean, provost, and president of West Chester University in Pennsylvania. At West Chester, Perrin is credited with guiding the growth of the university: admission applicants increased by 28 percent, annual giving by 100 percent, and external grant awards by 700 percent. From 1991 to 1993, Perrin was president of the national nonprofit Council of Postsecondary Accreditation. From 1993 to 1997, he was senior vice president at the University of Hawai'i as well as chancellor for the University of Hawai'i–Hilo and the University of Hawai'i–West O'ahu.

In 1997, Kenneth Perrin was appointed the third chancellor of Indiana University South Bend by IU President Myles Brand and served in that capacity until his retirement in 2002. During his time as chancellor, Perrin initiated scholarship programs with the alumni association and established The Perrin Project to bridge students, faculty, and staff with community activities such as volunteering. He oversaw the development and construction of IU South Bend's Student Activities Center, the pursuit of which was dubbed by some state legislators as the most active lobbying effort in state history. Perrin also established an art gallery on campus and began the process for funding a pedestrian bridge that crosses over the St. Joseph River. He also oversaw the campus's first capital campaign, which raised $3.6 million. In 1998, Wiekamp Hall opened, providing needed space for expanding academic programming on the campus. In addition, Perrin served the IUSB community as a member of the Memorial Hospital Board of Directors in South Bend, the South Bend Symphony Board of Directors, and the United Way Board of Directors. Perrin retired in 2002 with the titles chancellor emeritus and professor emeritus of psychology.

Perrin's service to his field, to his institutions, and to his communities has been recognized with several awards. In 1980, Perrin was elected a Fellow of the American Speech Language and Hearing Association for his distinction in the field. He received the West Chester Community Service Award (1983), Distinguished Alumni Award from California State University Long Beach (1988), Outstanding Leadership Award from Brian's Run for the Handicapped (1990), and the President's Medallion for Service from West Chester University (1991). In 2002, Perrin was awarded the President's Medal for Excellence by IU.

Kenneth Perrin married Shirley on April 1, 1960, and they raised two children, Steven Perrin and Lynnsey Perrin Hee. Ken Perrin passed away February 8, 2018. ꩜

RUTH J. PERSON
1945–

Chancellor, IU Kokomo,
1999–2008

Ruth J. Person

As the sixth administrative leader at IU Kokomo, Ruth Person served as the campus's fourth chancellor, becoming the second woman to hold that position. She moved on to become the seventh chancellor of the University of Michigan–Flint campus, and the first woman to hold that position.

Ruth Janssen Person earned a BA in history and psychology from Gettysburg College in Pennsylvania (1967) and an AMLS degree from the University of Michigan (1969). She holds an MA in administration from George Washington University School of Business and Public Management (1974) and a PhD in library and information science from the University of Michigan (1980). She is a member of Phi Alpha Theta, Beta Phi Mu, Pi Lambda Theta, Psi Chi, Kappa Delta Pi, and Beta Gamma Sigma, and attended the Harvard University Institute of Educational Management (1989).

Prior to coming to IU, Person had already built a successful academic career. She served for four years as vice president for academic affairs and professor of business administration at Angelo State University in San Angelo, Texas. She was also vice president for academic affairs at Ohio's Ashland University, associate vice chancellor for academic affairs at the University of Missouri–St. Louis, dean of the College of Library Science at Clarion University in Pennsylvania, and associate dean and faculty member of the School of Library and Information Science at The Catholic University of America in Washington, D.C. She was a fellow of the American Council on Education from 1990 to 1991.

Ruth Person joined Indiana University Kokomo in 1999 as chancellor with an additional appointment as professor of management in the Division of Business and Economics. She served on the president's senior management team and represented the IU regional campuses on the IU Foundation Board, the IU Integrated Image Committee, and the IU Master Plan Committee, and was a regularly requested counselor across all IU campuses. With her extensive expertise in academic affairs, she focused her energy on IUK's academic programs, eliminating most associate degree programs and implementing fourteen new degree programs in a wide range of disciplines which enhanced IU Kokomo's move toward becoming a full baccalaureate institution. Under her leadership, the campus developed freshman learning communities, new academic traditions, and expanded curricular and cocurricular

316

activities. Opportunities for nontraditional students expanded in part from accelerated evening and multiformat course offerings. Person also oversaw the expansion of facilities for faculty development and student learning as the campus developed a Center for Teaching, Learning, and Assessment and increased the number of resident full-time faculty members by 25 percent. Chancellor Person oversaw the construction of Hunt Hall, the campus's award-winning science facility. Furthermore, IU Kokomo greatly improved its information technology infrastructure by adding state-of-the-art technology in classrooms, conference rooms, and lecture halls.

When Chancellor Person left IU in 2008, President Michael McRobbie presented her with the President's Medal for Excellence as an enduring recognition of her contributions to Indiana University. Despite moving on, Person remains chancellor emerita and has maintained connections with IU through membership in the Arbutus Society (2016), 1820 Society (2017), and the IU Kokomo Campaign Leadership Group (2015–). In 2016, Person committed a bequest of $3.5 million for student scholarships, the largest gift to the IU Kokomo campus to date. Person named the fund the RMJ Scholars Program in honor of three women who believed strongly in the value of education: Florence Richardson McGee, Ruth Person's godmother; Ruth Mahoney Janssen, her mother; and Ruth Janssen Person.

In 2008, Person accepted the position as chancellor of the University of Michigan–Flint, a position she held until 2014 when she returned to full-time teaching as professor of management. Standout accomplishments during her six years as chancellor include establishing a Student Veterans Center, creating four new doctoral programs (including an EdD and a PhD in physical therapy), increasing enrollment from 6,200 to 8,500, securing $17 million to renovate the science building, and guiding UM–Flint to become a Carnegie Engaged Campus. She also served on the President's Council of the State Universities of Michigan and its board of directors (2008–2014).

Person's dedication and leadership extended beyond the classroom. While Chancellor at IUK, she served on the advisory boards of organizations ranging from the YWCA to the Kokomo-Howard County Public Library, the United Way of Howard County, Steak 'n Shake Company, and St. Joseph's Hospital. In Michigan, she has been a Garden and

Conservatory Ambassador at the Matthaei Botanical Gardens (Ann Arbor), as well as a volunteer Gamma Phi Beta Scholarship Advisor of the Beta Chapter. She has also been a member of the Academy of Management (2015–), an ACE Fellows Program Learning Contract Facilitator (2015–2016), and a member of the National Association of Corporate Directors (2010–). Furthermore, Person has served as director of Biglari Holdings, Inc. (2002–) and as trustee of the Biglari Foundation (2016–).

Ruth Person has received many recognitions for her outstanding service. She received a Doctor of Humane Letters from Indiana University (2016), the Key to the City of Flint (2014), the Order of Omega (2014), and the Gamma Phi Beta Carnation Award (2010). In recognition of her impact on the entire state of Indiana, she received the Distinguished Hoosier Award (2008). She has also received the 2008 Distinguished Alumni Award (School of Information, University of Michigan), the 2005 An Uncommon Woman Salute from the Kokomo Symphony Orchestra, the 2005 ATHENA Award from the Greater Kokomo Chamber of Commerce Women's Business Council, the 2004 Dr. Martin Luther King Jr. Exemplary Leadership Award from IU Kokomo, and the 2002 Distinguished Alumnus Award from Gettysburg College. In 1999, the American Association of University Administrators awarded her the John L. Blackburn Award for Exemplary Administrative Leadership and the Exemplary Models of Administrative Leadership Award. ❧

ORA H. PESCOVITZ
1956–

Vice President for Research Administration
(Interim), 2007–2009

Ora H. Pescovitz

I N ADDITION TO A THIRTY-YEAR AFFILIATION with Indiana University, Ora Hirsch Pescovitz's career has included positions as a doctor, professor, administrator, president, and corporate leader at institutions throughout the Midwest.

Born in 1956 in Chicago, her family had a tremendous impact on her life, both personally and professionally, teaching her to have faith not only in herself but also in the abilities of others. Her father Richard, a rabbi, marched with Dr. Martin Luther King Jr. in Selma, Alabama, and in Washington, D.C., and founded the Religious Action Center of Reform Judaism. Her mother, Bella, grew up in Russia during World War II and was on the first boat to arrive in Israel after it was granted statehood. Ora Pescovitz's parents encouraged her and her three brothers to work hard and maximize their potential, instilling in them the faith that they could accomplish anything and encouraging them to do work that benefits others and improves the world.

Ora Pescovitz attended public school in Maryland. She earned a BA in medical science from the Honors Program in Medical Education at Northwestern University, followed by an MD from the Northwestern University Medical School. She also studied for a year at Hebrew University in Jerusalem, Israel. Pescovitz completed residencies in pediatrics at the University of Minnesota (1979–1981) and the Children's Hospital National Medical Center in Washington, D.C. (1981–1982). She went on to serve as a Medical Staff Fellow in Endocrinology at the Developmental Endocrinology Branch of the National Institutes of Child Health and Human Development (1982–1985).

From 1985 to 1987, Pescovitz taught pediatric endocrinology and metabolism in the Department of Pediatrics at the University of Minnesota. In 1988, she joined Indiana University as associate professor of pediatrics, physiology and biophysics. From 1992 to 2009, Pescovitz was professor of pediatrics and physiology and of biophysics at Indiana University, and from 1998 to 2009, she was the Edwin Letzter Professor of Pediatrics at the Indiana University School of Medicine. She was also director of IU's Section of Pediatric Endocrinology and Diabetology. In 2000, Pescovitz was named executive associate dean for research affairs for the IU School of Medicine, a position she held through 2009. Concurrently from 2004 to 2009, Pescovitz was the president and CEO of Riley Hospital for Children, one of the largest children's hospitals in the United States. Finally, she was appointed IU's interim vice president for research administration (2007–2009).

As interim vice president for research administration, Pescovitz was responsible for the research infrastructure at all eight Indiana University campuses. She was responsible for creation and oversight of the Indiana Genomics Initiative (made possible by a $155 million grant from the Lilly Endowment), support of the BioCrossroads statewide life sciences initiative, oversight of the Clinical and Translational Sciences Institute, and growth in annual research funding at the IU School of Medicine from $133 million in 2000 to $231 million in 2009. As president and CEO of Riley Hospital for Children, Pescovitz was responsible for completion and implementation of a strategic plan to transform the quality of clinical care, education, research, and advocacy at the hospital; to construct the ten-story, $470 million, 675,000-square-foot Simon Family Tower; and to provide tertiary pediatric services throughout Indiana. Additionally, while at Indiana University, Pescovitz served on the Information Technology Strategic Planning Committee, the Advisory Committee to the Interim President, the President's Cabinet, and the board for the Borns Jewish Studies Program.

In 2009, Ora Pescovitz left IU for the University of Michigan, where she worked until 2014. At Michigan, Pescovitz served as professor of pediatrics and communicable diseases, executive vice president for medical affairs, and CEO of the University of Michigan Health System—becoming the first woman to serve in that capacity. During these years, she served as chair of the A. Alfred Taubman Medical Research Institute Scientific Advisory Board (2010–2012) and member of the Research Governing Council (2012–2014); member, University Musical Society Corporate Council (2010–2014); and member, Zell Lurie Institute Advisory Board (2010–2014).

From 2014 to 2017, Pescovitz worked as senior vice president and U.S. medical leader for Eli Lilly and Company in Indianapolis, Indiana. In this capacity, she has been a member of the Anthem/Lilly Joint Research Governance Committee, a member of the Titles and Promotions Committee, executive sponsor of both the Eli Lilly Early Career Professionals and the Eli Lilly Women Physicians' Network. During this return to Indiana, Pescovitz served as adjunct professor of pediatrics in the Department of Pediatrics, held the chair of the Indiana

University Center for Global Health/AMPATH-Kenya Development Board, and was a member of the Advancement Council for Indiana University's Richard M. Fairbanks School of Public Health.

In May 2017, Pescovitz was appointed Oakland University of Michigan's seventh president, taking office that July.

Ora Pescovitz has been very involved with both professional and civic organizations. Professionally, she has been the president of the Society for Pediatric Research (2000–2001) and the Lawson Wilkins Pediatric Endocrine Society (2004–2005). Moreover, she has served on the boards of directors for the National Association of Children's Hospitals, the National Association of Children's Hospitals and Related Institutions, the Children's Miracle Network, the Association of Academic Health Centers, and the National Institutes of Health. She has also been named to the Strategic Cabinet for the University of Florida Health System (2015–), and served as co-chair of the Health Planning Committee for Indianapolis Mayor Joe Hogsett's transition team (2015–2016).

Pescovitz's record of civic engagement includes serving on the Central Indiana United Way Board and Executive Committee, the Congregation Beth-El Zedeck Board and Torah Writing Committee, the Selection Support Committee for the Indianapolis Prize, and co-chairing the Seeing is Achieving Campaign for Prevent Blindness Indiana, the Michigan Israel Business Bridge Advisory Council (2012–2014), and the Board of Ann Arbor SPARK (2012–2014). In 2003, she was a founding member of the John Herron Art Society. She also serves on the Indianapolis Opera Board (2014–).

All of this has earned Pescovitz regional and national accolades. She was elected to the Alpha Omega Alpha Medical Honorary Society in 2005 and to the National Academy of Medicine in 2011. She has been the recipient of a Research Career Development Award from the National Institutes of Health (1991–1996), a Best Doctors in America Award (seven times since 1995), several leadership awards from *Becker's Hospital Review*, the IUPUI Science Medal of Distinction (2007), and the Robert H. Williams Distinguished Leadership Award from the Endocrine Society (2011). Her alma mater, Northwestern University, named her a Distinguished Alumnus in 2004 and presented her with a Northwestern University Alumni Association Alumni Merit Award in 2012. Her many honors include being named one of *Modern*

Healthcare's Top 25 Women in Healthcare (2009), a Sagamore of the Wabash Award for Excellence from Indiana Governor Mitch Daniels (2009), the Indiana University President's Medal (2009), being named Crain's Detroit Business "Newsmaker of the Year" (2010), being named a Michigan Women's Foundation Women Making a Difference Honoree (2012), Becker's Healthcare Leadership Award (2014), and the 2016 Touchstone Award Honoree from Girls, Inc.

Ora Pescovitz married Mark David Pescovitz, MD, on October 29, 1979, and they raised three children: Aliza Beth, Ari Samuel (BA 2008, BFA 2008, BS 2008), and Naomi Rachel. Mark Pescovitz, a renowned surgeon, scholar, and mentor at the IU School of Medicine, passed away in 2010. ᥬ

W. GEORGE PINNELL
1922–1991

Executive Vice President of the University,
1974–1988
Vice President and Treasurer,
1971–1974

K NOWN AS A PERCEPTIVE, EFFECTIVE ADMINISTRATOR and a supportive colleague, George Pinnell steadfastly served the students, faculty, and staff of IU for nearly forty years.

Born in West Virginia to parents George M. Pinnell and Anna Wagner, William George Pinnell was a United States Navy aviator during World War II (1942–1947). In 1946, he married Dorothy "Dot" Graham, and they had a daughter, Georgia. Pinnell operated a small business before enrolling at age 25 at West Virginia University (BA 1950; MA 1952).

Pinnell came to Indiana University to earn a doctorate in business administration, graduating in 1954, whereupon he immediately joined the faculty as assistant professor of real estate and assistant dean of the School of Business (now the IU Kelley School of Business). Thus began his long career as an educator and administrator at IU. Over the years, Pinnell held various administrative positions in the School of Business, including dean from 1963 to 1971. Noting Pinnell's abilities and the need to fill the vacancy left by the retiring Joseph A. Franklin in 1971, the Trustees and IU President John Ryan appointed Pinnell to be vice president and treasurer of Indiana University. In 1974, Pinnell became executive vice president of the university; and, in 1983, he assumed the additional post of president of the IU Foundation, working in both capacities until 1988, when he officially retired with the titles executive vice president emeritus and professor emeritus of business administration.

Pinnell's service to IU was not self-oriented but directed toward improving the quality of the university. The expression he used most often and the ideal he pursued unflaggingly was "academic excellence." As dean of the School of Business, he insisted upon academic rigor, urged curricular innovations upon a traditionally-oriented faculty, and initiated new international programs. He oversaw the planning and construction of the main Business School Building, which was completed in 1966. Although Pinnell remained fond of his business school colleagues and responded graciously to their requests for advice, as a central administrator he did not play favorites and was respected by all for his genuine interest in what they were doing and for his ability to make appropriate decisions, even when they were hard. As president of the IU Foundation, he moved the foundation closer to the needs of programs on IU's various campuses.

Beyond the bounds of IU, George Pinnell served on the boards of directors of The Kroger Co., Central Soya Co. Inc., Public Service Indiana, and American Fletcher Mortgage Investors. He was a member of Acacia social fraternity, and he was elected to many social and professional honorary societies including Beta Gamma Sigma, Beta Alpha Psi, Sigma Iota Epsilon, Alpha Kappa Psi, and Pi Alpha Alpha.

Other outside service included work on Evan Bayh's transition team when Bayh became governor, as well as earlier work on President-elect John F. Kennedy's Committee on Area Redevelopment. In 1959 he was part of Governor Matthew Welsh's 15-member Manpower Advisory Committee that worked with the Indiana Employment Security Division and the State Division of Vocational Education. In 1961 he was research director of the Indiana Post-High School Study Commission, whose work culminated in the formation of Ivy Tech (Indiana Vocational Technical College).

George Pinnell's dedication and service to the university were deeply appreciated and widely recognized. In 1987 President Ryan presented Pinnell with the President's Medal for Excellence, and in 1991 the IU Alumni Association honored him with the IU Distinguished Alumni Service Award. In 1988 when the University Faculty Council wished to establish an annual award to recognize faculty members and librarians who have shown exceptional breadth of involvement in service to the university, to their profession, or to the public, the faculty council voted to designate that award the W. George Pinnell Award for Outstanding Service. This award is a worthy and fitting memorial for an outstanding IU administrator and concerned citizen, and the award's annual recipients carry on the legend of service instilled by its namesake.

W. George Pinnell passed away March 18, 1991. In the faculty council's memorial resolution, Danilo Orescanin recalled that for Pinnell, "quality is an elusive characteristic that cannot be commanded or even bought. In his view quality is attainable only by means of relentless pursuit and nurturing." ❧

ELIZABETH BLUMBERG
POLLEY
1910–1994

Trustee, 1980–1986

A SUCCESSFUL BUSINESSPERSON, talented artist, and dedicated supporter of the arts, Elizabeth "Betty" Blumberg Polley served Indiana University as a trustee for two consecutive terms.

Born in Columbus, Indiana, on July 16, 1910, Betty Polley began her college education at Indiana University Bloomington before spending two years at the Herron School of Art and Design in Indianapolis en route to earning a BS in education from IU in 1931. She spent one summer at the Art Institute of Chicago and returned to IU to obtain an MS in 1938 and an EdD in 1952, both in education. Her academic interests were in general education with foci in art, music, theatre, philosophy, and psychology. As a student, she was involved in Chi Omega Sorority and Alpha Psi Omega dramatic club honorary. In the fall of 1965, Betty married Ben Blumberg (deceased 1971) and helped to raise four stepchildren. In 1982, Betty married Dr. Howard F. Polley of the Mayo Clinic and gained three stepchildren through that marriage.

Betty Polley began her career as an art instructor and supervisor at Indiana Central College (now the University of Indianapolis) immediately after completing her undergraduate degree. She then worked as chairman of the Art Department at Manual Training High School in Indianapolis. While there, Polley was also a part-time reporter and feature writer for the *Indianapolis News*. In 1950, two years away from finishing her EdD, Polley became associate professor of art at Indiana State University, a position she held for fifteen years. Her specialty was calligraphy, a beautiful art that required a delicate hand and an eye for aesthetics. After her first husband's death in 1971, she became the owner of Blumberg Farms; she also took over as vice president of the 624 Corporation and the Progress Building Corporation.

Betty Polley was extensively involved on the boards of many local, state, and national organizations. She served on the executive committee for the Red Cross, Wabash Valley Chapter; the board of directors for the Women's Department Club of Terre Haute; as a chamber member for Indiana Advocates for the Arts; as a member of the state curriculum advisory committee for Vincennes University; as a member of the Metropolitan Opera National Council; and as a member of the National Education Association. Polley received many awards and honors throughout her lifetime. She was an honorary speaker for the Indiana House of Representatives in 1978 and she represented the

United States in a three-country exhibition of artistic official documents at Buckingham Palace.

Polley was appointed to the Indiana University Board of Trustees in 1980. As a trustee, a professor, and a community volunteer, Polley's support dramatically advanced the arts at Indiana University and in the greater community. In 1976, she underwrote an Indiana University Opera Theater production of *Porgy and Bess* that toured in Terre Haute. Her dedication to the arts and her service to Indiana University were honored by President Thomas Ehrlich with the President's Medal for Excellence in 1988. To honor her substantial support for the IU Recital Hall and Music Library, a free performance of Mozart's *Symphony No. 41 in C Major, K. 551* (*Jupiter*) and Verdi's *Quattro Pezzi Sacri* was held after her death on January 17, 1994. ✺

LEON RAND

1930–

Chancellor, IU Southeast,
1986–1996

CHEMISTRY PROFESSOR, university administrator, and art museum docent Leon Rand served as chancellor of Indiana University Southeast for ten years.

Born in Boston, Massachusetts, on October 8, 1930, Leon Rand was the son of Max B. and Ricka (Muscanto) Rakisky. He received his bachelor's degree in chemistry from Northeastern University in 1953 before earning an MA (1956) and a PhD (1958) in organic chemistry from the University of Texas at Austin. During 1958 and 1959, Rand was a postdoctoral fellow in the department of chemistry at Purdue University.

After serving as instructor of chemistry at Southern State College in Magnolia, Arkansas, Rand moved to the University of Detroit, where he taught first as assistant professor and then as professor (1959–1968). He moved to Youngstown State University, where he was professor of chemistry from 1968 to 1981. Rand began his administrative career as chairman of the Department of Chemistry (1968–1978) before becoming dean of graduate studies and research (1974–1981) and acting academic vice president in 1980. Rand then accepted a position as the vice chancellor for academic affairs at the University of North Carolina at Pembroke (1981–1986).

In January 1986, Leon Rand became the chancellor of Indiana University Southeast. His tenure as chancellor marked a time of campus and academic growth. Rand was known for operating an open-door policy when it came to students. During his tenure, enrollment increased by 40 percent and the budget increased by 100 percent. An MBA program was added to the academic offerings, and more than $9 million in funds for scholarships and capital projects were raised. Numerous building projects were completed, including McCullough Plaza, Knobview Hall (1992), and the Paul W. Ogle Cultural and Community Center (1996), a complex which holds four indoor theaters, one amphitheater, and a popular art gallery.

In recognition of Rand's service and accomplishments at IU, President Thomas Ehrlich awarded him the Thomas Hart Benton Mural Medallion in 1994. Upon his retirement in 1996, Rand received the title chancellor emeritus. Among the honors he has received are: Outstanding Alumni Award from Northeastern University, Sagamore of the Wabash from the Governor of Indiana, Indiana Senate Certificate of Achievement, and Kentucky Colonel from the Governor of Kentucky. In retirement, Rand did not get too far from Indiana University, serving two years as special assistant to the chancellor at IUPUI.

Throughout the years, Rand has been involved with numerous professional and community organizations. He has been an active member of the American Chemical Society since 1950 and was active in the American Association of State Colleges and Universities for many years. While chancellor, he was also involved in many community organizations such as the Southern Indiana Chamber of Commerce, the Kentuckiana Metroversity, the United Way of Clark County, the Jewish Hospital in Louisville, the American Red Cross Louisville Area Chapter, and the Boy Scouts of America George Rogers Clark Area Council Advisory Board. His commitment to service has continued through his retirement years. Among other activities, he served as a board member of the Senior Academy at IUPUI until 2012. He has been an active docent for the Indianapolis Museum of Art since 1999.

Leon Rand married Marian Newton and together they have three children—Debra, Paul, and Marta—and eight grandchildren. Leon and Marian shared a love of classical music, the theater, long walks, and reading, with Leon a particular fan of mystery novels. Marian passed away in November 2012. ꗭ

Una Mae Reck
1946–

Chancellor, IU South Bend,
2002–2013

DILIGENT, TENACIOUS, AND PASSIONATE, Una Mae Reck was the first woman to serve as chancellor of Indiana University South Bend, retiring after an eleven-year tenure at the helm of IU's northernmost regional campus.

Una Mae Reck was born on November 22, 1946, in Houston, Texas, the first of three daughters raised by Ora Nell Lenert and Leon Henry Lange. Throughout her childhood, Reck's parents always stressed the importance of higher education and made sure that she became the first member of her family to attend college. Reck began her studies at the University of Houston but transferred to the District of Columbia Teacher's College in Washington, D.C., where she received a BA in elementary education in 1968. She then went on to earn an MA in reading from the Federal City College in Washington, D.C. (1972), and an EdD in curriculum and teaching from the University of North Carolina at Greensboro (1978).

Never forgetting her parents' lessons, Reck used her passion for education to benefit the lives of others, both as a teacher and an administrator. From 1968 to 1972, Reck taught first-graders in the inner-city Model School District of Washington, D.C., during the tumultuous period that followed the assassination of Dr. Martin Luther King Jr. From 1972 to 1979, Reck taught remedial and gifted elementary school children in the Appalachian Mountains of Boone, North Carolina. From 1979 to 1991, she worked as assistant dean, associate dean, and professor at the Reich College of Education at Appalachian State University, before becoming the dean of education at Kutztown University in Pennsylvania (1991–1998). In 1998, Reck became vice president of academic affairs at SUNY Fredonia, where she was the chief academic officer as well as, in the president's absence, chief executive officer.

In 2002, Una Mae Reck became fourth chancellor of Indiana University South Bend, and the first woman to hold that position at IUSB. As chancellor, Reck implemented what she referred to as "the parameters of engagement" on the South Bend campus: "communication, teamwork, integrity, respectability, and commitment." At the time of her retirement in 2013, she was credited with establishing the IU South Bend Elkhart Center, River Crossing student apartments (the first on-campus student housing at IU South Bend or any regional campus of Indiana University), a pedestrian bridge over the St. Joseph River,

IU South Bend's Center for a Sustainable Future, renovations to the Administration Building, the opening of the Civil Rights Heritage Center in the former city natatorium, and completion of the long-awaited Education and Arts Building.

At the retirement celebration held in her honor, Reck was named chancellor emerita, received the IU President's Medal for Excellence from Michael McRobbie, and was awarded a Sagamore of the Wabash from Governor Mike Pence. She was honored in 2012 by the YWCA North Central Indiana Tribute to Women as "Woman of the Year" for her accomplishments at IU South Bend.

Reck has been a member of numerous associations, councils, and organizations, including the American Association of State Colleges and Universities (AASCU), Council of Higher Education Accreditation (CHEA), National Association for Intercollegiate Athletics (NAIA), American Association of University Women, American Educational Research Association, Association of Teacher Educators, Delta Kappa Gamma Society, Phi Delta Kappa, Phi Kappa Phi, and the Association of Supervision and Curriculum Development. Reck has also served on the Memorial Hospital System Board, the South Bend Symphony Orchestra Board, the South Bend Regional Museum of Art Board, the St. Joseph County Chamber of Commerce Board, the Project Future Board, Northern Indiana Workforce Development Board, Indiana Campus Compact Board, Madison Center Hospital Board, Elkhart County Chamber of Commerce, and the Boys & Girls Club Board.

Reck has an avid interest in outdoor sports, particularly golf and tennis, and loves to spend time with her daughter, Alex, and her granddaughters, all of whom live in Bermuda. Reck and her dogs could often be seen jogging through campus at any hour of the day. ❧

Thomas E. Reilly Jr.
1939–

Trustee, 2005–2014

ALTHOUGH PASSIONATE ABOUT public higher education in Indiana, trustee "Tom Jr.," as he was known at Reilly Industries, Inc. (to distinguish him from his father), was educated at private universities and managed a global corporation.

Thomas Edward Reilly Jr. was born on December 31, 1939, in Indianapolis, Indiana. Growing up in Indianapolis, he attended Shortridge High School and played basketball. Since Reilly is a tall man, the story may even be true that he held Oscar "The Big O" Robertson to only 50 points while guarding him in a game! Reilly earned a BS in economics from Stanford University in 1961 and an MBA from Harvard University in 1963. Although his education prepared him intellectually to handle the challenges of global business, he believed that personality and character are the key attributes for a successful business career, because cultivating relationships required a person to spend significant time with the customer, supplier, or potential business partner.

After graduating from Harvard, Reilly joined the family business at Reilly Industries, Inc. After holding a number of positions in sales and new product development, Reilly became vice president and general manager of the Chemical Group in 1974. By 1981, he had assumed the presidency and developed a global strategy, implemented modern business processes, and diversified company operations by acquiring specialty chemical manufacturers. He transformed a basic old-line business—which included coal tar refining, creosoting, and chemicals—into a global leader in pyridine chemistry and added additional specialty chemical businesses to the company's portfolio. Under his leadership, the company acquired a West Virginia-based natural gas company (TREK), a brine operation in Utah, and a specialty chemical manufacturer in North Carolina (Morflex). He entered into the Vitachem joint venture with German chemical company Degussa and entered the MRM Toluic Company joint venture with Mitsubishi Gas Chemicals of Japan. In 2001, when the company's largest customer decided to build a plant in Nantong, China, Reilly agreed to invest millions of dollars to build the manufacturing plant to preserve the customer relationship and to expand the company's business in China. In typical Reilly fashion, the plant was completed on time, on budget, and was profitable. In 2006, Reilly Industries merged with Rutherford Chemicals to form Vertellus, and the company continued to expand internationally, acquiring businesses in India and the UK. As CEO, Reilly enjoyed mentoring talented young engineers, accountants, and business executives.

Tom Reilly's devotion to education began decades ago when he served on the board of directors for the school his children attended, Park Tudor School, and then as a trustee for Butler University. His conviction that education in Indiana needed to be transformed for the state to move forward lead him to chair the Subcommittee on Higher Education for the Indiana Government Efficiency Commission. The subcommittee reviewed Hoosier higher education and decided the state's economy depended on major changes in the entire system's organization. The *Report of the Subcommittee on Higher Education* issued in November 2004 became the strategic outline for many higher education reforms in Indiana. Tom Reilly once asked if anyone at Reilly Industries personally knew the president at Indiana University because he wanted to have a conversation about the role IU needed to play to better prepare students for jobs in the twenty-first century. In 2005, Reilly was appointed to the Board of Trustees at Indiana University and served three terms (2005–2014). As a trustee, Reilly advocated for innovative approaches to education in the State of Indiana and particularly at Indiana University. After retiring from the Board of Trustees, Reilly was appointed to the Dean's Council, the advisory board for the School of Public and Environmental Affairs (SPEA) and actively participates in many IU activities.

Reilly's leadership and ability to negotiate complex business deals in many countries brought him to the forefront of the U.S. chemical industry. He became president of the American Chemistry Council, a leading U.S. chemical industry trade association. In 2004, the Society of the Chemical Industry awarded Reilly the chemical industry's highest honor, the Chemical Industry Medal. In 1987, Governor Robert Orr awarded Reilly the Sagamore of the Wabash, the highest civilian honor in the State of Indiana.

In addition to numerous corporate boards (BDP International Corp., OneAmerica Corp., Herff Jones, Inc., Methodist Medical Group, Lilly Industries, Inc. and Bank One Corp.), Tom Reilly has also served on the boards of many community organizations such as the Indianapolis Children's Museum, the Indianapolis Zoological Society, and Crooked Stick Golf Club.

Reilly and his wife, Bonnie (Atchison), married on December 28, 1962.

When asked how he met a woman from Billings, Montana, Tom responded in his typical storytelling style: "A good friend of mine at Stanford went to Harvard Law School. I went to the business school. He was dating a law student who was working with Bonnie in the home of Professor Arthur Sutherland. He had an invalid mother-in-law who drank sherry and smoked Chesterfields. The two girls were there around the clock to keep her from all sorts of trouble. My friend called me and had me come over to meet Bonnie. I courted her about half of the time we were together in this creaky three-story house while Bonnie baby-sat the old lady." Together, the Reillys have two children, Nelson and Heather, and six grandchildren. ᴄ᷍ᴖ

DERICA W. RICE
1965–

AN INTERNATIONAL EXECUTIVE at Eli Lilly and Company and president of CVS Caremark, Derica Rice has given back to the State of Indiana through his dedicated service.

Born in Decatur, Alabama, on February 21, 1965, Derica W. Rice was one of seven children born to King and Inez Rice. Graduating second in his high school class, he was the first member of his family to attend college. Rice received an academic scholarship to attend Kettering University (formerly the GMI Engineering & Management Institute), where he received a BS in electrical engineering in 1988. Unsure of a career in engineering, Rice decided to continue his education at IU Bloomington, where he earned an MBA in finance from the IU School of Business in 1990 (later renamed the Kelley School of Business).

Shortly after graduation, Derica Rice joined Eli Lilly as an international treasury associate in the finance department. The presence of insulin vials in his mother's refrigerator may have been the determining factor in convincing Rice to accept a position at Lilly. Coming to the realization that the drug company may have given his mother, a type II diabetic, an additional twenty-five years with her family, Rice embarked on what would ultimately become a long and notable career with the Indianapolis pharmaceutical giant.

From 1990 to 1995, Rice held various positions as a sales representative, manager of global financial planning and analysis for the medical devices division, and global planning manager for pharmaceuticals. In 1995, he became finance director and chief financial officer for Lilly Canada. In 1997, he was promoted to executive director and chief financial officer for European operations based in London. From 2000 to 2003, Rice served as the general manager of Lilly operations in the United Kingdom and the Republic of Ireland. Continuing his rise in the company, he was promoted in 2003 to vice president and controller and served in that capacity until May of 2006, at which point he became chief financial officer of Eli Lilly and Company. In 2010, Rice acquired the additional title executive vice president of global services. In 2018, Rice left Lilly to accept the position of president at CVS Caremark, CVS Health Corporation's pharmacy benefit management business.

Derica Rice was first appointed to the Indiana University Board of Trustees by Governor Mitch Daniels in 2007 and reappointed by Governor Mike Pence. As an IU trustee, Rice served as chair of the

Finance and Audit Committee. He involved himself most with student affordability initiatives, facility modernization efforts, diversity initiatives, and curriculum oversight. In addition, Rice has served on the Board of Advisors of Indiana University–Purdue University Indianapolis since 2007. He chaired the IU Trustees' Health Affairs Committee and served as the trustee liaison to IUPUI and on the IU Kokomo Advisory Council.

Rice is a member of the boards of directors for Target Corporation and the Center for Leadership Development, as well as a previous member of the board of IU Health North and the Board of Governors of the Indianapolis Museum of Art.

The recipient of many honors, Derica W. Rice was named a Kelley School of Business Academy of Alumni Fellow in 2008. Selected as one of the "Most Powerful Executives in Corporate America" by *Black Enterprise Magazine* in 2009, Rice was also honored as one of *Diversity MBA Magazine*'s "Top 100 Under 50 Executives."

Derica W. Rice met his wife, Robin Nelson-Rice (BS 1987, MBA 1990), quite by serendipity during his orientation at IU. Mistaking his first name for a woman's, Residential Life staff assigned Rice to an all-female dorm suite, where he struck up a friendship with one of his suitemates. That friendship blossomed into romance and the couple married several years later. They have three sons, Solomon and twins Malachi and Isaiah. ⌘

HILDA RICHARDS
1936–

Chancellor, IU Northwest,
1993–1999

Her appointment as the first African American woman to serve as a chancellor at IU was only one of many pioneering firsts in Hilda Richards' career. Richards served as chancellor of Indiana University Northwest from 1993 to 1999.

Born in Missouri, Richards was raised by her supportive mother, Rose Avalynne Young, and her stepfather, Willis Young, after her father, Togar Ballard, died when she was six years old. Richards graduated cum laude from Hunter College with a BS in nursing education in 1961, and earned an MEd in curriculum and instruction and psychiatric nursing from Columbia University in 1965. She received an MPA in health administration from New York University in 1971, before returning to Columbia to pursue an EdD, which she completed 1976. She also received a nursing diploma from St. John's School of Nursing. Following the completion of her doctorate, Richards was an American Council on Education Fellow and received a certificate from the Institute for Education Management from Harvard University.

Richards began her professional life as a staff nurse at Payne Whitney Clinic of New York Hospital in 1956, where she was among the first Black nurses on the staff. She became an instructor of nursing in the Department of Psychiatry at City Hospital in New York, where she became head nurse in the Department of Psychiatry. From 1971 to 1976, while working on her PhD, she was director of nursing programs and chair of the Health Science Division at Medgar Evers College in New York City during the early days of that college's development. She then served for three years as associate dean of academic affairs for Medgar Evers College before she was appointed as the founding dean of the College of Health and Human Services at Ohio University (1979–1986). Richards moved to Indiana University of Pennsylvania from 1986 to 1993 as provost and vice president for academic affairs before coming to IU Northwest in 1993 as chancellor, succeeding Acting Chancellor Lloyd A. Rowe and Chancellor Peggy Gordon Elliott Miller.

The hallmark of Richards' tenure at IU Northwest was her ability to bridge relationships between the campus and the community. In consideration of the city's racial tensions at the time, Richards worked to build stronger relationships between the university and the community by focusing on the recruitment and retention of diverse faculty and students as well as by expanding students' educational and social opportunities.

Examples of this work include the Division of Nursing collaboration with the East Chicago Health Department and a total quality management project with the City of Gary. Richards oversaw upgrades to physical facilities and grounds, including the construction of a new academic/ activities building that housed the women's center, gymnasium, art gallery, and first campus computer center. Richards paid particular attention to nontraditional students and focused on issues of access, retention, and degree attainment across the eight community outreach sites operated by IUN throughout Northwest Indiana.

After her tenure at IUN, she served from 1999 to 2003 as president of the National Black Nurses Association (NBNA) in Washington, D.C., and then as immediate past president and conference coordinator from 2003 to 2007. She has been an active member of the NBNA since 1973, a national board member since 1974, the first vice president in 1984, and parliamentarian in 1998.

She has been active with the Men and Women for Prison Ministry organization, the National Coalition of Ethnic Minority Nurses Association, Inc., the AIDS Foundation of Chicago, and the Gary Educational Foundation. She also holds or has held memberships in Sigma Theta Tau, the international honor society of nursing, the American Nurses Association, the American Academy of Nursing, and the NAACP. She has volunteered with The Art Institute of Chicago, Horizon Hospice, as well as with the Northwestern University Memorial Hospital.

Richards has been the recipient of an honorary doctorate from Medgar Evers College (2005), a Living Treasure Award from The Virginia Satir Global Network (2006), was inducted into the Nursing Education Alumni Association Hall of Fame at Teachers College Columbia University (2001), and was inducted into the Institute of Excellence of the National Black Nurses Association (2006). Richards received the *Black Opinion Magazine* 1989 Achiever Award and was recognized for her Excellence in Leadership by the Chicago Chapter of the National Black Nurses Association (2007). She was featured in *Ebony Magazine*'s "100-Plus Most Influential Black Americans" yearly from 1999 to 2003.

Richards is the American mother of an Ethiopian woman, whom she supported through college, and grandmother to her two children. Richards also has a godson who is an honors alumnus from Harvard University. ᴄ᷂ᴸᴸ

LAURENCE D. RICHARDS
1946–

Chancellor (Interim), IU East,
2012–2013

PROFESSOR, ADMINISTRATOR, AND CIVIC LEADER Laurence Richards' work in higher education has spanned four decades including twelve years at IU.

The eldest of five siblings, Laurence "Larry" D. Richards was born in Michigan in 1946 to parents Kathryn (a special-needs teacher) and Charles (a professor of botany). His father gained some notoriety for the garden he designed and maintained on Great Wars Island, Maine. Richards grew up in Maine, attending public schools in the town of Orono, where he was a three-sport varsity athlete in high school, lettering in baseball, basketball, and football. He continued playing football at the University of Maine, graduating with a BS in electrical engineering (1968). He went on to earn an MS in aeronautical systems from the University of West Florida (1970), an MBA from Mississippi State University (1974), and a PhD in operations research from the Wharton School of Business at the University of Pennsylvania (1980). In between degrees, Richards served in the U.S. Marines as a pilot and flight instructor (1968–1974), earning the award of Naval Aviator in 1970.

After completing his PhD, Richards began a career as a university professor and higher education administrator. He began at La Salle University (1978–1979) before joining Colby College (1980–1984). He moved to Old Dominion University in Virginia (1984–1997), where he became the founding chair of the newly created Department of Engineering Management as well as the first executive director of the Center for Commercial Space Infrastructure, which by 1995 was the operating agent for Virginia's new Commercial Space Flight Authority and Mid-Atlantic Regional Spaceport on Wallops Island. He then moved to Massachusetts to accept a position at Bridgewater State University, where he served as the founding dean of the School of Management and Aviation Science (1997–2014). During this period he also served as acting vice president for academic affairs (2000–2002).

In 2004, Laurence Richards joined Indiana University as the executive vice chancellor for academic affairs and professor of management and informatics at IU East (2004–2015). During this period, Richards took on the responsibilities for enrollment services and dean of students (2008–2015), and also served as interim chancellor of IU East (2012–2013). While at IU East, Richards led the development of new graduate programs and the development of IU East Online. He then served as interim vice chancellor and dean of Indiana University–Purdue University Columbus (2015–2016) before retiring as professor emeritus of management and informatics in 2016.

Beyond Indiana University, Richards has served in several professional and civic organizations. He was a member of the American Society for Cybernetics (president, 1986–1988) and the American Society for Engineering Management (president, 1998–1999). He served on the Board of Aviation Commissioners in Richmond, Indiana (2009–2015, president 2013–2015). He also served as a trustee for Ivy Tech Community College's Richmond Regional Board of Trustees (2011–2015).

Richards has been honored as a Fellow of the American Society for Engineering Management (2002), awarded the Norbert Wiener Medal from the American Society for Cybernetics (2007), and named an Academician of the International Academy for the Systems and Cybernetics Sciences (2013).

In 1969, Laurence Richards married his wife, Jane, a mathematics teacher, and together they raised two boys, Douglas and Gregory. ᨑ

F. C. RICHARDSON
1936–

Chancellor, IU Southeast,
1996–2002

BOTANY SCHOLAR AND UNIVERSITY ADMINISTRATOR F. C. Richardson served IU in two different periods, first as both a professor and a dean at IU Northwest (1967–1984) and later as the third chancellor of IU Southeast (1996–2002).

Born in Whitehaven, Tennessee, F. C. Richardson was the sixth of eight siblings raised by Rich and Lillian Richardson, a minister and a housewife, respectively. Early on, his family instilled in him the importance of education, and Richardson became the first member of his family to attend college. He studied at Rust College (Holly Springs, Mississippi), funded by a singing scholarship (he had sung with the glee club in high school). He was soon recruited to play first-string guard for the basketball team, which earned him an athletics scholarship that covered the second half of his degree. After receiving a BS in biology in 1960, Richardson served in the U.S. Army, receiving an honorable discharge in 1963. He then attended Atlanta University (now Clark Atlanta University), earning an MA in biology with highest honors in 1964. At the insistence of an encouraging professor, Richardson went on to earn a PhD in botany from the University of California, Santa Barbara, in 1967.

F. C. Richardson first joined Indiana University in 1967 as assistant professor of botany at IU Northwest, where he worked until 1984. During this time, he rose in rank and responsibilities, becoming associate professor (1971–1982), chair of the department of biology (1971–1972), dean of the College of Arts and Sciences (1972–1984), and professor of botany (1982–1984). He then left Indiana for twelve years to take several teaching and administrative positions at other institutions. From 1984 to 1985, he worked at Jackson State University as professor of biology and vice president for academic affairs. From 1985 to 1989, he worked as vice president for academic affairs at Moorhead State University. From 1989 to 1996 he was president of Buffalo State College as well as professor of biology.

In July 1996, Richardson returned to Indiana as professor of biology in the Division of Natural Sciences (now the School of Natural Sciences) and chancellor of Indiana University Southeast. He was given the additional title of chancellor liaison, Office of the President, in 1999. Under his leadership, IU Southeast's enrollment reached a new high, and he successfully increased the number of full-time faculty by 21 percent. Richardson also created the Quality Services Initiative to provide students with efficient and effective support services. He oversaw the expansion and renovation of the Life Sciences Building and initiated planning for a new library. He also completed a three-year, $15 million capital campaign and increased institutional endowments by over 500 percent, in addition to securing state funding more than $20 million. He improved access for minority students and increased minority enroll-ment by 67 percent. His continuous quality improvement program ulti-mately changed the culture of the campus, improving both institutional and student academic performance. Although he officially retired in 2002 with the titles chancellor emeritus and professor emeritus of biol-ogy, Richardson continued to be involved with IU, and served on the IU Northwest Board of Advisors from 2011 to 2014.

Richardson has served on numerous boards and councils, including the Louisville Area Workforce Development Council, the New Albany Rotary Club, the Negro Educational Review, the Botanical Society of America, the Southern Indiana Chamber of Commerce, the Louisville Ballet, the Lincoln Heritage Council for the Boy Scouts of America, the Kentuckiana Metroversity, the DeHaan Family Foundation Project, the American Council on Education, and the Greater Louisville Health Enterprises Network. He has also served on the board of trustees of Rust College (Holly Spring, Mississippi) and on the board of directors of Methodist Hospitals of Gary, Indiana. He was a founding president and Executive Steering Committee member (1999–2013) of the Millennium Leadership Initiative within the American Association of State Colleges and Universities, designed to prepare underrepresented minorities and women for college presidencies.

Over the years, Richardson has been recognized with several hon-ors, including the President's Medal for Excellence in service to Indiana University (2002) and being named a senior fellow by the American Association of State Colleges and Universities (1996), as well as receiv-ing a National Science Foundation Graduate Fellowship (1965–1966) and a University Doctoral Fellowship from the University of California (1966–1967). He is the author of various scholarly works, including arti-cles on the power of literacy education, the culture of academic institu-tions, and American educational reform.

Richardson is married to Bernice, a former teacher and principal, with whom he has three children: Darrell, Ramonica, and Melvin. ❧

R. RAY RICHARDSON
1937–

Trustee, 1992–2001

ATTORNEY AND CIVIC LEADER Ray Richardson has spent his entire life in service to the people of Indiana and Indiana University.

An Indiana native, Robert Ray Richardson was born July 13, 1937, in Logansport to Frances Richardson Steele and Robert Richardson. He received a BS in political science from Purdue University in 1959, and a law degree from the IU School of Law in 1962 (now the IU Maurer School of Law). While at IU, he was a member of the IU Student Senate. He is a senior life member of the Indiana Bar Association. Richardson worked as an attorney for a private practice in Greenfield, Indiana, where he has been a county attorney from 1969 through 2017.

Richardson served for nine years on the Indiana University Board of Trustees, elected to three terms by the alumni of Indiana University. As a trustee, Richardson served as chairman of the Trustees' Committee on University Policies, and in addition, served on President Myles Brand's Strategic Directions Steering Committee and on the trustees' Campus and Community committee. Richardson, described as a studious trustee, advanced several initiatives during his service to Indiana University. At his request, all chancellors devised and implemented methods to improve graduation rates, which resulted in a wide variety of tutoring opportunities and a restructuring of the freshman math course. Awards to faculty for teaching were expanded and emphasized. For the first time at Bloomington, faculty members could obtain tenure based primarily on their teaching ability. At all campuses except Bloomington, hundreds of full-time, non-tenure-track faculty members were hired to replace large numbers of part-time instructors.

Richardson committed himself to serving his Indiana communities beyond IU. He was a member of the Indiana House of Representatives from 1966 to 1990. He was a member of the American Judicature Society and a former volunteer division chairman with the American Heart Association, the American Cancer Society, and United Way. He is also the co-founder of the Hancock Hope House, a shelter in Greenfield, Indiana, serving homeless individuals and families. He is a fifty-year member of the Greenfield Kiwanis Club.

Ray Richardson is married to his wife, Paulette (BS 1984), and has two children, two stepchildren, and five grandchildren. Paulette was a housing development analyst for the Indiana Housing and Community Development Authority before her retirement in 1998. ᕙᕗ

LAUREN K. ROBEL
1953–

Executive Vice President and Provost,
IU Bloomington, 2012–

After coming to Indiana University as a law student in 1980, Lauren Robel became a law professor in 1985, associate dean of the law school in 1991, dean in 2003, and provost of Indiana University Bloomington in 2012.

Born in Omaha, Nebraska, in 1953, Lauren Robel lived in fifteen cities before graduating from high school due to her father's service with the United States Air Force. After he retired in his last duty station (Montgomery, Alabama), her father resumed his education, attending Auburn University alongside Robel and two of her three siblings. Robel earned a Bachelor of Arts degree in English Literature, completing an additional two years of graduate study in the field. Her first daughter, Anna, was born when Robel was an undergraduate. Robel first arrived in Bloomington as a law student in 1980. Despite entering law school as a single working mother, Robel graduated summa cum laude with a JD in 1983.

After graduation, Robel held a clerkship with the Honorable Jesse Eschbach in the Seventh Circuit Court of Appeals in Chicago. She and her husband, Stephen Thrasher (d. 2015), whom she married in 1983, welcomed their second daughter, Katie, during Robel's clerkship. Along with Stephen's son, Daniel, the family returned to Bloomington in 1985 to accept Robel's appointment as assistant professor in the IU School of Law (later renamed Maurer School of Law). With a focus on federal jurisdiction, Robel quickly earned acclaim for her courses on constitutional law and civil procedure and her research on federal procedure and the federal courts. She became associate professor in 1987 and a professor of law in 1990. The following year, she was appointed associate dean of the law school, a position she held until becoming dean in 2003. During her associate deanship, she was honored with the Val Nolan Chair in Law, endowed by IU Law alumnus and business leader Mickey Maurer (JD 1967) and named for his favorite professor.

After nearly ten years as dean of IU Bloomington's Maurer School of Law, Lauren Robel became provost of Indiana University Bloomington in 2012. Appointed by IU President Michael A. McRobbie, Robel took office as provost while simultaneously serving as president of the Association of American Law Schools. Among her chief responsibilities during her first year was implementing one of the largest academic transformations in IU Bloomington history: the recommendations of the

New Academic Directions report, which called for several new schools and interdisciplinary programs including global, online, and student success initiatives. Robel also worked closely with faculty and the university administration to shepherd the creation of the Hamilton Lugar School of Global and International Studies; transition of the School of Health, Physical Education, and Recreation to a School of Public Health; merging of the School of Library and Information Science with the School of Informatics and Computing (now the School of Informatics, Computing, and Engineering); creation of The Media School; evolution of the Hope School of Fine Arts into the School of Art, Architecture, and Design; and the creation of an Integrated Program in the Environment drawing on the strengths of several schools. In partnership with IUPUI Chancellor Charles Bantz and Vice President for International Affairs David Zaret, she also helped orchestrate the opening of IU's new international Gateway offices, which serve as a portal for Indiana University's academic and alumni activities in regions around the world. Robel was also a key figure in the development of IU Corps and the Center for Rural Engagement, which received a $10 million dollar grant from the Lilly Endowment.

Throughout her twenty-seven years at the law school, Robel continued to serve pro bono, often working with students, as appointed counsel in criminal, habeas, and civil rights cases for the Seventh Circuit Court of Appeals. She was also active in the Bloomington community, serving as chair of the Bloomington Human Rights Commission from 1986 to 1991; president for two years and then member of the Habitat for Humanity of Monroe County Board of Directors; and co-chair of the United Way Campaign for Indiana University from 2005 to 2007. ᴄᴈᴜ

JOHN W. RYAN
1929–2011

President, Indiana University, 1971–1987

THE FOURTEENTH PRESIDENT of Indiana University, John W. Ryan served the institution for over thirty years including sixteen as president, and was instrumental in the formal recognition of eight IU regional campuses. Even after his retirement, Ryan continued an active public role as a liaison, public speaker, and representative for IU.

Born on August 12, 1929, to Leonard John Ryan and Mary Maxine Mitchell, John William Ryan grew up in Chicago, Illinois, as one of six siblings, including a brother Leonard and sisters Patricia, Maureen, Mary, and Ellen. After graduating from high school, Ryan earned a BA from the University of Utah. In 1951, he came to Indiana University as a graduate student, earning an MA in political science. After working as a research analyst in the Department of Revenue for the Commonwealth of Kentucky from 1953 to 1955, he returned to IU to work on a PhD in public administration. During this time, he spent two years in Bangkok, Thailand, at Thammasat University as a visiting research fellow with Indiana University's international development initiative. He returned to the Bloomington campus, where he worked as assistant director of the Institute of Training for Public Service from 1957 to 1958, completing a PhD in political science in 1959. This international training was a formative experience that shaped the global perspective he maintained throughout his career.

Ryan began his administrative career at the University of Wisconsin as associate director of the Bureau of Government (1958–1962). Consistently seeking new challenges and professional growth, Ryan left Wisconsin to serve at several other universities before coming to IU. He held the position of professor of political science and also served as executive assistant to the president and university secretary at the University of Massachusetts, Amherst (1962–1963); vice president for academic affairs at Arizona State University (1963–1965); and finally chancellor at the University of Massachusetts, Boston (1965–1968)—the Boston campus's first ever chancellor. During these first ten years as an administrator, Ryan gained the practical leadership experience and the appreciation for regional campus missions that prepared him for the challenges of leading IU.

In 1968, John Ryan returned to Indiana University as vice president and chancellor for regional campuses. His familiarity with IU and his demonstrated administrative leadership skills led the trustees to appoint

Ryan as president of the university on January 26, 1971, after the sudden resignation of President Joseph L. Sutton. As president, Ryan reshaped the university in significant ways that continue to echo today. One change was the major administrative reorganization that he implemented in 1974, which recognized Bloomington and Indianapolis as the core campuses of IU. He also oversaw the creation of four new schools on the Bloomington campus: the Schools of Journalism (1974), Continuing Studies (1975), Optometry (1975), and Public and Environmental Affairs (1972). Highlights of his many additional accomplishments include the completion of the Indiana University Art Museum (now the Eskenazi Museum of Art), which was designed by architect I. M. Pei starting in 1973 and completed in 1982. Also completed in 1982 was the William Hammond Mathers Museum, and the razing of the Tenth Street Stadium. He was also instrumental in getting the Andrew Wylie House entered on the National Register of Historic Places (1977) as well as the Old Crescent buildings entered onto both the Indiana Register of Historic Places (1979) and the National Register of Historic Places (1980).

One hallmark of Ryan's administration was the formal recognition of the campuses at Fort Wayne, South Bend, Gary (IU Northwest), Kokomo, and Jeffersonville (IU Southeast)—elevating their status from extension centers to degree-granting campuses. Ryan also guided the development of the long-time cooperative program in Richmond into the university's sixth regional campus, IU East, and development of the relocated IU Southeast Campus in New Albany. In addition to developing IU's regional campuses, Ryan formalized the Office of International Affairs and led in IU's continuing focus as a global university.

In 1987, John Ryan retired with the titles president emeritus of Indiana University and professor emeritus of political science and of public and environmental affairs. In his final remarks as president, John Ryan quoted H. G. Wells: "It is possible to believe that all in the past is but a beginning of a beginning, and that all that is and has been is but the twilight of the dawn." That comment was prophetic. Within a matter of months after retiring as IU President, John Ryan began another career of service and leadership that brought both him and IU much acclaim. He served in interim roles as president at Florida Atlantic University and the University of Maryland at Baltimore, he spent two years at the Agency for International Development in Washington, D.C., and he served for four years as system chancellor of the State University of New York (1996–1999), which is the largest university system in the world. In 2004, SUNY established the John W. Ryan Fellowship in International Education, awarded annually to honor contributions to international education. Indiana University has also established a John W. Ryan Fellowship Fund within SPEA and the John W. Ryan Award for Distinguished Contributions to International Programs and Studies.

John Ryan received many awards in recognition of his outstanding service to the university, community, state, and the nation. He was a member of the Kappa Sigma social fraternity, who named him Kappa Sigma Man of the Year in 1975 and which dedicated a library at their national headquarters in his honor in 2017. He also was a member of Phi Kappa Phi, Phi Alpha Theta, Beta Gamma Sigma, and Pi Sigma Alpha honorary fraternities. In addition to sixteen honorary degrees, Ryan has received numerous awards and honors. Among them, he was named a Sagamore of the Wabash by Indiana Governors Otis Bowen and Robert Orr and received the Edmund F. Ball Award from the Indiana Public Broadcasting Society; Knight Commander (Second Class), Most Exalted Order of the White Elephant from the King of Thailand; Hungarian People's Republic Order of the Star; Knight Grand Cross, the Equestrian Order of the Holy Sepulcher of Jerusalem; Commander, Order of Merit, Polish People's Republic; Horatio Alger Award; and the Ellis Island Medal of Honor. In September 2009, IU President Michael A. McRobbie presented Ryan the University Medal, IU's highest award and the only medal that requires approval from the Board of Trustees. The university has also presented Ryan the Distinguished Alumni Service Award, the Thomas Hart Benton Mural Medallion, and an honorary doctorate.

John Ryan married D. Patricia "Pat" Ryan in 1949, and together they had three children: Kathleen Elynne Ryan Acker, Kevin Dennis Mitchell Ryan, and Kerrick C. Ryan. As first lady, Pat Ryan managed the planning and interior decorating for three houses, volunteered in the community, raised funds for the university, planned programs, and served as her husband's trusted confidante such that John is said to have considered her a "partner in the presidency." Pat not only served as first lady of IU, she did so while raising three teenagers and completing a BA in psychology and sociology at IUB (1979). Together Pat and John Ryan advanced the vision that Herman Wells created for a global university and they cultivated many programs and relationships around the world that are still bearing fruit today. Their leadership of the university is remembered as one that projected the warmth and collegial spirit of IU. Even after John stepped down as president, Pat Ryan served as a mentor and friend to those who followed in various university roles that called for outreach and friendships with leaders of Indiana.

John W. Ryan passed away in Bloomington, Indiana, on August 6, 2011, at the age of 81, with his loving family by his side. Pat still resides in Bloomington. ᴄᴇ᷎

MICHAEL M. SAMPLE
1952–

Vice President for Government Relations, 2018–

Vice President for Public Affairs
and Government Relations, 2007–2018

Vice President for University Relations, 2005–2007

V ICE PRESIDENT Michael M. Sample holds a BA in political science from Indiana University as well as a Certificate in Advanced Management from Oxford University's Templeton College in England. Prior to graduating from IU Bloomington in 1977, Michael Sample served in the U.S. Army from 1972 to 1974. He then worked for seven years as a special assistant to U.S. Representative Elwood H. (Bud) Hillis, splitting his time between Indiana and Washington, D.C. In 1983 he joined PSI Resources, the predecessor company to Cinergy Corp. and Duke Energy, where he initially served as the company's federal affairs representative in Washington, D.C., before being named vice president for government relations and corporate communications in 1986. He later became vice president for international business development at Cinergy and was responsible for initiating and developing international business ventures, including successful investments in South America and the United Kingdom.

Following the election of Mitch Daniels as governor of Indiana in 2004, Sample served on the gubernatorial transition team, focusing on utility regulation issues and chairing a committee to nominate candidates for commissioners of the Indiana Utility Regulatory Commission. Sample also served for one year (2003) as the executive director of Hoosier Voices for I-69, an advocacy group for construction of a new interstate highway between Evansville and Indianapolis.

Sample joined Indiana University in 2005 as vice president for university relations. After President Michael McRobbie reorganized the leadership structure in 2007, Sample became vice president for public affairs and government relations with responsibility for IU's governmental efforts at the state and federal levels as well as university-wide programs in marketing, internal and external communications, media relations, and other public outreach activities. After another administrative reorganization in 2018, Sample focused solely on government relations and in addition has served as director of the IU Center on Representative Government, which was founded in 1999 by former Congressman Lee Hamilton, who serves as its senior advisor.

Sample is married to Jhani Laupus, who has a degree in history from IU and a law degree from the Indiana University McKinney School of Law. Together, they have two sons, Andrew and James, both graduates of IU Bloomington. ☙

ROBERT B. SCHNABEL
1950–

Vice President for Research (Interim), 2009–2010

VICE PRESIDENT Robert B. "Bobby" Schnabel was born December 18, 1950, in Queens, New York, to Edith Bachert (an administrative assistant and community volunteer) and Bruno Schnabel (an accountant and business person). Both of his parents immigrated to the U.S. as young adults fleeing from the Nazis, his mother from Germany and his father from Austria. Bobby Schnabel was deeply influenced by his parents' journeys and by their stories of life before, during, and after WWI, and escaping the Nazis before WWII. He was also inspired by his great-aunt Hildegard Bachert, who in 2018, at age 97, is co-director of Galerie St. Etienne in New York City, a post she has held since 1978; and by his maternal grandparents, especially his grandmother Frieda Reis Bachert, who was a gifted amateur painter and who helped support the family with her sewing after arriving in the United States.

Growing up in Queens, Bobby Schnabel attended public schools PS 117, PS 217, and Jamaica High School. He attended Dartmouth College (1967–1971), graduating with a BA in mathematics, then Cornell University, earning an MS and a PhD in computer science (1973–1977). At Dartmouth, he served as manager of the football team and was inducted into Phi Beta Kappa. In between college and university, he served in the U.S. Army National Guard, and continued to serve part time until 1977.

Schnabel spent the first thirty years of his career at the University of Colorado at Boulder (1977–2007). He arrived as an assistant professor (1977–1980) and rose through the ranks from associate professor (1980–1988), receiving tenure in 1983, to professor (1988–2007). He served as department chair (1990–1995), associate dean for academic affairs in the College of Engineering (1995–1997), and vice provost for academic and campus technology and chief information officer (1998–2007). He was founding director (1997–2007) of the Alliance for Technology, Learning, and Society Institute, including the minor in technology, arts and media; the MS in technology, media, and society; and the PhD in technology, media, and society. He also co-founded the National Center for Women & Information Technology (NCWIT), a nonprofit chartered in 2004 through the National Science Foundation (NSF) and dedicated to increasing the participation of women in the field of computing.

Schnabel joined Indiana University as a professor of informatics and of computer science and as dean of the School of Informatics and

Computing (2007–2015) (now the School of Informatics, Computing, and Engineering), also serving as interim vice president for research (2009–2010). In that role, he formulated the structure of the Office of Research that laid the groundwork for the appointment of his successor, Jorge V. José. During Schnabel's tenure at IU, he oversaw the establishment of the BEST (Building Entrepreneurs in Software and Technology) program (2011), the merger of the School of Informatics with the School of Library and Information Science (2013), the establishment of the Data Science Program (2014), the establishment of the Intelligent Systems Engineering Program (2015), and the planning of Luddy Hall (2011–2015). Undergraduate enrollment in informatics at IU Bloomington tripled, while women undergraduate majors grew by a factor of four, graduate enrollment doubled, and funding tripled. Schnabel retired in 2015 as dean emeritus and professor emeritus.

From 2015 to 2017, Schnabel held the position of CEO at the Association for Computing Machinery (ACM) and since has been affiliated again with the University of Colorado at Boulder. He serves on the advisory committee for the NSF Directorate for Computer and Information Science and Engineering and on the board of code.org. In the past, Schnabel served as chair of the ACM Education Policy Committee; as chair of the advisory committee for the Computing Alliance of Hispanic Serving Institutions; and on the boards of the Kinsey Institute, TechPoint, and the Indiana University Research and Technology Corporation.

The most notable honors and awards received by Robert Schnabel include the Indiana University President's Medal (2015), TechPoint Trailblazer in Technology Award (2014), Computing Research Association A. Nico Habermann Award (2012, with Lucy Sanders and Telle Whitney), University of Colorado Boulder Faculty Service Award (1998), University of Colorado Boulder Faculty Teaching Award (1987), and the University of Colorado Teaching Recognition Award (1980). He was also named a White House "Champion of Change" for Women in STEM (2011), an ACM Fellow (2010), and a SIAM (Society for Industrial and Applied Mathematics) Fellow (2009).

Robert Schnabel married Edith (Edie) Stevenson on June 7, 1981. Together they have raised two adopted children born in South Korea: Heidi Schnabel and Cory Schnabel. ⌒❧

SUSAN SCIAME-GIESECKE
1954–

Chancellor, IU Kokomo, 2012–

PROFESSOR OF SPEECH COMMUNICATION and Chancellor Susan Sciame-Giesecke has been a constant presence at IU Kokomo for over forty years.

Susan Sciame-Giesecke was born in Rockford, Illinois, on October 17, 1954, to nurse Florence Nieciag and postman Lacy Sciame. Growing up, Susan was inspired by the strong women in her family. One example is her paternal grandmother, Frances, who immigrated to the United States from Italy on a ship, by herself, with a baby and unable to speak English, with only a note describing where to go once she landed in order to reunite with her husband, who had preceded her in order to establish a home. A second inspirational woman was her mother, Florence (one of seven siblings), whose own mother died when Florence was born, leaving Florence to be adopted by a neighbor. At the age of 18, Florence enrolled in a nursing program at St. Anthony's Hospital in Rockford, Illinois, leaving home with one suitcase and the goal of becoming a nurse.

Although her parents sent her to private schools for her early education (St. Bernadette's for elementary and Boylan Central Catholic for high school), Sciame-Giesecke later attended public institutions for her higher education. She earned an associate degree from Rock Valley Community College in Rockford, Illinois (1974), before attending Ball State University in Muncie, Indiana, to complete a BS in speech communication (1976). She then earned an MS in speech communication (1977) from Illinois State University in Bloomington, Illinois. During these years she was a member of the Speech Team (1972–1976). Approximately fifteen years later, she earned a PhD in speech communication (1995) from Indiana University Bloomington.

After graduating from Illinois State University, Sciame-Giesecke began her career in higher education as assistant professor of speech in the Division of Arts and Sciences at Indiana University Kokomo in 1977, rising to professor in 2013. Along the way, she also held many administrative positions. She served as chair of the Humanities Division (1998–2006), dean of arts and sciences (2001–2009), executive vice chancellor of academic affairs (2009–2012), interim vice chancellor of student affairs, and interim vice chancellor of administration and finance (2011). Some of the major accomplishments during these years include creating a theatre program (1977); a communication arts degree program (1984); a center for teaching excellence (1996); and a freshman learning community program that increased retention from 48 percent to 63 percent (1998). In 2008, she chaired the Higher Learning Commission reaffirmation of accreditation self-study. In addition, she served as director of the Indiana University Enhancing Minority Attainment Conference (2000–2008), director of the Indiana University Faculty Leadership Institute (1996–2002), and director of the FACET Retreat Planning Team.

In September 2012, Sciame-Giesecke was given the additional title of interim chancellor of Indiana University Kokomo, a position made permanent when she was appointed as IUK's seventh chancellor on April 15, 2014. During her tenure as chancellor, she facilitated an increase in enrollment and eleven new degree programs ranging from New Media Communication and Applied Sociology to Master of Nurse Practitioner and Master of Counseling. The campus added a new wellness and fitness center, gym, advising center, and a substantial amount of public art. The campus also completed a $14 million renovation of the major classroom building, a new outdoor courtyard, and a new art gallery in downtown Kokomo. Since 2012, Sciame-Giesecke has helped IU Kokomo raise nearly $11 million for scholarships, research, student travel, and other opportunities, including a gift of $1 million from IU alumna Kathleen Ligocki to establish the Kathleen Ligocki Scholars Program at IU Kokomo, and a bequest of $3.5 million from Chancellor Emerita Ruth J. Person, which is also to be used for student scholarships.

Beyond the university, Sciame-Giesecke has been active within several community and regional civic organizations. These have included serving as chair of the Family Services Association Board of Directors (responsible for the domestic violence shelter and homeless veterans shelter), chair of the Greater Kokomo Economic Development Alliance (responsible for the Chamber of Commerce, Visitors Bureau, Economic Development Council, Inventrek New Business Incubator, and the Downtown Association), board member of the North Central Regional Partnership; national board member of the University Economic Development Association, director of the Regional Leadership Institute, president of Altrusa, Rotary member, and chair of the Howard County Women's Network.

For her contributions to the university, community, and the State of Indiana, Sciame-Giesecke has been recognized with the Sagamore of the Wabash (2014), Kokomo Chamber of Commerce Athena Award for Outstanding Community Service (2010), Indiana University Kokomo Alumni Association Distinguished Service Award (2007), IU Kokomo Martin Luther King Leadership Award (2003), John L. Blackburn Award for Outstanding Administrative Model (2003), Teaching Excellence Recognition Award (1997), FACET Teaching Award (1991), and inclusion in the Rock Valley Community College Alumni Hall of Fame (2007).

Susan Sciame married Daniel Giesecke on August 17, 1985, and together they have two children: Lindsey and Lauren. ⌒✿⌣

JOHN A. SEJDINAJ
1959–

Vice President and Chief Financial Officer,
2016–

Vice President John Sejdinaj built his career in finance, first in banking and then at the University of Notre Dame before joining Indiana University.

Born in Oak Park, Illinois, on March 25, 1959, to Irene Rant (anesthesiologist) and Isa Sejdinaj (cardiovascular and general surgeon), John A. Sejdinaj grew up in an immigrant household to parents who came to the United States in 1951. Sejdinaj attended private schools in Elgin, Illinois (St. Thomas More Elementary and St. Edward High School). He earned a BA from the University of Notre Dame (1981) followed by an MBA from DePaul University (1984). As an undergraduate he was active in the Glee Club.

For the first nine years of his career in finance (1985–1994), Sejdinaj worked at the First National Bank of Chicago. He began as operations officer in the Trading Products Group before rising to the position of vice president in the Public Banking Department. His next move was a return to his alma mater, Notre Dame, where he worked from 1994–2016. Sejdinaj joined Notre Dame as director of fixed income and cash management (1994–1996). He became director of budget and planning (1996–1999) and then simultaneously took on the position of assistant vice president for finance (1999–2002). In this capacity he not only coordinated the university's annual operating budget but prepared the university's capital plan, coordinated all debt issuance, and organized the Office of Student Financial Services. From 2003 to 2016 Sejdinaj served as vice president for finance, overseeing all financial aspects of the university aside from investments, which included the Controller's Group, the Office of Budget and Financial Planning, and the Office of Treasury Services.

In 2016, John Sejdinaj joined Indiana University as vice president and chief financial officer, succeeding MaryFrances McCourt and relieving Joan Hagen, associate vice president and university controller, who had served as acting CFO during a three-month interim period. As vice president and CFO, Sejdinaj oversees the budgetary and financial management for IU's statewide network of campuses and sites. In his early tenure, Sejdinaj implemented reviews of IU's human resources operations, the Responsibility Center Management budgeting model, and the reduction of administrative burdens on faculty and staff. One of the first challenges he faced at IU was to rectify a nearly $70 million budgetary shortfall projected for fiscal year 2021. In collaboration with the Office of the Vice President for Information Technology and Chief Information Officer, in 2017 Sejdinaj initiated Project Recharge, an overhaul of the university's financial systems to improve user experience, add new functionality, and modernize IU's financial and purchasing applications.

Over the years, Sejdinaj has served on numerous community organization boards. Some of these include the Tuition Plan Consortium (board chair), Fischoff National Chamber Music Association (board president), South Bend Center for the Homeless (board treasurer), Sisters of Saint Francis (Investment Committee), Saint Joseph Regional Medical Center (integrated Finance Committee), Alliance for Catholic Education (Advisory Board), Logan Center (board treasurer), Innovation Park at Notre Dame (board treasurer), St. Adalbert Parish (Finance Committee), and University of Note Dame England (Advisory Board).

John and Jennifer Sejdinaj married in 1986. Their son, Alexander, graduated from the IU Jacobs School of Music in 2011.

JANET C. SHIRLEY
1934–

Secretary of the Board, 1988–1990

Secretary of the IU Board of Trustees Janet Shirley's long relationship with IU dates from her time as an undergraduate in the 1950s to the authorship of her book on the IU Alumni Association (IUAA) in the 2000s.

Janet Lee Carter was born October 4, 1934, in Indianapolis, Indiana, but grew up in Park Ridge, Chicago, Illinois. She earned a BA in English at IU Bloomington in 1956 before attending Butler University, where she earned an MS in education (1972) and an MA in personality theory religion (1978). In college, she was a cheerleader and an active member of Pi Beta Phi Sorority, the IU Student Foundation (and a member of its steering committee), Pleiades, and the Panhellenic Association.

After graduation, Shirley worked at the IU Foundation (IUF) for nine years. She was assistant to the IUF president (1978–1982), administrative assistant for a major fundraising campaign (1982–1984), and then that campaign's associate director (1984–1987). She designed and wrote "The Plan" for The Campaign for Indiana and prepared analysis of the campaign objectives. In 1988, she joined the IUAA Alumni Affairs Office as director of administration. At the same time, she served for two years as secretary to the Board of Trustees (1988–1990). From 1990 to 1993 she worked as director of alumni relations at IUPUI, where she conducted a year-long alumni planning forum, organized and implemented the IUPUI Alumni Association, founded and directed the Good Friends Volunteer Program, and organized the IUPUI Letterman's Club. She also received the Community Service Award from the Governor's Voluntary Action Program. From 1994 to 1999, she served as associate executive director of the IUAA. Her book, *The Indiana University Alumni Association: One Hundred and Fifty Years, 1854–2004*, was published in 2004.

Janet Carter married David F. Shirley (BS 1956), who is the CEO of Allen Funeral Home in Bloomington and the owner of Shirley Brothers Company, Inc. He was an active Phi Gamma Delta fraternity member and was a member of the Scabbard and Blade Club and Skull and Crescent honorary society. Together, the Shirleys have four children: David (BGS 1993), Deanna (BS 1985, JD 1988), Donald (BA 1986), and Daniel (BA 1988). ✒

PATRICK A. SHOULDERS
1953–

Trustee, 2002–

Aᴛᴛᴏʀɴᴇʏ ᴀɴᴅ ᴄɪᴠɪᴄ ʟᴇᴀᴅᴇʀ Patrick Shoulders has been a staunch supporter of Indiana University and the State of Indiana for more than thirty years.

A native Hoosier and one of three siblings, Patrick Alan Shoulders was born in Evansville on March 26, 1953, to Jeanne M. Nicholson, a homemaker and secretary, and Harold R. Shoulders, a draftsman. He grew up with strong family and community ties, learning early the importance of service to the community. His grandfather, Richard Nicholson, despite dropping out of high school to work in the family grocery business, after retirement went back to finish high school, enrolled in college, and authored a book about his father (Patrick's great-grandfather). Patrick's grandmother, Ruth Nicholson, raised nine children and was very active in her community; she took great pride in genealogy and enrolled Patrick in the National Society of the Sons of the American Revolution.

Patrick Shoulders attended Harper Elementary School and William Henry Harrison High School before enrolling at Indiana University, receiving a BA in English in 1975. He then was admitted to the IU School of Law–Indianapolis (now the McKinney School of Law), graduating with a JD (magna cum laude) in 1978. An active student, he was involved as president of Sigma Nu Fraternity and served on the IU Student Foundation, Interfraternity Council, and the Judicial Board. Upon graduation from law school, Shoulders returned to Evansville, passed the bar in Indiana, Kentucky, and several federal court systems before joining the firm Kahn Dees Donovan & Kahn (1978–1987), eventually making partner. He then left to join Ziemer Stayman Weitzel & Shoulders, where he remains as a partner. He concentrates his practice in litigation, labor, and employment law. He has been named an Indiana Super Lawyer annually since 2005, has been elected to the Federation of Insurance and Defense Counsel, and is a member of the American Board of Trial Advocates. Shoulders has also been extensively active in the Indiana Continuing Legal Education Forum (ICLEF), having served as the co-chair and founder of the Trial Advocacy Skills College held annually by the organization; the Indiana State Bar Association, serving as a chair of the Litigation Section, chair of the Litigation and Citizenship Education Committee, and member of the state bar's Board of Governors; and chair of the Fellows of the Indiana Bar Foundation. He is a Fellow of the American College of Trial Lawyers and the American

Bar Foundation. He has also served as president of the Evansville Bar Association and was awarded its highest honor, the James Bethel Gresham Freedom Award.

Patrick Shoulders began his service to Indiana University more than twenty-five years ago when he began working as a volunteer in his local alumni club. Since then, he has served the university and its alumni as director of the Indiana Public Policy Institute, president of the College of Arts and Sciences Alumni Board, president of the national IU Alumni Association, a board director of the Center on Philanthropy (now Lilly Family School of Philanthropy), a member of the Alumni Board of the IU School of Law–Indianapolis (now the IU McKinney School of Law), and as a member of the Friends of the Kinsey Institute. He has also been a member of the IU Foundation Board since 2002, has served on the Varsity Club Board of Directors and the Well House Advisory Board, and he and his wife are members of the President's Circle and Hoosier Hundred from a lifetime of giving. Because of a vacancy, Shoulders was appointed to the IU Board of Trustees in January 2002 by Governor Frank O'Bannon for a three-and-a-half-year term and was subsequently elected by the IU alumni body five times, in 2005, 2008, 2011, 2014, and 2017. He has served as vice president of the Board of Trustees for over eight years as well as chair of academic affairs and the board's liaison for the Bicentennial Celebration; he often provides humming musical accompaniment to trustee meetings.

Shoulders has been involved in a range of community activities, including serving as director of the IHSAA Foundation (2016–), president of the Evansville Parks Foundation, Museum of Arts and Sciences, and the YMCA. He has also been chair of the WNIN Auction and founder and director of the Arts Fest 12K River Run. He has served as a Civic Theater Board Member, Public Defender Commissioner, and a member of the Evansville-Vanderburgh County Unification Study Committee, the Indiana Youth Institute, the Indiana Equal Justice Fund (treasurer), Acordia Business Benefits of Evansville, and chairman of the City of Evansville Bill of Rights Bicentennial Celebration. Shoulders also enthusiastically rallies the participants at the start-line of the Hoosiers Outrun Cancer annual race each year.

Extensive volunteer efforts have earned Shoulders the titles of

Sagamore of the Wabash and Kentucky Colonel. He has been inducted into the Evansville Vanderburgh School Corporation Hall of Fame (2012), was presented with the Lifetime Achievement Award by the Vanderburgh County Democrats, was named Distinguished Barrister by *The Indiana Lawyer* (2012) and received the William G. Baker Award from the Indiana State Bar Association. He was presented with the Leadership Evansville Trustees Award (2014). In 2005, he received the Maynard K. Hine Medal, the highest honor bestowed by the IUPUI Alumni Association, for his unique and significant contributions to that campus. Also in 2005, he received the Wells Leadership Award by Sigma Nu Fraternity. And in 2016, he was presented with the Chancellor's Medallion at IU Southeast.

The Shoulders family consists of lifetime IU Alumni Association members Lisa (BA 1975), whom Patrick married July 12, 1975, son Andrew (BA 2004), daughter Samantha (BA 2000), and son-in-law David (BA 2000). Shoulders also has triplet granddaughters, whom he hopes will be members of the IU Class of 2028. ⸱

JACQUELINE A. SIMMONS
1955–

Vice President and General Counsel, 2012–

XTENDING A RELATIONSHIP WITH IU that began in graduate school
at the IU School of Law in 1976 (later renamed the IU Maurer
School of Law), Jacqueline "Jackie" Simmons has been the vice president and general counsel for Indiana University since 2012 and an
adjunct professor at the Maurer School since 1991.

Born August 27, 1955, in South Bend, Indiana, to Annette Lambert
and Jack Simmons, a catering company manager and a pipefitter and
steamfitter, respectively, Jacqueline Simmons developed a love for reading and education at an early age. As a first-grader at John J. O'Brien
Elementary School, she was skipped to a fourth-grade reading class
by a teacher who remained a source of encouragement throughout her
career. Simmons attended James Whitcomb Riley High School, then the
University of Notre Dame, where she received a BA in government with
honors in 1976. She received a JD cum laude in 1979 from the IU Maurer
School of Law. While in college, she was an active member in the band
and orchestra, as well as a journalist for the school newspaper. In law
school she was active with the *Indiana Law Journal* and the Student
Bar Association. Simmons also worked 30–40 hours per week during
college and law school.

After graduation, Simmons worked as an associate for Ice, Miller,
Donadio & Ryan (1979–1982). She then served two years as environmental counsel for Chemical Manufacturers Association (1982–1983)
and as an environmental associate for Kirkland & Ellis (1983–1984)
before returning to Ice, Miller, Donadio & Ryan, where she became
environmental associate, then partner, then chair of the Environmental
Practice Group (1984–1994). Subsequently, she worked with Reilly
Industries (1994–2006), beginning as corporate counsel, then as general counsel, and finally as vice president and general manager. She then
worked for Baker & Daniels (2006–2012) as partner, then as chair of the
Environmental Practice Group, and finally as chair of the International
Practice Group.

In 2012, IU President Michael McRobbie appointed Simmons vice
president and general counsel at Indiana University. In this position, she
directs the university's in-house counsels and outside counsel retained
to represent the university's interests, and supervises other offices as
assigned by the president, including Internal Audit and Affirmative
Action. She has implemented two management systems to track and

monitor the university's legal matters, budget, and documents, which has contributed to legal cost savings of more than $1 million since 2014. She has advised on many projects, including the closing of the IU Health Proton Therapy Center and Cyclotron, and the restructuring of the IU Health Board of Directors. She testified before the Indiana House and Senate on behalf of IU to oppose a constitutional ban on gay marriage and filed an amicus brief in the *Fisher v. University of Texas* case (2015) in support of affirmative action in college admissions. In addition to her administrative duties, she holds an adjunct faculty position at the IU Maurer School of Law (since 1991), has served as president of the IU Law School Alumni Board, and has been chair of the IU Law School Board of Visitors. She has worked with the IU Alumni Association and was a founding member of the IU Women's Philanthropy Council. She has also served as general counsel member of the Big Ten Academic Alliance.

Simmons has a record of active civic engagement. Her work with bar association offices and committees includes: the American Law Institute (board member), the Indiana State Bar Association Environmental Section Educational Outreach, Committee on Lawyer Certification, Environmental Section Newsletter editor, and the IU Panel on Lawyer Satisfaction. She has served on the Julian Center Board (2008–2012), as vice chair of the Indianapolis Symphony Board (1999–2008), on the board of directors for Providence Cristo Rey High School (2012–2016), and on the Indiana Repertory Theatre board (2016–). Simmons was the first woman elected president of the Notre Dame Club of Indianapolis. She has been active with the American Heart Association, Go Red for Women, American Coke and Coal Chemicals Institute, and the Indiana-Japan Society. She has also authored several pieces in the *Indianapolis Business Journal.*

Simmons has received several honors. In 2013, she received the *Indianapolis Business Journal* Woman of Influence Award. From 2008–2010 she was recognized among the Best Lawyers in America for Environmental Law. In 2004, Simmons was inducted into IU Law School Law Fellows. In 1987, she was a delegate to the Soviet Union and Poland for the American Center for International Leadership Conference on International Environmental Issues.

She wed Thomas F. Schnellenberger Jr. in 1977. They have three children: Jason Thomas, Jenna Marie, and Claire Elise (BA 2010). ᴄᴓᴖ

CHRISTOPHER SIMPSON
1955–2008

Vice President for Public Affairs
and Government Relations, 1996–2001

W RITER, EDUCATOR, and public relations consultant Christopher Simpson served Indiana University for seven years.

Born in 1955 in Anderson, South Carolina, to Lois Shoolbred and David Simpson, James Christopher Simpson earned a BA in history and psychology from Clemson University in 1977 and an MA in journalism from the University of South Carolina in 1990.

Prior to coming to IU, Simpson worked at the University of South Carolina and the University of Oregon. While at South Carolina, Simpson developed and implemented one of the first university system-wide integrated marketing efforts, which led to increased fundraising and student applications. He was an educator as well, teaching enhanced media relations, media training, and crisis communications to leaders at more than 1,000 independent schools, colleges, universities, and associations in the United States, Mexico, Canada, and Europe. Simpson worked as a writer for *The Washington Times* and served as the newspaper's Capitol Hill Bureau chief and assistant national editor. He later served as press secretary to United States Senator Strom Thurmond, handling media and PR in the senator's office. He held similar responsibilities for the Senate Judiciary Committee and Senate Armed Services committees.

Christopher Simpson joined IU under President Brand in 1994 as special counsel to the president. In that capacity, he oversaw two new committees on government relations, one for Federal Relations and one for State Relations, chairing the latter. His capabilities in chairing this committee as well as his management of other government relations efforts, such as U.S. Deputy Secretary of State Warren Christopher's visit to IU in March of 1995, led President Brand to appoint Simpson the additional title of associate vice president for government relations, effective July 1, 1995. Upon Douglas Wilson's retirement in February 1996, Simpson became interim vice president for public affairs and government relations for four months before Brand appointed him permanently that July.

As vice president for public affairs and government relations, Simpson raised the university's profile nationally, leading to increased public and private support and new student enrollment. The five-year IU integrated marketing campaign, which focused on building stronger ties to the community statewide, regionally, and nationally, generated $11 million in new revenue for the Bloomington campus. Simpson also was responsible for the system's branding, media relations, publications, digital communications, and federal relations efforts. During this period, he continued to serve as special counsel to the president. Simpson was also active in the community, serving as co-chair of the IU United Way Campaign and on the board of the Monroe County Humane Society and the IU Kokomo Board of Advisors.

He and his wife, Millie, founded Simpson Communications together in 2002, with offices in Indiana and Washington, D.C. He was CEO and partner to the organization as it evolved into SimpsonScarborough, a firm known for assisting colleges and universities in their development of brand strategies. Simpson's professional experiences culminated in the publication of his book, *Weathering the Storm: How to Protect Your Brand in the Worst of Times.*

Simpson and Millie had two children together, David and Sara. He was an avid outdoorsman, and owned his own sailboat, named Athena. He also enjoyed skiing (and was an active member of the National Ski Patrol), bicycling, scuba diving, kayaking, and fly fishing. He raised llamas commercially and was both a master gardener and an avid cook. Christopher Simpson passed away in 2008 in Williamsburg, Virginia, after a battle with cancer. ❧

R EAL ESTATE BROKER, CIVIC LEADER, and IU alumna Donna Spears
has been serving Indiana University and her communities for
nearly thirty years.

Born in July 1957 in Gary, Indiana, Donna Spears was raised by her
mother, Jeannette, who worked in management at the East Chicago
Housing Authority. Her father, Charles Berry, worked at Inland Steel.
Donna grew up in East Chicago, Indiana, and attended public schools.
A significant early influence was her great-grandmother Susie Gertrude
Wilson, with whom she lived from ages 2 to 6 on her farm in Michigan.
Growing up, Donna was inspired by her great-grandmother's entrepreneurship, philanthropy, creativity, and her engagement in real estate
and home ownership at a time when it was not common or, in many
cases, not legally permitted for African Americans. In 1967 at age 10, she
spent six weeks on the IU Bloomington campus, living in the Campus
View apartment building. Those weeks were a life-altering international
experience, and she decided immediately that she would attend IU. And
so she did, enrolling after having graduated at the top of her class in
high school. As a first-generation college student, she was guided to
attend Indiana University by the Groups Scholars Program. She completed an AS in dental hygiene at the IU School of Dentistry (1978), a
BS in public health education at the IU School of Medicine (1979), and
an MPA in health system administration at the IU School of Public and
Environmental Affairs (1981). Much of her college life was spent studying hard in the library to maintain her scholarships, and in 1976 she was
named a Founders Scholar for her 3.8 GPA. In her free time, she was a
member of the IU African American Dance Company (AADC) under the
direction of Professor Iris Rosa, who was from East Chicago, Indiana,
and for whom she also worked part-time as a graduate assistant.

In her early career, Spears worked as a dental hygienist, the license
for which she still retains. Her entrepreneurial spirit arose in the 1990s,
when she became the owner of Fitness Foundations, a company focused
on public health education, fitness consulting, and personal training
(1992–2005). She then worked for the Academy of Motion Picture Arts
and Sciences (2003–2006). In 2005, Spears became a licensed real
estate agent. In 2011, she graduated from the Indiana Association of
Realtors Leadership Academy and was named to the Graduate Realtor
Institute Board of Governors. She currently serves on the executive

committee of the Indiana Association of Realtors and is an associate broker for Coldwell Banker Lingle in Richmond, Indiana.

Throughout her life, Donna Spears has been a devoted alumna, serving Indiana University in many capacities. That includes being a member of the IU East Advisory Board, the IU Alumni Association (IUAA) Executive Council, Woodburn Guild Board, IUAA Board of Managers (national chair 2009–2010), founding member of the Women's Philanthropy Leadership Council (2010), and Colloquium for the Women of Indiana University (co-chair 2017, chair 2019). In 2018, alumni elected Spears to the IU Board of Trustees after she campaigned on a platform that promised attention to recruitment, educational quality, tuition affordability, and economic development initiatives.

Beyond IU, Spears has served in several professional and civic organizations. Most notable are her terms on the governing boards of the following organizations: Richmond Art Museum, Richmond Symphony Orchestra, Economic Development Council, Indiana Youth Institute, Indiana Association of Realtors, Girls Inc. of Wayne County, and the Wayne County Boys and Girls Club. She also assists with the Richmond High School and IU East golf teams, having acquired the Titlist Performance Institute's levels 1 and 2 certifications.

Some of Spears' most notable awards and special achievements include being awarded the IU East Chancellor's Medallion (2016), featured on TLC's television program *My First Home* (May 2010), named Realtor of the Year by the Wayne County Realtor Association (2008), awarded the Pam Frantz Community Service Award (2008 and 2017), and receiving the IUAA Gertrude Rich Award (2006).

Donna met her future husband on the Bloomington campus in the summer of 1976 and in 1980, Donna and Alan M. Spears were married at Beck Chapel. Alan is also an IU graduate (BS political science 1979; MPA School of Public and Environmental Affairs 1981; JD McKinney School of Law 1990).

ABBEY RAE STEMLER
1986–

I T IS NO SURPRISE that Abbey Rae Stemler has become so much a part of Indiana University. When she was young, her sister made her an IU Cabbage Patch Kid costume. Stemler was at IU Bloomington from undergraduate through graduate school, when she served as a trustee, and later returned to join the faculty of the Kelley School of Business.

Born on January 12, 1986, Stemler attended New Albany High School, graduating as salutatorian and class president. One of the first in her family to go to college, she attended IU Bloomington, earning a BA with highest distinction in 2008, completing an individualized major in the anthropology of mental health and illness, a major in psychology, and a certificate from the Liberal Arts and Management Program (LAMP). As an undergraduate, Stemler received many honors and awards, including the IU Hutton Honors College Lloyd G. and Mildred Balfour Scholarship for four consecutive years, the Clara Jovan Goodbody Award, the Palmer Brandon Prize, and the Beryl Showers Holland Fellowship. Stemler continued her studies in a dual-degree graduate program at IU, completed in 2011, with a JD from the Maurer School of Law and an MBA from the Kelley School of Business. It was during her two years of graduate school from 2009 to 2011 that Stemler served IU on the Board of Trustees as its eighteenth student trustee.

After completing her graduate degrees, Stemler practiced law at Bose McKinney & Evans LLP in Indianapolis, Indiana, where she had previously worked one summer while in law school. In 2012, she left to establish a private practice as an attorney in Bloomington. Stemler has also been an entrepreneur, founding and managing three small businesses in Bloomington between the years 2011 and 2016 (One–Eighteen LLC, Two-Zero Five LLC, and Needler Management LLC), for which she acquired and managed various properties, including a mixed-use commercial/residential building in downtown Bloomington. Also in 2012, Stemler began lecturing in the Department of Business Law and Ethics at the Kelley School of Business, where she became assistant professor in 2015. Her practical experiences as an attorney and entrepreneur reflect her research interests, which focus on small business and start-up finance and the legal aspects of entrepreneurship in the sharing economy. They also inform her teaching, enabling her to bring real-world examples into the classroom. Stemler is an award-winning instructor and teaches a variety of courses including entrepreneurship law, business law, and critical thinking. She has been published in journals such as the *Emory Law Journal*, the *Fordham Urban Law Journal*, the *Vanderbilt Journal of Entertainment and Technology Law*, and the *Northwestern Journal of International Law and Business.*

In 2006, Stemler co-founded a program called The Virtú Project, which teaches students about entrepreneurship and investment while raising money for the Timmy Foundation (now Timmy Global Health), a charity devoted to expanding health care and health education around the world, particularly in developing countries. Her work with the Timmy Foundation also led her to taking a group of high school students on a trip to Quito, Ecuador.

Stemler continues to serve Indiana University in various capacities, including as a member of the Bloomington Faculty Council, faculty coach in the Global Business Institute, and mentor in the CEWiT Emerging Scholars Research Experiences for Undergraduate Women program. She has also served as president, program chair, and secretary of the Midwest Academy of Legal Studies in Business. ᴄᕕᒪ

WILLIAM B. STEPHAN
1959–

Vice President for Engagement, 2007–

Vice President for University Relations and Corporate
Partnerships, 2004–2005

Vice President for Public Affairs
and Government Relations, 2001–2004

A TTORNEY AND UNIVERSITY ADMINISTRATOR William B. "Bill" Stephan has served Indiana University since 2000, although his relationship with IU began as a graduate student at the Indiana University School of Law–Indianapolis (now the Robert H. McKinney School of Law) in the early 1980s.

An Indiana native, William B. Stephan was born May 18, 1959, and raised in Gary, Indiana. As a youth, he played baseball through high school and worked a variety of jobs ranging from delivering newspapers to working on the underframes of Amtrak passenger train cars during college summers. Stephan received a BS in economics from Arizona State University in 1981. In college, he participated in intramural athletics, helped oversee student government election processes, and worked in a security position for university events and concerts. After completing his BS, he decided to go to law school for the broader array of career options that he believed it would provide him. He earned a JD from the IU School of Law in Indianapolis (now McKinney School of Law) in 1984.

An attorney by profession, Stephan has worked as a chief magistrate for the Marion County Juvenile Court, as well as an administrator for former Indianapolis Mayor Stephen Goldsmith (1992), where he specifically focused on the mayor's Building Better Neighborhoods Initiative, an initiative that would become a model for strengthening low-income neighborhoods across the country. In addition, Stephan served as chief of staff and special counsel to the mayor.

Stephan has been a member of Indiana University's administrative team since 2000, when he became assistant vice president for economic development in the Office of the Vice President for Information Technology. He then took the post of vice president for public affairs and government relations (2001–2004). In 2004, then-IU President Adam Herbert restructured the administration and renamed the position vice president for university relations and corporate partnerships, in order to better reflect the responsibility of developing relations between the university and external entities. Stephan left IU in 2005 to become senior vice president for corporate communications and community relations for Clarian Health Partners (now IU Health), one of the nation's largest health care systems.

Stephan returned to IU in the fall of 2007 when IU President Michael McRobbie appointed him to the newly created position of vice president for engagement, which focuses on economic development in the State of Indiana. In this position, Stephan has been responsible for statewide economic engagement activities on behalf of the university, as well as technology commercialization, marketing and communications functions, events, and conferences. In July 2018 Stephan assumed the additional responsibility for IU's federal relations activities, working closely with Vice President for Government Relations Mike Sample, and in January 2019, he assumed joint responsibility with Sample for IU state relations activities.

Stephan's other activities within IU have included serving on the IU School of Informatics and Computing Dean's Advisory Council (now the School of Informatics, Computing, and Engineering), the Kelley School of Business Board of Visitors, the McKinney School of Law Board of Visitors, and several search committees. He also served as the university's corporate liaison to Clarian Health Partners (now IU Health). Moreover, as chairman of the Board of Indiana University Research and Technology Corporation (IURTC), Stephan oversaw its reorganization in 2017, establishing the new IU Innovation and Commercialization Office and launching the IU Philanthropic Venture Fund. In 2018, IURTC was named Tech Transfer Unit of the Year by Global University Venturing.

Active not only within the university, Stephan serves on multiple boards in civic organizations across the State of Indiana. Some of these include the board of directors of the Greater Bloomington Chamber of Commerce (chair, 2014–2015), the American Lung Association of Indiana (chair, 2012–2014), the board of governors for the Economic Club of Indiana (2012–2017), the Indiana Chamber of Commerce Board of Directors (2016–), the Boy Scouts of America/Crossroads of America Council (2014–), as well as the Executive Committee for the Association of Public and Land-Grant Universities' Commission on Innovation, Competitiveness, and Economic Prosperity (2014–). He also served as president and CEO of the Indianapolis Private Industry Council, on the National Association of College and University Business Officers Board of Directors, on the Advisory Council for the Purdue Discovery Park, and on the board of directors for the Indiana University Research and Technology Corporation (2010–).

William Stephan and his wife, Carol, have two children, Laura and Paul, both of whom attended Indiana University. ❧

CYNTHIA P. STONE
1956–

Trustee, 1993–1996

Trustee Cynthia Stone began her association with Indiana University in 1974 as a student and has since worked for IU in a variety of staff and faculty positions for more than thirty-five years.

Born in Worcester, Massachusetts, Cynthia Pearl Stone was a first-generation college student and credits her paternal grandmother, Pearl, with influencing her to work hard, study, and dream big dreams. An only child of divorced parents, Cynthia was raised by her grandmother in New England, where she was encouraged to study music and dance from a young age. After graduation from Doherty Memorial High School in Worcester, Cynthia was recruited to IU by her ballet teacher, Marina Svetlova, chair of IU Ballet. She graduated from IU Bloomington with a BA in special education and minors in ballet and voice (1978), later earning an MA in instructional systems technology (2008). Stone was an engaged student, serving as an usher at the Musical Arts Center, secretary of Wright Quad Student Government, member of the IU Judo Club, member of IU Ballet and Opera Theatre, an orientation assistant, and she played intramural softball.

In 1981, Stone began working for IU as a clerical by day and was a graduate student by night. In 1986, she began as a training and communications coordinator in the Physical Plant. Over the next eighteen years, she developed educational programs and communications and instructional materials for more than 1,000 employees, conducted training, and designed a variety of multimedia tools. She also collaborated with the IU Foundation to engage donors for landscaping projects.

Because Stone believed that both women and staff in general needed a stronger voice in the university, she decided to run for the trustee position. She was elected by the IU alumni body to serve from 1993 until 1996, becoming the first university employee elected as well as the first openly gay member of the Board of Trustees. During her tenure on the board, Stone worked tirelessly on behalf of IU employees, especially on women's and family issues, and issues related to undergraduate education. Stone is credited with expanding childcare facilities on all campuses and was instrumental in the $2 million investment that IUPUI made to open a childcare center.

During Stone's tenure as a board member, her partner of twenty years, Donna Payne, was diagnosed with brain cancer and died in 1995. Stone experienced firsthand the negative impact of IU's health insurance

policy that excluded domestic partner benefits. As a result, she vigor-
ously pursued policy changes that would recognize all types of diversity
at Indiana University, including pushing for domestic partner benefits.
Although she was unable to change the insurance policy before her
trustee term ended in 1996, Cynthia Stone's strong advocacy for women
and same-sex domestic partners did not end. She served on a university
task force to study the issue of same-sex domestic benefits, resulting in
the decision by IU in 2001 to extend health care benefits to same-sex
domestic partners. Stone is an IU Alumni Association Board Member,
serving on the IUAA Executive Council and as a board member on the
GLBT Alumni constituent group. She worked with the IU Foundation
Academy for Women to organize the Women and Workplace Conference,
among other initiatives. For her tireless advocacy for the LGBTQ community, she received the 2011 Spirit Award from the LGBTQ Student
Support Services Office for mentoring and advising women's and GLBT
student groups.

Cynthia Stone's service extends to the broader community of
Bloomington. Many have benefited from her involvement in Women in
the Arts, Girl Scouts of Tulip Trace (and she was an Indiana Delegate to
the National GSUSA Convention in 2003), the Interfaith Winter Shelter
(coordinator, 2010–2015), Community Kitchen of Bloomington, and the
Bloomington Feminist Chorus.

Stone was an adjunct faculty member at Ivy Tech State College
(1989–1995), receiving the President's Award for Outstanding Teaching
in 1994. She began an adjunct appointment with the IU Kelley School
of Business in 1999. From 2007 to 2014, she was a full-time lecturer in
the Kelley School, advancing to senior lecturer in 2014 before retiring
in May 2017. Stone has been nominated and won several awards during
her time at IU, including being a finalist for the 2015 Trustee Teaching
Award and being named one of the Bloomington campus's "favorite professors" by IU varsity athletes in fall 2011. She was also the Outstanding
Women's Staff Member of the Year for work on personal safety, awarded
by the Indiana University Office for Women's Affairs (2002–2003).

Stone resides in Bloomington with her partner, Amy M. Benckart
(MS library science 1989), granddaughter of legendary IU football coach
Bo McMillin. After thirteen years together, Cindy and Amy were legally
married in Delaware in the summer of 2013. ༺

RICHARD B. STONER
1920–2008

Trustee, 1972–1992

INDUSTRIALIST, CIVIC LEADER, and staunch supporter of Indiana University Richard Burkett "Dick" Stoner served twenty years as a trustee, extending a relationship with IU that first began as an undergraduate in 1937.

Richard Stoner, one of seven children, was born May 15, 1920, in Ladoga, Indiana, to Edward and Florence Stoner. He graduated from Tipton High school in 1937 and entered Indiana University, earning a BS in finance and banking in 1941. Stoner interrupted his studies to serve as a captain in the Finance Department of the United States Army from 1942 to 1946, after which he attended Harvard School of Law on the Walter Kessler Scholarship, earning a JD in 1947.

While a student at Indiana University, Stoner was actively involved in campus life. He was senior class president, president of the Union Board, president of Sigma Nu Phi fraternity, chairman of the junior prom, associate editor of *Arbutus*, and was a member of Beta Gamma Sigma, Phi Eta Sigma, the Sphinx Club, Blue Key, Dragon's Head, and Skull and Crescent.

Professionally, Richard Stoner worked at the Cummins Engine Company for more than fifty years, holding various key administrative and executive positions including vice chairman, director, executive vice president, and corporate general manager. In addition, Stoner served on the board of directors for several companies, including the Bank One Corporation, Public Service Indiana, and American United Life Insurance. In 1970, he was inducted into the Kelley School of Business Academy of Alumni Fellows.

In 1972, Richard Stoner joined the Board of Trustees when appointed by Indiana Governor Edgar D. Whitcomb, and during his twenty years of service, Stoner was reappointed by Governors Otis Bowen, Robert Orr, and Evan Bayh. At the beginning of his second term, he began serving as president of the board, a position he held until the end of his tenure. During his time on the Board of Trustees, the University's student enrollment rose by nearly 30,000 students, the School of Public and Environmental Affairs had its inauguration, the Herman B Wells Scholars Program was launched, and each campus saw the development and addition of major buildings. During his tenure on the board, and particularly during his time as chairman in the early 1980s, Richard Stoner voiced his opposition to legislative cuts in funding for higher education, worrying that if they continued, decreased funding could eventually lead to the elimination of public higher education in Indiana. Stoner also had an overlapping tenure on the IU Foundation Board of Directors and served one year on the IUPU Columbus Advisory Board. In 1993, after his retirement from the Board of Trustees, Stoner received the IU Distinguished Alumni Service Award. In addition, he received honorary degrees from Butler University in 1973 and from Indiana University in 1994.

Stoner was always conscious of and responsive to the needs of his community and worked with numerous public service organizations throughout his life. While president of the Bartholomew County School Board, he worked with Cummins Engine Company to make funds available to the community to attract the country's leading architects to design buildings for its schools and other public buildings. In 1968, Stoner led the Indiana State Policy Commission on Post High School Education, speaking out on civil rights, equal education, and employment opportunities for minorities and the economically underprivileged. He was the president of The Indiana Forum, the Area 4 President of the East Central Region Boy Scouts, and a member of the Board of Directors of the Indiana State Chamber of Commerce. A model of active and responsible citizenship in the political arena, Stoner was a delegate to the Democratic National Convention from 1956 to 1988, Democratic Chairman of the Ninth District from 1961 to 1966, and an Indiana Democratic National Committeeman from 1966 to 1988.

Richard Stoner was married to Virginia B. Austin, with whom he raised six children: Pamela, Richard, Benjamin, Janet, Rebecca, and Joanne. At the time of his death on March 15, 2008, he was the proud grandfather of fourteen grandchildren and four great-grandchildren. ᗢ

WILLIAM H. STRONG
1952–

Trustee, 2010–2013

ACCOUNTANT AND CIVIC LEADER William Strong has been active in business, politics, and the arts in addition to serving Indiana University as a trustee.

William H. Strong inherited his Midwestern work ethic from his mother, Geneva Overpeck Strong, and his father, Charles L. Strong, who worked in a Southeastern Indiana coal mine before working his way through Indiana University to graduate in December 1941. Born April 1, 1952, in Indianapolis, Indiana, William Strong attended Fall Creek School, Eastwood Junior High School, and North Central High School en route to Purdue University in West Lafayette, where he graduated with a BS in industrial management in 1973. While an undergraduate, he studied abroad at the University of Vienna, receiving a Certificate of Language in 1972. In 1974 he entered The Kellogg School at Northwestern University, becoming a Certified Public Accountant (1975) and earning an MBA in finance and accounting (1976).

His first job was at Price Waterhouse in Chicago. In 1979, he moved on to Salomon Brothers in New York, becoming managing director in 1987. At the time, he was the youngest person to be named a managing director in investment banking at Salomon Brothers. Two years later in 1989, he was named joint-head of the Global Merger and Acquisition Group. In 1991, Salomon Brothers named him head of international investment banking in London, England. In 1993, he joined Morgan Stanley as vice chairman (1993–2011) and became co–CEO of Morgan Stanley Asia Pacific in Hong Kong (2011–2014). William Strong was appointed as a Trustee of Indiana University in 2010 by Governor Mitch Daniels. As a trustee, Strong served as a member of the committees on finance and audit, health affairs, and compensation and benefits. In 2013, he was appointed to the Global Advisory Board of Northwestern University's Kellogg School of Management. While still in Hong Kong, Strong was named an adjunct professor in the Department of Finance at The Chinese University of Hong Kong (2012–2014), and also named to the Financial Services Development Council (2013–2015) by Leung Chun-ying, the chief executive of Hong Kong. Upon returning to Chicago, Strong served as senior advisor at Morgan Stanley (2014–) while devoting his main attention to Longford Capital Management, a private investment company where he is chairman, managing director, and chairman of the Investment Committee (2014–).

Strong is very active in the political world. He was a delegate at the 2008 Republican National Convention. As finance chairman for the State of Illinois during Senator John McCain's presidential campaign, Strong broke the record for most money raised for a Republican presidential candidate in Illinois. In the 2012 presidential campaign cycle, he served as national cochairman of the presidential campaign of Governor Tim Pawlenty of Minnesota. Since 2015, he has served as finance chairman of the Illinois Republican Party. Strong takes an interest in the military as well, serving as a member of the Board of Visitors of the United States Military Academy at West Point, New York, from 2006 to 2008, having been appointed by President George W. Bush. In July of 2008, at the request of the Office of the Secretary of Defense, Strong led an economic mission to Iraq which involved traveling to Basra, Babil Province, and Baghdad to encourage investment in the rebuilding of Iraq.

Strong is a member of several financial associations including the Economic Club of Chicago, the American Institute of Certified Public Accountants, the Illinois CPA Society, the Council of Advisors to the Treasury Markets Association of Hong Kong (2012–2014), and the National Association of Securities Dealers (now the Financial Industry Regulatory Authority) in the United States. In 2007 *The Dealmaker* named him one of the top investment bankers in the United States.

Strong is also a patron of the arts, serving on several boards around the world. He has been on the board of trustees of the Chicago Symphony Orchestra since 1994, serving as chairman of the board from 2001 to 2006, and is now a life trustee. He is also a member of the board of governors of the Hong Kong Philharmonic Society Ltd. He was a trustee of the Newseum in Washington, D.C. (2006–2015), a museum dedicated to celebrating the First Amendment of the United States Constitution. Strong was also involved with Colgate University in New York, serving as chairman of the Colgate Society of Families, and was the driving force behind The Palace Theater, a student venue for Colgate. In 2008, the American Jewish Committee gave him the Civic Achievement Award.

In December 1974, he married Sandra J. Sharp. They have three children: Ryan, an attorney in private practice; Fletcher, a litigating attorney; and Meredith, a public relations senior account manager. ❧

ANN WHITLOCK SWEDEEN
1944–

Trustee, 1986–1992; 1994–1997

A CIVIC LEADER, BUSINESSWOMAN, and supporter of the humanities, Ann Swedeen served Indiana University for over fifteen years, including three terms as a trustee.

Ann Whitlock Swedeen was born July 3, 1944, in Cincinnati, Ohio. She traces her paternal lineage's arrival in America to 1641, and counts several notable ancestors including Ephraim Lockhart Whitlock (1755–1825), who served as an officer under General George Washington and became a founding member of The Society of the Cincinnati (1783), and grandfather J. W. Whitlock, who built and raced the Hoosier Boy series of stepped-hydroplane boats, setting the Ohio River Cincinnati to Louisville speed record of 59.9 mph in 1924. Ann's father, Stewart Blair Whitlock, was a civic leader and the president of the Whitlock Chair Company of Rising Sun, Indiana. Her mother, Eleanor Greive Whitlock, was a beloved wife and mother of four children and grandmother to three, a poet laureate of the Indiana Federation of Women's Clubs, and clerk of the circuit courts for Ohio County, Indiana.

Following two years as a student at John B. Stetson University in Deland, Florida, Swedeen attended Indiana University Bloomington from 1964 through 1971. She earned a BA in music education (1967) and an MAT in music and multiple arts (1971). At Stetson, she was active in the Gamma Chi chapter of Alpha Chi Omega. At IUB, she was a member of the Singing Hoosiers and the IU Student Foundation's Little 500 Committee. Swedeen continued her education at Ball State University (BSU), earning an MA in student personnel administration (1975) and an EdD in educational administration in higher education (1977).

Ann Swedeen's early career includes work as director of public information at WIPB-TV (1975–1977) and at Ball State University as assistant professor and academic advisor of undergraduate programs (1979–1981). In 1981, she joined Ball Corporation (Muncie, Indiana) as manager of corporate relations and speechwriter for the chairman of the board (1981–1996). She received the company's 1994 Community Service Award, one of the highest awards given to employees. And in 1996, she received the Indiana Women of Achievement in Business and Humanities award from Ball State University. From 1996 to 2001, she was the Indiana Humanities Council's director for international affairs and programs. From 2002–2004 she was major gifts officer for the Indiana State Museum Foundation while also serving as managing consultant for the Federation of Alliances Francaises, USA. She has also worked as regional consultant at the Indiana Partnerships Center of the Indiana Academy for Parent and School Leadership (2008–2010) and as management consultant for Indiana Youth Institute Consulting Services (2002–2017).

Elected by IU alumni to the Board of Trustees three times, Swedeen served from 1986 to 1992 and 1994 to 1997. As a trustee, she served as chair of the IU Hospitals Advisory Committee (1994–1997), the IU External Relations Committee (1989–1992), and the IU Personnel Committee (1987–1992). She also served on the IU Foundation Board of Directors (1989–1992), the board of directors for the IU Advanced Research and Technology Corporation (1996–2004), the IU East Board of Advisors (1986–2004), and the Board of Visitors for the IU Center on Philanthropy (now the Lilly Family School of Philanthropy) (1989–2002). She was one of sixteen trustees nationwide on the Association of Governing Boards of Universities and Colleges, Washington D.C. She was part of the fundraising campaign cabinets for the IU Alumni DeVault Center and the IU School of Nursing, and a member of the IU Friends of Music Board of Directors, Well House Society, Hoosiers for Higher Education, and the IU Alumni Association (life member).

Swedeen's civic involvement extends beyond Indiana University. She has served as president of the Indianapolis Woman's Club (2014–2015); elder on the Council of Elders at the Second Presbyterian Church of Indianapolis (2010–); board chair for the Alliance Francaises d'Indianapolis (2007–2009); Volunteer Liaison for the French-American Foundation of Paris (1997–2005); board chair, Indiana Youth Institute (2001–2004); board chair, Indiana Council for Economic Education—Purdue University (2003–2004); board chair, Indiana Association of United Ways (2000–2001); board chair, Muncie-Delaware County United Way (1995–1996); board of directors, Indiana Grantmakers (1994–1996); and board of directors, Indiana Public Broadcasting Stations (1989–1991).

In August of 1969, Ann married James E. Swedeen, who earned his BA from Indiana University (1969) and an MA from Ball State University (1975). They have one son, Blair Andrew Swedeen, who holds a BA from the IU Kelley School of Business (1997) and an MBA from the University of Chicago (2003). ꙮ

SUE H. TALBOT

1938–

F ELLOW TRUSTEES DESCRIBE Sue Hays Talbot's work ethic as one consisting of commitment, integrity, and enthusiasm. Time and again she has demonstrated these qualities in her service to IU as an officer, advocate, and general ambassador.

A lifelong resident of Bloomington, Talbot has been part of Indiana University from childhood. She grew up a couple of blocks from campus, where her mother, Dorotha Armantrout, was an IU catalog librarian and her father, Roy Hays, was a film projectionist at the Indiana Theatre. For middle and high school, she attended University School, which at that time was housed in the IU School of Education. Talbot began her undergraduate work in 1956 but paused her studies to take care of her first child. She later finished by taking courses part time, completing a BA in education in 1966. She later returned for an MA (1971) and again for a PhD in school administration (1992).

Upon earning her education degree, Talbot began teaching first grade at Bloomington's Arlington Heights Elementary, moving to University Elementary a few years later. Reflecting her view that all are deserving of a quality education, she became an advocate for methods to mainstream children with disabilities into the regular classroom, building on a belief that all children should have an opportunity to learn. Within a few years, Talbot's teaching gained state and national recognition, and in 1978 she was named Indiana Teacher of the Year and was runner-up for National Teacher of the Year.

That recognition increased the demand for Talbot's expertise. She began adjunct teaching for the Indiana University School of Education, sharing her enthusiasm for classroom teaching with pre-service teachers and conducting statewide workshops. The Indiana State Board of Education asked her to serve on the Teaching and Licensing Board. Then in 1986, Governor Robert Orr asked Talbot to serve as special assistant for education in order to help author the "A+ Plan," the governor's signature education initiative.

Following two years as the governor's education point person and a few more in the classroom, Talbot used her boundless energy to promote the interests of Indiana University. Talbot directed the IU School of Education's Leadership in Education Administration Development program. She was also the president of the Indiana University Alumni Association. Capitalizing on her governor's office experience and relationships formed through IU as well as her role as an educational leader, she worked on behalf of IU in the state relations office to help promote university interests in state government. That led quite naturally to a position as the founding director of Hoosiers for Higher Education (HHE), the grassroots advocacy and lobbying organization sponsored by the IU Alumni Association. Under her leadership, HHE didn't just grow—it flourished. HHE began in 1991 with just over 100 participants, but by the time Talbot ended her directorship, it counted more than 10,000 members. In 2001, she was elected by IU alumni to serve three terms on the IU Board of Trustees. Since stepping down from the board in 2010, she has remained engaged with IU by serving on the IUAA past chairs council, the IU Foundation, and the Women's Philanthropy Council (honorary).

Talbot has been equally engaged in civic activity. She has held leadership positions with the First Presbyterian Church, the IU Credit Union Board of Directors, the Salvation Army, the Hospital Advisory Committee, the Bloomington Municipal Facilities Board, and the Woman's Club of Bloomington.

Sue Talbot's record of achievement has earned accolades and admiration from Indiana and beyond. Hoosiers for Higher Education named a Distinguished Member Award in her honor; the IU Alumni Association has named her the recipient of the President's Award and also of the Gertrude Rich Award; Indiana University has given her the Distinguished Alumni Service Award (2011); the IU School of Education has honored her with its Distinguished Alumni Award; IU President Tom Ehrlich presented her the Thomas Hart Benton Mural Medallion; the dean of students awarded her the Ward G. Biddle Visionary Award; the Chamber of Commerce bestowed on her its Lifetime Achievement Award; and twice the State of Indiana has bestowed her with a Sagamore of the Wabash. In 2016, she was recognized by the Bloomington Chamber of Commerce with the Women Who Excel award.

Sue and her husband, Robert Merrill "Bob" Talbot Jr. (BS 1961), have three children: Michelle Talbot (BS 1983), Lisa Talbot Deinlein (BS 1983), and Robert "Bud" Talbot III (BS 1996; MS 2000). They saw the fourteenth family IU degree bestowed on their granddaughter Natalie Deinlein Meador in 2008, and the fifteenth family IU degree bestowed upon grandson Rett Deinlein in 2012. ❧

A TTORNEY, ENTREPRENEUR, AND CIVIC LEADER John Talley has served
IU since his undergraduate days, when he was the fifth student to
sit on the Board of Trustees.

John R. Talley earned a BA in English and political science at Indiana
University Bloomington in 1982 and was a student director for Union
Board, a member of the Dean of Students Advisory Board, the Board of
Aeons, and Blue Key and Mortar Board honorary societies. As a senior,
he received the Elvis J. Stahr Distinguished Senior Award in recognition of his outstanding contributions to student life at IU. The following year, he entered the IU School of Law–Indianapolis (later renamed
the McKinney School of Law) and applied to be a student trustee of the
university.

As a member of the IU Board of Trustees, Talley served on the
Student Affairs Committee, Medical Center Hospitals Committee,
Natatorium and Track/Field Advisory Board, and the Real Estate and
Legal Committee, in addition to serving as trustee representative to
IUPUI and IU Kokomo. His success on the board was aided by his deep
involvement in student activities as an undergraduate at IU.

Talley earned a JD from the law school at IUPUI in 1985, graduating
magna cum laude, and was the recipient of the George O. Dix Award.
Talley was admitted to the American Bar Association, Indiana State Bar
Association, and the Indianapolis Bar Association.

From 1985 to 1990, Talley worked as an attorney at Indianapolis
firm Barnes & Thornburg before joining Indiana Gas Company, Inc.
as assistant counsel for regulatory affairs (1990–1992), director of federal regulatory affairs (1992–1994), and director of gas supply (1994–
1995). He then served as vice president at Indiana Energy Services, Inc.
from 1995 to 1996. In 1996, Talley co-founded ProLiance Holdings, an
energy-related holdings company that is jointly owned by Vectren and
Citizens Energy Group. He is also the president of ProLiance Energy
and ProLiance Transportation and Storage, the company's largest
subsidiaries.

Talley has also been active in his communities and in the State of
Indiana. He is a director of the 500 Festival, the Economic Club of
Indiana, the Indiana Manufacturers Association, the Indiana Chamber
of Commerce, Ransburg YMCA, and the United Way of Central Indiana.
He was elected to the board of trustees for Franklin College for a term

beginning in 2013 and has been involved with the Greater Indianapolis Progress Committee and the Ivy Tech Community College Foundation.

Talley's service to Indiana University has continued long after his term on the Board of Trustees. He has been an IU Alumni Association Executive Council member at large (1986–1989), a board member for the Whittenberger Society (1985–1997), and a member of the McKinney School of Law Board of Visitors (2011–).

John Talley and his wife, Lesa, also an Indianapolis-based attorney, and their children reside in Indianapolis. ᔑ

NEIL THEOBALD
1956–

Vice President and Chief Financial Officer,
2007–2012

BEGINNING HIS CAREER at Indiana University in 1993 as an associate professor at the School of Education, Neil Theobald became vice president and chief financial officer of the university in 2007.

A Midwesterner by birth, Neil Theobald was born in Peoria, Illinois, where his father's ancestors had moved from Germany in the nineteenth century. His mother, Agnes, was a bank teller and his father, Milo, was a shipping clerk. Neil became the first member of his family to attend college. After receiving an academic scholarship to Trinity College (Hartford, Connecticut), he earned a bachelor's degree in economics in 1978, winning the Ferguson Prize in Economics for his senior thesis. While at Trinity, he also played baseball and wrote for the sports section of the school newspaper. He went on to earn an MEd from the University of Washington in 1986 and a PhD in education finance in 1988.

Theobald worked as a pricing analyst and taught mathematics for a public junior high school before teaching at the University of Washington (1988–1993). In 1993 he came to Indiana University–Purdue University Indianapolis to work as an associate professor of education, and in 1995 he became associate professor at Indiana University Bloomington, advancing to professor in 2002. He also served on the Bloomington Faculty Council's Budgetary Affairs Committee (1999–2002). In 2002 he was appointed vice chancellor for budgetary administration and planning, a four-year term in which he procured salaries through the Commitment to Excellence funding for 96 exemplary faculty members and found matching funds for more than $150 million in undergraduate and graduate scholarship gifts. From 2006 to 2007, he served as senior vice provost and special assistant to the president, during which time the campus was able to add 120 tenure-track faculty members, increase the campus financial aid endowment by over twice its previous amount, and increase the mean SAT score of the incoming class through merit-based financial aid strategies. In 2007, he was named vice president and chief financial officer, the first tenured professor to be appointed as a Big Ten CFO since the early 1970s. Under his leadership, IU's credit ranking was upgraded in 2010 to Moody's highest level (Aaa)—making IU one of only eight Aaa-rated public universities in America. Along with Treasurer MaryFrances McCourt, he created a multifaceted financial literacy program and promoted on-time graduation, which led to a $70 million (17 percent) decrease in student loans over four years.

Theobald left IU to become the president of Temple University (2012–2016), where he contributed to the university's growth and financial stabilization. Temple achieved Advanced Carnegie Classification as a Research 1 institution, set research funding records in each year, and doubled annual invention disclosures from 51 to 115. They ended 2016 with a budget surplus of $74 million and doubled fundraising from $38 million to $84 million. The university set undergraduate enrollment records, with the freshman class growing over these three years, and Theobald also oversaw the development of the Temple Option to diversify the student body and the "Fly in Four" program to help reduce student debt. Since 2018, Theobald has served as vice president for finance and administration at the University of Wyoming.

Beyond the universities at which he worked, Theobald was also committed to professional service within his field and service to his communities. He served on the editorial board for *Educational Evaluation and Policy Analysis* (1997–2002), and he has worked for the *Journal of Education Finance* (1993–2002), the *Review of Economics and Statistics* (1998–2002), and the *Economics of Education Review* (1997–2002). From 2000 to 2001, Theobald was the president of the American Education Finance Association. He also served on the board of directors of the Greater Philadelphia Chamber of Commerce, the board of directors for the Urban League of Philadelphia, and as chair of the Philadelphia Regional College and University Presidents' Council. In addition to his commitments to higher education, Theobald has also been a board member for the Indiana Urban Schools Association, the Indiana Public School/University Partnership, the Alliance of Business Leaders and Educators State Education Finance Committee, the Governor's Council on Education Reform, and the nonprofit Cougars for Better Education.

Theobald has received several awards for his work and for his teaching. In 1990, he was presented the Jean Flanigan Outstanding Dissertation Award by the American Education Finance Association (now the Association of Education Finance and Policy). He is a three-time recipient of the Teaching Excellence Recognition Award from Indiana University (1997, 1998, 1999), as well as a recipient of the Jack A. Culbertson Award in Education Administration, given by the University Council for Educational Administration at the University of

Washington, for his outstanding contributions to the field of education administration. In 1997, he was a visiting professor for the Department of Economics at the University of Edinburgh. In 2003, he was honored with a Distinguished Alumnus Award from the College of Education at the University of Washington. In 2014, he was named "Most Admired Education CEO" by *Philadelphia Business Journal*.

In his free time, Theobald has been a coach for youth baseball, softball, and basketball. He and his wife, Sheona (Mackenzie), married in 1982 and have three children: Roddy, Kinnear, and Mattie. 〜

HUGH LEE THOMPSON
1934–2007

Chancellor, IU Kokomo, 1980–1990

As THE FOURTH CHANCELLOR of Indiana University Kokomo, Hugh Lee Thompson was a highly respected educator and administrator as well as an ardent and steadfast advocate for regional campus development. During his tenure, he oversaw tremendous growth on the Kokomo campus.

Hugh Thompson was the son of Frank Leslie and Althea Electa (Brown) Thompson, and was born in Martinsburg, West Virginia, on March 25, 1934. He graduated from Martinsburg High School in 1952 and was granted a BA from Shepherd College (West Virginia) in 1956. In college, he was a member of the football, basketball, and swimming teams. He earned an MA from Pennsylvania State University in 1958 and a PhD from Case Western Reserve University in 1969.

Prior to assuming the chancellorship of IU Kokomo, Hugh Thompson spent fourteen years as a professor and administrator at several institutions. He began teaching courses in education at Pennsylvania State University, the University of Akron, and Baldwin Wallace University. At Baldwin Wallace, he began the transition into administration by holding positions as assistant professor of education (1966–1969) and director of institutional planning (1969–1970) while serving as assistant to the president (1966–1970). He was the coordinator for Associated Colleges of Cleveland (1970–1971), then assumed the presidency of Sienna Heights College in Michigan (1971–1977) and the presidency of Detroit Institute of Technology (1977–1980).

In 1980, Hugh Lee Thompson became Indiana University Kokomo's fourth chancellor. Under his adept leadership, the campus doubled in physical and academic size. He took the helm at IU Kokomo with two buildings; when he left in 1990, the campus had forty-eight acres including a new student center, a Purdue University wing, a campus observatory, and more than twenty new degree programs. Thompson cultivated community support for the university in north central Indiana, including the campus's longtime friendship with Tipton County entrepreneur Ed Kelley, whose name adorns the Kelley Student Center and the Kelley House on campus. Two memorials to Thompson's tenure exist at Indiana University Kokomo: the Hugh L. Thompson Room, which was dedicated in the Main Administration building on campus in 2007; and the Thompson Minority Scholarship, named in honor of Pat and Hugh Thompson, which provides educational opportunities to deserving students. Upon Thompson's resignation, Vice Chancellor for Academic Affairs and Professor of Botany Arthur C. Gentile was given the additional appointment of acting chancellor, which he held until the appointment of Emita Hill in April 1991.

Thompson left IUK to serve as president of Washburn University in Topeka, Kansas, following which he served as academic vice president at both Clarke College (Iowa) and Meyers University (Ohio).

Thompson was very active in civic, philanthropic, and religious organizations at each of his home locations. He served on the boards of directors of Goodwill Industries, the Chamber of Commerce, the Lutheran Church, the Finance Board of Lenawee County, the YMCA, and Detroit Public School's Advisory Board. He worked with the PTA, Cleveland Catholic Charities, and aided Berea officials in preparing federal proposals. In Kokomo, Thompson was a member of the board of directors of the Creative Arts Council, Kokomo-Howard County Chamber of Commerce, American Cancer Society, United Way, Kokomo Civic Theatre, and the Kokomo Symphonic Society. He was a member of the Rotary Club, Cross Lutheran Church, Kokomo Development Corporation Board, and the Christian Business Men's Committee.

Thompson's professional memberships included the American Association for Higher Education, American Association of University Administrators, American Management Association, National Urban Education Association, Association of Institutional Research, Society for College and University Planning, National Association of College Admissions Counselors, Phi Delta Kappa, Kappa Delta Pi, American Association of Presidents of Independent Colleges and Universities, Economic Club, Capitol Hill Club, the Engineering Society of Detroit, and the Michigan Academy of Science, Arts, and Letters.

Thompson's social affiliations included the Columbia Club, Elks Club, Kokomo Country Club, Masons, Scottish Rite, Shriners, Worldwide Sportsman's Club, Detroit Athletic Club, and the Detroit Club.

Hugh Thompson married Patricia Smith of Hagerstown, Maryland, on October 16, 1952, and they had four daughters: Cheri, Linda, Tempe (BGS 1982), and Vicki. At the time of his death, they had ten grandchildren and three great-grandchildren. Thompson died on March 15, 2007, in Florida, where he had lived since 1999. ❧

RANDALL L. TOBIAS
1942–

Trustee, 2013–2016

H OOSIER BUSINESSMAN AND PHILANTHROPIST Randall Tobias has supported Indiana University in a variety of ways including as a trustee and as the founder of centers for leadership excellence and international development.

Randall L. Tobias was born March 20, 1942, in Lafayette, Indiana, to parents Fern Harwood and Roy Tobias, a teacher and banker, respectively. He grew up in Remington, Indiana, and attended public schools. He earned a BS in business from the Indiana University School of Business in 1964 (renamed the Kelley School of Business in 1997).

From 1964 to 1966, Tobias served on active duty as an artillery officer assigned to the faculty at the United States Army Artillery School at Fort Sill, Oklahoma. In 1966, he joined AT&T, where he held a number of positions with Indiana Bell Telephone Company before being transferred in 1977 to the company's Illinois Bell subsidiary in Chicago, where he became vice president (1978–1981). In 1981, he was assigned to AT&T's global headquarters in New Jersey, where he later ran the company's worldwide long distance and network businesses as chairman and CEO of AT&T Communications. He helped lead AT&T through the difficult period following the breakup of the Bell System in 1984, serving both as vice chairman of AT&T (1986–1993) and as chairman and CEO of AT&T International (1991–1993). In 1993, Tobias joined Eli Lilly and Company as chairman, president, and CEO. After retiring on January 1, 1999, he focused his attention on a number of business, community, and philanthropic interests and on teaching and writing. His book on leadership lessons learned, *Put the Moose on the Table*, written with his son, Todd Tobias, was published in early 2003.

In 2003, President George W. Bush nominated Tobias to serve as the first United States Global AIDS Coordinator, reporting directly to the Secretary of State. In this position, Tobias was responsible for launching the President's Emergency Plan for AIDS Relief, and for directing all U.S. government international HIV/AIDS assistance across the globe.

Since his undergraduate days, Randall Tobias's relationship with IU has grown significantly. In 2004, the Tobias Family Foundation founded the Tobias Center for Leadership Excellence at Indiana University–Purdue University Indianapolis. In 2013, Indiana Governor Mike Pence appointed Randall Tobias as a trustee of Indiana University for a single term (2013–2016). And in 2016, he and his wife, Deborah, founded the

Tobias Center for International Development at the IU Hamilton Lugar School of Global and International Studies. He is currently on the board of directors for the IU Foundation.

Tobias has served on a number of corporate boards, including AT&T, Eli Lilly and Company, Chemical Bank of New York, Agilent Technologies, Kimberly-Clark Corporation, Knight-Ridder, Inc., and ConocoPhillips Petroleum Company. He served for twelve years as a trustee of the Colonial Williamsburg Foundation, and for thirteen years as a trustee of Duke University including three years as board chair.

Among his numerous honors, Tobias was named pharmaceutical industry CEO of the year by *The Wall Street Transcript* in 1995, and CEO of the year in 1996 by *Working Mother* magazine. In 1997, he was named one of the top twenty-five managers of the year by *Business Week* magazine and recognized as the Norman Vincent Peale Humanitarian of the Year. He received the Positive Ally Award from the National Association of People with AIDS in 2005, and in 2006 he was named an honorary fellow of the American College of Healthcare Executives. In addition, Tobias was conferred honorary Doctor of Laws degrees from Indiana University, Wabash College, Butler University, Gallaudet University, and Ball State University, as well as an honorary Doctor of Engineering degree by the Rose-Hulman Institute of Technology. Indiana University–Purdue University Indianapolis (IUPUI) awarded Tobias the Urban University Medal. He has been inducted into the IU Kelley School's Academy of Alumni Fellows and has also received the Indiana University Distinguished Alumni Service Award.

Randall Tobias was married to Marilyn Salyer from 1961 until her passing in 1994. Together they had two children: Paige and Todd. On June 19, 2010, Randall married Deborah Flanagan. ᥫ

ERIC A. TODD
1968–

Trustee, 1991–1993

L AWYER, IU ALUMNUS, AND FAMILY MAN Eric Todd spent seven years at Indiana University and served as the ninth student trustee before embarking on a career in law.

Born in 1968 in Indianapolis to Paul Todd, a human resources professional, and Judy (Rodocker) Todd, a registered nurse, Eric Allen Todd graduated from Yorktown High School. He entered Indiana University, graduating with a BA in political science in 1990 before earning a JD in 1993. As a student at IU, he was active in many organizations, including the IU Student Association, Phi Gamma Delta fraternity, the Judicial Board (chief justice), the Board of Aeons (president), the Hearing Commission, and Alpha Lambda Delta (vice president). He was on the Homecoming Court at IU.

While he was in law school, Todd was appointed by Governor Evan Bayh to a two-year term as a member of the IU Board of Trustees, the ninth student to serve on the board. He was a member of the board's student affairs, external affairs, and real estate/legal affairs committees in addition to serving as the trustee liaison to the IUSB campus. He was lauded for his thoughtful consideration of all concerns that arose during his term, as well as for a perceptive understanding of constituencies within the university, care in analyzing the issues, willingness to express his views, balanced judgment, and good company. He was recognized with the Thomas Hart Benton Mural Medallion for Outstanding Service to Indiana University, Blue Key, Mortar Board, was a member of the Order of Omega, and was both an Epler Scholar and a Forrest Jump Scholar. His connection to the law school continues, and he served on the Law School Alumni Board from 2007 to 2010.

At the beginning of his career, Todd clerked for the Honorable Edward W. Najam Jr. of the Indiana Court of Appeals. He then went on to practice law, focusing on employment and labor disputes of all kinds, such as individual disputes, unions, and class action suits. He has represented clients in arbitrations, before state and federal courts, the Equal Employment Opportunity Commission, the United States Department of Labor, and the National Labor Relations Board. He made partner at Stinson Morrison Hecker LLP, before becoming managing shareholder of the St. Louis, Missouri, office in the law firm of Ogletree, Deakins, Nash, Smoak & Stewart, P.C. Todd was selected as a Missouri Super Lawyer in 2011 through 2013, and he is AV rated by Martindale Hubbell.

He is admitted to practice in the states of Missouri, Illinois, and Indiana; U.S. District Court of Eastern and Western Districts of Missouri; U.S. District Court, Central and Southern Districts of Illinois; U.S. District Court, Southern District of Indiana; and U.S. Court of Appeals, Seventh and Eighth Circuits.

In addition to a law career, Todd has also been very active in charitable organizations, particularly ones that work with children. From 1999 to 2005 he was on the board of directors for the Christian Service Center, now Gateway Homeless Services. Gateway is a 24-hour shelter for women and children, as well as an educational and support center for adults and children alike. Todd served as president of the board, as an Executive Board member and secretary, and was also the chairman of the Personnel Committee. He was also on the board of directors of the St. Louis Downtown Children's Center from 1995 to 2000. The center provides daycare for children of parents who work in downtown St. Louis, making sure that working parents do not have to choose between their employment and good care for their children. It is also a school devoted to innovative learning methods. Todd has been on the board of directors for Kids in the Middle since 2006 and served as its board president. Kids in the Middle is an organization devoted to helping children cope with the divorce of their parents.

Eric Todd has two daughters, Emma and Kelsey (IU Kelley School MBA 2013). In 2014, he married Emily Beutel. ⌀

SACHA I. WILLSEY URBAN
1969–

Trustee, 2001–2003

BUSINESSWOMAN AND CIVIC LEADER Sacha Ilona Willsey Urban served as a student trustee at Indiana University for a two-year term while completing a master's degree.

Born in Zurich, Switzerland, in 1969, Urban came to the United States in 1991. She attended Indiana University, earning a BA in religious studies with highest distinction in 2001, with a minor in Spanish, followed by an MPA in nonprofit and public management in 2003. She was a member of the Theta Alpha Kappa National Honorary Society of Religious Studies and Theology, and a member of the Golden Key National Honor Society. She also received a baccalaureate in law and economics from Kantonsschule Zuercher Oberland in Wetzikon, Switzerland.

Urban was the fourteenth student appointed as a trustee of the university. During her time on the Board of Trustees, Urban witnessed the Indiana University–Purdue University Indianapolis campus reach new heights. The campus experienced explosive growth at the turn of the century, and Urban was on the board that approved many projects that facilitated this growth. Urban was a strong believer in the importance and the power of the student voice, and while a trustee at IU, she also worked with the Indiana University Student Association, playing a vocal and pivotal role in bridging the two entities to initiate the school's "Vote Hard" campaign, which registered more than 10,000 formerly non-registered voters on IU campuses.

Urban has worked as a contract negotiator and principal contact with artists and illustrators for Sunrise Publications (1991–1994), has worked with Business Forms Plus in San Diego, California, and with Bank Finalba AG in Zurich. She has also worked with United Way of Central Indiana (2003–2004) as a major gift associate, cultivating and developing donors for the UW Alexis de Tocqueville Society. In 2014 she accepted a position as manager of community giving at TriCity Family Services, where she is responsible for the annual fundraising plan, agency promotions, grant writing, and also serves as race director for TriCity Family Services' Annual Snowflake Shuffle 5K/10K run/walk.

Urban is known as a dedicated believer in the ability to create meaningful change. A philanthropist, fundraiser, and advocate, she is heavily involved in the fields of human health and services, the arts, higher education, social justice, and local community advancements. In 2002, she was an invited speaker at the Monroe County First Public Forum on Childhood Cross-Cultural Education, a forum created to educate the public on the individual, civic, and economic benefits of teaching foreign languages and cultures to children. She has been a member of the Indiana University Alumni Association, the St. Charles Chamber of Commerce Board of Directors (2016–), and a board member for the Open Door Clinic (2006–2014), as well as an associate with the Indiana University Foundation Well House Society, and has participated in countless colloquiums, receptions, galas, and dedication ceremonies for Indiana University.

Sacha Urban was first married to Ari Vidali, with whom she came to the United States, in 1991. She has two children, Jonah and Ilona, with her second husband, Jeffery Willsey. She currently lives in the greater Chicago area with her husband Milan Urban Jr., who she married in 2007. She is fluent in six languages and enjoys running, reading, gardening, and healthy cooking. ❧

JOHN D. WALDA
1950–

Trustee, 1990–2001

THROUGH TWO SUCCESSFUL CAREERS, first as a respected attorney and second in academia, John Walda has established himself as a local and national leader in higher education policy and management. John David Walda was born in 1950 in Fort Wayne, Indiana, to Martha and David, a legal secretary and a banker, respectively. He attended Indiana University Bloomington, receiving a BA in English and political science in 1972 and a JD in 1975. As an undergraduate, he was class president from 1968 to 1970, and again in 1972. He was also a member and president of the Board of Aeons, the student advisory board to the university president, and he was active in both the IU Student Association and the IU Student Foundation.

Walda's career began when he joined the Fort Wayne law firm of Barrett & McNagny in 1975; he left the firm as partner in 2001. From 2002 to 2004 he served as Indiana University's executive director of federal relations and corporate partnerships, building relationships and raising the profile of IU among influential Washington, D.C., organizations and political figures. In 2005, he returned to the legal profession as a partner at Bose, McKinney, and Evans, and he also worked as a senior vice president for federal relations for the consulting firm Bose Treacy Associates, LLC. Since 2006, Walda has served as president and CEO of the National Association of College and University Business Officers, a membership organization of more than 2,500 colleges and universities that advances the economic viability and business practices of higher education institutions in fulfillment of their academic missions through professional development, research, and advocacy.

In 1990, Walda was appointed to the Indiana University Board of Trustees and was reappointed to two terms by Indiana Governors Evan Bayh and Frank O'Bannon. He was president of the board from 1992 to 1993 and 1994 to 2001. In addition to his trustee service, Walda was the national president of the IU Alumni Association and chairman for Clarian Health Partners (now IU Health). He held all three of those positions simultaneously from 1996 to 1997. Walda continues to serve as a director of the Indiana University Foundation.

Walda has been a leader in many professional and educational organizations. He was the first chairman of the Indiana State Lottery Commission and has been a member of the AAU Council on Federal Relations, the NASULGC (now the Association of Public and Land-Grant

Universities) Council on Government Relations, the American College of Trial Lawyers, American Inns of Court, the Libel Defense Resource Center, and the Allen County, Indiana State, Montana State, and American Bar Associations. He was the chairman of the board of the Association of Governing Boards, the national association for university trustees. He has served on the board of directors for the American Council on Education and was member and past-chair of the Steering Committee for the Washington Higher Education Secretariat. He has also served as a trustee at Stetson University (2011–) and Carroll College.

Walda has been very active in community matters as well, serving on the board of directors for Junior Achievement of Northeast Indiana, the Allen County Parks and Recreation Department, the Headwaters Park Commission, the Indiana Area Health Education Centers, the Yellowstone Park Foundation, and the Fort Wayne Civic Theater and Art Museum. He has been the director of Mad Anthony's as well as president of the Junto Club of Fort Wayne. He is currently a director and officer for Yellowstone Forever, the association which supports programs and projects in Yellowstone National Park.

Walda has been the recipient of numerous awards and distinctions, including the 1999 Award of Merit from the Indiana Hospital and Health Association and a Presidential Citation from the Indiana State Bar Association. He is a Fellow of the American College of Trial Lawyers and was the Democratic nominee and candidate for the U.S. House of Representatives in 1978 and 1980.

John Walda was married to Julie Inskeep from 1974 to 1999, with whom he had two children: Laura (BA 2004, MPA 2009, JD 2009) and Kirk (BS 2006). In 2001, Walda married Martha Clark Walda and together they reside in Washington, D.C. ❧

George E. Walker
1940–

Vice President for Research
and Dean of the Graduate School, 1991–2003

D URING THE TWELVE YEARS that George E. Walker served Indiana University as the vice president for research and dean of the Graduate School, he labored across the IU system as an advocate for faculty research and was recognized nationally as a leader in research and graduate education.

Walker's own experiences of higher education began at Wesleyan University (Middletown, Connecticut), where he received a BS in 1962 and was a member of Sigma Chi Fraternity. He then pursued graduate studies in theoretical nuclear physics at Case Western Reserve University, earning both an MA and PhD. He undertook postdoctoral training at Los Alamos National Laboratory and Stanford University.

In 1970, Walker joined Indiana University as assistant professor of physics. He rapidly moved up the ranks with promotions to associate professor in 1973 and to professor in 1976. He won grants from the National Science Foundation to support his research and that of his graduate students, and was the two-time recipient of an Outstanding Contributions to Graduate Education award. He was elected a Fellow of the American Physical Society. From 1976 to 1979 he served as associate dean of the College of Arts and Sciences. In 1986, he was appointed chair of the Department of Physics. During these years, Walker initiated and saw to completion the establishment of the Nuclear Theory Center. He also held appointments as a theoretical physicist with the Lawrence Livermore National Laboratory Physics and Advanced Technology Committee, chairing its Physics and Advanced Technology Directorate Advisory Committee; he has also been a member of the Nuclear Division Advisory Committee.

During Walker's tenure as vice president and dean of the University Graduate School (1991–2002), IU enjoyed an increase in sponsored research funding from $113 million in 1990 to $339.5 million in 2002. In addition to facilitating and celebrating the research and creative activities of individual faculty, he administered dozens of centers, institutes, and museums while also establishing several new ones, including the Center for Genomics and Bioinformatics, the Center on Congress (now the Center on Representative Government), and the Center for Mathematics Education. With his help, IU's Cyclotron Facility contributed to an era of particle physics research and was transformed into a state-of-the-art facility to treat patients at IU's Midwest Proton

Radiotherapy Institute. He also coordinated awards from the $4 million President's Arts and Humanities Initiative, championed intercampus research collaboration, and enhanced graduate education opportunities. After Walker stepped down from the post of vice president in 2002, he stayed on an additional year as special assistant to the vice president for research until 2004, when he retired with the title professor emeritus of physics. Some of Walker's continuing ties to IU are seen in his ongoing roles as a member of Hoosiers for Higher Education, the Friends of Music, and service on the board of the Stone Age Institute.

Since leaving IU, Walker served as the director of the Carnegie Initiative on the Doctorate at the Carnegie Foundation and, beginning in 2006, senior vice president for research development and graduate education at Florida International University. In 2010, he was named vice president of research and graduate studies at Cleveland State University.

Over the course of his career, Walker became a force on the national scenes of research administration and graduate education. He served as president of the Association of Graduate Schools of the Association of American Universities, chair of the board of the Council of Graduate Schools, and a member of the National Advisory Board of the National Survey of Student Engagement. He sat on the Graduate Record Examinations Board, the National Association of State Universities and Land Grant Colleges board of directors, and the National Research Council Committee on Methods of Forecasting Demand and Supply of Doctoral Scientists and Engineers. Walker has held appointments with the North Central Association of Colleges and Schools, the Commission of Institutions of Higher Education, and the Test of English as a Foreign Language (TOEFL) Policy Council. Walker has also been a member of the National Advisory Board of the Center for the Integration of Research, Teaching, and Learning (CIRTL).

George Walker met and married his wife while they were graduate students at Case Western Reserve University. They have three children: Beth, Patricia, and Christopher. ◈

MELANIE S. WALKER

1959–

Trustee, 2016–

USINESS EXECUTIVE AND CIVIC LEADER Melanie Walker has served IU as a trustee since 2016.

Melanie S. Walker was born June 17, 1959, in Ithaca, New York, to Ruth Steiger, an artist, and Richard Landon Walker, a farmer-turned-entrepreneur in road construction. Walker's early years were spent on a productive farm, from which she could see the Cornell University campus across the valley. She grew up daydreaming of being a college student on that campus. After attending public elementary and junior high schools in Ithaca, she completed high school at the private Brooktondale Christian School in Brooktondale, New York. She then matriculated to Albany Business College, earning an AAS in retail marketing in 1979, after which she attended Cornell University, earning a BS in industrial and labor relations in 1985. She credits "a good dose of luck and a larger dose of determination" with her eventual entrance to and graduation from Cornell and making her daydreams come true. Walker also cites as inspirational three of her male ancestors, who she had researched for a family genealogy, each of whom served the United States in a different great war: Bennett Landon, a great-great-grandfather who served in the Civil War; Richard Landon, a great-uncle who served in World War I and died at the Battle of Verdun ten days before the Armistice was signed; and Bennett T. Landon, who died in World War II on D-Day as he was maneuvering a landing craft tank to the beach.

During her early career, Melanie Walker gained experience in the field of human resources in three very different organizations: Cornell University (as an employee relations specialist), Mobil Oil and Chemical (as a human resources specialist), and Schlegel Corporation (as an employee relations manager). In 1990, she joined the Tsuchiya Company of Nagoya, Japan, working at their first North American subsidiary, TASUS Corporation, as a human resources manager before being promoted to human resources, legal, and finance manager. In 1994, at age 34, Melanie Walker broke the glass ceiling to become the first female president of a Japanese-owned manufacturing company in North America. In 2005, she was named CEO and president of the TASUS Corporation/Tsuchiya Group North America. During her twenty-three years as president, she established four Tsuchiya facilities throughout North America, including the Tsuchiya Group North America headquarters in Bloomington, Indiana.

In 2016, Walker was appointed as an Indiana University Trustee by Governor Mike Pence. Walker has also been a member of the IU Research and Patents Management Advisory Board, formed by President Myles Brand; the Deans Council at the IU School of Public and Environmental Affairs; the IU Manufacturing and Public Policy Steering Committee; and the Steering Committee of the Indiana University Women's Philanthropy Council.

Walker has also been involved in a variety of professional and civic organizations. These include serving on the board of directors for the Indiana Economic Development Corporation, the Japan American Society of Indiana, Indiana University Manufacturing Policy Institute, the Applied Research Institute, Susie's Place Child Advocacy Center, Bloomington Economic Development Corporation, Greater Bloomington Chamber of Commerce, and the Monroe County Community Foundation. She also was president of the American Heart Association Executive Leadership Team, member of the State of Indiana Workforce Innovation Council, speaker and member of the SelectUSA Investment Summit in the U.S. Department of Commerce, and State of Indiana Delegate to the White House Conference on Small Business.

Melanie Walker was married to Wade Hart (1984–1994). She had two children: Stormy Ray Walker and the late Landon Marion Hart. ༄

Ray Wallace

1960–

Chancellor, IU Southeast, 2014–

A PROFESSOR OF ENGLISH and an accomplished administrator, Ray Wallace has dedicated his entire career to improving the quality of higher education.

Ray Wallace was born March 28, 1960, in Antrim County, Northern Ireland, to Eveleen Rooney, a civil servant in the British Ministry of Defense, and Harry Wallace, a textile worker. Wallace attended public primary and grammar schools in Antrim and Magherafelt in Northern Ireland. Growing up, he found inspiration in his aunt Pat Dundas, a well-read educator, and in his uncle John McCartney, a university-educated civil servant. Wallace also took a turn serving his country as a young man, representing Northern Ireland in track and field (1977–1981). And it was an athletics scholarship that enabled Wallace to attend Eastern Illinois University, where he earned a BS in physical education and English (1981) and an MA in English (1982) before completing a Doctor of Arts in English at Illinois State University (1985).

Prior to coming to Indiana University, Wallace taught for many years as a professor of English and held various administrative positions at the University of Hawai'i–Hilo, the University of Tennessee-Knoxville, Kennesaw State University, and Northwestern State University of Louisiana. At Troy University he served as dean of arts and sciences (2001–2003). At Clayton State University, he served as dean of the College of Arts and Sciences (2003–2007). Moving to the University of Arkansas-Fort Smith, he served as senior vice chancellor (2007–2014). During his tenure at UA-Fort Smith, Wallace's accomplishments included stewarding twelve new undergraduate degrees and fourteen new minors through the university system and state regulatory board; re-establishing a university-wide honors program; developing a Center for Excellence in Teaching and Learning; signing sixteen memoranda of understanding with overseas universities for faculty and student exchanges; and introducing initiatives involving outreach to high school and community college students.

In 2014, Ray Wallace joined Indiana University as chancellor of IU Southeast, relieving Interim Chancellor Barbara Bichelmeyer, who had served in that capacity since the retirement of Sandra Patterson-Randles in 2013. As chancellor, Wallace has been working with alumni affairs and advancement/foundation offices in ongoing fundraising efforts. Although enrollment at IUS peaked at 7,256 in 2011, it fell due to the economic recession to a low of 5,874 in 2017; during this time, Wallace has overseen small gains in enrollment among women and minorities, from 13.1 percent in 2014 to 15 percent in 2016. And with renewed attention to flexible evening and online programs for adult and working students, the number of nontraditional students (age 25 or older) among new admits in fall 2017 grew 11 percent from the year before, while the number of enrolled graduate students increased 7 percent over fall 2016. Although declining enrollments resulted in a $1.3 million dollar budget deficit in 2017, Wallace responded by working with units across the campus to balance the budget, achieving approximately $1.7 million in efficiencies for the fiscal year 2018–2019. He also moved to increase enrollments by establishing Crimson Advantage, a credit transfer agreement with Jefferson Community and Technical College (JCTC) to enable their graduates to easily enroll in BA programs at IUS. Wallace has also overseen the addition of more than fourteen new programs, ranging from a BA in history and a Bachelor of Interdisciplinary Studies in Arts and Humanities (B.I.S.) to an MBA with a concentration in healthcare administration, to a program in professional sales housed in the newly endowed Judge Carlton and Sue Sanders Professional Sales Center. In April 2017, Indiana University Southeast was honored for its diversity and inclusion efforts at One Southern Indiana's 29th ONE Awards program with the Brown-Forman Corporation Diversity Champion of the Year Award.

Ray Wallace and his wife, Susan, have a son, Reed, a daughter-in-law, Jill, and two grandsons, Noah and Zachary. ᥣᥣ

HERMAN B WELLS
1902–2000

University Chancellor, 1962–2000
President, Indiana University (Interim), 1968
President, Indiana University, 1938–1962
President, Indiana University (Acting), 1937–1938

A$_{\text{T}}$ HIS RETIREMENT FROM THE PRESIDENCY IN 1962, Herman B Wells received an honorary Doctor of Laws summa cum laude from Indiana University. It occupied a unique place in his growing list of honorary degrees, which eventually totaled twenty-eight. In 1962, at only 60 years of age, Wells received a lifetime appointment to the new post of university chancellor, created by the IU Board of Trustees to retain his administrative knowledge while allowing him latitude in developing his portfolio.

Wells had identified two major possibilities for his post-presidential career: fundraising on behalf of the university and organizing international education. He pursued both by continuing to serve as president of the IU Foundation (as he had during his presidency) and by becoming the chairman of the board of the new Education and World Affairs organization, headquartered in New York City. Wells resigned as chair of the board in 1970, a change that was precipitated by his increasing duties back at Indiana University. In spring 1968, IU President Elvis Stahr, feeling embattled by student activism, stated his wish to resign, and the trustees called on Wells to step in as interim president. Inexorably, Wells found himself drawn into the day-to-day administration of the university as he served as executive officer from July through November. Moreover, the university was preparing for its upcoming sesquicentennial in 1970, which included a major fundraising campaign. As the 150th Birthday Fund got underway in 1969, the IU Foundation was reorganized, and Wells was made chair of the board. The fund's original goal of $25 million was surpassed, and when the books were closed in July 1972, the foundation had raised $51 million—double its starting goal. As Joseph Sutton assumed the IU presidency at the end of 1968, Wells gave up the title of interim president and concentrated on his activities as university chancellor. In the last half of the 1970s, Wells embarked on writing his autobiography, his most sustained literary production. Published in 1980, *Being Lucky: Reminiscences and Reflections*, was, in equal parts, an engaging autobiography, a manual of higher education management, and an artful spoof of his stellar career.

Wells turned 80 in 1982, and he remained remarkably active throughout his eighth decade and well beyond. His work on behalf of the IU Foundation continued, and he was co-chairman of the Campaign for Indiana, a major effort to enlarge the endowment, concluded in 1989.

Among the many projects for which he sought funds, the IU Art Museum was near the top of the list. Completed in 1982, the museum marked the architectural finale to the Fine Arts Plaza. Over the preceding forty years, Wells patiently assembled funds and mobilized the university's will for this magnificent complex of facilities surrounding the Showalter Fountain, including the IU Auditorium, the Fine Arts Building, the Lilly Library, and the Art Museum (now the Eskenazi Museum of Art), dedicated to artistic expression and humanistic understanding.

A gala birthday celebration was held for Wells when he turned 90, complete with a published book, *Herman Wells Stories: As Told by His Friends on His 90th Birthday.* Confined to a wheelchair, with fading eyesight and hearing, he still managed to work regularly at his Owen Hall office and was a fixture at campus events. State, national, and international honors accumulated, and in 1993 WTIU produced a video documentary, *The Vision of Herman B Wells.*

In his ninety-eighth year, his body weary and his mind intact, Wells passed away in his campus home on the evening of March 18, 2000, while the student body was away on spring break. The funeral held on March 22 was exactly sixty-two years to the day after his selection as president of Indiana University. In October 2000, a seated bronze statue of Wells was dedicated in the Old Crescent, located close to the Rose Well House overlooking Dunn's Woods. His outstretched hand is burnished gold through the touch of countless individuals coming to pay respect to him. ᏬᎶ

Bradley C. Wheeler
1964–

Vice President for Communications
and Marketing, 2018–

Vice President for Information Technology
and CIO, 2007–

B EGINNING WITH THE VALUES AND WORK ETHIC of a small Oklahoma farming community, Brad Wheeler became a globe-trotting technology professor and university chief information officer.

Born in Hinton, Oklahoma, population 1,300, Bradley Charles Wheeler learned at a young age that resourcefulness was crucial to success, and that useful solutions come out of really diving into a problem, taking it apart (sometimes literally), and putting it back together. This ability to dissect a problem, solve it, and enjoy the satisfaction of doing so has proven invaluable throughout his career.

Wheeler's family farmed, and also owned a General Motors car dealership. Farm work started early, and in the sixth grade, Wheeler started working in the dealership parts department after school and on weekends. That eventually led to working nearly every job, from changing oil to washing cars to finance and accounting. The dealership introduced him to his first computer (a Wang), and in the ninth grade Wheeler taught himself to program that system, developing a payroll system that saved hours in preparing the weekly payroll. Thus began his fascination with technology.

After graduating from Hinton public schools, Wheeler enrolled at Oklahoma State University, receiving a BS (1987) and an MBA in business management (1989). He came to Indiana University Bloomington in 1990 and earned a PhD in less than three years from the IU School of Business in 1993 (renamed the Kelley School of Business in 1997), with a major in information systems and minor in small group communication.

Even as tenure-track jobs were scarce during the 1991–1993 recession, Professor Maryam Alavi chose him for a key assistant professor role at the University of Maryland, College Park's MBA program. There, his career began with early success in grants, top-tier publications, and teaching awards. In 1996, he received an unexpected invitation to return to IU Bloomington, and jumped at the opportunity to take a position as assistant professor of information systems (1996–2001) in the Kelley School of Business. His research and teaching launched him into working with companies and teaching executive education all over the world (including six continents and more than thirty countries), and eventually led to his tenure and promotion to associate professor (2001–2007).

Wheeler's path changed in 2001, when he assumed a part-time, university-wide position as the first associate dean for teaching and learning IT. He served under Michael McRobbie, IU's first vice president for IT and chief information officer (CIO). As McRobbie's responsibilities grew, he moved Wheeler through five different leadership roles in six years, including directing IU's highly advanced supercomputing and research systems. Along the way, Wheeler co-founded the Sakai and Kuali open source software foundations, pioneering a community source investment model that has dramatically reduced the costs of enterprise systems for higher education. He has been principal investigator, co-principal investigator, or research team member on over $11 million of sponsored research at Indiana University.

In 2007, McRobbie became IU's eighteenth president, and named Wheeler vice president for information technology and chief information officer. Having just been promoted to the academic rank of professor, Wheeler took the helm of IU's $125 million IT budget and 1,000-person staff. Despite his executive role, he still finds time to engage with leading international companies (mainly through executive education) and to work with universities around the world. Since becoming VP for IT and CIO, Wheeler's portfolio has included steering the continuing expansion of national and international leadership in high-performance research networks with Internet2, the National Science Foundation, National Oceanic and Atmospheric Administration, and the State of Indiana's I-Light network. In 2011, he moved all IU regional campus IT staff to be part of University Information Technology Services (UITS), and in 2014, he created the IU Clinical Affairs IT Services in partnership with the vice president for university clinical affairs. In 2016 he created University Auxiliary IT as part of University Information Technology Services. Along the way, Wheeler has served as interim dean in the IU Bloomington School of Informatics and Computing (2015–2016) (now the School of Informatics, Computing, and Engineering), on the board of directors of the IU Kinsey Institute (2013–2017), on the board of directors for IU Health Bloomington Hospital (2012–), as co-founder and chair of the board for Unizin Consortium (2014–), preferred director and member of the board at Kuali, Inc. (2014–), as well as co-founder and member of the board of directors at the Kuali Foundation, Inc. (2006–). In 2018, Brad Wheeler was given an additional title and set of responsibilities when President Michael McRobbie named him Vice President for Communications and Marketing.

In recognition of his global reputation as an IT leader, Wheeler has twice been named a Top 100 CIO by *CIO Magazine* (2009 and 2012). In 2012 he was named one of *The Chronicle of Higher Education*'s 12 Tech Innovators Who Are Transforming Campuses and one of *Government Technology*'s Top 25 Doers, Dreamers, and Drivers in Public Sector Innovation. In 2013, he received the EDUCAUSE Leadership Award. In 2015 he received the inaugural CTO of the Year Award from the *Indianapolis Business Journal*.

Reflecting on his journey, Wheeler deeply values those early skills of hard work and problem solving that he learned working on the farm and in the car dealership. The 4-H Club, highly influential faculty at Oklahoma State University and Indiana University, and wonderful environments like the city of Bloomington were instrumental to leading a kid from a small town to the extraordinary global opportunities of IU's leadership team. ॐ

JOHN J. WHELAN III
1968–

Vice President for Human Resources, 2018–

A HUMAN RESOURCES SPECIALIST with experience in both the private sector and higher education, John Whelan brought his customer-centric philosophy to Indiana University in 2014.

John J. Whelan III was born in February of 1968 in Meadowbrook, Pennsylvania, to Margaret Weld, who was a real estate broker, and John J. Whelan Jr., who worked in the human resources field. They raised him in Pennsylvania and Massachusetts, where he attended elementary school at Our Lady of Good Counsel in Southampton, Pennsylvania; Medfield Middle School in Medfield, Massachusetts; and secondary school at Xaverian Brothers High School in Westwood, Massachusetts. He then attended the University of Notre Dame, earning a BA in American studies (1990) as well as a JD from the Law School (1996). As an undergraduate, he ran varsity track and field alongside author Nicholas Sparks and Heisman trophy winner Tim Brown. He is admitted to practice law by the Bar of the Commonwealth of Massachusetts (1996) and the Bar of the U.S. District Court of Massachusetts (1997).

Before entering the human resources field, Whelan worked for several service organizations such as the South Bend Center for the Homeless (1991–1993) and the Notre Dame Legal Aid Clinic (1994–1996). Whelan then embarked on a career in human resources, accumulating nearly 20 years of experience before coming to IU. He began as a human resources generalist at Brown Brothers Harriman Co. in Boston (1996–1998) before working at the Gillette Company as a compensation analyst (1998–1999) and human resources manager (1999–2001). Next, he joined Bristol-Myers Squibb, where he worked as human resources manager at their Evansville Supply Center (2001–2002) and then as assistant director/manager of human resources for their Mead Johnson division (2003). Whelan was then hired at the University of Notre Dame, where he served in human resources leadership as director of HR business partners (2003–2009). He also served as a faculty member in Notre Dame's Mendoza College of Business (2007–2009). Whelan then spent five years at Baylor University in Waco, Texas, first as associate vice president for human resources and chief human resources officer (2009–2014) and then as vice president (2014), as well as a being a member of the president's cabinet during Ken Starr's tenure (2009–2014). At both Notre Dame and Baylor, Whelan helped to change the way human resources operated by focusing on being more attentive to the needs of university leadership, faculty, and staff.

Indiana University hired John Whelan as associate vice president for human resources in June 2014. In this position, Whelan placed an emphasis on being customer-driven. He reorganized human resources across all of IU's campuses to ensure they operate as a single office with uniform policies. To achieve this goal, he strengthened the sense of community among human resources employees and worked to boost morale of employees on all campuses, which he did by using confidential employee surveys in order to gather input to craft positive improvements and to help create buy-in. He has also guided the development and implementation of HR2020, IU's first-ever human resources strategic plan, which launched in 2015. The university-wide comprehensive plan aims to systematically address and improve broad issues such as workplace satisfaction, health and wellness, hiring and promotion, training, parental leave, workplace safety, controlling benefit costs, as well as employee diversity, equity, and inclusion. On July 1, 2018, Whelan was promoted to be IU's first vice president for human resources, responsible for the more than 20,000 IU employees across the state.

Beyond Indiana University, Whelan is a member of several professional and civic organizations. He serves on the national board of directors of the College and University Professional Association for Human Resources (CUPA–HR), a term that lasts 2014–2020, and is board chair for 2018–2019. He is also a member of the Society for Human Resources Management (SHRM), World at Work, and the National Association of College and University Attorneys (NACUA).

John Whelan married Molly O'Neill on June 17, 1994. Together they have five children: Aidan (IUB class of 2020), Gavin (IUB class of 2021), Maeve, Grania, and Sinead. ◈

Anna M. Williams
1989–

Trustee, 2015–2017

W HILE COMPLETING a dual degree master's program, Anna Williams served a two-year term as the twenty-first student trustee at Indiana University.

Born on March 5, 1989, to Kelly Gaffney, an English Teacher, and Randy Williams, a businessman, Anna M. Williams grew up in Indianapolis. She attended Newby Elementary School and Speedway High School, both public schools, before entering Indiana University, completing a BA in international studies in 2010.

After graduation, Williams moved to Spain and taught English as a Foreign Language, earning a Certificate in Foreign Language Instruction from the Universidad Pontificia Comillas in May 2013. While studying for this certificate, Williams worked as an English instructor at Colegio San Jose in Madrid, Spain (2012–2013). In this position, she taught intensive English immersion courses across a multidisciplinary curriculum. She also worked as a translator at Global Voices in Madrid, Spain (2012–2014), where she translated Spanish political, economic, and human rights news reports and commentary into English, as well as wrote first-hand reports of protests, political movements, and the economic crisis in Spain for English audiences.

In 2014, Williams returned to the United States to pursue graduate work at Indiana University Bloomington. Williams enrolled in a dual-degree program and graduated in May 2017 with an MA in public affairs, with a concentration in economic development and policy analysis, and an MA in European affairs, with a concentration in international trade. While a graduate student, she taught Spanish grammar, sociolinguistics, and culture as an associate instructor for the Department of Spanish and Portuguese, and she was named an AI Recognized with Distinction for her teaching. She was also awarded the Gene Coyle Academic Excellence Scholarship, Greater Good Leadership Scholarship, Mellon Foundation European Endowment Research Scholarship, and an EU Studies Fellowship. Furthermore, she was a U.S. Department of Education Foreign Language and Area Studies Fellow in Turkish studies.

In the midst of her graduate work, Anna Williams was appointed to the IU Board of Trustees and served one term (2015–2017). As a trustee, Williams was involved in supporting the change from individual campus admissions applications to a single, streamlined process for all eight campuses in order to improve the student experience, lower application fees by 90 percent, and integrate systematic processes of the university. While pursuing her graduate studies, Williams also held two summer internships. Her first was as an international trade intern with the Trans-Atlantic Business Council in Washington, D.C. (2015). There, she worked with the U.S. Congressional Transatlantic Trade and Investment Partnership Caucus and the EU delegation to the U.S. in shaping negotiation strategies for SME (small and medium-sized enterprise) growth opportunities, providing briefings on trade, financial services, and life sciences issues. Her second internship was in International Corporate Affairs and Global Pricing, Reimbursement, and Access at Eli Lilly and Company in Indianapolis, Indiana (2016). She conducted comparative analysis of financial, performance-based, and innovative pricing strategies and developed a proactive pricing messaging, training session, and interactive visualization tool. Since completing her graduate studies, she has been senior associate at Eli Lilly and Company in Indianapolis.

Williams is a member of several professional associations and organizations, including Young Professionals in Foreign Policy, Step Up Women's Network, and Chicago Council on Global Affairs.

Anna Williams married Zachary Waninger in December 2017. ༄

EDGAR G. WILLIAMS
1922–2012

Vice President for Finance
and Chief Financial Officer, 1986–1988

Vice President for Administration,
1974–1986

ATALENTED ADMINISTRATOR and management expert who helped lead the university through its major 1974 reorganization, Edgar Williams had a long career at Indiana University that spanned 40 years. Born May 4, 1922, in Poseyville, Indiana, to Noley Wesley Williams and Anna Lena (Wilsey), Edgar Williams lost his mother at age six and was raised by his maternal grandparents, Mr. and Mrs. John S. Wilsey. He was schooled in Phoenix, Arizona, and Poseyville before attending Evansville College with his childhood sweetheart, Joyce Grigsby, whom he married in 1944. After working in the U.S. Army Medical Corps as a second lieutenant, he earned a BA in economics and political science in 1947. He then studied business administration (management) at Indiana University, earning an MBA in 1948 and a DBA in 1952. While at Evansville College, he was a member of the basketball and football teams, the Athletic Board, and Phi Zeta Fraternity, and of Pi Gamma Mu, Beta Gamma Sigma, and Sigma Iota Epsilon honorary societies. Williams credited Professors John Mee, Arthur Weimer, Les Waters, Eddie Edwards, and Ed Hedges as the most influential educators in his career. Williams was a Ford Foundation Postdoctoral Fellow at Harvard University and Stanford University and held faculty internships at DuPont, Inc., Chrysler Corporation, and Eli Lilly and Company.

After completing his doctorate, Williams began his academic career in 1948 as assistant professor of management at IU Bloomington. He advanced to associate professor in 1955, professor in 1960, departmental chair in 1963, and associate dean for administration in 1965. As dean, he served as liaison to programs in East Pakistan, Yugoslavia, and Thailand, while also traveling on university business to Venezuela and Great Britain. He became executive assistant to the president in 1972, vice president for administration in 1974, and in 1986, President Ryan re-designated that position to be vice president of finance and chief financial officer. Williams held that position until his retirement in 1988. He then became special advisor to the president and was also interim director of intercollegiate athletics and of human resources, and president of the Distinguished Alumni Service Association. Williams holds the distinction of serving under six IU presidents: Herman Wells, Elvis Stahr, Joseph Sutton, John Ryan, Thomas Ehrlich, and Myles Brand. Upon his retirement, he was given the titles vice president emeritus and professor emeritus of business administration.

One of Williams' accomplishments was his participation in the major 1974 reorganization of the university. He helped to define how the regional campuses could be organizationally successful, the unique relationship between IU and Purdue at IUPUI, and the conception of the core campus of Bloomington and Indianapolis. During that process, his vice-presidential portfolio expanded to include overseeing budgets, computer systems, registrar and admissions, and management services. His contributions to professionalizing the business affairs of the university include the planning and paying off of several million-dollar deficits in computing centers, setting up reserves for repair and rehabilitation of academic and residential facilities, and contributing to the development of athletics programs and facilities. He credited his successes to his associates at IU, particularly the friendship and support of Thomas R. Bossort Jr., John F. Mee, Arthur M. Weimer, L. L. Waters, W. George Pinnell, John W. Ryan, Ralph Floyd, Bob Knight, William Armstrong, J. Terry Clapacs, and Curt Simic.

Williams was a management expert who published essays and articles throughout his career, for both scholarly journals and book-length collections. He consulted for more than sixty-five manufacturing companies, hospitals, government agencies, national health associations, financial institutions, and retail establishments, specializing in executive development, general management, personnel and human relations, corporate strategy, and systems management.

Throughout his life, Williams was the recipient of countless awards, including the Graduate School for Savings and Loan Executives Gold Key, an Alumni Certificate of Excellence from the University of Evansville, two Sagamore of the Wabash honors from Indiana Governors Robert Orr and Evan Bayh, the IU President's Medal for Excellence and the Thomas Hart Benton Mural Medallion presented by President Thomas Ehrlich, and the Distinguished Alumni Service Award. He was named an Honorary "I" Man as well as a member of the Indiana University Athletic Hall of Fall.

Edgar and Joyce Williams were married for 68 years; they had two children, Cynthia and Thomas, and two grandchildren. An accomplished fisherman, golfer, and St. Louis Cardinals fan, Edgar G. Williams passed away in 2012 at the age of 90 in Bloomington. He wrote about his experiences in a personal memoir, *For the Life of Me* (2004). ◑

DOUGLAS M. WILSON
1941–

Vice President for University Relations
and External Affairs, 1988–1996

A<small>S A LEADER IN HIGHER EDUCATION</small>, Douglas Wilson has spent his career advancing the goals of public higher education in Ohio, Indiana, and Oregon.

Douglas M. Wilson was born in May of 1941 and grew up in Hamilton, New York, home to Colgate University, where his father, Charles R. Wilson, was professor of history and a campus administrator. His mother, Elizabeth Cook Wilson, a homemaker, sent him to a fine New England prep school. From there he enrolled at Miami University in Oxford, Ohio, where he earned a BS in education (1964), an MA in history (1969), and completed graduate coursework in educational administration. During his college years, he was a teaching assistant in the history department, a member of Phi Alpha Theta and Phi Delta Theta, and the yearbook photography editor.

Wilson began his career as an educator by spending a year teaching at Rocky River High School near Cleveland, Ohio, before returning to Miami University Ohio to work for three years as alumni secretary and then for ten years as director of the Office of Alumni Affairs. He spent two years at the University of Oregon as director of development and executive director of the University of Oregon Foundation and then as the assistant vice president for development. In 1982, he once again returned to Miami University Ohio, this time to serve as vice president for university relations (1982–1988). During these years, Wilson was also an Elder in the Presbyterian Church of Oxford, Ohio.

In 1988, IU President Thomas Ehrlich appointed Wilson as vice president for university relations and external affairs, a position he held until 1996. At IU, Wilson is credited with advancing the national and international reputation of Indiana University, managing the public relations challenges and triumphs of a difficult economic era in the history of American higher education, and implementing a university-wide communications plan that focused on the interrelationship between teaching and research, the impact of IU on society, the connection between IU and the State of Indiana, and establishing the university as a good investment for the state, students, and supporters. Wilson also held an adjunct professor appointment in the School of Education Department of Higher Education.

After stepping down as vice president for university relations and external affairs, Wilson held several other positions. From 1996 to 1998 he served as president of the IU Advanced Research and Technology Institute, and from 1998 to 2001 he was executive director of the Office of Corporate and Foundation Relations at the Indiana University Foundation. In 2001, he served part time as executive director of the Pulaski County Community Foundation.

Nationally, Wilson was a well-respected and highly sought-after member of professional commissions and councils, including the Council for Advancement and Support of Education, Association of Governing Boards, National Conference on Volunteers, Alumni Administration Institute of the Council for Advancement and Support of Education (CASE), and the National Conference on the Young Alumnus.

Wilson made it a goal to be involved with community service. While at IU, he linked the university to important organizations across the state. He was the president of the Bloomington Pops Board of Directors, co-chair of the Monroe County United Way Campaign, President of the University Club, Citizens Advisory Board for Crane Naval Station, IU Varsity Club Advisory Committee, IUPUI Board of Advisors, and was on the board of directors for the Foundation of Monroe County Community Schools, the IU Friends of Music, Bloomington Mayor's Round Table, Bloomington Rotary Club Foundation, Bloomington Chamber of Commerce, and the Greater Monroe County Chamber of Commerce. He was also a member of the Mayor's Round Table and the Long Range Planning Committee of the Monroe County Community Schools Corporation.

For his service to the university and to his communities, Wilson has been recognized with multiple honors. He has been the recipient of the Sagamore of the Wabash by Governor Frank O'Bannon, two Thomas Hart Benton Mural Medallions from Indiana University Presidents Myles Brand and Thomas Ehrlich, the Diane L. Breeden Catalyst Award from the Bloomington Chamber of Commerce, and was named Oxford Citizen of the Year.

Douglas Wilson married Susan Roberson in 1964, and she passed away in 1989. He married Kathy Kruger, a professional development consultant, in 1991. Wilson has three children: Hilary, Haley, and Grant. His hobbies include photography, rose gardening, and travel. ᘐ

JAMES C. WIMBUSH
1959–

Vice President for Diversity, Equity,
and Multicultural Affairs, 2013–

Professor, administrator, and educational leader James Wimbush has served IU since 1991.

Born January 25, 1959, in Danville, Virginia, to Inez Saunders and James Costella Wimbush, James C. Wimbush Jr. attended Southside Elementary School in Danville before the family moved to Martinsville, Virginia. He finished his schooling in Martinsville at Mt. Olivet Elementary School and Laurel Park High School. He then earned a BS at Averett College (now University) in 1981, where he was a member of the Averett Leadership Society. Upon graduating, Wimbush received several awards: Cougar Spirit Award, Outstanding Business Student Award, and the C. L. Davenport Award for General Excellence—the highest honor Averett College bestows upon a student for excellence in leadership, scholarship, and character.

Between 1981 and 1986, Wimbush was an active member of the Jaycees. He was named Jaycee of the Year by the Princeton Jaycees (1983–1984), was presented with the Ed Gilger Award by the West Virginia Jaycees (1984), and was West Virginia State Speak–Up Champion (1985).

In 1986, Wimbush attended Virginia Polytechnic Institute and State University, earning an MS in human resources management and industrial and labor relations (1988) and a PhD in management (1991). As a graduate student, he won the Jack Hoover Award (1991), the highest honor the students and faculty of the Department of Management can bestow upon an instructor for exemplary teaching. He was also a member of the Beta Gamma Sigma Honor Society, inducted in 1992.

After completing his PhD in 1991, Wimbush joined Indiana University as a professor of business administration. He began his university administrative career in 1999 as associate dean of the faculties (1999–2004). During this period, he also served as chairperson of doctoral programs in business (2000–2001), MBA Program chair in the IU Kelley School of Business (2001–2003), and chair of the Department of Management in the IU Kelley School of Business (2003–2009). He was also appointed dean of the University Graduate School (2006–). In 2013 he took on the additional role of vice president for diversity, equity, and multicultural affairs. A member of the IU Athletics Committee since 1998, he also served as chair (2004–2008).

Wimbush has served on several local and national boards and

committees. Recent examples include serving as chair of the Graduate Record Exam (GRE) Board of Directors (2011–) and as chair of the CGS Advisory Committee on Minorities in Graduate Education (2009–). He has been a member of the Commission on Pathways through Graduate School and Into Careers, which is a collaboration between Educational Testing Service and the Council of Graduate Schools (2011–). He has also been a member of the joint Commission on the Future of Graduate Education (2009–), which released the 2010 report *The Path Forward: The Future of Graduate Education in the United States.* He also served on the Association of Graduate Schools (AGS) of the Association of American Universities 2012 Executive Committee; was elected as a member of the Council of Graduate Schools (CGS) Board of Directors in 2010, and then to the 2011 and the 2012 Executive Committees, and then as chair of the board (2013–2014); as president, Association of Graduate Schools (2014–2015); and as vice-chair, Kinsey Institute Board of Directors (2015–2016).

Wimbush has received numerous awards for his teaching and professional service. Representative examples of teaching awards include citations for teaching excellence from the MBA Core program (1995), from the dean of the Kelley School of Business (1995, 1996, 2000), and from the Golden Key National Honor Society (1995), as well as the Harry C. Sauvain Teaching Award from the business school's Teaching Excellence Committee (1995) and the IU Teaching Excellence Recognition Award from the Board of Trustees (1997). Furthermore, Wimbush has been a Wachovia Distinguished Speaker at the R. B. Pamplin College of Business of Virginia Tech (2008) and a Fulbright Senior Specialist at the Economics Institute in Zagreb, Croatia (2008). He was inducted into the Edward A. Bouchet Society as an Honorary Member at Howard University (2008). And in 2012, he received the Bill Orwig Medal, the highest honor bestowed upon a non-alumnus of Indiana University for distinguished service to Indiana University Athletics.

On June 6, 2015, James Wimbush married Kerry L. Werst. ∽

LESTER M. WOLFSON
1923–2017

Chancellor, IU South Bend,
1969–1987

DESCRIBED AS "A MAN OF HUMANITY AND LETTERS," Chancellor Lester Wolfson was responsible for the development and success of IU South Bend more than any other individual. He led the campus through its formative and maturing years against many challenges at the university, state, and national levels. His chancellorship is credited with tripling student enrollment, increasing physical facilities from one building to eight, developing the largest number of master's degree programs on any IU regional campus, and infusing all degree programs with solid foundations in the liberal arts and sciences.

Lester Wolfson was born September 13, 1923, in Evansville, Indiana, to William and Bess (Silverman) Wolfson. His father was the proprietor of a small lunchroom, and his mother managed a women's hat shop. Later, his family moved to Grand Rapids, Michigan, where as a student at Union High School, Wolfson excelled by participating in debate, dramatics, vocal music, and student government; editing the school newspaper; winning local and state speech awards, local and national essay awards, the Keck Prize for creative writing, and the Dillingham Memorial Cup for scholarship and leadership. He graduated in 1941 as co-valedictorian. It was the inspiration of a high school English teacher that led Wolfson to pursue scholarship and teaching over a legal career.

Wolfson earned his BA (1945), MA (1946), and a PhD (1954) from the University of Michigan, where he was elected Phi Beta Kappa his junior year and won the Association of American Colleges Award for the graduating senior judged to have the greatest promise of distinguished college teaching. He was a Horace Rackham Pre-doctoral Fellow; was a member of Phi Eta Sigma, Phi Kappa Phi; was a Hunt Scholar, a Student Aid Foundation Scholar, a University Scholar and Fellow; and was the recipient of a Hopwood Essay Award. His master's thesis was "Matthew Arnold as Hebraist and Hellenist." His doctoral dissertation was "A Rereading of Keats's Odes: The Intrinsic Approach in Literary Criticism." At IUSB he frequently quoted from Keats in his eloquent addresses to the faculty.

Wolfson began his career in higher education as an instructor of English at Wayne State University (1950–1953) and then as an assistant professor of English and speech at the University of Houston (1953–1955). For family reasons, he declined an offer from the University of Wisconsin–Madison in 1955 and instead took a position at Indiana

University's Gary extension school (now Indiana University Northwest) as assistant professor of English (1955–1961), advancing to associate professor (1961–1964). He moved to IU South Bend in 1964 and was promoted to professor in 1967.

The move to IU South Bend in 1964 proved to be a significant turning point in Wolfson's career, as he shifted from teaching to administration, an area in which he excelled. In 1964, Wolfson began his tenure at IUSB as director and assistant dean of University Extension. As the campus expanded, Wolfson's title likewise changed, reflecting the evolution of his leadership role: dean (1966–1968), dean and acting chancellor (1968–1969), and finally chancellor (1969–1987). In retirement, he held the title of chancellor emeritus, but in his own words, "Despite anything else, I think my proudest title is professor of English."

Wolfson is remembered for using his low-key and civilized leadership to build a genuine university of learning and scholarship. Upon his arrival, he found a single building, opened three years earlier, some 2,000 students, mostly part-time, and a full-time faculty of only twenty. Degree programs were authorized in 1965, and the first class of 31 received their degrees in business and education in 1967. Upon his retirement twenty years later, the campus enrolled just under 6,000 students and had a full-time faculty of 153. The class of 1987 numbered 654 and received associate, bachelor's, and master's degrees in sixty-three undergraduate and nine graduate programs.

Wolfson's dedicated leadership was recognized by both the university and the state. Named in honor of his distinguished service to IUSB, the Lester M. Wolfson Literary Award in creative writing is presented annually to deserving students. Furthermore, the IUSB publishing arm, which focuses on local and regional subjects, is known as the Wolfson Press. In 2011, IUSB held a tribute to Chancellor Wolfson, dedicating a bronze bust created by retired art professor Tuck Langland in the lobby of Northside Hall. In recognition of his distinguished contributions to IU and the State of Indiana, Wolfson was named a Sagamore of the Wabash in 1987. He received an honorary Doctorate of Humane Letters from Indiana University in 1988 and was inducted into the South Bend Hall of Fame in 1991. The book *A Campus Becoming: Lester M. Wolfson and Indiana University South Bend 1964–1987*, by IUSB Professors Emeriti Patrick J. Furlong and Tom R. Vander Ven, chronicles the early days of IUSB and Wolfson's leadership, and includes many examples of his annual addresses to the faculty and remarks at graduation.

In his active years he published articles and reviews, and he served the community by sitting on the board of directors of several organizations, including the South Bend Symphony Orchestra Association, the Michiana Arts and Sciences Council (president 1974–1975), the Michiana Public Broadcasting Corporation, the Stanley Clark School, the Civic Center Foundation, and the Memorial Hospital of South Bend. In retirement, he enjoyed baseball and all forms of great music, especially grand opera.

Lester Wolfson married Esther Evans in July 1949. She too was a graduate of the University of Michigan, and later earned an MS in elementary education at IU South Bend. Together, they raised three children: Alice, Margaret, and George, all Indiana University graduates. Their two grandchildren, Daniel and Catherine, are also IU graduates. Esther Wolfson died in December 2003. Three years later, Lester married Frances Savett, a long-time family friend. Lester passed away February 10, 2017, in South Bend, Indiana. ❧

DAVID ZARET
1951–

Vice President for International Affairs, 2011–2018

A S A PROFESSOR AND ADMINISTRATOR, David Zaret spent his 41-year career serving Indiana University by helping to expand and strengthen the university's presence internationally.

Born in New York in 1951, David Zaret received a BA in sociology from Amherst College in 1973, graduating magna cum laude. He received a PhD in sociology from Oxford University in 1977.

Zaret joined IU Bloomington as an assistant professor of sociology in 1977. He was promoted to associate professor in 1984 and professor in 1992. His scholarship focuses on historical sociology, comparative history, and social theory. Zaret has also been a senior associate member at St. Antony's College of Oxford University and a visiting fellow at the Institut für Soziologie at Heidelberg University in Germany. From 1999 to 2005, Zaret was executive associate dean of IU's College of Arts and Sciences. In 2006 and again in 2010–2011, he served as interim dean of the College. He has also served as senior advisor to the provost (2010). Zaret was appointed IU vice president for international affairs in 2011. In this position, Zaret was responsible for leading the continued implementation of IU's International Strategic Plan. He oversaw IU's Office of Overseas Study, the Office of International Services, IU's Global Gateway Network (including the launch of offices in Europe, India, China, and Mexico), the Office of International Partnerships, the Office of International Development, the IUPUI Office of International Affairs, and the Honors Program in Foreign Languages. During this time, he participated in approximately twenty international trips to about thirty countries, establishing new partnerships with universities and institutions while strengthening existing ones, including with: the National Institute for Development Administration, which IU helped to establish in Thailand in 1968; study abroad partnerships in Madrid, Spain and Bologna, Italy—two of the oldest ongoing formal study abroad partnerships in the country, started in 1968; and IU's partnership with the University of Warsaw, a relationship that began in 1978.

Zaret is also the chief executive officer of IU International Consulting and Research, LLC (2013–). He sits on the board of directors of the Institute for International Business in the Kelley School of Business (2011–). In addition to serving on dozens of IU committees, task forces, and councils, Zaret has been the director of undergraduate studies and the director of graduate studies for the Department of Sociology. He served as a trustee of South East European University (2011–2016). He also served a term as president of the IU Bloomington chapter of the Association of American University Professors.

Professionally, Zaret has been active nationally for many years as a reviewer with the National Endowment for the Humanities. He has served on the editorial boards for the *American Journal of Sociology*, *American Sociological Review*, *Studies in Historical Social Change*, and *History of Sociology*. His published work includes *Origins of Democratic Culture* (Princeton University Press, 2000) and *The Heavenly Contract: Ideology and Organization in Pre-Revolutionary Puritanism* (University of Chicago Press, 1985). His article "Petitions and the 'Invention' of Public Opinion in the English Revolution" (*American Journal of Sociology*) won the Barrington Moore Award for Best Published Article from the Comparative-Historical Section of the American Studies Association.

Zaret is the recipient of numerous honors and awards, including fellowships and grants from the National Endowment for the Humanities, the American Council of Learned Societies, the Lilly Foundation, and the American Sociological Association. For several years he was a member of the core faculty for the IU Honors Division (now the Hutton Honors College), and he has received several departmental and campus teaching awards. At Zaret's retirement in 2018, IU President Michael McRobbie awarded him the President's Medal for Excellence.

David Zaret is married to Julie Knost, who was director of IU's Office of Affirmative Action (retired in 2018). They have two children: Anna and Max (BA 2018).

About the Editors

KEITH BUCKLEY is director of the Jerome Hall Law Library and senior lecturer in law. Keith Buckley was appointed reference librarian in 1980, became collection development librarian in 1999, and was appointed assistant director for public services in 2012. He was appointed interim director in January 2017 upon the retirement of Linda Fariss and named director and senior lecturer in December 2017. He teaches Advanced Legal Research, Legal Research in the Legal Research and Writing Program, and Legal Bibliography and Law Library Administration through the School of Informatics, Computing, and Engineering's Department of Information and Library Science. Buckley is currently researching the treatment of women and families under the Civil War pension statutes during the early twentieth century. His other areas of study include nineteenth-century gravestone carving.

DEREK F. DiMATTEO is associate instructor of English, managing editor of *Africa Today*, and PhD candidate in the Department of English at Indiana University. Derek DiMatteo's research interests include American literary and cultural studies since 1945, globalization and the transnational, critical university studies, and pedagogy. Before coming to IU, he was instructor of general studies at Lakeland University Japan, and he also taught high school English in the United States and in Japan, where he lived for nearly nine years. He has been a column editor at the journal *The Language Teacher* and a copyeditor and production assistant at book publisher O'Reilly Media. He holds an MA in English literature from IU, an MAT in English education from Tufts University, and a BA in English from Wesleyan University.

LINDA FARISS is former director of the Jerome Hall Law Library and senior lecturer in law emerita. Linda Fariss was named interim director of the library in June 2011 and appointed director in 2012; she retired on January 31, 2017. Prior to her appointment as director, Fariss held several appointments in the library, including as the long-time associate director; in that position she was directly responsible for all public service areas and served as human resources officer for the law library and liaison to the law school for all personnel matters. Throughout her tenure, Fariss was active in law school and university committees. Along with Keith Buckley, Fariss taught Legal Bibliography and Law Library Administration through the IU School of Library and Information Science (now part of the School of Informatics, Computing, and Engineering). Also with Keith Buckley, Fariss wrote a history of the Maurer School of Law, to be published by IU Press in November 2019. She received her BS and MLS from IU, where she was a member of Beta Phi Mu. She received her JD *magna cum laude* from the Maurer School of Law, where she was elected to the Order of the Coif.

KELLY KISH has been at Indiana University since 2000 and is currently director of the Indiana University Bicentennial and deputy chief of staff in the Office of the President. She holds a BA in government and politics/Russian area studies from the University of Maryland, and an MA in higher education administration and a PhD in higher education administration from IU. Her scholarship focuses on historical perspectives of higher education organizations, governance, and decision making. As deputy chief of staff, she manages presidential initiatives including university honors and awards, presidential student initiatives, and committees and task forces and serves as the president's liaison to the Board of Aeons. In 2015, she assumed the additional position of director of the IU Bicentennial, overseeing a multi-year, multicampus, academically focused program of twenty-seven signature projects, two grant funds, and a student internship program.

COLLEEN PAUWELS was the director of the IU Law Library from 1978 to 2011, and became acting director in 1978 and permanent director in 1983. During those years, she transformed the library into a facility that was named the country's Best Law Library in 2004. She oversaw the expansion of the physical facilities, the collection, the technology, and the staff. She also became the school's unofficial historian, publishing several articles on the history of the law school. She received her MLS from IU in 1975 and her JD in 1986 from the IU School of Law (now the Maurer School of Law). In honor of her many contributions to the law school, Pauwels was inducted into the law school's Academy of Law Alumni Fellows in 2013. She died on April 24, 2013, at the age of 67.

Periods of Service
of Trustees
and Officers

INDEX

A NOTE ON PRODUCTION

The cover of this volume features the seal of Indiana University. The seal bears the name of the university in Latin, *Indianensis Universitatas*, as well as the institution's motto, Light and Truth, *Lux et Veritas*. The year the university was founded, 1820, is shown in Roman numerals.

The font used throughout is Georgia Pro. The text paper is Accent Opaque Smooth, 70 lb. text. The dustjacket is Endurance Silk, 100 lb. text. The cover is 100 percent cotton plain weave cloth, scarlet. The book is Smyth sewn.

Jeremy Hackerd was project manager, Heather Barber was production manager, Derek F. DiMatteo was copyeditor, Dennis Hill was designer, Mary Spohn was production editor, and Kay Daniel provided production assistance and quality control.

Printed by Mossberg & Company Inc.
Roger A. Brown, National Account Executive